Under the Editorship of

DAYTON D. McKEAN
University of Colorado

✤ CONTENTS ✤

✦ PREFACE ✦

This collection of readings is designed to be used as a supplementary readings book with most textbooks in public administration. Emphasis is placed on recent research findings in the field of public administration to provide the kind of reading material and presentation which a textbook does not give the student. The selections reflect behavioral and inter-disciplinary contributions as well as institutional and descriptive materials.

The following points summarize my approach to the book:

1. The descriptive and analytical treatment of the textbook can be given increased meaning by the presentation of research findings and developments.
2. The emphasis on recent research findings should give the student positive examples of the thinking of researchers and practitioners in the field of public administration.
3. Each chapter contains a short introduction which provides a general background to the topic but does not attempt to summarize or digest the readings.
4. Some of the longer selections have been abridged where it is possible to do so without distorting the original views of the authors. The emphasis, however, has been to present fewer selections at greater length rather than a large number of heavily edited selections.

I am grateful to the authors and publishers of these selections for their permission to reprint and specific acknowledgements have been made at appropriate places in the text.

MAURICE E. O'DONNELL

1

The Study of Public Administration

In the relatively short time that public administration has been a subject for study and research at the university level, it has undergone a number of changes in approach and theory. Wallace Sayre in his article summarizes these changes and indicates where he feels the discipline is and what it stands for today.

The study and practice of public administration have never been far apart. Many persons have had governmental experience which has added much to the perspective they can contribute to the subject. Paul Appleby is such an example of the practitioner at a high executive level whose later writing and teaching contributed much to an understanding of the subject.

Public administration has also benefited from interdisciplinary research in business administration, sociology, anthropology, and psychology. The more recent theoretical developments in the field are an outgrowth of the multi-disciplinary approach.

American administrative practices have been put to a different kind of test when applied to developing nations in an attempt to help these nations develop effective administrative systems. One outgrowth has been a more systematic approach to the study of comparative administration and a re-examination of some of the principles which we have tried to export in developmental administration programs.

Premises of Public Administration:

Past and Emerging ❖ Wallace S. Sayre

When the first textbooks in public administration appeared in the United States a little more than thirty years ago (Leonard D. White's *Introduction to the Study of Public Administration* (Macmillan Co., 1926), and W. F. Willoughby's *Principles of Public Administration* (Johns Hopkins Press, 1927), they were based upon premises and concepts about the executive branch and its administrative agencies which had been at least a half century in the making. The civil service reform movement beginning in the late 1860's and culminating in the Pendleton Act of 1883, Woodrow

Reprinted from the *Public Administration Review*, the journal of the American Society for Public Administration, Vol. XVIII, No. 2, 1958, pp. 102–105, by permission of the publisher.

Wilson's essay on "Public Administration" in 1887, Goodnow's *Politics and Administration* in 1900 (MacMillan Co.), the work of the New York Bureau of Municipal Research and its counterparts throughout the country, the scientific management movement in industry, the reorganization movement (including the Taft Commission studies of 1910-12, the Illinois and New York reports of 1915), the city manager movement beginning in 1910, the Budget and Accounting Act of 1921, the Classification Act of 1923, the New York state governmental reorganizations under Governor Smith — all these, as well as other events and writings, helped to provide the raw materials for the syntheses attempted in the pioneer textbooks in public administration. These texts, in turn, not only provided the first effective teaching instruments for the new field of study; they also codified the premises, the concepts, and the data for the new public administration.

The Textbooks' Codification

The main elements of this codification of 1926-27 may be very briefly summarized:

1. The politics-administration dichotomy was assumed both as a self-evident truth and as a desirable goal; administration was perceived as a self-contained world of its own, with its own separate values, rules, and methods.

2. Organization theory was stated in "scientific management" terms; that is, it was seen largely as a problem in organization technology — the necessities of hierarchy, the uses of staff agencies, a limited span of control, subdivision of work by such "scientific" principles as purpose, process, place, or clientele.

3. The executive budget was emphasized as an instrument of rationality, of coordination, planning, and control.

4. Personnel management was stressed as an additional element of rationality (jobs were to be described "scientifically," employees were to be selected, paid, advanced by "scientific" methods).

5. A "neutral" or "impartial" career service was required to insure competence, expertise, rationality.

6. A body of administrative law was needed to prescribe standards of due process in administrative conduct.

In these pioneer texts the responsibility of administrative agencies to popular control was a value taken-for-granted; the responsiveness of administrators and bureaucrats was not seen as a problem because everyone then understood that politics and policy were separate from administration, which was concerned exclusively with the execution of assignments handed down from the realm of politics.

The events of the 1930's — depression, New Deal, the rise of Big Government — served at first to confirm the premises of the texts. The expansion of government, especially the great growth in the size, complexity, and discretionary power of administrative agencies, was regarded as making all the more relevant and urgent the tools of rationality which public administration offered to the practitioners in the new and expanded agencies of the executive branch. Many of the teachers and the students of public administration themselves became practitioners.

The *Report* of the President's Committee on Administrative Management and its literary companion-piece, the Gulick and Urwick *Papers on the Science of Administration* (Institute of Public Administration, Columbia University), both appearing in 1937, represent the high noon of orthodoxy in public administration theory in the United States. In the Gulick and Urwick *Papers* were brought together eleven essays constituting the classic statements then available in the United States and Europe, in business and public administration, of the elements believed to be embodied in *the science* of administration. (It is perhaps worth noting that of the ten authors only Gulick wrote as a political scientist.) The *Report* of the President's Committee, for its part, set forth in eloquent language the prescriptions of public administration made orthodox by the texts of 1926-27. The significant and impressive managerial changes in the executive branch of the national government which were made as a result of the *Report* strengthened the prestige of public administration as a body of precepts.

Post-War Dissent

But the high noon of orthodoxy had a brief hour of prominence. World War II interrupted the further development of public administration research and literature, and at the close of the war the resumption took the form of dissent and heterodoxy. Prewar orthodoxy, it is true, was reasserted in the *Reports* of the two Hoover Commissions, in most of the textbooks, and in the rash of post-war administrative surveys at state and local government levels. There was, however, a strong ferment of dissent in the monographic literature, in the journals, and elsewhere. The dissent took three main lines:

1. *The assault upon the politics-administration dichotomy.* This keystone of pre-war orthodox public administration had always been viewed with some skepticism by a considerable number of political scientists (particularly by those mainly concerned with political theory or with the political process); to them, all administrative agencies and their staffs seemed to be involved in politics. This view was now to recruit strong support from within the public administration fraternity itself. The first textbook to appear after the war — Fritz Morstein Marx (editor), *The Elements of Public Administration* (Prentice-Hall, 1946), with fourteen political scientists among its contributors — brought a new, if still mild, emphasis upon the involvement of administrators and administrative agencies in policy formation, in the use of discretionary power, and in the general political process. In 1949 Paul H. Appleby's influential monograph, *Policy and Administration* (University of Alabama Press), boldly and persuasively described administration as "the eighth political process." In 1950 the second post-war text — Herbert A. Simon, Donald W. Smithburg, and Victor A. Thompson, *Public Administration* (Alfred A. Knopf) — presented a systematic exposition of public administration as a political and group process. In 1952 the first casebook in public administration — significantly titled *Public Administration and Policy Development*, Harold Stein (editor), (Harcourt, Brace and Co.) — emphasized in each of its case studies the political role of the administrator; and, in the introductory essay, Harold Stein wrote incisively of "public administration as politics." These several illustrations serve to reveal the stages by which public administration as politics, as involved deeply in policy and values, was firmly established in the literature of public administration within a few years after the war. Even the most orthodox texts yielded some ground on the doctrine that politics and administration were separable.

2. *The assault upon the claims to science and to universal principles of administration.* The premises which pre-war public administration had borrowed primarily from scientific management were of course necessarily subjected to criticism by all those who were asserting that administration was a political process. These critics were soon joined by the students of the history and development of administrative

theory. When, for example, Dwight Waldo published in 1948 his important study, *The Administrative State: A Study of the Political Theory of American Public Administration* (The Ronald Press), he demonstrated how value-loaded, how culture-bound, how political — in short, how "unscientific" — were the premises, the "principles," the logic, of orthodox public administration.

To these powerful critical voices there was soon added a third group: the prophets of a new science of administration. The outstanding representative of this school of thought has been Herbert Simon whose *Administrative Behavior: A Study of Decision-Making Processes in Administrative Organizations* (Macmillan Co., 1947) not only attacked the orthodox "principles" of public administration as being merely "proverbs" but also presented a new administrative science based upon the argument of logical-positivism that facts must be separated from values. For Simon, the orthodox politics-administration dichotomy was to be replaced by the new fact-value dichotomy.

These critics have successfully made their point. The claims to scientific principles and to their universal applicability have been placed on the defensive although they have not entirely disappeared from the literature of public administration. But the claims of a new science of administration have not been widely accepted.

3. *"Sociological" studies of bureaucracy.* Another stream of ideas and knowledge contributing to the post-war growth of dissent from orthodoxy has been the "sociological" study of the public bureaucracies as representing in themselves a form of political power. The primary impact of these studies has been upon the orthodox doctrines of the neutral career service. Philip Selznick's *TVA and the Grass Roots* (University of California Press, 1948), for example, revealed a career bureaucracy deeply involved in the political process, demonstrating that the creation and maintenance of a career bureaucracy is more a problem in values and politics than a problem of administrative science.

Emerging Reformulations

The post-war decade of dissent and heterodoxy has not yet revealed the clear outlines of an emerging new body of comprehensive doctrine. But perhaps we can anticipate some of the major components of the reformulation now in process. The premises around which the new consensus — perhaps to become a new orthodoxy — would seem to be forming, may be stated somewhat as follows:

1. Public administration doctrine and practice is inescapably culture-bound. It is also bound to more specific values: to varying conceptions of the general public interest, to particular interest-group values, to the values of a specific administrative organization or bureaucracy at a specific time.

2. Public administration is one of the major political processes. The exercise of discretionary power, the making of value choices, is a characteristic and increasing function of administrators and bureaucrats; they are thus importantly engaged in politics.

3. Organization theory in public administration is a problem in political strategy; a choice of organization structure is a choice of which interest or which value will have preferred access or greater emphasis. Organization is, therefore, as Robert A. Dahl and Charles E. Lindblom suggest in *Politics, Economics and Welfare* (Harper & Bros., 1953), a determinant in bargaining.

4. Management techniques and processes have their costs as well as their benefits. Each new version has a high obsolescence rate, its initial contributions to rationality

declining as it becomes the vested interest of its own specialist guardians and/or other groups with preferred access.

5. Public administration is ultimately a problem in political theory: the fundamental problem in a democracy is responsibility to popular control; the responsibility and responsiveness of the administrative agencies and the bureaucracies to the elected officials (the chief executives, the legislators) is of central importance in a government based increasingly on the exercise of discretionary power by the agencies of administration.

Making Sense Out of Things in General

✢ PAUL APPLEBY

One of the points of Alfred North Whitehead's concluding chapter in *Science and the Modern World*, some four decades ago, is that the idea of professionalism is a modern one, and that the development of professions is both essential to the advance of civilization and dangerous to that advance. The danger he saw was the inevitable limitation of specialization which some one else has explained in a pithy dictum: "Any special way of looking at things is a myriad of ways of *not* looking at them."

In some realization of the problem Whitehead posed, persons academically or administratively concerned with the conduct of affairs have been disposed to draw a sharp distinction between "specialists" and "generalists." One result of this distinction was the useful dictum I have heard attributed to Harold Laski: "Experts should be on tap, not on top." But the usual thing is that many experts are perennially unhappy about the "ignorance" and "superficiality" of administrators and politicians. Each variety of specialist inevitably regrets that other people don't have the same kind of specialized equipment.

In the United States, the mutually inspired frustration of administrators and politicians, more or less on the one side, and of the many varieties of specialists on the other "side," is especially marked. Here, we have carried the development of specializations and sub-specializations further faster than anywhere else in the world. Here, we experienced an unprecedented pioneer situation in which rugged individualism had its greatest, and shortest, day as we moved into an even more completely unprecedented condition of high interdependence at a tempo still rapidly accelerating. Here, too, the frustration was furthered by the philosophical emphasis Emerson gave to individualism, which he identified as a wholly modern idea.

The terms "political science," "public administration," "sociology," and many kindred ones also represent modern ideas, of course. I was a student at Grinnell College when Jesse Macy — the first teacher denominated a "political scientist," I believe — was still teaching there. Nowadays there are many different varieties of specialisms within political science and other new disciplines. So, too, with the functional fields off campus, where specialization has spawned jobs for powder-puff

Reprinted from the *Public Administration Review*, the journal of the American Society for Public Administration, Vol. XXII, No. 4, 1962, pp. 175–180, by permission of the publisher.

cutters, tie-painters, packaging experts, public-relations counsellors, opinion poll-sters, and countless others, even while technological advancements have been carry-ing the phenomena of change and complexity into synthetics, automation, cyber-netics, fission, fusion, space exploration, and even space utilization.

Need for Instrumentalities Concerned with Making Sense in General

Time was when I might have justified my existence by identifying myself with the "generalists." But, I never much liked the term, and in the face of all that has occurred it seems fantastically presumptuous and absurd. No longer can there be any individual who is truly very much of a generalist. Yet, if the specialists are going to save themselves and keep civilization on the march, they are going to have to submit willingly and cooperatively to coordination of some adequate kind and dimension.

A few decades ago, most of the rationalization about such matters chiefly begot new varieties of experts; general administration was to be achieved through pur-chasing agents, accountants, planners, budget examiners, personnel examiners and classifiers, and a good many more. Additional values were served, but new dimen-sions were added to complexity, too. Meanwhile, new nations have emerged, millions of persons have been newly invigorated, great developmental programs undertaken, and relationships between peoples and nations have been increased in number and broadened in scope; potentialities for enrichment of life on the planet have opened widely with great suddenness, along with an increase in possibilities of stress and frustration.

If the conditions thus depicted are to be kept tolerable, if life is to be made reward-ing at a sufficient tempo for enough of the planet's population, development of the instrumentalities especially concerned with making sense in general is a need greater than any other. Difficult as are the technical assistance problems of the experts, these activities can be successful, in fact, only as more general success is attained. Some of the success needed, of course, is at the level of the United Nations and the World Court and others of the U.N. galaxy of organs. Some of the success needed some time in the future, of course, will be at levels higher than those on which the U.N. entities are established. But for the immediate future and for as long ahead as anyone can see, the primary needs are at the level of individual nations. Can they succeed as nations? Can they succeed as nations dedicated to the service of mass well-being and the enrichment of individuality? They are subsidiary needs of a similar sort below the level of entire nations; there are single agencies, departments and bureaus, single programs to make sense of in their own terms as well as in whole-nation terms. But, there is no chance for any of these particulars, if the nations that make their success possible themselves disintegrate.

Making Over-all Sense Requires Institutional Decisions

In recent paragraphs I have spoken disparagingly of "individualism" and with great concern for "individuality." The former was a doctrine, essentially unsocial and anarchic. The greatest development of *individuality* is achieved in a highly organized society which proliferates, nurtures, and makes mutually serviceable many diverse specialisms. As the anthropologist Malinowski declared, both freedom and tryanny can be achieved only through institutions. The difference between tyranny and freedom is a consequence of differences in social institutions. Only primitive life and primitive individuals are possible in disorganization. Universities, as one of the prime sources of specialisms, should be proportionately concerned about making over-all sense out of diverse learnings, interests, functions, persons and aspirations.

Making over-all sense is in one important aspect an intellectual problem, of course, in the special province of the discipline of philosophy. For me this has always been a most attractive field. But philosophy has had to pursue the course of specialization, too, dividing itself into parts representing different efforts to make *partial* over-all sense. In any case, however, general sense can be formulated verbally only in abstract terms, whereas both individual and social problems in actual life have to be met in specific and concrete actions. We do not, in fact, turn over to the philosophers our society's most weighty decision making responsibilities of a specific sort. It should not be surprising when we observe that the most philosophical and most revered of our American newspaper columnists is at his best when he is most abstract, and at his poorest when he is most specific in judgments attempted on behalf of society.

Even the man of action in a post of high responsibility is at his best as a usual thing when he makes relatively general decisions and *delegates* more specific decision making. The general intellectual contribution of the observer, the philosopher, the theorist, the commentator, is important chiefly for its indirect value. It contributes something additional to the total of interactions of interests, ideas, and responsibilities of those most deeply immersed in the decision making activities.

The more important and complex a problem, the less equal to it is the widom of any individual. Social widom is something more. In a democratic society most distinctly and extensively, no matter how heavily decision making weighs on particular individuals, decisions in some fashion or other emanate from the society. This is so because the decision makers reach decisions under the discipline of the society, with eyes and ears keenly sensitive to society, experience tuning them to society, their future dependent upon society. And it is so because the decision makers arrive at decisions through a subtle and intricate processs of intra-institutional interaction in an institution very especially informed and itself highly representative of interaction within the society at large.

Institutions of the Past Need More Study

The word "politics" is usually thought of as the phenomenon of "partisanship" in a particular setting. Actually, of course, it comprehends the whole living and acting process of governance, of which parties are only one feature, however important. And, of course, we quite sensibly refer to "campus politics," "departmental politics," "church politics," and many more. "Politics" is to be defined usefully as "the business of recognizing, treating, balancing, or resolving the differences of interests and functions of individuals and groups." More particularly, it is this business at the level of sovereignty; it is governance. It is the ultimate authoritative level of making sense of things in general. Political institutions are the vehicles of the sovereign generalizing processes of whole societies. Administration at its highest and best is a complement to the over-all generalizing process we call "politics."

In Professor Merriam's book on "Power," his chapter on "The Morbidity and Mortality of Power" might just as well be read as "The Morbidity and Mortality of Social Orders." The point is that after millions of years we still know much too little about establishing, maintaining and developing political orders that can further civilization and advance general welfare. Mankind has done it by fits and starts — and stops.

The United States is rightly thought of as a young nation. Yet it is the second oldest political order of any great pretensions now existing. Recall the Mayas, the Long-Ears of Easter Island, the society that built the amazing first version of the Great Wall of China in pre-history days, the society that built the pyramids, the Greece of Alexander, the Roman Empire, and all the others that rose and fell. Why did they fall? What were their weaknesses in structure and operations? How little we really know about them in these terms! The length of spears used by Alexander's army had much to do with its cellular structure, but the organizational form of infantry continued pretty much the same long after weapons changed. Why did the Moslem advance not succeed in France even though it had swept everything before it until then? Charles Martel's soldiers had armor, the Moslems had cavalry; he determined to mount his armored troops, and to do it took over *control* of the farmlands while leaving its ownership to the nobles and clergy, putting him in a position to deploy men and horses. He stopped the invaders but by means which changed the internal order of France with enduring consequences, some eventually having debilitating effects. Not far apart in time, British developments were in very different directions. Whether we accept the conventional interpretation, basing almost everything on Magna Charta or the picture detailed by the historian A.B. White of the University of Minnesota in *Self-Government at the King's Command*, the rise of democracy was in important ways a structural phenomenon, too.

The study of past political structures and procedures needs much more attention so that understanding of the current scene may be greatly enlarged. This is a fascinating field, and perhaps no other is of equal importance. But how little of our effort is spent in seeking this kind of understanding! It pertains to our conduct of governance at every level.

Making a "Mesh" of Things

About a quarter of a century ago, the Department of Agriculture experimented with a special field team of extremely bright and able young men. Until that time, every person employed by the Department outside of Washington had been an employee of some one of the Department's bureaus, with responsibility confined to it. But these young men were employees of one of the Secretary's staff offices, and, thus, were truly "departmental employees." I was called in to give them a briefing talk. Among other things, I said to them, "Don't make much effort to find over-lapping and duplication. Those things are largely creatures of the imaginations of persons ignorant of the ways of bureaucrats. If they are to be found at all, they are temporary and self-curing. The bureaus are so jealous of their prerogatives that if someone in another bureau seems getting close enough to appear to be capable of the least encroachment, hair-pulling and shin-kicking start at once. We don't have much overlapping," I said, putting the fingers of one hand over the fingers of the other. Then pulling the two hands some distance apart, I added, "What we actually have is this: wide gaps between what we do in the bureaus." Then fitting the ends of my ten fingers between each other, I concluded, "What we need is this." One of the bright young men thereupon said, "You're telling us that it is our job to help make a *mesh* of things."

This is still my point, but I am now talking about all levels of governmental forms and all levels of action in them. As we differentiate ourselves in equipment and function, we can continue to succeed in our efforts to advance civilization only if we avoid making messes of things by finding out more about building and operating institutions that make a mesh of things.

The Political Structure Must Provide for Diverse Views

I am most of all an administrator, and in the past I have talked most about administration. I certainly realize that administrators have important roles in the grand coordinating effort to which I am directing attention. But the more I see of things, the more crucial I see the more frankly political structures and functions to be — most notably a good party system.

Because I have spent a good deal of time in India during the last decade, I am often asked, "Who will succeed Nehru?" I answer that I haven't even an inkling of a guess. When in a company where more can be said, I say that while I have the highest respect for Mr. Nehru, and while I agree that the choice of his successor is a very important question, I think questions about the political structures that will exist at the time of his passing will prove to be even more important. What kind of party system will there be then? To what extent will state structures at that time follow linguistic or religious lines? How much will the nation then be relying upon the states to carry on essential national development activities? How much will the nation then be dependent upon the local "panchayat raj" for carrying on the development program?

Mr. Nehru's most frequently necessary plea to his countrymen is that they forsake "communalism" and put the good of the whole of India first. The government has found it necessary to make very important concessions to parochialisms, and the danger is that the political structures will sprawl and thus endanger the preservation of Indian unity and effectiveness. India will continue to succeed after Mr. Nehru is gone, if communication between leadership and the citizen millions is feasible on a sufficient scale, if political structures provide ample expression for diverse views, and if other facilities provide for their translation and sublimation into majority politics. For these functions there can be no substitute for a good party system — very preferably a system that provides the values of a two-party arrangement.

The problems I point to are not simply problems of India. They are problems everywhere, if we are to keep enriching civilization and maintain generally conditions of order that produce governmental institutions both humanely considerate and decisive. It is not hard to find various examples.

Every few years in New York State there is a drive within the City of New York to "secede" from the state. The argument is that the city differs from the state so much that its interests can not be served by the state. The differences are, indeed, substantial, and the representational pattern is highly inequitable. Yet in spite of the inequity, the very fact that the city and the state have so many differences has frequently caused New York legislation to lead the whole nation in providing patterns for the handling of public problems. The great virtue of the state is its extraordinary cosmopolitanism. The most homogeneous of our states are the most parochial and backward ones.

Society is enriched by diversity of activity, knowledge and ideas, and democracy is heightened by facilitation of interchange in terms of concerns thus diversified. Social and political structures should take account of these things, and, at the same time, take account of human nature in the social context. Barbara Ward not long ago in an admirable *Saturday Review* article incidentally reflected upon some of the phenomena involved in all this, saying that politics goes corrupt most commonly in municipal government and in local trade unions. She attributed this to apathy. A minister in Madison, Wisconsin, wrote to the *Review* to say, I think correctly, that the explanation needs broadening. He said:

Local elections go askew and civic government goes corrupt precisely because the voters *do* know the candidates and office holders. They belong to the same Rotary Club and PTA, their youngsters date each other, their wives ring doorbells for the Community Chest together. How can you accuse a friend of corruption? It's not apathy, not that we don't care or don't know — it's that we do care and do know those guys too well. We care so much about our wives and kids and jobs that we don't dare run risks against the rascals. It's easier to slay the devil at a distance.

This explains shortcomings less drastic than corruption, too; policy issues are ignored, slovenly performance in public office is overlooked; and these things are highly important. Political structure should be designed to make more of these things manageable by citizens, more issues more readily recognized and dealt with. Political structures need first of all to confront citizens with differences in points of view and interest, challenging their parochialisms. Secondly, they need to provide successively higher levels of responsibility of broader scope, to which issues may, when necessary, be elevated.

France for a good many decades provided another, national, example. Under the extraordinary leadership of de Gaulle, unprecedented unity has been maintained for a few years, but the organic structures do not support formation of majorities, do not give many important interest groups confidence of hearing or influence, or demonstrate clear defeat for their demands. Most citizens have suffered chronic political frustration. There are inadequate facilities for interplay of interests and their coordination in majority policy. One, therefore, can not be confident that de Gaulle's great achievements will be a part of his political estate, capable of being carried forward by his political heirs and assigns.

Latin America provides frequent displays of political insecurity and frustration in country after country. Often the constitutional charters resemble our own, while the performances under them differ radically. The opportunity to get orderly political expression of issues that need attention, and the ability to make orderly determinations, are alike irregularly and uncertainly available. Because political succession is not suitably provided for, politics in these nations focuses too exclusively on succession and opens succession to undesirable methods — military or other versions of usurpations that inhibit politics of the proper sort. There is too little way for area and interest problems to be handled politically, and too little way for these matters to be politically or procedurally appealed to higher jurisdictions of popular character and accountability.

Adequate political organization is a very difficult matter with numerous aspects. Of course, people do play a part as individuals. Some persons are more capable of being relatively generalist in function than most others are, and we need to give thought to ways in which we can increase their number and their capacities. But, in doing so we must remember that we are looking for ways to improve the performances of governmental *institutions*. Individuals may develop more institutional skill; institutions may be better structured and managed. And the weight attached to coordination in terms of over-all sense in making these provisions needs to be increased.

To set up a "Dairy Bureau" merely because dairy farmers think it would dignify and emphasize their interests doesn't help make general sense. Or, to establish "a department of Cabinet rank for Education" to please educators. The theory of structuring departments to make "coherent missions" — which has been popular for a decade or more — may make over-all sense harder to achieve; it would resemble the sundering of New York City and New York State, or Michigan and Detroit. Rather, we should be exploring ways to rise above our parochialisms and to find common interests in the riches of a cosmopolitan reality.

Professional civil servants in cities, counties, states, and in national government — or very many of them — might have membership in a common service and be subject to flexibility in assignment to suit times, workloads, and program changes. We should allow substantial indemnification for those whose usefulness to an incoming administration has been damaged by a too high-level association with the outgoing administration. We probably should begin to develop a pooled retirement system for professional public servants as a contribution to flexibility and professional competence.

Political Experience Builds Generalizing Ability

Similarly, we need to give more attention to the development of really good politicians, and should make more political appointments to important governmental posts. Too many ambassadors are experts who are put on top instead of on tap. Too many cabinet members are appointed for their presumed expertness in clientele or subject-matter fields instead of for their political competence to deal with diverse interests and functions. Such appointees inevitably serve as special pleaders for the interests they represent, and make more difficult the distillation of general good sense. This is why the late Charles Gates Dawes often remarked, out of his experience as Budget Director and Vice President, that "the Cabinet comprises the President's worst enemies." The President is pre-eminently responsible for making over-all sense, and he needs much help.

As citizens we need to appreciate more the importance of political experience — especially elective experience over a considerable period of time — on the part of those who seek high office. Really suitable top political leaders are very "rare birds." There is no one professional field, no one type of education or private experience, that surely equips for governorships, cabinet posts, the Presidency and other high political places. But, the importance of extensive political experience is clear. It builds generalizing abilities, not specialism. And nothing so educates able politicians for participation in making sense for society than running for office over and over again.

My reference is to educable politicians. In politics, as in every other field, there are those who do not merit promotion because what they regard as an equipment of "fifteen years of experience" is really only one year of experience repeated fifteen times. I know one man who is a perennial candidate for Governor or United States Senator, getting from fifteen to ninety votes each time. His old automobile's windows are constantly plastered — illegally — with fanatical and incoherent ravings. Obviously, he is not preparing himself for the Presidency.

There are a good many politically ineffective citizens, too, who while not running for office readily predict high popular tides that never appear, and have no least notion of what is politically feasible. No matter how large the community and how much larger the nation where such people live, these citizens suffer from a chronic sort of political autointoxication.

Harder to identify as politically of small competence are a few persons who are elected repeatedly from highly homogeneous states and remain thoroughly insensitive to politics in national terms. Because of their out-of-step conduct, the press gives them much attention and often leads citizens to an inflated view of the importance of the views they express.

We have, in fact, insufficient means for giving any large number of politicians cosmopolitan political experience. Yet from the beginning we have found our most effective national leaders from the ranks of those electively experienced and widely acquainted with people and affairs.

The case of Washington is perhaps a little less than typical, but probably the record would surprise most voters. He was not elected President, and did not make the brilliant success as President he did make simply because he had been a victorious military commander. He first ran for office at the age of 25, and was defeated. He ran again the next year, won, and held political office constantly thereafter until the day he left his seat in the Continental Congress while he was being elected Commander-in-Chief. He knew the whole country extraordinarily well. He was in the public service all but seven of his adult years, and in definitely political rather than professional or specialized posts for a total of 25 years.

. . . to Come to the Aid of the Party

If we are actually to develop more outstanding political leaders, we must increase the total number from which to select. To do this, we need to make politics and politicians more revered. We need also to provide more economic security for politicians.

We need to provide for politicians more generalizing staff aides, and to carry the same idea further into all the organs of government — at the levels of division and section heads, for example. But most of all, we need to structure and to understand government as the prime general instrument for making over-all sense out of a pluralistic and dynamic society.

For this all-important purpose, we need to insure at least proximate majority government, outlawing elections by units instead of by majority vote, requiring bi-partisan or non-partisan redistricting in accord with population changes, and requiring run-off elections whenever candidates otherwise victorious would have secured less than 48 or 49 per cent of the total vote.

Almost every election, in almost every jurisdiction, should be in doubt until the votes are counted. And voters should realize more than ever before the importance of politics and the importance of parties. They should, more often than now, feel that when they vote they are for the time being voting for a party. Citizens can hardly hope to be able to appraise appropriately the performance of all office-holders and governmental programs in the various functional fields and levels of government. Citizens can arrive at proper judgments if they hold a party responsible. Parties are the best means yet devised for securing majority rule and fixing responsibility. These are the prime essentials, if we are to avoid making a mess of things.

Trends in the Comparative Study of Public Administration ✣ Fred W. Riggs

Three trends in the comparative study of public administration during the past half-century may be discerned. The first is by now fairly clear, but the second and third are perhaps only just emerging. The first is a trend from *normative* toward more *empirical* approaches. The second is an emergent emphasis on "*nomothetic*" in contrast with predominantly "*idiographic*" methods. And the third involves a shift from *non-ecological* to *ecological* modes of thought. I shall deal with each trend in succession.

1. The Shift from Normative to Empirical Approaches

By a normative approach I understand one in which the chief aim is to prescribe "ideal," or at least "better," patterns of administrative structure and action. This approach is implicit in most of the so-called "principles" of public administration. It reached its height in the "scientific management" movement with its stress on the "one best way."

As the study of public administration advanced, it became apparent that no simple formula of "efficiency" or "public interest" would provide adequate and clear guides to action. Hence the literature of public administration became more and more cautious. It elaborated multiple and often conflicting criteria for action, gradually increasing its stress on empirical description and "explanation," finally even abandoning the effort to prescribe. The results may be seen in the writings of Herbert Simon and the sociologists of administration, as well as in the studies published by the Inter-University Case Program.

To discern such a trend is not, of course to say that empirical work has replaced normative. Rather, the new emphasis has grown up by the side of the old, challenging and to some extent displacing it, but the older movement is still vigorously alive. Perhaps the crucial point is a growing awareness of the difference between empirical and normative work, and insistence that each has its own appropriate methods, criteria and uses.

This trend in the general field of public administration has its counterpart in comparative studies. Indeed, the analysis of alien and contrasting administrative systems has intensified our awareness of the relativity of our own cultural norms and hence the limited relevance of our most prized administrative values.

An early example of a comparative study, exhibiting an unabashed normativism, is Dorman B. Eaton's *Civil Service in Great Britain: A History of Abuses and Reforms and Their Bearing upon American Politics*. This book was a bell-wether for a substantial outpouring of studies of foreign — chiefly British — administrative practices, the goal of which was to hold up models for emulation here at home. Woodrow Wilson's famous and influential essay falls into this category. More recent examples include the work of Leonard D. White on foreign civil service, coming at a time

"Trends in the Comparative Study of Public Administration," by Fred W. Riggs, reprinted by permission of the International Institute of Administrative Sciences from *International Review of Administrative Sciences*, No. 1 (1962), pp. 9–15.

when the depression and the New Deal brought a reconsideration of our administrative heritage. Other essays which examine the relevance of British administrative practices for America include papers by Donald Price and Rowland Egger.

This normative approach to comparativism, which we might label the "mirror for Americans" style, has, since World War II, been largely replaced by a similar but reverse method that might be called the "mirror for others" style. The angle of vision has been changed to reflect American practice as a model, especially for the peoples of the "underdeveloped" countries. In this category are to be found a growing flood of reports and studies by experts, visiting consultants, technical assistants, and even, to some extent, by the young, Western-trained specialists in public administration of the new States. Among these essays are to be found some keenly discerning work, quite sophisticated in its recognition of the relativity for overseas application of American, British, French or other Western norms.

An outstanding example of this genre is Paul H. Appleby's report on Indian administration. As with many studies of this type, it contains much empirical, analytic material, but underlying the presentation are implicit assumptions about the character of a good administrative system which give the whole treatment a basically normative flavor.

Since the establishment of the United Nations and its public administration program, there has also emerged a type of generalized normative essay which might be called the "mirror for all" style. Here the author attempts to synthesize from the "good" features of several systems those which may be recommended for all. Such endeavors seek to identify the "universals" of the administrative process. An outstanding example is the report, in the form of an elaborate questionnaire, of the United Nations Special Committee on Public Administration Problems; under contracts with the United Nations and Unesco, the International Institute of Administrative Sciences prepared various reports which perhaps fall in this category. Although these reports all include a good deal of empirical data, the basic orientation is the quest for ideal patterns and the identification of difficulties or obstacles to be overcome, and problems to be solved.

It is possible to discern in this literature a growing interest in descriptive and analytic information for its own sake. Thus the normative study of comparative administration merges gradually into the empirical and explanatory. Increasingly, I believe, the more recent writings tend to characterize existing situations, and to offer explanatory notes or hypotheses. I turn then, to the empirical trend in the comparative study of public administration.

Within this empirical category, however, it is necessary, to make a basic distinction between the *idiographic* and the *nomothetic* approaches. Hence in discussing the empirical data, it is convenient to deal with:

2. The Shift from Idiographic toward Nomothetic Approaches

First, by way of definition, let us say that any approach which concentrates on the unique case — the historical episode or "case study," the single agency or country, the biography or the "culture area" — is basically *idiographic*. By contrast, an approach which seeks generalizations, "laws," hypotheses that assert regularities of behavior, correlations between variables, may be called *nomothetic*. Obviously these are polar types, and many studies fall between the extremes, combining idiographic and nomothetic elements in varied proportions.

The trend which I find to be incipient is a shift from interest in predominantly idiographic studies to those which give more and more attention to nomothetic elements.

The classic type of idiographic approach takes the form of a "country study," as in the "comparative government" works devoted to the description and analysis of government in a single country. Often several such area essays are packaged in a single volume under the title, "Comparative Government," with, perhaps, an introductory comment by the editor on points of similarity and difference in the systems described. Normally such country studies include a chapter on the "British Civil Service," the "French Bureaucracy," etc., in which can be found a characterization of each national administrative system.

Some of the IIAS reports mentioned above have considerable data of this type. One of the obvious first steps for the new centers and institutes of public administration is to issue reports on the formal structure of government and administrative organization in their country. However, established research centers have also sponsored reports on public administration in several countries, a notable example being the series published by the Royal Institute of Public Administration.

Many of these works also include a good deal of analytic comment and analysis. The volume by Stene and Associates, for example, is notable in this regard. They are similar in this respect to a growing number of studies which, in addition to some structural description, focus mainly on interpretation and explanation of the phenomena described. These include a substantial series of works on foreign bureaucracies by American political scientists.

These American studies are now joined by a growing literature written by scholars in the countries concerned, especially in England and France.

In a rather different style are some contributions to the study of particular bureaucracies by sociologists. A notable example is the report on Egypt by Morroe Berger. Such works may be compared with the sociological studies of American bureaucracy Bendix, Selznick, and Blau.

Another type of idiographic study uses the historical method. A monumental administrative history is Leonard D. White's four-volume survey of American public administration. There are several histories of the Indian Civil Service and valuable studies of the Philippine and traditional Chinese civil service.

A different kind of historical approach of considerable value for comparative purposes is the "case study" in which an administrative decision is made the focal point for historical exposition. The well-known publications of the Inter-University Case Program are undoubtedly the most outstanding. So far these cases have dealt almost exclusively with American situations, but a new series of overseas cases is in preparation. Also, several of the overseas institutes have launched their own case studies programs, notably the institutes in the Philippines and Viet Nam. One extraordinary case study by José Abueva has come from the Philippine Institute.

Finally, there are works which, though predominantly idiographic in method, bring together data on several or even many administrative systems. We might call this the "classified-data" method. The major works by Herman Finer and Carl Friedrich probably belong in this category. Although they do include a good deal of theorizing about government, basically they classify governmental structures, then juxtapose information about these cognate structures in many societies. Such works, while dealing with government as a whole, include contributions on public administration in chapters dealing with bureaucracy and the civil service.

An important recent administrative work in this category is Brian Chapman's *The Profession of Government.* This book describes various aspects of civil service systems as exemplified in European practice. A work which falls between the one-country and the classified-data type is C. H. Sisson's *The Spirit of British Adminis-*

tration; And Some European Comparisons which, as its title suggests, deals primarily with the British system, but interlards material on similar features of French, German and Swedish practice.

In works of this last type are to be found generalizations, attempts to draw from the concrete experience of several countries hypotheses or "laws" of wide applicability. Insofar as this happens, a nomothetic approach is in use. Let us turn, then, to those studies which seek explicitly to formulate and test general propositions.

3. Nomothetic Approaches: Homological and Analogical

My personal opinion is that the term "comparative" should be restricted, strictly speaking, to empirical, nomothetic studies. However, nomothetic analysis would scarcely be possible without idiographic data. Hence the country reports and case studies provide an indispensable foundation for comparative analysis. It should be added, of course, that nomothetic analysis provides the theories, the conceptual schemes or criteria of relevance which — whether explicitly stated or not — guide the historian and area specialist in his selection of data. Hence the idiographic and nomothetic approaches are not alternative, but complementary, modes of study. Neither can be fruitful without the other.

It should be noted that American studies must be included in nomothetic analysis. Certainly we cannot frame generalizations about government which ignore our own experience. In the context of idiographic work, of course, there is a strategic justification for stressing information about foreign systems of government. The strategic reason is the greater availability of material on American government which lends urgency to the study of other systems. However, it might clarify the situation to call the idiographic study of non-American systems "government of foreign areas," rather than "comparative government."

Nomothetic studies themselves may be subdivided into two main types: one concerned primarily with similarities and differences of structure, i.e., the *homological;* and the other concerned with functions and related variables, the *analogical*.

(a) *Homological* study starts by identifying and describing structures in different systems which have parallel characteristics. In a sense, this is the method used in the works by Finer, Friedrich and Chapman mentioned above. However, to become nomothetic, the analyst must go beyond description to formulate generalizations. These largely take the form of explanatory hypotheses intended to account for the indicated similarities and differences.

Unfortunately, the number of works applying this method to public administration is still quite limited. An interesting example is by S. Y. Teng, who traces important features of the civil service examination system in British and modern Indian practice to a common origin in China.

Such works still have a largely idiographic method, however, since they seek mainly to trace a single course of events with little attempt to generalize therefrom. They fall in the category of "history of ideas." For a more developed illustration of the homological method, one must look to other disciplines. A good example is in the work of A. M. Hocart. Hocart is able to shed some light on the processes of dispersal of traditional political institutions from a common origin through study of homologues in different societies, both contemporary and historical. His work has the advantage also of being quite explicit about the methodology used.

Arnold Toynbee's method, in his monumental *Study of History*, includes a great deal of homological work — from which the author derives certain "laws" of change — but it is also analogical in important respects.

Some authors in public administration have used the study of contrasting structures to advantage. An example is an essay by Samuel Finer in which contrasting trends in the evolution of the British and American patronage systems are explained. A somewhat similar approach is used by Robert Dahl in his analysis of contrasting British and American practices.

Possibly if more attention were devoted to studies of similar and contrasting developmental sequences for institutions and ideas, some generalizations of considerable value for planned change, for "administrative reform," would be made. A new research program of the Maxwell School at Syracuse is launching a systematic study of the processes of "institution building." It illustrates the current interest in this subject which, of course, is basic to the technical assistance enterprise of the United Nations and other agencies. The danger, of course, is that by concentrating on the normative, the hoped-for results, not enough energy will be spent studying actual processes of change, even when — perhaps especially when — the changes were not planned or intended.

(b) My own interest is primarily in nomothetic studies of the *analogical* type. Here the fundamental unit is not a structure but the consequences of structure, i.e., function. Functions can often be characterized in terms of variables, i.e., a shared but changing aspect of something. For example, commodities have the function of being for sale, and hence of having a price. Price is thus a common variable, and separate items may be compared in terms of price. Climates may be compared in terms of temperature. We may compare countries in terms of population, per capita income, the degree of centralization of government, the extent to which the population is "mobilized" for mass communications, etc. Systematic ways of identifying and dealing with such variables are described in the works of the "functional-structuralists."

Many aspects of an administrative system can be analyzed in terms of such functional variables. It then becomes possible to place each system, to "measure" it, in terms of its position on the scale or index for each variable. From such identifications we may move on to postulate relationships, i.e. how changes in one variable tend to be associated with changes in other variables. Such hypotheses may then be tested by looking at the empirical data from a number of actual societies. When we find instances which deviate from the predicted relationship, we are forced to modify or change the hypothesis. In this way, just as in the natural sciences, we may move gradually toward a verified — and verifiable — "science" of public administration. This is the direction in which I hope we can move in the comparative study of public administration. My own work is dedicated primarily to the investigation of paths toward this goal. However, I cannot claim to have found the way. Certainly, our basic concepts are still too vague. They are not yet "operational." Correlations can only be suggested in the most general way, with little progress in finding ways to put them in mathematical or quantitative form.

One of the most interesting works in its attempt to formulate and test general propositions is Daniel Lerner's *The Passing of Traditional Society*. This work is primarily in communications analysis, but it has important implications for administrative study, and gives a good example of the nomothetic method of comparative analysis. In the same connection, we might mention the pioneer work of Karl Deutsch.

Formal attempts to apply functionalism to the comparative study of government have as yet had limited success. The most ambitious experiment is probably the volume by Gabriel Almond and James Coleman, which grew out of the work of the

Committee on Comparative Politics of the Social Science Research Council. Unfortunately, much of this work is still idiographic in approach. The most nomothetic part is the final section by Coleman in which an attempt is made to define and relate variables, such as degree of economic development and centralization of power. Unfortunately, we still lack anything in comparative administration which even approaches this experiment in comparative politics.

4. From Non-Ecological to Ecological Approaches — A Need

In concluding I wish to add a few words about a trend, which I discern only on the horizon, to shift from a predominantly non-ecological to an ecological basis for comparative study. John Gaus was one of the first to urge an ecological view-point in the study of public administration. Unfortunately, few appear to have taken his injunction seriously. For studies of American administration this is not a fatal weakness since, here, administrative institutions are sufficiently autonomous or detached from their total environment to enable them to be studied abstractly, as though they could be explained in terms of their own structure and laws. For most countries of the world, however, this non-ecological viewpoint can only produce misleading impressions. Certainly, in traditional societies politics and administration can only be thought of as undifferentiated aspects of a total system.

In modern, transitional societies, there has been a tendency to establish formal political and administrative institutions, but they remain formalistic. That is to say, effective behavior is still determined, to a considerable extent, by traditional structures and pressures, the family, religion, and persisting socio-economic practices. Hence it is possible to understand politics and administration in these countries only ecologically, i.e. by relating these non-administrative factors to the administrative.

Once we have gone through the difficult exercise of learning how to think ecologically when dealing with foreign countries, we may surprise ourselves by discovering that we can also understand our own government better by ecological analysis. Why, we should inquire, have our institutions become so differentiated? What is it which enables us to treat administrative structure as a thing apart?

I cannot quote to you here a sample of writings to demonstrate my point, to prove a trend from non-ecological toward ecological frames of reference. It is possible, of course, to mention works which devote considerable attention to the geography, history, religion, social structure, etc. of a country being examined. Administration and politics are included as parts of a total system. The country handbooks recently prepared by the Human Relations Area Files are illustrative. Unfortunately, these works often fail to tell us just how the geography or the history or the social structure actually affects the administrative system. Hence the method is not truly ecological, for ecology implies not just a characterization of environments, but rather analysis of the patterns of interaction between the subject of study and its environment.

My point, then, is not to claim a trend, but rather to indicate a necessity for the future. The comparative study of public administration, I believe, will remain relatively sterile and limited in its significance unless, and until, it learns how to change from a predominantly non-ecological to an ecological method.

5. Conclusion

There is no proper conclusion to this paper. Perhaps all that is left to say is a caveat. If what I have said sounds arbitrary, extreme, it is because I have exaggerated and polarized my points for the sake of clarity. An actual essay or paper before you will rarely be a pure case of any of the methods I have spoken of. Rather, it will typically be a mixture, in some degree, of all of them. If we could visualize the range of possible variations in approach to comparative study on a three-dimensional graph, it might take the following form:

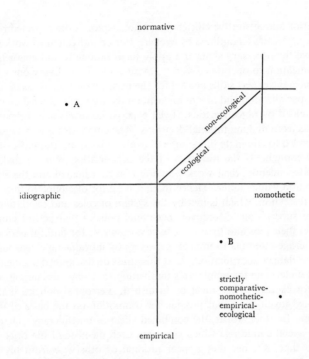

In terms of the graph, we may visualize any actual study as having the combination of characteristics given by a point on the three coordinates, as at A or B. I should also say that the tendency has been, and will be, for comparative study to move, in method and outlook: from the top, down; from the left, right; and from the rear toward the front. While all studies that could be plotted on this graph might be thought of as "comparative" in a broad or vague sense, my own preference would be to consider as "truly" comparative only those studies which are empirical, nomothetic, and ecological.

Theory and Development of Bureaucracy

✤ Peter M. Blau

The superior administrative efficiency of bureaucracy is the expected result of its various characteristics as outlined by Weber. For an individual to work efficiently, he must have the necessary skills and apply them rationally and energetically; but for an organization to operate efficiently, more is required. Every one of its members must have the expert skills needed for the performance of his tasks. This is the purpose of specialization and of employment on the basis of technical qualifications, often ascertained by objective tests. Even experts, however, may be prevented by personal bias from making rational decisions. The emphasis on impersonal detachment is intended to eliminate this source of irrational action. But individual rationality is not enough. If the members of the organization were to make rational decisions independently, their work would not be coordinated and the efficiency of the organization would suffer. Hence there is need for discipline to limit the scope of rational discretion, which is met by the system of rules and regulations and the hierarchy of supervision. Moreover, personnel policies that permit employees to feel secure in their jobs and to anticipate advancements for faithful performance of duties discourage attempts to impress superiors by introducing clever innovations, which may endanger coordination. Lest this stress on disciplined obedience to rules and rulings undermine the employee's motivation to devote his energies to his job, incentives for exerting effort must be furnished. Personnel policies that cultivate organizational loyalty and that provide for promotion on the basis of merit serve this function. In other words, the combined effect of bureaucracy's characteristics is to create social conditions which constrain each member of the organization to act in ways that, whether they appear rational or otherwise from his individual standpoint, further the rational pursuit of organizational objectives.

Without explicitly stating so, Weber supplies a *functional* analysis of bureaucracy. In this type of analysis, a social structure is explained by showing how each of its elements contributes to its persistence and effective operations. Concern with discovering all these contributions, however, entails the danger that the scientist may neglect to investigate the disturbances that various elements produce in the structure. As a result, his presentation may make the social structure appear to function more smoothly than it actually does, since he neglects the disruptions that do in fact exist. To protect ourselves against this danger, it is essential to extend the analysis beyond the mere consideration of functions, as Robert K. Merton points out. Of particular importance for avoiding false implications of stability and for explaining social change is the study of *dysfunctions*, those consequences that interfere with adjustment and create problems in the structure.

A re-examination of the foregoing discussion of bureaucratic features in the light of the concept of dysfunction reveals inconsistencies and conflicting tendencies. If reserved detachment characterizes the attitudes of the members of the organization toward one another, it is unlikely that high *esprit de corps* will develop among them. The strict exercise of authority in the interest of discipline induces subordinates, anxious to be highly thought of by their superiors, to conceal defects in operations from superiors, and this obstruction of the flow of information upward in the hierarchy impedes effective management. Insistence on conformity also tends to engender rigidities in official conduct and to inhibit the rational exercise of judgment needed for efficient performance of tasks. If promotions are based on merit, many employees will not experience advancements in their careers; if they are based primarily on seniority so as to give employees this experience and thereby to encourage them to become identified with the organization, the promotion system will not furnish strong incentives for exerting efforts and excelling in one's job. These illustrations suffice to indicate that the same factor that enhances efficiency in one respect often threatens it in another; it may have *both* functional and dysfunctional consequences.

Weber was well aware of such contradictory tendencies in the bureaucratic structure. But since he treats dysfunctions only incidentally, his discussion leaves the impression that administrative efficiency in bureaucracies is more stable and less problematical than it actually is. In part, it was his intention to present an idealized image of bureaucratic structure, and he used the conceptual tool appropriate for this purpose. Let us critically examine this conceptual tool.

Implications of the Ideal-type Construct

Weber dealt with bureaucracy as what he termed an "ideal type." This methodological concept does not represent an average of the attributes of all existing bureaucracies (or other social structures), but a pure type, derived by abstracting the most characteristic bureaucratic aspects of all known organizations. Since perfect bureaucratization is never fully realized, no empirical organization corresponds exactly to this scentific construct.

The criticism has been made that Weber's analysis of an imaginary ideal type does not provide understanding of concrete bureaucratic structures. But this criticism obscures the fact that the ideal-type construct is intended as a guide in empirical research, not as a substitute for it. By indicating the characteristics of bureaucracy in its pure form, it directs the researcher to those aspects of organizations that he must examine in order to determine the extent of their bureaucratization. This is the function of all conceptual schemes: to specify the factors that must be taken into consideration in investigations and to define them clearly.

The ideal type, however, is not simply a conceptual scheme. It includes not only definitions of concepts but also generalizations about the relationships between them, specifically the hypothesis that the diverse bureaucratic characteristics increase administrative efficiency. Whereas conceptual definitions are presupposed in research and not subject to verification by research findings, hypotheses concerning relationships between factors are subject to such verification. Whether strict hierarchical authority, for example, in fact furthers efficiency is a question of empirical fact and not one of definition. But as a scientific construct, the ideal type cannot be refuted by empirical evidence. If a study of several organizations were to find that strict hierarchical authority is not related to efficiency, this would not prove that no such relationship exists in the ideal-type bureaucracy; it would show only that these organizations are not fully bureaucratized. Since generalizations about idealized states defy testing in systematic research, they have no place in science. On the other hand, if empirical evidence is taken into consideration and generalizations are modified accordingly, we deal with prevailing tendencies in bureaucratic structures and no longer with a pure type.

Two misleading implications of the ideal-type conception of bureaucracy deserve special mention. The student of social organization is concerned with the patterns of activities and interactions that reveal how social conduct is organized, and not with exceptional deviations from these patterns. The fact that one official becomes excited and shouts at his colleague, or that another arrives late at the office, is unimportant in understanding the organization, except that the rare occurrence of such events indicates that they are idiosyncratic, differing from the prevailing patterns. Weber's decision to treat only the purely formal organization of bureaucracy implies that all deviations from these formal requirements are idiosyncratic and of no interest for the student of organization. Recent empirical studies have shown this approach to be misleading. Informal relations and unofficial practices develop among the members of bureaucracies and assume an organized form without being officially sanctioned. Chester I. Barnard, one of the first to call attention to this phenomenon, held that these "informal organizations are necessary to the operations of formal organizations." These informal patterns, in contrast to exceptional occurrences . . . are a regular part of bureaucratic organizations and therefore must be taken into account in their analysis.

Weber's approach also implies that any deviation from the formal structure is detrimental to administrative efficiency. Since the ideal type is conceived as the perfectly efficient organization, all differences from it must necessarily interfere with efficiency. There is considerable evidence that suggests the opposite conclusion; informal relations and unofficial practices often contribute to efficient operations. In any case, the significance of these unofficial patterns for operations cannot be determined in advance on theoretical grounds but only on the basis of factual investigation. . . .

Public Administration: Toward the Future ✤ ANDRÉ MOLITOR

In the public administration of today and tomorrow, specific problems are and will be set, first to the industrialized and economically developed countries, secondly to countries in the process of development, and thirdly on the level of international and supranational administration. May I suggest that we should conduct our inquiry in those three directions in turn. It will, of course, be a cursory inquiry but will nevertheless open up certain prospects. This survey will consequently deal with the problem of administration towards the future on those three parallel planes, on which are found the major patterns in which present-day public administration is embodied.

"Public Administration: Toward the Future," by André Molitor, reprinted by permission of the International Institute of Administrative Sciences from *International Review of Administrative Sciences*, No. 4 (1961), pp. 375–381.

These three "embodiments" of public administration doubtless have much in common. But in each case their peculiar features involve individual problems, so that it is appropriate for us to examine them separately.

I. The Problems of Public Administration in Industrialized and Economically Developed Countries

In this first group of countries, I include, among others, the Union of Soviet Socialist Republics and the European People's democracies as well as Northern America and the Western European democracies.

In spite of the extreme differences in political systems and economic structures, the countries of Europe arrayed under Soviet allegiance appear to me, as far as public administration conditions are concerned, closer to the Western democracies than to the countries in the process of development. I would, however, point out that, since I have not enough first-hand experience of the Communist systems, I am forced to take the Western democracies as the starting-point for my thinking and as the source of any supporting examples.

If I were to attempt to put in a nutshell the fundamental problem that has to be faced, today and in the near future, by the public administration of industrialized and economically developed countries, I should say that it must cope with, and adapt itself to, a new and drastic technical revolution, and to the present and future effects of that revolution on economic and social life.

The revolution is as far-reaching as the First Industrial Revolution of the early nineteenth century. And we remember the tremendous impact which that had on society and on the organization of public services. Let us think, for example, of the administrative upheaval that Great Britain had to pass through a century ago, so as to adjust itself to the new tasks of the Industrial Era. We have every reason to imagine that, during the next twenty years, our administrative authorities will be expected to make a tremendous effort to adapt themselves. And if they fail to undertake that effort, or to carry it through, serious consequences that are already felt in some countries, will follow for the community.

Let us go into all this a little more closely. My task here is not to describe the present technical revolution, or its economic and social effects. We are involved in what Lewis Mumford, as long as thirty years ago, in his book *Technique and Civilization*, described as the transition from the "Palaeotechnical Era," the era of the steam-engine, to the "Neotechnical Era" we are now entering, that of atomic energy. As I have said, the Second Industrial Revolution is as radical and as important as the First. Yet it differs from it in many features in which the technical order affects the sociological order. It has recourse, to a much greater extent and in every field, to scientific method. It tends to control and to absorb the impact of the Machine Age. At all levels, it needs better qualified technical staff, a fact which leads to greater concern for training. The First Industrial Revolution brutally upset the former social order and distorted the face of the earth. The Second is more careful to spare and to restore the social fabric. It gradually eliminates the proletariat. It is beginning to focus its attention on leisure as much as on work. It aims at a harmonious arrangement of man's habitation, and at the conservation of Nature that man had wantonly squandered and destroyed during the last century.

What, then, are the general implications of this turning-point of history, for public administration, for its objectives and its means of action? May I submit a few remarks on that point.

1. The administration of yesterday did not, as has long been maintained, merely perform mechanical tasks. Even then, it took part in general policy-making. But it did so at a time when there was but little State intervention and little concern for medium-term and long-term forecasting.

Economic and social evolution, and the development of the Welfare State have brought about a change in the role of the State. They have led us to expect a minimum amount of planning, or at least of programming, in the work of the authorities and consequently of the administration, even in the countries most traditionally distrustful of the State and attached to freedom of enterprise. This trend appears likely to be maintained in the coming years. It will always, to some extent, remain opposed to the concern, which is legitimate enough in itself, for protecting the citizen against arbitrary authority, the vagaries of bureaucracy or — what is perhaps even worse and in any case is more insidious — the temptation to make people happy in spite of themselves.

Whether the administration of tomorrow will be at the service of a system in which general planning is highly developed, or part of a political system in which wider scope will be left to voluntary effort, it cannot, in any case, without running the risk of considerable national backwardness, do without at least a medium-term or even a long-term programme outlook, and without the proper means for that programming.

The generalization of that outlook appears to me to be connected with the second stage of technical civilization, to which corresponds a second phase of State intervention better regulated and co-ordinated than the first.

2. The generalized trend towards an administration more aware of its general political aims, and more desirous of making its own work part of a national progress, is powerfully supported by the development of considerable equipment for scientific inquiry and for the analysis of the various facets of economic and social life.

In matters where, until recently, empiricism and improvisation prevailed, the resources of the social sciences have been developed since a generation ago. Those sciences are still young but are making swift progress, and are taking advantage of the perfecting of new and powerful means and resources. The collection and classification of statistical data, the analysis of economic conditions and structures, sociological surveys, electronic data processing, and the advent of operations research give us grounds for great hopes.

But we should be realistic and not be too eager to imagine an administration of the future in which political and governmental action may be determined and decided beforehand, which would be unfortunate in many ways. Let us rather say that there is some likelihood, in the fairly near future, that means of analysis will be available to the administration that will enable it to submit to the authorities a choice of courses of action, increasingly based on collected rational data, that will more accurately indicate the risks and consequences of any selection.

These are a few factors which seem to me calculated to have a great influence on the administration of tomorrow, in determining government objectives and decision-making. The influence of science and techniques on the performance of the day-to-day tasks entrusted to many a public administrative agency might well be examined on similar lines. Even now, the very advanced stage of mechanization reached for certain tasks such as the settlement of expenditure, book-keeping and statistics has simplified the work of many offices. A few weeks ago, I received a letter from the first fully automated post office in the United States of America, and doubtless in the world. It most appropriately came from a city called Providence (Rhode Island). I daresay that public administration in general is less suitable than private enterprise for the widespread use of these methods, owing to the peculiar nature of certain duties devolving upon the public service. It is nevertheless true that a vast amount of progress is still to be made in that field. Its impact will be twofold. The citizen will benefit by the increased efficiency of the administrative machinery and, at the same time, a multitude of tedious tasks will be eliminated and no longer crush those who perform them with their boring monotony. It may be added that certain advances in sociology and applied psychology will perhaps make it possible to utilize administrative personnel in a more flexible and suitable manner, especially through wiser selection and by putting the right man in the right place.

But, again, this does not mean that every problem will be solved, and that improved techniques, or the development of scientific research in our bureaucracies, is likely at short notice to lead us to the Brave New World. Besides, the course of life is such that, as soon as any problems are solved, new ones always arise.

3. All this tends to prove that public administration today and tomorrow is much more influenced by the technical factor than it was yesterday. Although general administrative duties remain vital, the multiplication and specialization of tasks involve increasing recourse to specialists and technicians.

That being the position, some people take pleasure in reminding us of the dangers of the technicians controlling the statesmen, and in raising the bogey of a techno-bureaucratic tyranny. The problem deserves to be considered in the light of a tradition which, at least in political democracies, has always insisted on keeping exports on tap and not on top and on leaving the last word to men who, though without technical qualifications, are entrusted by the will of the nation with tasks of political leadership. Likewise, the wholesale and necessary recourse to technicians is open to question. Is there no risk of the disappearance, from among the groups of leading administrators, of the essential concern for comprehensiveness, which combines the technical aspects of a problem and converts them into a possible course of action on the level of a general policy? It is increasingly necessary, in the industrialized and economically developed countries, to maintain this concern for comprehensiveness among leading administrators, including technicians. That presupposes that one of the vital problems of the administration of today and tomorrow should be solved on those lines by the constant education of the chief administrators, which should smoothly lead them from technical preoccupations to that concern for all-comprehensiveness whose true name is wisdom.

Plato, in *The Republic*, describes this wisdom that is required of rulers and consists in "bringing the mind's eye to contemplate the essence of goodness and thenceforth using it as a model for governing the State, private individuals and oneself, and in taking upon oneself . . . the burden of authority and of the administration of business with the common good alone in view . . . ." Holy writ, too, describes the wisdom of the scribe who may be looked upon as the ancestor of our senior civil servants . . .

4. Another factor which has an important influence on public administration, as well as on many other fields of social life, is the swift progress of events in our times. A few years ago, the French philosopher Daniel Halévy wrote a brilliant little *Essay on the Acceleration of History* in which he shows how, since the earliest times, the rate at which decisive events have followed one another in the technical, political,

social and other spheres has increased until the present time. The acceleration has by now become frantic. In the field of science and technology, for instance, an invention can hardly reach the industrial utilization stage before it is made obsolete by some other discovery, which the producers are literally compelled to put into "cold storage" until the first is worked out as a commercial proposition. This illustration, taken from the field of science, is repeated in every field of social life. The administration, which is the expression of authority that provides a framework for social life as a whole, is faced with this hallucinating sequence of events. By nature, it is slower than the events, since it is the instrument of authority intended to provide them with continuity and coherence and to fit them into a programme of action through a choice of possible courses. Moreover, in industrialized countries, administrative structures and procedures often date from a period when the pace was a great deal slower. That sets the administration of today and of tomorrow a tremendous task of adaptation. To be sure, it is out of the question that the machinery of authority should give way to the confusion of events and go adrift. The administrative machinery cannot, without serious danger to itself and the public, allow too great a lag between its rate of action and the rate of events. Beyond a certain limit, the result would be a cultural lag or, worse still, a rout. The authority then has no control over occurrences whose meaning it no longer grasps, and the administrative apparatus merely beats the empty air as events get beyond its control. If the administration wishes to play its part properly, it should not run after events, but keep abreast of them, and even act in advance of them. That is doubtless a difficult task. It calls for those virtues that are the opposites of the shortcomings, such as cumbersomeness, slowness, routine and lack of flexibility, for which the public service is criticized. It need hardly be pointed out that the problem is essentially one of training. And, in that respect, it appears imperative to stress once more the importance of the in-service training of all civil servants, and especially those at the top level. In the administration, as elsewhere, the main cause of the lag behind events often arises from the fact that the responsible officials, even if they have received unusually good training at the start, are satisfied to spend that intellectual capital during their entire careers, and are not systematically urged to readjust their ideas and imaginations to current conditions. Such was the case of the generals who fought in 1940 as if they were still in 1918, and of the colonial administrators who were outstripped by their wards. Other examples might be quoted.

A biologist has defined life as the aggregate of organized forces struggling against death. And we may say that it is essential for administrations to wage an unceasing campaign against the cristallization of outlooks, which is a kind of death. In that connection there is no better cure than taking part in a permanent educational and readjustment activity. To be sure, we cannot tell whether the rate of acceleration of history will continue to increase. As a matter of fact, one can hardly imagine how it could. But, in any case, it is and will remain increasingly necessary for our public administrators to be prepared to adapt themselves to the changing world of tomorrow.

5. I also feel that, in the bulk of the countries with ancient administrative traditions, the civil service, or in other words the aggregate of the men who form the administration, is becoming and will continue to become less isolated from the remainder of the nation. The comparative isolation of the civil service in relation to the other social forces of the country has, above all, occurred where the administrative personnel is governed by the so-called "career system," which considers the

exercise of public office as a lifelong vocation. Even in those countries, the administration now no longer appears to be as isolated from the remainder of the citizens as it was two or three generations ago. I think that there is a wide variety of reasons for this. In the first place, there is a standardization of conditions of employment in the private sector, so that the large and medium-sized enterprises become bureaucratic, owing to the application everywhere of a social security system the equivalent of which was formerly the privilege of public servants. On the other hand, the nature of the duties that devolve upon the State places the civil servants in ever closer touch with the general body of citizens. The representatives of an authority which has become more technical and less regalian no longer appear to be as far apart from the people as they used to be. It is probable that this trend will be maintained during the coming years, provided that the technical nature of the duties does not set up a fresh screen between the people and the men at the helm.

The above remarks far from exhaust a possible inquiry into the prospects of public administration in the industrialized and economically developed countries. But I cannot devote any more time to it, because we still have to examine two other important aspects of our subject.

II. The Prospects of Public Administration in Countries in the Process of Development

The second fundamental problem of public administration for the coming years is how to organize the administrative structures and the civil service in countries in the process of development. I use the term "countries in the process development" because I have not been able to find a better one. The term "under-developed countries" is sometimes used, but is inadequate, and the countries in question rightly feel offended because, in most of them, economic and social under-development goes hand in hand with an ancient, genuine and advanced culture. Another term is "newer countries," but some of them are among the oldest kingdoms on earth. Yet another term is "countries that have recently attained independence," but many of them have been independent for centuries. However that may be, the countries in the process of development are faced with an administrative problem of extraordinary magnitude. Its solution is a prerequisite for their progress and — let us say so frankly — for the general balance of power in the world.

The problem is many-sided. For our present purposes, I shall select only two of its aspects. The first is the problem of manpower. The countries under consideration have to recruit and train qualified officials who have acquired the peculiar turn of mind expected of public servants. The second aspect of their problem is how to perfect administrative structures and processes, so that progress and development may take place under the best possible conditions.

1. With regard to manpower, I shall say a few words about training. The training, at every level, of talented groups of administrators is one of the essential requirements of the countries in the process of development. The experience of the former colonies that have recently been emancipated supplies proof of this. Among them, some start off with a fair number of sufficiently trained civil servants. And, although it may be observed that they do not get off the mark without difficulty, they do so more smartly than others, which set off without the necessary nucleus of trained men and are terribly handicapped.

In that field, and indeed, by definition, demand is always greater than supply. By that, I mean that there is hardly an instance of any country attaining either independence or development with a really sufficient number of qualified administrators at its disposal. The problem is always how to make up a deficiency. But the deficiency may be greater or smaller according to whether or not steps have been taken in time to organize the training system. Besides, during a number of years, those countries will have to be satisfied with civil servants the majority of which will have received a so-called "accelerated" training, i.e. a faster one than a full and well-balanced process would normally require. Such are the difficulties attached to their coming of age.

As to requirements in the field of the training of administrators, they assume two forms. First, that of the administrative skills demanded of them. But that is not the most complicated problem. The most complicated problem consists in developing in administrators and civil servants the turn of mind and what I might call the special ethics of the public service. Skills are obviously vital, as is the organization of administrative structures and procedures. But the behaviour of the State's servants towards the public service, the notion they have of their duties, their sense of the general interest, their concern for the public welfare, their independence with regard to private interests, and their willingness to sacrifice their personal interests to the common weal, are all characteristics which, in any case, can only be maintained with difficulty in any body of civil servants. They have to be developed in societies which have hitherto been organized on highly different principles. It would be untrue to say that these characteristics are not found in societies in the process of development. But they have not had an opportunity to flourish there in connexion with a general notion of the State and of the public service, which to those countries is a pronounced novelty that calls for a rearrangement of social values.

It must be admitted that this turn of mind, the ethics of the public service, is difficult to develop. It cannot be created artificially out of nothing. It presupposes a general condition of morals and customs. It calls for a system for selecting administrative elites in an environment in which the general system of education has already prepared the way. It also requires the formation in the administration of a sound tradition which provides the civil servant with a background and turns his mind towards the imperatives of the service. All that takes time. Perhaps not quite as much time as to grow a real English grass-lawn, but quite a long time all the same.

2. As to administrative structures and processes, the essential concern of the authorities in a country in the process of development will be to adapt the structures and procedures to the real state of the country, and make them flexible enough to develop gradually.

In that respect, a frequent temptation should be resisted, that of transferring and setting up, in countries in the process of development, structures and processes of administrative action and management that are found suitable in countries that have gone much further forward on the road to development and industrial civilization. This applies to the administrative system in the same way as to the actual political system. Nowadays, we see too many developed countries that are full of good intentions towards "younger" countries suggest that they should adopt, as an ideal pattern and without carrying out the essential transpositions, their own techniques and their own methods of administration, which are those of a highly industrialized civilization. Similarly, in the political sphere, they tend to propose the adoption of the most refined forms of political democracy, whereas those forms could only be a much more advanced stage of the process which the "younger" countries are only beginning to undergo.

For their part, countries in the process of development sometimes suffer the same temptation to press on and scorch the road, and to adopt administrative techniques they think are sound, because they have been successfully tried and tested in a different context. In both cases, the view is mistaken and its consequences may be serious. While it may be admitted that public administration, rests upon a given number of very general principles of application, it is even more true that a national administrative system may and must be closely related to the historical background and the stage of evolution of the country concerned. The fact, in my opinion, is merely the application to the field of administration of a general law which holds good for all social machinery — for the educational apparatus, for instance. Purely and simply to transfer to one country an administrative system suitable for another that is more developed economically or socially is an artificial operation involving great dangers and leading to bitter disappointment.

Most of the industrialized nations have for decades, and even for centuries, carried out tasks of public administration in the territories they have colonized. Such tasks may be variously appraised from the point of view of value judgements. As the case may be, their work may be put forward as a venture aiming at imperialistic exploitation, or as the conferring of the blessings of civilization on destitute countries.

The truth is usually a mixture of both points of view, and cannot be sorted out. As in most human actions, light and shade are intermingled. But, however that may be, the European nations have fulfilled an historical role whose administrative aspects are highly significant. That phase of their action is vanishing altogether. During the coming years, those nations — and many others, such as the United States of America and Israel — will, instead, be confronted with a new task, that of technical co-operation and of helping the younger countries in various fields. And assistance in problems of public administration will then take up a large share of the total assistance. As well as actual colonial administrative action, many countries have, in any case, already been carrying on technical assistance missions, which have only recently been known by that name, in the field of public administration.

Technical co-operation in the field of public administration between the industrialized countries and countries in the process of development must, like the action of the international organizations in that field, be conducted with much tact and caution in the spirit I have just described. It calls, on the one hand, for much unselfishness and, on the other, for much wisdom and sense of discrimination. By joint action, the receiving countries should be persuaded to perfect whatever administrative solutions are in keeping with the requirements and with the factually assessed potentialities of the stage of evolution reached.

. . . .

What I have just said about public administration in the countries in the process of development is, I think, sufficient to show that we have there one of the major aspects of the administrative problems of today and tomorrow. The stability and well-being of what has been called the "uncommitted world" and, indirectly, the general peace of the entire world depend largely on the solutions that will be applied in those countries to the administrative problem, through the establishment of public services adapted to their real needs, and staffed with civil servants technically trained and morally prepared for the performance of their tasks, with a view to both serving the authority and respecting the citizen. One should not attempt to conceal the almost unlimited proportions of this programme of action nor the patience and tenacity it requires of those called upon to carry it out, either in the countries concerned, or in the countries and international organizations that supply them with technical co-operation for their administrative planning.

III. International and Supranational Administration

I still have to speak briefly of the third aspect of public administration in the world of today and tomorrow, International and Supranational Administration.

In spite of upheavals that disturb it, real and apparent discordance, and struggles between States and between classes, the world is progressing towards unity.

At the end of the last World War, Wendell Wilkie wrote a book called *One World*. More than ever, the world really appears to have started on a process of unification. A closer and closer network of relations encircles the globe. First, they may be material, and transport provides the finest example of this, since my country is now only six hours away from yours by air. But the relations are also intellectual and moral, for there are increased means of disseminating information, and concern for identical problems creates, for instance, a world public opinion that is roused everywhere when any part of the earth is perturbed. The development of the international public institutions and of their administrations is connected with that fundamental phenomenon of our times. When, on the eve of the Second World War, the League of Nations foundered helplessly, it was possible to believe for a while that international institutions were an incidental development. They are nothing of the kind. Their present extension is a major event in the evolution of the world, and there is no turning back from it, whether they are world-wide or regional institutions, or political or specialized organizations.

The international administrations will, during the coming years, have to solve a certain number of important administrative problems. Fundamentally, no doubt, the questions do not differ from those which national administrative authorities have to solve. But yet, the very facts of the situation involve problems peculiar to those organizations.

In that connection, I think it worth while to distinguish the staffs of the international administrative agencies or their headquarters, if you prefer to call them so, from their field services.

I shall only refer for the record to the special problems of the field services of international administrative agencies. Nearly all those problems come within the scope of the technical assistance and co-operation I have already mentioned when dealing with administration in countries in the process of development. On the other hand, I feel that I ought to enlarge a little upon the general administrative problems of the international organizations and on the problems their headquarters are called upon to solve. In fact, it is a case of having to create entirely new administrative machinery out of nothing, and to make it work as smoothly and efficiently as possible. To the observer interested in political and administrative science, the great public international organizations therefore appear to be a new and highly original expression of officialdom.

The first problem international administrations, as well as national administrations, have to consider is manpower. They have to recruit highly qualified personnel, make rules for them, and organize their working conditions. In doing so they have to select between the career system or a system of unstable employment. They have to adopt recruitment techniques that will enable them to have at their service, without irritating interference from Member States, highly qualified officials who will be loyal to the charter and ideals of the organization. They have to combine those requirements with legitimate or unjustified relics of nationalism, and particularly with a distribution of employment vacancies proportionate to the relative importance of the Member States. The methods of recruitment and training of the officials raise a whole series of general and technical questions, and give rise to many projects among which I would mention, by way of illustration, the possible establishment of an international civil service training school.

When the international civil servants have been recruited, they have to be adapted to life abroad and to extremely variegated work surroundings in which outlooks, administrative traditions, ways of thought and technical processes are highly varied and at times conflicting, and in which there is the added hindrance of language difficulties. With all those odds against it, the international administrative institution has to frame a set of administrative principles, that is, a coherent intellectual tradition that will impart life and spirit to its work.

It has to give itself a structure and procedures consonant with its objectives while avoiding, as much as possible, the cumbersomeness with which all bureaucracies are afflicted, but which principally affects international bureaucracies, where the most priceless applications of Parkinson's Law may be found.

International administrations are faced with additional difficulties that arise from the very nature of the institutions they serve and the aims they pursue.

Many international organizations entirely lack decision-making powers, and are bodies for study, research or consultation. That is, for instance, the case of the Council of Europe. Others act as a forum for high-level debates and recommend large-scale action. But the enforcement of many of their decisions rests with each Member State, or at least requires its consent or co-operation. As a result of that position, action, an essential factor in the concept of administration, does not predominate in international organizations. Whence the danger of an unrealistic atmosphere being bred and propagated in those institutions. Whence also the importance given to procedural formalities, and the danger of a feeling of frustration being prevalent among the staffs of the institutions, for they hardly ever see the actual results of their efforts.

On the other hand, whenever an international administration has real powers of action and decision-making, it offers the essential features of a complete administration. Its powers arouse that sense of urgency and efficiency which is the only real driving force of administrative action. Such is the case with the few institutions endowed with supranational powers. It is also the case with technical co-operation services.

Similarly, in many international administrations at the present stage there are, strictly speaking, no contacts with the persons or, if interest groups are involved, the bodies under administration. There are consequently the same dangers as in national administrative agencies that have no contacts with the public, and are threatened with living on the fringe of factual reality.

Further, in connection with international administrations, a final problem arises as to the distribution of authority, and it has direct repercussions on the working of their administrative services. For obvious structural reasons, the national pattern of distribution of authority, which has become traditional in democracies, between a Parliament and an Executive is not reproduced in the same simple form at the top of the international organizations. Their constitutional structures are highly varied, and newly-formed institutions proceed tentatively. It is therefore difficult at this stage to examine the real distribution of authority, the components of the decision-making process, the methods for the control of implementation, and so on. Hence, it is often difficult to say precisely where the administrative components, i.e. international civil servants, fit into the machinery, and what effective part they play in the exercise of authority and in general policy-making, as also to what extent they are effectively supervised when they take action. It may also be wondered whether, at times, the conditions are not fulfilled for the excessive development of a technocratic authority in the hands of international administrators and experts, who are insufficiently supervised by the political authority. It should be fully emphasized that, in every way, the international administrative institutions are still in their infancy and are passing through a period of trial and experiment, even though they already have tens of thousands of officials in every part of the world and have fine achievements to their credit.

But two things appear to be certain. The first, as I have already pointed out, is that there is no going back on the development of international administration. Short of a world-wide catastrophe, those administrations are destined to become one of the permanent features of world organization. The second point is that international administration will be one of the main features of the public structures of tomorrow, and that the international civil service, in spite of its present problems and difficulties, is, socially and professionally, a new departure which, in various forms, will be called upon to break new ground in the development of the world of tomorrow.

2

Organizational Theory

Organization theory as it developed toward a "science" in the 1930's has been the subject of much criticism and revision during the last twenty years. Indeed, contemporary organization theory, generally called "behavioral," represents an interdisciplinary approach and views organizations as social institutions in which the individual is concerned with such factors as his role and status, relationship to the work group, his perception of authority and leadership, and the role of the organization in society.

Studies in this area emphasize the fact that modern man's life is the product of living in a society in which most of his life is organized for him. Organization theory is not concerned with personality, but, as Victor Thompson writes, the bureaucratic structure, "can tolerate considerable variations in personalities . . . organization theory is only concerned with those aspects of behavior which are determined by organizational structure."

Many of the findings cited in such studies deal with private as well as public institutions, thus making the conclusions more general than if they distinguished between behavior and events in the two kinds of organizations. It is a search for "universals" in organization at the broadest and highest level.

Organization Theory: An Elephantine Problem ♣ DWIGHT WALDO

. . . .

A Look Backward

Writers on theory of organization make much of recent and rapid development — "even ten years ago, it would not have been possible to bring together such a group of papers." Indeed, this sense of recent origins and rapid development tends to be shared widely among the behaviorally oriented who are concerned with the

Reprinted from the *Public Administration Review*, the journal of the American Society for Public Administration, Vol. XXI, No. 4, 1961, pp. 216–221, by permission of the publisher.

development of "administrative science," whether or not they are identified with organization theory by name or intent. No doubt the self-conscious pioneer always is inclined to deprecate his forerunners so that his own exploits may appear the greater, but there is a sense in which the current writers are quite correct. Volume XI of the *Encyclopedia of the Social Sciences* (1933) contains the entry "Organization, Administrative," by Herman Finer, and the entry "Organization, Economic," by Walton Hamilton (in addition to the piece by L. D. White, "Administration, Public," in Volume I), but there is no entry for Theory of Organization or Organization Theory. It is wholly predictable that the new edition of this work, now in the planning, will have a lengthy essay under one of these headings. There *are* new data, new ideas, new interminglings of disciplines, and fresh strong impulses, all in addition to the idea that it is useful to try to theorize about organization "as such."

Nevertheless, there are many themes in the contemporary writings with roots and analogues in the past, more than the contemporary writers would appear to believe; as anyone can verify who will, for example, leaf through the pages of the *Papers on the Science of Administration* (1937). In the study of administration one can find for at least two generations back, firm declarations that what up to this point has been art, experience, guess, and intuition is now about to become Science, that momentous and converging developments now make this possible for the first time, that what has seemed diverse is about to be unified by general, abstract principles or theories, etc. As to theory of organization, specifically, the *Papers* are introduced by Luther Gulick's famous "Notes on the Theory of Organization." In a more general sense much of social science (if I may use the term) through the centuries has dealt with theory of organization. John Gaus once suggested that Plato's *Republic* be viewed as a treatise on personnel administration; alternatively, it might be viewed as a treatise on organizing a government. In short, when one of our writers states that some years ago a discussion of organization theory would have dealt with such things as line and staff and span of control, whereas present writers deal with all manner of different things, he is correct; but it is not yet clear what the new theory *is*, nor how great is the net gain.

From Administrative Theory to Organization Theory

The rise to popularity of organization theory probably can be attributed to various sources, among them the oft-cited fact that ours is an Age of Organization and that this pervasive phenomenon is a natural subject for attention. It is plausible, however, that fashions in social science methodology and philosophy have played a part. In general, among those concerned with the Scientific approach to the study of "cooperative action," there has been something of a movement away from the terms "administration," "administrative," and "administrative theory" to the terms "organization," "organizational," and "organization theory." It is hypothesized (to use a favorite expression of our authors) that the mood and methods of behavioralism are responsible for this movement, and my speculation runs as follows.

The behavioralists want above all else, of course, to be Scientific in the study of social phenomena, taking as their model what they conceive to be the outlook and methods of physical science. The general goal is a value-free generalization about how the subject phenomena behave, given specified conditions. "Values" are proper data for scientific generalizations, but the social scientist, as scientist, has no concern for their "intrinsic validity" (if I may be forgiven the term). Technologies and applied sciences take the theories achieved by pure science and use them in the realization of human values. To be sure, this is desirable and gives further import-ance to the enterprise of pure science; but pure science is higher on the Scientist's value-scale than applied science. Pure science is *purer*, untainted by the humanness of values.

Now, administration, private or public, is an applied science — if it is not indeed a profession, an art, or something less. "Administrative theory" suggests an engage-ment with the world, a striving after values. One can, to be sure, make a respectable compromise, and seek a "normative science," one in which values are posited but not justified, striven for but not examined; and some would argue that for adminis-trative (or organizational) science this not only is the best approach, but the only feasible one. But even in this case particular organizational values must be dealt with aseptically.

"Organization," on the other hand, suggests something "out there." Organiza-tions are value-saturated, of course, but the researcher can be free not only from the values of particular organizations, but from the administrator's natural involvement with the organization's values. He can become an anthropologist, so to speak, completely detached from the society he observes. Organization theory — "how things are" — suggests, in short, less value-involvement than administrative theory — "how things should be done (at least if you want to achieve such-and-such)."

The Meaning of Theory

Since our undertaking is an examination of theory of organization, with a view to assessing the present status of this theory, a proper next step is to ask: What is theory? *This* is a tangled skein, for certain; but fortunately our involvement can be brief. One or two distinctions will serve our purposes.

As used in this discussion, an organizational theory means simply a conceptual scheme, the aim (but not necessarily the achievement) of which is to enable us to understand, to predict, and to control (if we wish) organizational phenomena. We regard it as quite legitimate to use the term theory in treating of the ethical, the valuational; but we shall not use it here in that connection, except as such considera-tions are involved in descriptive or causal theories of an "if-then" variety.

On the other hand, we avoid the strict meaning of the term given in the physical sciences (or at least by their interpreters), according to which a theory not only is a tight logical structure with empirical referents, but can be refuted by a single con-trary empirical finding. (Presumably, nobody would argue that we have yet achieved much if any organizational theory by *these* criteria.) Most importantly, we shall not distinguish between *theories* and *models*, meaning by the latter conceptual representations of organizational phenomena, the first aim of which is *understanding* as a step toward prediction and control, but which, compared to theories, are generally looser in logical structure and less precisely, and differently, related to their empirical referents. Some would prefer to call "models" many or all of the conceptualizations reviewed below. They may, if they wish!

"About It, and About"

Those who not only do much of their living in organizations but deal with them professionally, so to speak, may feel that it is very obvious what organization "is," and that attempts to construct theories of organization are at best an unnecessary elaboration, at worst a positive obfuscation. There is, to be sure, a case for knowl-edge gained from personal experience, for the intuitive, for direct sensual perception; for some purposes such knowledge, not theoretical constructs, is of the essence.

However, only the mildest sort of commitment to the position that through study administration can become more scientific (not necessarily A Science) suffices to arouse a concern for organizational theory. What is the "stuff" of organization? How does it move? To have any answer that can be stated in general terms, even if the level of abstraction is not high, is to have a theory of organization.

A definition of organization is a theory of organization — at least a crude sketch of a theory — for it must necessarily try to state in general, more or less abstract, terms what the essentials are and how they relate. Who has not tried his hand at framing a one-sentence (or even one-paragraph) definition of organization has denied himself an educational experience of high value. The abstract nouns and adjectives that are the conventional building blocks will be found to be unbelievably complex, awkward, misshapen. At the end, one may believe he knows less rather than more about organization, but he is likely to have a new respect for semantics and more understanding of the problems of the scientific enterprise in its application to human affairs.

Personally, I am of two minds about the value of taking the problem of definition seriously, head-on, as a part of the scientific enterprise or (and) constructing useful theory. On the one hand it seems cavalier, even outrageously slipshod, to try to proceed to a careful examination of any phenomena without an attempt to define, that is, to understand and agree upon, what the object of examination is, at least in general terms and as now understood. On the other hand, one can argue persuasively that the scientific enterprise has no close and necessary relationship to conventional definitions, that the verbal difficulties outweigh the scientific gain, that the problem of definition can really only be solved by by-passing it and proceeding to activities that eventually will "define" in meaningful, operational terms.

The first of these positions is best represented by E. Wight Bakke, whose "Concept of the Social Organization" is an essay in definition. It worries him that, though there is a large and growing literature dealing with organizations and organizational behavior, "seldom does one find a careful and systematic description of the nature of the 'thing' with whose internally and externally directed activity the hypotheses are concerned." (p.16) After twenty pages of wind-up, Bakke delivers the following one-sentence definition:

A social organization is a continuing system of differentiated and coordinated human activities utilizing, transforming, and welding together a specific set of human, material, capital, ideational, and natural resources into a unique problem-solving whole engaged in satisfying particular human needs in interaction with other systems of human activities and resources in its environment. (p. 37)

This is followed by thirty-five pages in which the meaning of the definition is explained, its implications explored. To me, the essay is rewarding, but also, eventually, confusing and mystifying. Frankly, I don't understand what The Fusion Process is, unless it consists of phenomena with which, under different names, I have long been familiar.

Various of the other writers . . . attempt definitions, but most of them are content simply to ignore the problem — indeed, given their limited concerns, they are justified in ignoring it. We turn to the recent *Organization* (1958), by James G. March and Herbert A. Simon, to illustrate the other extreme. This work is a presentation of all organization theory, as the authors conceive the subject, in summary, schematic form; and it might be presumed, therefore, to begin with a careful definition of a title stated in one word, no qualifiers, no subtitle. Instead, the book begins simply:

This book is about the theory of formal organizations. It is easier, and probably more useful, to give examples of formal organizations than to define the term. The United States Steel Corporation is a formal organization; so is the Red Cross, the corner grocery store, the New York Highway Department. . . . But for present purposes we need not trouble ourselves above the precise boundaries to be drawn around an organization. . . . We are dealing with empirical phenomena, and the world has an uncomfortable way of not permitting itself to be fitted into neat classifications.

This reasoning is very appealing to me. But I still find myself wondering about the significance of "*formal*" in the first sentence, about the criteria by which a formal organization is differentiated from a non-formal or un-formal organization, and whether the authors really mean to assert that a corner grocery store is a formal organization (and if so, what would an *in*formal organization look like?).

The Classical Theory

The theory of organization best known to American students of administration, of course, is that developed largely in the Scientific Management movement during the early decades of this century. This theory, designated "classical" by March and Simon, is (for students of public administration) closely associated with the noted *Papers on the Science of Administration*, which contains the well-known essays by Gulick, Urwick, Fayol, Mooney, and others. It is the theory that, taking efficiency as the objective, views administration as a technical problem concerned basically with the division of labor and the specialization of function. It is the theory which (in Gulick's famous essay) distinguishes four organizational bases: purpose, process, clientele or materiel, and place; and designates the work of the executive as concerned with POSDCORB — Planning, Organizing, Staffing, Directing, Co-ordinating, Reporting, and Budgeting. Its symbol is the organization chart.

For the readers of this *Review* no more need be said in explanation or elaboration. But what should be said in trying to see such theory in perspective?

Since publication of the *Papers* in 1937, a generation of younger students have demolished the classical theory, again and again; they have uprooted it, threshed it, thrown most of it away. By and large, the criticisms of the new generation have been well-founded. In many ways the classical theory was crude, presumptuous, incomplete — wrong in some of its conclusions, naive in its scientific methodology, parochial in its outlook. In many ways it was the End of a Movement, not the foundation for a science.

Nevertheless, not only is the classical theory still today the formal working theory of large numbers of persons technically concerned with administrative-organizational matters, both in the public and the private spheres, but I expect that it will be around a long, long time. This not necessarily because it is "true," though I should say that it has much truth in it, both descriptively and prescriptively; that is to say, both as a description of organizations as we find them in our society and as a prescription for achieving the goals of these organizations "efficiently." But in any event a social theory widely held by the actors has a self-confirming tendency and the classical theory now is deeply ingrained in our culture. Granted, the new girl in the typing pool may know little of it but, on the other hand, she very certainly would not even have heard of a Feedback Loop or a Bavelas Communication

Net. Not only is the simplicity and wide diffusion of the classical theory in its favor, we have made cultural adjustments to it: at every level from the heights of Pittsburgh to the new girl in the typing pool, we know when to take it seriously, when to charge it with error or injustice, when to acknowledge it formally while we ignore it informally.

Bureaucracy

The map of the organizational world associated with the term bureaucracy and the name Max Weber is also "classical," in the sense that it has been with us for some time and has had many "believers," much attention. It, too, has been much subject to criticism during the past decade, both on scientific and moralistic grounds. As to the former, March and Simon treat such theory rather peremptorily, placing it in effect in their "paleolithic" period.

Bureaucratic theory enjoyed a vogue in this country following the publication of two translations of Weber's relevant writings immediately after World War II. In general, Weber's description of bureaucracy as one type of organization merely puts in formal terms what most of us are familiar with in working for or dealing with government bureaus or business corporations: it is the familiar picture of a hierarchy of authority organizing and in turn shaped by the division of labor and the specialization of function, with full-time positions filled in principle on merit, regular career ladders, etc. But it was the frame in which this familiar picture was placed that made it exciting to some. Speaking for myself, not only was I greatly stimulated on first reading, I am sure I could now read Weber on bureaucracy for the tenth time with fresh insights.

The point is that Weber related what is "natural" for us by deep inculturation, to history, to economic life, to technological development, to political philosophy, to social structure and processes. Bureaucratic-type organization as *the* most efficient way of doing things develops, he argued, in conjunction with certain other developments in a society, and it acts upon and in turn is shaped by these environing factors.

Though the Weber vogue has subsided, he inspired and continues, even if indirectly, to inspire considerable scholarship — I venture to call it scientific inquiry — from various students, particularly and naturally from the sociologists. Much of what is written "refutes" some aspect of Weber; much more "qualifies" some aspect of Weber. But this is the natural pattern of the scientific enterprise, and that there continues to be need to refute or qualify this or that bureaucratic hypothesis is a tribute to the strength and vitality of the theory. Certainly any striving toward a general organizational theory through the comparative route cannot ignore bureaucratic theory; nor until a more accurate and revealing picture of the total organizational world is created, can anyone ignore bureaucratic theory if the objective is the central one of a liberal education: to understand one's world in relation to oneself.

Simon's Three-Fold Schemata

Simon, and March and Simon, have set forth two more or less complementary conceptualizations — theories, schemata, maps, or models, I am not sure what is the proper term — for viewing, classifying, and understanding organizations and organization theory.

The first of these, chronologically, is set forth in Simon's essay "Comments on the Theory of Organizations," published in 1954 in the *American Political Science Review* and reprinted in the volume by Rubenstein and Haberstroh. Here we begin with a definition:

Human organizations are systems of interdependent activity, encompassing at least several primary groups and usually characterized, at the level of consciousness of participants, by a high degree of rational direction of behavior toward ends that are objects of common acknowledgement and expectation.

As an empirical matter, Simon feels that organizational phenomena are different from those of institutions on the one hand, and primary groups on the other; and while the differentiation on either side is far from sharp, he feels that the organizational "level" meets appropriate tests for scientific study and theory construction — tests of internal cohesion and differentiation from the next level.

Addressing himself to the organizational level, so to speak, he then discusses "Major Problem Areas." He makes clear that he does not purport to be presenting finished theory: "Until we know what frames of reference are going to be the most useful for organization theory, it will surely be desirable to retain alternative frameworks, and to take considerable pains to develop means for translating from one framework to another." (p. 159) The major problem areas he conceives as: (1) the process of decision making in an organization, (2) the phenomena of power in organizations, (3) rational and non-rational aspects of behavior in organization, (4) the organizational environment and the social environment, (5) stability and change in organizations, and (6) specialization and the division of work.

Returning in conclusion to a justification of his focus, Simon states:

The characteristics of this level that gives it its particular flavor are the following: (a) its focus on relations among interlocking or non-interlocking primary groups rather than on relations within primary groups; (b) it is largely concerned with situations where *zweckrationalität* plays a large role relative to *wertrationalität* (as compared with the study either of small groups or of cultures); (c) in these situations the scheme of social interaction becomes itself partly a resultant of the rational contriving of means and the conscious construction and acting out of "artificial" roles; and (d) explanation of phenomena at this level requires the closest attention to the fluid boundaries of rational adaptation, including the important boundaries imposed by group frames of reference, perceptual frameworks, and symbolic techniques.

There is no ostensible attempt to relate *Organizations* to this earlier "Comments on the Theories of Organizations," but the two fit together, after a fashion, to form a larger schema. That is, we can assume that the three-fold distinction between institutions, organizations, and primary groups remains; and that a new three-fold distinction introduced in *Organizations* is theory of organization, i.e., theory about the organization "layer." This does not seem too arbitrary, despite the fact that organizations are now designated "social institutions" (p. 2) and that the book contains considerable summary of the theory of primary groups.

Be that as it may, there is a new three-fold schema introduced. Three "models" are discerned, each concentrating on a partial aspect of the human organism, and, though overlapping, coming in chronological sequence:

Thus, the model of the employee as instrument is prominent in the writings of the scientific management movement. In the last several decades the second model, emphasizing attitudes and motivations, has gained the greater prominence in research in bureaucracy, human relations, leadership and supervision, and power phenomena. The third model, emphasizing the rational and intellective aspects of organizational behavior, has been less extensively used than the other two, but is represented particularly by the work of the economists and others on the planning process, and by the work of psychologists on organizational communication and problem-solving.

Though *Organizations* is not organized in three distinct "parts," as this language suggests, nevertheless the theory summarized in the book is ranged along a scale, beginning with the "classical" and ending with the planners. The schema is obviously one of large scope, great adaptability, and considerable usefulness. . . .

Toward a Theory of Organizational Behavior ❖ ROBERT PRESTHUS

During the recent past the analysis of organization has shifted from a preoccupation with structured rationality to an emphasis upon individual behavior. Much of this emphasis has been sociological, that is, it is concerned mainly with small groups and with the ways in which such groups shape the alignment and use of power in the organization. The following analysis attempts to add another dimension to this main drift by pulling together the insights of several social sciences into a general theory of organizational behavior. Such efforts seem required, however crude and abstract they may be at this early stage in the development of administrative science.

In line with Merton's plea for more attention to the interplay between bureaucratic structure and personality, some psychological formulations are brought to bear upon two major variables, the total organizational situation and the individual. Such a framework seems well suited to the complexity of organizational behavior, which is the product of interaction among the whole culture, a given organization, and an individual personality which itself is the result of the genetic composition and unique experience of any given individual. In this context an organization may be viewed as a miniature society in which traditional social controls over the individual appear in sharp focus. The organization draws upon the accumulated learning and experience of the individual, who brings to it certain socially inculcated attitudes that encourage a satisfactory accommodation to the organization's major values and expectations. Obviously not all individuals achieve this kind of accommodation, but the vast majority do so at varying levels of identification and self-realization.

Without denying the influence of informal, small-group liaisons, we assume that individuals have several reference points other than their immediate work group, including the organization as a whole. This concept of differentiated reference foci is suggested by the dichotomy between "cosmopolitans" and "locals," between

"Toward a Theory of Organizational Behavior," by Robert Presthus, from *Administrative Science Quarterly* (June, 1958), pp. 46–67; 70–72. Reprinted by permission of the author and publisher.

those whose loyalty is bound up with their own organization (locals) and those whose referential context is profession-wide and national (cosmopolitans). Here we are concerned mainly with "locals" who tend to accommodate successfully. While our theory necessarily includes an "ambivalent" type who tends to reconcile in-apposite adjustment by resignation, aggression, and withdrawal, this inquiry is directed toward those "upward-mobiles" and "indifferents" to whom the organizational bargain is either satisfactory or at least insufficiently unsatisfactory to provoke disengagement. The question thus becomes, What aspects of the dynamic interplay between the total organizational situation and the individual encourage these different kinds of accommodation? Part of the answer seems to lie in the individual's perception of the organization as a social instrument and in the ways that the organization engages the deep-seated attitudes of the individual toward authority.

In this general framework, organization is defined as a system of structured inter-personal relations, that is, individuals are differentiated in terms of authority, status, and role with the result that personal interaction is prescribed or "structured." Anticipated reactions tend to occur, while ambiguity and spontaneity are decreased. It is hypothesized that the resultant psychological field has exceptional influence upon learning and accommodation to the organization. A related hypothesis is that behavior will tend to be more predictable in complex, structured organizations than in so-called voluntary associations. These assumptions reflect Harry Stack Sullivan's interpersonal theory of psychiatry and particularly his view that "the human organism is so extraordinarily adaptive that not only could the most fantastic social rules and regulations be lived up to, if they were properly inculcated in the young, but they would seem very natural and proper ways of life." It would seem that the rational character and demands of the typical big organization will surely appear less than "fantastic" to its members.

According to Sullivan, personality is the result of a "self-system" worked out through successful (anxiety-reducing) accommodations to the wishes of successive authority figures, such as parents, teachers, supervisors, and so on. The theory of anxiety is central, since anxiety is the principal medium by which the individual is exposed to the values of those in authority. Sullivan's conclusions as to the signif-icance of the anxiety-conformity-approval syndrome can be summed up as follows: "I believe it fairly safe to say that anybody and everybody devotes much of his life-time and a great deal of his energy . . . . to avoiding more anxiety than he already has, and if possible, to getting rid of some of this anxiety."

It is assumed here that anxiety is probably the most critical variable in organiza-tional behavior, when such behavior is defined as an interpersonal process occurring in a highly structured environment. Such behavior is always associated with in-dividual reactions to authority, which in turn are mediated by anxiety and the structure of the immediate interpersonal situation. It is important to add that anxiety occurs along a continuum, ranging from extreme, disorganizing fear to the natural uneasiness felt by most people in a strange situation. For our purposes, anxiety is defined as an unpleasant tension that, in Sullivan's terms, guides the development of the self-system, is present in some measure in all interpersonal relations, and is the main influence determining how such relations develop. This degree of tension may be called "adaptive anxiety" because in most cases it facilitates personal accommodation. In terms of organizational needs, such anxiety and the "security operations" that seek to overcome it are usually functional.

This is not to say that anxiety reduction is the *only* motive for accommodation. Individuals seek opportunities for joy, love, self-realization, and power, which are not necessarily tied to anxiety, although they may be. Certainly, because power in our society can usually be equated with the control of organized resources, organizations provide unusual opportunities to satisfy this drive. But for the majority such expansive states as deep emotional satisfaction, love, and self-realization are not usually obtainable within the organization, which instead tends to stifle the spontaneous, idiosyncratic satisfactions that individuals seek. The "professional mask," the pleasant detachment, the rivalry, and the anxiety that characterize interpersonal relations in big organizations are germane. For most of us, impersonality, limited discretion, built-in power inequities, and the fact that work often becomes a means of buying more meaningful off-the-job satisfactions suggest that less positive motives such as anxiety reduction warrant closer analysis.

Something may now be said about the relation of anxiety to learning. Anxiety is apparently a kind of free-floating dread that affects most interpersonal relations to some degree. Unlike fear which has objective referents, anxiety is often vague. Moreover, whereas fear usually relates to physical injury, anxiety relates to threats against personal esteem. But anxiety also has a positive role: it facilitates learning by sharpening both motivation and perception. As Sullivan concludes, "The first of all learning is called out to avoid recurrence of the extremely unpleasant tension of anxiety, which is, and always continues to be, the very antithesis of everything good and desirable . . . the child soon learns to discriminate *increasing* from *decreasing* anxiety and to alter activity in the direction of the latter. The child learns to chart a course by the anxiety gradient."

Broadly, then, this analysis is grounded in the environmental school of psychology, which, without denying the biological foundation of human behavior, believes that cultural values play a major role in determining man's character. While this school is a minority one in psychology, its formulations seem to me to be most useful in analyzing organizational behavior. Believing that social institutions shape behavior, this school turns to anthropology and sociology as well as biology to understand man. The theory and research of cultural anthropology reinforce the view that environmental conditions largely shape individual behavior and personality, since biological impulses such as pugnacity and competitiveness take quite different forms in different societies. The attending emphasis upon anxiety follows, since it becomes the primary mechanism for exposing the individual to cultural pressures. In the context of organization, it is significant that both Fromm and Thompson agree that the so-called "marketing character," who can be equated with the successful "other-directed" organization man, will "often tend to automaton conformity." Finally since individual reactions to organizational stimuli are the result of learning, the concepts of perception and reinforcement are enlisted to help explain behavior in a structured environment.

These several formulations underlie the present assumption that the patent status and power apparatus of organizations sharpens anxiety and thus increases the probability that behavior will reflect organizational premises. Complex organizations have an exceptional influence upon individual behavior because they are organized systems of expectation. Their status and authority symbols function as patterns of manifest stimuli that reinforce the human tendency to honor majority values. The probability of compliance is increased by the fact that organizational behavior is group behavior of an exceptionally structured kind.

All human behavior occurs within some normative framework, consciously articulated or (more frequently) tacitly assumed. In big organizations there is a fairly consistent hierarchy of values, culminating in a final ideal, the "good of the organization." Among the advantages of such a criterion is its flexibility and ambiguity — it can be manipulated to meet most exigencies. Because the organization must always compete for popular approval, consumer loyalty, and legislative protection and because its power must be constantly nourished, its major values become important tactical instruments. They are personified by the leaders of the organization and explicit in its traditions, and they provide behavioral cues for its rank and file. The assumed best interest of the organization thus provides a standard for determining policy, evaluating individual performance, defining loyalty, and rationalizing injustice if injustice becomes necessary. Obviously this standard may be misapplied in any given instance, but this possibility is not significant here because the decision makers always try to apply it rationally.

Imperatives such as these are reflected in the psychology of the organization. They result in a conscious effort to increase its predictability and internal discipline. The organization tends to become a routine of skill, energy, and opinion. The structured interpersonal relations with which this analysis is concerned are part of this rational climate. They increase the probability that individual behavior will reflect organizational necessity. The individual is conditioned to accept the legitimacy of obedience, for example, by the very fact that he has been hired to do a specific job with explicit obligations, by the provision of rules and regulations that limit his discretion, and by the definition of his place in a hierarchy of authoritative relationships. But such situational factors become most meaningful in terms of the psychological impact they have upon members of the organization. The resultant attitudes, it must be said, obviously help the organization achieve its objectives, but they also have certain unanticipated consequences that are dysfunctional in terms of such goals and of personal adjustment.

We turn first to learning theory, because individual accommodation to the organization is essentially a matter of learning. Learning may be defined as a modification of behavior resulting from repeated exposures to a certain kind of stimuli. Learning proceeds according to a stimulus-response mechanism; its effectiveness depends upon various factors, including the number and strength of existing habits, perception, and the strength of the drive evoked by the stimulus. Perception is the process of becoming acquainted with the environment. Its motives include anxiety and what seems to be an instinctive tendency to use our sense organs functionally. Random observation suggests that we appraise new social situations in order to orient ourselves, to decide what role is required. Our perception of a situation defines our behavioral limits in the sense that its speed and accuracy determine the appropriateness of the role we choose.

Obviously differences in intelligence, emotional maturity, and motivation influence perception and behavior. Some individuals have a limited social sensitivity, that is, their reactions are inappropriate to the "normal" expectations of a given situation. Such behaviors reflect, in part, inadequate or distorted perception. Among higher animals, whose perceptual organization is acquired (learned), the sensitivity toward, range of, and discrimination among stimuli are greater than in lower animals, who depend largely upon inherent perceptual facility. Man is highly susceptible to learning because he is more aware of stimuli and more selective than other animals. It is also clear that perception is bound up with environment, since the latter provides the potential stimulus field. This leads to a basic assumption: *In the structured milieu of a big organization, we can assume that both perception and conditioning are facilitated by the manifest, authoritative nature of the stimuli.*

Reinforcement is also vital to learning, since it makes possible conditioning through rewards and punishments. We know that responses which are followed by reinforcement will be learned; they will result in changes in the individual's behavior or response patterns. Individuals develop certain tensions reflecting needs for food, water, sex, recognition, power, security, and so on. The behaviors which satisfy these needs are reinforced because they reduce the tension generated by the need. The reduction of tension is thus an unusually powerful reinforcement. Learning is also mediated by attitudes, that is, dispositions to act in a certain way. We learn things that agree with our preconceptions much easier and retain them longer than those that seem alien. Through this process of selective perception a steady reinforcement of accepted values occurs. The reinforcement that accompanies the reduction of other tensions also operates with regard to the anxiety reduction achieved by deference to authority.

Reinforcement and motivation, building upon individual needs and the perceived means to meet them, lead to learning and habit formation. Through learning, the individual gradually selects from among several potential behaviors those which seem to have the best consequences in a given situation. The rationality of his choices will vary according to his intelligence, knowledge, information in a given situation, social perceptivity, and so on. *In a bureaucratic setting, the predictability of behavior and the probability that it will be functional in organizational terms are greatly enhanced by the limited number of behavioral alternatives.* Functional responses are reinforced by rewards. In bureaucratic occupations an obvious example is the granting of frequent yet small pay increases. We can assume that the stimuli which elicit desired reactions are manipulated in terms of organization needs. Such manipulation occurs at various levels of sophistication, but the harnessing of social science research to commercial objectives, advertising and sales psychology (e.g., the impact of repetition), opinion surveys, consumer research, the professionalization of charity fund drives, and so forth suggests the growth in the systematic molding of human behavior.

Something must now be said about authority, which is among the main conditions of organized behavior. Authority is usually defined as the ability to elicit compliance whether or not the employee believes an order ought to be obeyed. In the sense that the leader must be able to secure consent from his followers, it is clear that authority, like power, is reciprocal. This definition of authority is acceptable if we remember that the symbol "consent" has more than merely permissive connotations and that consent is only the final, manifest expression of many complex motivations, mediated by the current interpersonal situation and the personalities of those concerned. We must ask *why* the individual accepts authority.

To say that authority is defined by consent suggests that the subordinate has a real choice between acceptance and refusal, that his response to an authoritative order is an "either-or" proposition. But this view not only neglects the disparities in power and security between the organization and the individual and between different individuals in the same organization; it also posits too great a degree of free will and too simple a social situation. Here again psychology and anthropology are helpful. As we have seen, from infancy on the individual is trained to defer to authority. He develops over time a generalized deference to the authority of parenthood, experience, knowledge, power, and status. Moreover, in any given dependency situation, many factors operate to negate the "either-or" notion. There are so many degrees of compliance, ranging all the way from enthusiasm to resignation that outright rejection of an order becomes a gross and unlikely alternative, particularly among highly socialized (aggression-repressing) members of the organization. (We assume that most middle- and upper-level members will tend to be highly socialized owing to the technical demands of organization and the extended education required to gain the necessary skills.) We assume that consent will be normal. In a structured situation, when consent is withheld it is expressed in socially acceptable terms: orders are evaded, misunderstood, forgotten, or projected upon someone "better qualified," and so on. In any event, so long as subordinates know that a superior controls ultimate sanctions to compel obedience if his orders are resisted, how can authority validly be defined as a matter of consent?

When authority and the symbols that define it are organized and patent and there are known sanctions to encourage desired reactions, we seem to have left the permissive level of influence for the authoritative level of power. In terms of a continuum of sanctions, we can say that authority is a condition that is subject to being reinforced by sanctions, while influence usually secures compliance without reference to sanctions. This difference accounts in part for our assumption that interpersonal relations in big organizations tend to rest upon authoritative premises rather than upon influential ones. This is not to say that organizations do not use influence. With the possible exception of those in military organizations, interpersonal relations are usually articulated in permissive terms, but there is little reason to suppose that those concerned are unaware of the relative power disequilibrium. Moreover, aside from other motives for consent such as personal ambition, anxiety reduction, and the desire for group approval, the very fact that an order emanates from someone with higher status and more power tends to induce consent based upon an assumed legitimacy of his role. This is only another way of saying that the very fact of hierarchy in complex organizations encourages compliance.

Obviously authority in organizations does not always function hierarchically. In addition to informal loci of power, there is the fact that technical skill demands recognition. Thus a superior must often defer where technical considerations are decisive. Yet as the experience of the atomic physicists suggests, the control of technical personnel in terms of recruitment, promotions, security, and the ends to which the product will be put is usually determined by authority according to the formal hierarchy. The conflicts between administrators and scientists and researchers on this score are well documented.

An appraisal of authority must also include the fact that big organizations are composed of many subhierarchies, each bound together by authority, interest, and values in a way similar to that in the total organization. Each has its internal power structure headed by a leader who is supreme within his own system, but who is a nonleader when viewed from the perspective of the larger hierarchy. This devolution of power has important consequences. It ensures discipline, since the life chances of those in each subhierarchy are determined largely through representations made on their behalf by such subleaders. As a result, an upward-looking posture characterizes the whole organization. The will of the minority is transmitted downward through the organization by the subleaders, reinforcing their own authority and status vis-à-vis their subhierarchy.

Here the ambiguity of personal and organizational goals may be seen. To retain his position and preserve the hope of future rewards, each subleader must simultaneously promote organization-wide values and yet retain the loyalty of his immediate associates by defending their interests against both competing subhierarchies and neglect by the elite. Although ambivalence may result, his career is in the hands of the elite, and we can assume that he will give priority to its will, as he must if he is to fulfill his role as an agent for carrying out its policy. He will be measured by the loyalty and affirmation with which organization policies are effected. Thus the tribute that the upward mobile subleader pays for marginal power and localized status is upward-directed anxiety and ambiguous interpersonal relations.

In sum, authority includes legal, psychological, moral, and technical factors. Their relative weights vary with the particular situation, mainly in terms of how manifest and compelling the authoritative stimuli are. Thus the hypothesis: *The more obvious and powerful (structured) the stimuli in a given interpersonal situation are, the more predictable and constant the response.*

Despite the complexity resulting from the interplay of these situational and psychological factors, we can assume that bureaucratic structure produces exceptional probabilities that individuals will defer. We know that the recognition that one occupies a hierarchical position clearly subordinate to others encourages deference. We also know that a positive assumption of authority on whatever grounds enhances compliance. Haythorn found that "when one member of a group was aggressive, self-confident, interested in an individual solution to a task, and showed initiative, the other members of the group showed less of such behavior than they normally did." This tendency reflected the group's desire to avoid conflict. The way that group values are imposed will be considered presently, after we have seen how the organization encourages the loyalty and obedience of its members.

As Donald Calhoun has suggested, this is done by convincing the followers of the legitimacy and rationality of the organization, mainly by equating authority with ethical and ideological principles. Of course, all institutions strive to find some basis other than sheer power for their authority. Evocative symbols and rituals are enlisted to inspire loyalty to the organization. If loyalty is to be thought merited, the values and motives, as well as the routine behaviors, of the organization must be seen as selfless; if possible the organization must appear to be the embodiment of certain universal ideals that are beyond individual criticism. This process may be called legitimation.

Max Weber posited three kinds of legitimacy: legal, traditional, and charismatic. The first is based upon the assumption that the organization seeks the good of everyone and merits support accordingly. Traditional legitimacy is the belief that the organization and its values are hallowed by age and experience and ought not be challenged by any time-blinded individual. Charismatic legitimacy is based upon an irrational faith in the values and goals of the organization and its leaders. The charismatic personality is able to inspire among his followers a desire for sacrifice and devotion.

Most organizations enlist all of these legitimations in justifying their claims to loyalty, and the appeals are usually articulated in terms of the general welfare. It is necessary, however, for organizations to simplify what is really happening, since their objectives are actually more complex and less disinterested than this. While they do in part seek to advance the common good, they are also concerned with perpetuating the organization and its individual prerogatives and with mediating conflicting demands within the organization. As Calhoun says, however, if mass loyalty is to be maintained, all three activities must be rationalized in terms of the first objective. Since it is impossible to define the general welfare, much less achieve it, the organization is obliged to draw upon another ideological resource, the myth that it is founded upon unquestionable, unchanging principles.

Once these principles are accepted, it becomes possible to attribute any patent shortcomings, blunders, and injustice of the organization to its members, leaving its ideals intact. This sacrificial behavior is seen in the dramatic "confessions" that occur periodically in the Communist party, but mechanisms that differ mainly in degree are employed by most big organizations. Necessity demands that failure be personalized and projected in a way which shows that human error was involved rather than organizational legitimacy. Certain highly self-conscious organizations, among which one can safely include the Marine Corps, the medical profession, and the Foreign Service, exhibit this collective idealization, often evoking exceptional loyalty from enchanted members. By contrast the individual may appear to himself to be ineffectual. The ritual, continuity, and power of the organization reinforce this self-perception.

Another psychological aspect of big organization is the illusion of unanimity among its members. Differences of interest and opinion are ignored in an effort to present a public image of discipline and unity that will enhance the organizations' competitive chances. Dissent is confined within the organization. Once a decision has been hammered out, everyone must accept it, since further discussion would impair the desired solidarity. In part, the tendency of organizations to limit participation reflects a desire to avoid the appearance of internal disharmony that active participation entails. The common organizational requirement that communications be cleared through a "public information" agency is germane. The remarks of uninstructed members can thus be dismissed more easily as unauthorized. It follows that only certain individuals are actually responsible spokesmen. These are its priests, who explain the organization to the outside world, interpret its catechism, and rationalize any disparity between its ideals of service and its daily behavior.

To increase the probability that individual behavior will reflect the unanimity principle, various appeals are invoked. Affirmative stimuli include inspirational calls for loyalty, sacrifice, perpetuation of the organization's ideals, and so forth. Negative stimuli are latent but powerful. The organization depends mainly upon the sensitivity, the learned deference behaviors, the anxiety-reduction needs, and the ambition of the individual. Such psychological mechanisms reduce the need for sanctions. This climate permits us to view the complex organization as an institution of learning which calls upon deep-seated individual needs and experiences to support ends that in point of time and significance are often prior to those of any given individual. In effect the individual's "self-system" of successful accommodation to authority is coopted by the organization, and the stimuli that initially induced its development are systematically reinforced in ways described below.

Some of the implications of learning theory for organized behavior can now be specified. We suggested earlier that organizations elicited an exceptionally strong tendency to defer and, generally speaking, that it seemed reasonable to assume that the consistency of individual responses was correlated with the power and ease of recognition of stimuli. Psychologically speaking, the very definition of a "structured field" is that stimuli are stable, obvious, and compelling, in the sense that they define appropriate behavior. Learning is a function of perception and motivation, and both depend upon the quality and the number of stimuli, as well as upon individual sensitivity and receptivity. We have also defined bureaucratic structure as a system of manifest, authoritative stimuli, reinforced by known sanctions and a high reward potential. A related hypothesis follows: *Individual responses will be more certain and constant in bureaucratic structure than in so-called "voluntary associations."* To put it another way, big organizations have decided influence on individual behavior patterns, which are defined as a consistent way of reacting to interpersonal situations.

Perhaps the most common kind of manifest and authoritative stimuli are status and prestige indexes. In organizations status and authority are designated by appropriate symbols including title, size of office, accessibility, and income. In this sense the organization presents a "structured field." Such indexes, which differentiate members on the bases of authority, prestige, skill, and seniority, enhance the structured character of organizations by providing a network of signals that curtail spontaneity, limit alternatives, and generally define interpersonal relations. For this reason status consciousness tends to become a built-in part of bureaucratic psychology, as well as a necessary personal skill.

The present importance of status symbols seems to reflect a change from an economy of scarcity to one of conspicuous consumption. But conspicuous consumption is difficult to achieve today because mass production and productivity have made the symbols of material success available on so large a scale. The resulting disenchantment of once-favored classes is interestingly seen in the Middle East, where the periphery of material benefits is slowly being expanded through industrialization and inflation. There the elite feels deprived, owing to the loss of indexes that once set it apart. In the United States the diminution of this psychic income suggests that subtle, nonmaterial distinctions will become more highly valued, since they will be more difficult to establish.

The social framework of status also includes the fact that its symbols tend to become a substitute for values no longer attainable. The declining opportunity for individual autonomy through self-employment, which reflects the trend toward size, concentration, and difficulty of entry; the employment of the "independent" professions on a salary basis; the devaluation of professional training and increased status anxiety — all seem related. The effort to achieve status through word magic is suggested in the attempts to borrow prestige by assigning status-laden titles to socially devalued jobs: news analyst for reporter, mortician for undertaker, executive for salesman, engineer for all sorts of routine jobs, and the widespread co-optation of the honored symbol "professional."

The American assumption of upward mobility, generation by generation, is thus related to status idealization. A cross-cultural comparison with class-bound European and Middle East societies suggests that in time sheer age, the maturing of the economy, and declining occupational mobility in the United States will tend to aggravate status consciousness, resulting in greater reliance upon inherited distinctions as objective means to status become more difficult to achieve. A free and easy democracy requires a social and economic situation in which there is relatively free access to abundant natural resources. A mature society checkmates this competitive situation as the lessons of power are learned by previously disadvantaged groups, and an uneasy equilibrium between major interests tends to follow. In this milieu big organizations turn to subtle status rewards as compensation for personal dependence and limited mobility. The honoring of seniority is an obvious example, as is the small gap between initial and upper-level incomes in the bureaucratized occupations.

As a rule those who have organizational power possess exceptional status and prestige reinforcements, such as size and *decor* of office, expense accounts, and staff and secretarial assistance (ideally including a handsome private secretary whose loyalty and maternal protectiveness may achieve Freudian intensity), that formalize access and encourage attitudes of deference. Such stimuli are patent and compelling, and we can assume that the responses to them will be more predictable than in less structured situations. Their effectiveness is increased by the fact that status anxiety is common in big organizations.

In addition to being obvious and authoritative, organizational stimuli are relatively constant. Authority and its symbols are structured so that the individuals who personify it may change, but the *system* of authority relationships remains. Indeed, bureaucratic structure may be defined as a relatively permanent system of authority relationships. As a result there is little ambiguity or uncertainty about rights and obligations which attach to the "position" rather than to its incumbent. In comparison with social and political power, which is often vague and transitory, organizational power is obvious and definable. Moreover, insofar as organized behavior is group behavior, the authority of legitimated stimuli is increased by sheer numbers. The acceptance of organization values by the majority fosters a consensus that makes dissent seem quixotic.

As was discussed earlier in this paper, such conformity responses have a basis in individual learning and experience, namely, in the successive authority relationships that begin in childhood. It may be assumed that the individual develops considerable sensitivity to authority in all interpersonal situations. An example of the resulting pattern of anticipated reactions is the effect of rank insignia in the military. The mere sight of a high-rank symbol, identifiable at twenty paces, evokes a whole battery of conditioned responses from those affected. The relationship is reciprocal; all concerned know what their proper roles are. Deference, degree of familiarity, tone of voice — indeed the whole character of the interpersonal situation is mediated with ease and dispatch by this single evocative cue. For most organizations the operational consequence of such signals seems clear: the more patent and authoritative the stimulus, the more prompt and certain the response. Related functional aspects of status systems include the recognition of individual achievement and the legitimation of formal authority.

An interesting latent consequence of status-directed behavior is an exaggerated picture of conformity demands, which is often dysfunctional because it aggravates the fear of action and responsibility often seen in big organizations. As A. K. Davis shows, the military situation encourages an "affirm and conform" pattern of accommodation, reflecting the overemphasis on authority and status anxiety. This distorted perception reflects the anxiety of the individual to please his superiors. Since the elite is remote and its will in specific instances cannot be known definitely, the individual seeks to anticipate its expectations. As a result such expectations may seem more compelling than they really are. The individual is not inclined to underestimate them for fear of alienating those upon whom his career chances rest, and he thereby increases the burden of his anxiety. This rule of exaggerated response seems to be a common dysfunctional consequence of big organization.

Despite such consequences, the over-all psychological situation is generally economical, ensuring internal discipline, dispatch, and a minimum of overt interpersonal conflict. Bureaucracy's task is simplified because the reactions it evokes are already deep-seated, having been inculcated by a succession of social institutions. Since birth the individual has been conditioned to operate in a structured environment. Noncoercive sanctions including custom, mobility expectations, and potential rewards practically eliminate the use of gross instruments of control. Because obedience becomes almost automatic, its significance is easily overlooked, or it may be repressed as an uncomfortable reality in a society where individualism is a pervasive theme. This notwithstanding, authority relations in any society become institutionalized between parent and child, teacher and student, leader and follower, officer and man, boss and worker, and so on. Although the resulting power situation may be activated by imperative cues, usually the mere presence of an authority figure, his spoken name, or an appropriate stimulus such as a title or military rank is sufficient to provoke desired responses. We have seen that organisms become conditioned to whole classes of stimuli. The patterns of obedience initiated by parents become generalized to accommodate a whole range of such authoritative stimuli.

We can assume that the anxiety evoked by authority sharpens the individual's perception of organization cues. Pavlov was among the first to argue (on the basis of empirical observation in mental institutions) that anxious people acquire conditioned responses with exceptional rapidity and stability. More recent evidence supports this view. Eysenck sites a study in which normal individuals required twenty-five repetitions of a nonsense syllable accompanied by a buzzer stimulus before a conditioned response was established, whereas anxiety neurotics required only eight repetitions. Similarly, a study by Franks comparing neurotics, normals, and hysterics found that conditioning was much faster and more efficient among neurotics. If, as Sullivan insists, most of us spend much of our time trying to reduce the anxiety we already have and to avoid getting more, we can assume that anxiety reduction by deferring to authoritative others will be a common behavior in complex organizations. Because the range of potential responses is thus limited, behavior becomes more predictable.

Since complex organizations are composed of many small groups representing different skills and values, the structure and the psychology of such groups must be considered. For this analysis a selected aspect of group theory seems most useful. While small groups serve as instruments for mediating idiosyncratic personal needs and for wielding informal power, they also contribute to the "structured field" being examined here. It is well known that after an initial exploratory period small groups become stratified; authority becomes structured in a way similar to that in the larger organization. Freud argued that small-group behavior was best understood as an extension of the early family situation in which the father's role of authority was assumed by the group leader. We can safely conclude that each group develops its own social structure and its means of controlling its members.

From the perspective of a given individual, his own group tends to become "the organization." Usually he performs a given task in company with other specialists, organized in a hierarchy on the bases of skill, seniority, empathy, physical strength, or whatever the going indexes of evaluation are. Since his work satisfactions and his life chances are often bound up with this group, the individual may develop considerable loyalty to it, regarding other groups as competitors. He will probably form personal alliances within the group, and he will tend to rank each member. Some individuals will be accorded leadership, while others will be catalogued as followers. The point of reference for such ranking is often the individual's perception of his own status in the group, as well as the degree to which each member seems to have internalized the group's norms.

This process of structuring gives the small group a hierarchical quality, validated by the tacit endorsement of the entire group. The members apparently seek an equilibrium so that anticipated reactions become the basis of interaction. If groups are to function, such structuring must exist. In any informal group situation, once a goal is set certain individuals gradually assume positions of leadership; in a relatively brief time the resulting pattern becomes crystallized because it meets both operational and emotional needs. In such situations the individual tends to seek "consensual validation" of his own attitudes by comparing them with those of the group. That is, he tends to look elsewhere, to the group and its authority figures, for cues that define approved opinions.

. . . .

Compliance in organizations is thus encouraged by a variety of sanctions, most of which invoke the anxiety-conformity-approval syndrome but vary considerably according to the situation and the personalities concerned. Given dominant values of success and security, middle-class child training and education seem to foster a high degree of adaptive anxiety, discipline, and repression of aggression in outside-the-home interpersonal relations, whereas a lower-class milieu is somewhat more tolerant of aggression. In industrial work situations ridicule, censure, and even blows are used to discipline nonconformants. On the other hand, in organizations engaged in highly technical work requiring considerable education and training (correlated in turn with middle-class social expectations), we find that sanctions are apt to be rather more Machiavellian and that rewards meet status needs to a greater extent than they do economic ones.

Any useful theory must account for such differences, and research in the framework outlined above would have to differentiate among organization members according to class, motivation, educational background, and attitudes toward authority, since these factors play a significant role in accommodation. I would propose three general patterns of accommodation to the bureaucratic situation: the upward-mobiles, the indifferents, and the ambivalents. (There is some evidence that items in the Adorno "F" scale are helpful in identifying each type.) A preliminary sketch of each ideal type follows. Type one is characterized by an ability to identify with the long-range, abstract goals of the total organization and to make these a meaningful basis for participation, in other words, to accept the legitimacy and rationality of the organization. Allied with this attitude is a capacity for action despite conflicting alternatives and contradictory aims; the organization's values are accepted as decisive. An acceptance of the demands and operational necessity of the organization's authority and status systems seems another functional attitude. For example, it is well known that the successful executive tends to regard his superiors as friendly and sympathetic. These formulations permit us to suggest a third major research hypothesis: *Individual patterns of accommodation to the organization are associated with attitudes toward authority and with socioeconomic status.*

Type two, the indifferents, seem to comprise the most common pattern of accommodation. Rejecting majority values of success and power, the indifferent's orientation is essentially *extravocational*. His work is separated from the assumed-to-be more meaningful aspects of life. His references lie outside the organization, which merely provides the income necessary to indulge off-the-job satisfactions; and unlike the upward-mobiles, these activities rarely reinforce his organizational role. His relationship with the organization is essentially an economic bargain in which he sells his time and energy for a certain number of hours per week but jealously guards the remaining time as his own.

The third type of adjustment pattern is to be seen in the ambivalents, who comprise that small minority who can neither resist the appeals of power and success available through the organization nor play the role required to attain them. The ambivalent seems to need security, which the organization's structure and power could provide, but he is temperamentally unable to make the accommodation necessary to obtain it. This conflict seems to reflect inapposite views toward authority and an aggressive sense of individuality which will not permit him to accept the organization as a collective instrument seeking ends that are beyond those of any individual in point of time and significance. He is thus unable to make decisions in terms of organizational premises, exhibiting instead a particularistic point of view which places friendship and similar subjective values above the objective universalistic values that ensure success in the upward-mobiles' case. As E. G. Mishler has shown, "particularism," or the preference for individual over against collective (organizational) values, is "associated with the rejection of authority, a permissive view of dissent, an acceptance of one's own impulses, and an objective appraisal of one's parents." On this basis it seems appropriate to suggest a relationship between particularism, which is organizationally dysfunctional and characteristic of the ambivalent type, and universalism, which is organizationally functional and characteristic of the upward-mobile type.

Conclusion

Several psychological formulations that may contribute to the understanding of individual behavior in complex organizations have been suggested. Sullivan's interpersonal theory of psychiatry, which assumes that the social environment has a major role to play in shaping personality, provided the framework for a theory of individual accommodation to the organization defined as a social microcosm. Anxiety is central to this theory, since it seems to provide the principal mechanism for determining individual reactions to organizational authority. The organization is defined as a system of structured interpersonal relations, in which preorganizational attitudes of the individual toward authority are geared into the organization. In psychological terms, the patent assignment of authority, status, and role in the complex organization constitutes a structured field which eases functional behavior because appropriate behaviors are designated by the situation. Anticipated reactions tend to govern. Three research hypotheses were suggested: The more patent and authoritative (structured) the stimuli in a given interpersonal situation, the more predictable and constant is the response; individual behavior will be more constant and predictable in complex organizations than in so-called voluntary types of associations; and individual patterns of accommodation to the organization are associated with attitudes toward authority and with socioeconomic status. Finally three ideal-types of individual accommodation were suggested.

Hierarchy, Specialization and
Organizational Conflict ❖ VICTOR A. THOMPSON

Many elements undoubtedly combine to make up that particular ordering of human behavior which we call bureaucratic organization, but two are of rather obvious and particular importance. These are the social process of specialization

"Hierarchy, Specialization and Organizational Conflict," by Victor A. Thompson, from *Administrative Science Quarterly* (March, 1961), pp. 485–492; 498–500; 502–505; 507–508; 511–515; 517–519. Reprinted by permission of the author and publisher.

and the cultural institution of hierarchy. A great deal of insight into these organizations can be gained by tracing out the relations between specialization and hierarchy. Particularly, many underlying tensions or conflicts can be illuminated in this fashion.

Modern bureaucracy attempts to accommodate specialization within an hierarchical framework. A hierarchy is a system of roles — the roles of subordination and superordination — arranged in a chain so that role 1 is subordinate to role 2; 2 is superordinate to 1 but subordinate to 3; and so forth until a role is reached that is subordinate to no other role (but perhaps to a group of people, such as a board of directors or an electorate).

A role is an organized pattern of behavior in accordance with the expectations of others. Social scientists often refer to the pattern of expectations as a person's social position — his rights and duties in a particular interactional situation — and his role as behavior appropriate to his position.

Roles are cultural items and are learned. The roles of subordinate and superior (i.e., man–boss roles) are likewise learned cultural patterns of behavior transmitted from generation to generation. We will refer to these roles in shorthand fashion as hierarchical roles.

Defining position as a system of rights and duties in a situation of interaction, and role as behavior appropriate to a position, we will first turn our attention to a discussion of the rights and duties associated with hierarchical roles.

First let us consider the role of a "superior" — the superordinate role. When a person is designated as the "boss," what does this mean? In the first place, it means that he has a right to veto or affirm the organizationally directed proposals of his subordinates, subject to no appeal. Furthermore, the superior's rights include a near-absolute power over the organizational ambitions and careers of subordinates, such as raises or promotions. Although there are many promotional arrangements, nearly all depend heavily and ultimately on the kind word from the "boss."

Hierarchical relations overemphasize the veto and underemphasize approval of innovation. Since there is no appeal from the superior's decision, a veto usually ends the matter. An approval, however, will often have to go to the next higher level where it is again subject to a veto. Thus, an hierarchical system always favors the *status quo*. In a collegiate body, individual members have a free constituency to which they can appeal and get a hearing. However, even in collegiate bodies (e.g., legislatures) there is some hierarchy, and so the *status quo* is also favored in these bodies. The advantage is on the side of those who oppose innovations (e.g., new legislation); the advantage is on the side of the veto. (Here we do not refer to collegiate bodies which are hierarchical creations such as a Russian Soviet.)

The superior is generally considered to have the right to expect obedience and loyalty from his subordinates. Although Weber thought that the separation of public (i.e., organizational) from private (i.e., personal) rights and duties was one of the hallmarks of modern bureaucracy, bureaucratic demands upon subordinates extend to many aspects of their personal lives. The right to obedience is only another aspect of the right to command. It should be noted that this is the right to command autocratically and arbitrarily, as Weber indicated. Although there are many superiors who do not supervise autocratically and arbitrarily, they nevertheless have the right to do so.

The superior has the right to monopolize communication, both official communication between the unit and the outside world and communication between the members of the unit. The right to monopolize outgoing communication is often expressed by the insistence upon "going through channels" and bitter resistance to the use of specialist, nonhierarchical channels. The right to dominate internal communication is less often pressed. In autocratically supervised units, however, communication often comes close to a one-way, star-shaped pattern — a restriction of communication to the superior-subordinate relationship only.

The superior has the right to deference from his subordinates, the right to be treated with extra care and respect. What makes this right significant is that it is one-way. The superior has a right to be somewhat insensitive as to subordinates' personal needs. The ranking of roles with regard to the amount of deference due them is what we mean by the "status system." Although specialties are also status ranked, by far the most visible and virile ranking in organization is ranking according to hierarchical position. Thus, the status system of an organization corresponds very closely to the hierarchy of superior-subordinate roles. It will be discussed below.

From these primary rights of the superior flow, logically, certain secondary rights — the right to determine the personnel of the unit and its organizational form; the right to initiate activities (set the unit's goal) and to assign them (confer jurisdiction); the right to settle conflicts (make decisions). His power of command makes it possible for him to create nonhierarchical authority by ordering his subordinates to submit to the influence of persons other than himself in various specialized areas — the delegation of authority. In this way the propriety of specialist influence can be assured.

The rights associated with hierarchical positions are cultural givens. Actual behavior associated with these positions will be modified by personality, any one person being more or less authoritarian than another. Actual behavior may also be modified by the social process within the groups of people which compose the organization. Thus a superior may form strong affective attachments to his subordinates; he may identify with them. Having become their friend, so to speak, he will find he has assumed the duties of friendship, most of which are at war with his hierarchical rights and usually with his duties to his superior. In extreme cases of this kind, a specific individual may engage in almost no behavior appropriate to his hierarchical position; he may not enact his hierarchical role. It is not unusual in such a situation for a person so entrapped to be considered useless by the hierarchy and to be replaced. Perhaps most people in hierarchical positions find their roles compromised in this fashion to a greater or lesser degree.

Above what might be considered a market minimum, the good things, the satisfactions which the organization has to offer, are distributed according to hierarchical rank, hence status rank. These goods, in addition to money, include deference, power, interesting activities and associations, inside knowledge, conveniences, and the like. Because these goods are distributed according to status rank, and access to any rank is controlled by hierarchical position, these positions acquire great power even over those who might not recognize all the rights of the position as they have been outlined above. Likewise, these positions become great personal prizes as means to personal (as opposed to organizational) ends, and as such are the objects of a constant struggle.

The superordinate role is chiefly characterized by rights. If it has duties, they constitute the correlatives of subordinate rights. On the other hand, the subordinate role is chiefly characterized by duties — all those duties which constitute the correlatives of the superordinate's rights. They are the duties of obedience, of loyalty, of deference; the duty to accept a superior's veto without attempting to appeal around him (is anything more organizationally immoral than attempting to "go around" a superior?); and so on. In our modern democratic culture there are demands for rights of subordinates — rights to personal dignity, to be treated on the basis of merit, to extraorganizational freedom from organizational superiors. All of these "rights" are ambiguous because they conflict with superordinate rights, and this conflict has not yet been worked out in our culture. That is to say, the doctrines of democracy and liberalism which underlie our state have made almost no impact upon our bureaucratic organizations. The only nonlabor-union movement in this direction has been the attempt by some personnel people to introduce rudimentary elements of procedural due process into the bureaucracy; but because of the persistence of the old role definitions and the actual power of hierarchies the assurance of procedural due process is problematical in any particular organization and more or less dependent upon the personalities or connections of the people involved.

Since a large part of the role behavior associated with hierarchical positions is concerned with deference or prestige, it would be well to take a closer look at the status system. Prestige has been defined as the invidious value of a role. We have defined the "status system" as a hierarchy of deference ranks and seen that it corresponds to the hierarchy of subordinate-superordinate roles. Although positions can be differentiated without ranking, they are usually ranked.

Since a person's hierarchical position is a matter of definition, of defined rights and duties, it should be clear at the outset that any special deference paid to the incumbent may constitute a confusion of person and role. That is to say, a person may be entitled to deference by virtue of one or more of his qualities, but his role is not one of his qualities. A person is perceived by others, however, through his roles, his public or perceived personality being the sum of his various roles.

The confusion of office (role) and person is a very old phenomenon; it was part of the charismatic pattern. In fact, status can be regarded as the continuation of charismatic attitudes and practices. It has often been noted that people impute superior abilities to persons of higher status. Furthermore, this imputed superior ability is generalized into a halo of general superiority. Thus, persons of very high status are called upon to help solve problems of every conceivable kind — problems about which they could have no knowledge whatsoever. In public affairs, this halo effect of status requires high-status persons to speak out on all sorts of matters from a position of almost complete ignorance. They are, therefore, forced to develop plausible-sounding jargons and propositions which come to constitute pseudo technologies in terms of which many of our public problems must be publicly analyzed and discussed. If, with this handicap, real solutions are found to these problems, they must be found by unsung "staff" specialists who must perforce solve the problems in ways which do not jolt the pseudo technologies too profoundly.

It has already been pointed out that status has a dominant position in the distributive system. Studies with small groups show that high-status persons get the most satisfactions from such groups. Studies of military behavior suggest that high-status persons are more interested in preserving the system of status ranking than are low-status persons. Above a certain level it would seem that salaries are to some, rather large, extent a function of status — the higher the status, the higher the salary. In fact, it would seem that salaries operate chiefly as symbols of status rank. That the perquisites and conveniences of the work situation are distributed according to status rather than organizational need is common knowledge, and it has been argued that they are distributed in inverse ratio to need. These perquisites also act as symbols and, along with other symbols such as salaries, methods of payment, clothing, insignia, titles, and the like, help to maintain the status system by increasing its visibility. The amount of deference a person receives is made manifest by the good things others give him, and so, in one sense, the status system *is* the distributive system.

. . . .

. . . Hierarchical roles, as culturally defined, have strong charismatic elements connected with them. Current conceptions of organization are clearly based upon charismatic assumptions concerning these roles. It will be recalled that current formulations of bureaucratic organization (which we have called "monistic" and Weber "monocratic") conceptualize organization entirely in terms of hierarchy, as follows:

1. The person in each hierarchical position is told what to do by the person in the hierarchical position above him, and by no one else. He in turn, and he alone, tells his subordinates what to do. They, and they alone, do the same for their subordinates. These instructions establish the division of work, namely the organization. The authority to do anything is cascaded down in this way, and only in this way, by the process of delegation.

2. Each subordinate is guided (supervised or directed) in carrying out these instructions by his superior and no one else, who, in turn, is guided in this guiding by his superior and no one else, etc.

3. Each superior "controls" his subordinates in carrying out the instructions by holding them responsible for compliance with the instructions or with performance standards associated with them. The subordinates are responsible to their superior, and no one else; he, in turn, is responsible to his superior and no one else; etc. Thus all authority comes from the top and is cascaded down by progressive delegations, while responsibility comes from the bottom and is owed to the next superior and to no one else.

. . . .

In modern bureaucracy specialization is incorporated into the older hierarchical framework. Consequently, our problem is to describe and explain the interactions between specialist and hierarchical roles and the kind of order resulting therefrom.

The behavior of people in organizations is purposive in two senses. First, this behavior must be minimally oriented to a common (organizational) purpose or it would not be meaningful to speak of an organization. Second, behavior within organizations is oriented to personal goals. Consequently, we are interested in role interaction in the promotion of organizational goals and in the pursuit of personal goals. The first interest stresses capacities (abilities, powers), while the second stresses tastes, i.e., motivation.

Activities and relations oriented to the objective, externalized goals of the organization stress instrumental considerations. These activities and relations reflect an institutional framework characterized by specificity of function and the norms of rationalism and universalism. They grow out of specialization and out of advancing science and technology. On the other hand, the relations most closely associated with personal goals in bureaucratic structures stress rights or authority rather than instrumental considerations. These relations are characterized by diffuseness of function (in relation to personal goals) and particularism. They are the relations of hierarchy. The subordinate's obligations to his superior which rise out of his dependence upon the superior for the satisfaction of his personal goals (needs, satisfactions, motivations, and so on) are diffuse and ill-defined; and since objective standards governing the relationship tend to be absent (e.g., bills of rights) particularistic norms appear in their place (who one knows, mannerisms, appearance, out-of-office behavior, and so on). The institutional pattern of functional diffuseness and particularism associated with out hierarchical relations is older than the pattern of functional specificity and universalism associated with specialization. Bureaucracy is thus seen to be compounded of the old and the new, of hierarchy and specialization.

We have defined a specialist as a person skilled in a number of programs — fairly complex sets of organized activities of a practical nature. As problem-solving mechanisms, organizations can be viewed as a breakdown (factoring) of a general problem (accomplishing the organizational goal) into simpler and more specific sets of organized activities until actual programs are reached. New problems for an existing organization are likewise factored. If this factoring is done in defiance of existing specialties (hence programs), new and usually unacceptable specialties are created with all their implicit problems of tension, co-operation, and coordination. Such factoring would not be freely undertaken by specialists and could thus be only an act of authority. For these reasons, problem factoring, hence the definition of organization structure, is being forced into specialist hands (though note; the hierarchical role includes the right to do this job and it is almost universally claimed as an "executive function" by writers). The overwhelming need for co-ordinated (hence co-operative) activities among specialists makes this development inevitable.

Associated with the factoring of the organization's goal is the delegation of jurisdictions (i.e., the creation of nonhierarchical authority relations). Previously we emphasized the principal system of authority in organizations — the hierarchy. The authority relations of hierarchy are the relations of a superior to a subordinate. The superior's right to command, however, makes it possible for him to create (delegate) nonhierarchical authority relations. He can command his subordinates to accede to the influence of another person in some defined area or specialty. He can therefore centralize activities or create interdependencies. Since this power of a superior is not necessarily restricted by any formula or operational standard, it is essentially political power — the personal power to confer favors. To the extent that this power is exercised in accordance with the needs of specialization, it constitutes a *pro forma* legitimizing of a technical reality, an official promulgation of a technically existing interdependence.

. . . .

Since problem solving in organizations is a specialist activity, it is a group rather than an individual activity. A decision by a group of specialists must be almost unanimous, and modern organizations try to make decisions about organization goals by unanimous groups. In matters involving the personal goals or ambitions of employees, however, autocratic hierarchical decision is still the rule. Although group decision is an inevitable result of specialization (hence interdependence), it is also a result of the perceived need for group decision. Thus, there may be and probably usually is more group consultation in modern bureaucratic organizations than the objective facts of interdependence warrant. This overworking of group processes, the exaggeration of interdependence, appears to result from conditions within the hierarchy rather than from specialization. Since the hierarchy, by definition, is an allocation of rights rather than abilities, this emphasis on the right to be consulted, the right of review, is understandable. The relation of the hierarchical role to the decisional process is a relation of right (competency or jurisdiction). "Has everyone with a legitimate interest been consulted?" Furthermore, the more joint decision is engaged in, the more the immediate superior will be called upon to settle differences, and hence the greater his influence will be. When only single recommendations can reach him, he becomes largely a captive of his organization. It is not surprising, therefore, that the superior will see the need for joint decision whether it exists or not and that he may be tempted to create technically unnecessary interdependence by delegating authority in defiance of the criteria of specialization. However, in addition to the right to be consulted, and desire for enhanced influence, excessive insistence upon joint decision reflects insecurity growing from dependence upon specialists, which increases both in time and with elevation in the hierarchy.

Although, in general, group decision can be greatly superior to individual decision as a problem-solving device, bureaucratic structure severely limits the effectiveness of the group process. For the small-group-thinking process to be most effective, a substantial degree of group cohesion is required. This cohesion greatly increases the ability of the group members to accept and back up affectively one another's analyses and suggestions. It minimizes autocratic procedures and behavior which create tensions, dry up spontaneity and creativity, and attack co-operativeness. Although many spontaneous, nonhierarchical, informal group discussions constantly take place in organizations, the decisions which commit the organization, the official ones, take place in hierarchically structured situations including hierarchically structured groups. Although attempts are often made to hide the hierarchical structure in the formal group-decision process, to pretend that it is not there, the hierarchy is *in fact* present and all group participants know it. Consequently, because of hierarchical control over personal goals, everything said and done in the group situation must be evaluated from the standpoint not only of its relation to the organization's goals but also of its relation to personal goals. In bureaucracy, ideas do not stand on their merits alone. It is not only an opinion or an idea that wins but also a man. The situation is inherently competitive rather than co-operative, and, as Kurt Lewin has pointed out, competition attacks group solidarity and consequently the ability of the group to employ specialization in pursuit of the group goal.

An organizational decision-making group is ostensibly a small problem-solving group and so all the experimental data concerning the latter are relevant to the former. These data roughly indicate that the problem-solving process goes through three stages — orientation (the statement of the problem, definitions, and the like), evaluation (setting up the relevant values and norms), and control (attempts to influence decision or solution). It is necessary to get agreement at each phase before a joint decision at the control end can be achieved. One of the prerogatives of the superior position in hierarchically structured groups is to monopolize the orientation phase — to define the problem ("we are meeting here for the following purpose"). If the problem is thus hierarchically defined, the resulting decision cannot be called a group decision. Although in specific cases particular superiors may forego the exercise of this right, common experience indicates that the right is frequently claimed. Such a hierarchical statement of the problem will almost certainly have inarticulate premises relating to personal goals (or informal group goals), and this fact contributes to the difficulty of obtaining an effective solution.

In a nonstratified group, positive and negative responses of other members act as controls over participants both in the direction of goal accomplishment and of eventual consensus (true group decision). In the stratified (hierarchical) group, high status or prestige protects a person from group influence but increases the power of his own positive and negative reactions as controls over others in the group. The group must therefore yield to him.

It has been observed in experimental groups that the perception of leadership (who is the leader?) is related to the quantity of activity rather than its quality. Furthermore, as groups increase in size, a larger and larger proportion of the activity is addressed to the perceived leader, and he addresses himself more and more to the group as a whole. The process tends to become one of informal lecture with questions and answers (with the familiar rimless wagon-wheel or star pattern of communication). In the formal organizational group, the position of "leader" is predefined — he is the person with the highest hierarchical position. Thus, even apart from the *rights* of his position there is a strong tendency for him to dominate the group process.

In a group with considerable cohesion, "questions provide a means of turning the process into the instrumental-adaptive direction of movement, with a low probability of provoking an effective reaction, and are an extremely effective way of turning the initiative over to the other." Questions, however, prevent the asker from improving his status because the initiative is given to another and so are much less likely to be used in a competitive, stratified group.

In the experimental group without formal structure, the idea man is most disruptive of group equilibrium and hence is most likely to arouse hostility. He is also most likely to be perceived as the group leader. In the formally structured group, the idea man is doubly dangerous. He endangers the established distribution of power and status, and he is a competitive threat to his peers. Consequently, he tends to be suppressed.

These potential weaknesses in the group thinking process in formally structured groups raise the question of how effective organization decisions are made in our modern bureaucracies. Four possible answers suggest themselves, all of which are no doubt true to some extent. First, the problems taken up for formal group decisions may not usually have a high degree of importance to the organization's success, and a *de facto* delegation of important decisions to specialist, informal group processes actually takes place. Secondly, it is likely that a considerable degree of self-restraint in the exercise of hierarchical decisional rights must be and usually is practiced. In the third place, it is possible that formal bureaucratic decisions are not as effective as they could be. And, finally, much of the effective decisional process in organization is camouflaged by myths and fictions to give it an apparent consistency with the culturally sanctioned rights of hierarchy.

. . . .

The full exercise of hierarchical rights results in autocratic rule, or "bureaucratic" supervision as the term "bureaucratic" was used in the previous paragraph. Whereas a person in a hierarchical position can be expected to dislike the insecurity of his own position and the application of autocratic practices to himself, he may be less sensitive to his subordinates' reactions to such practices, may even need to impose autocratic discipline as an outlet for aggressions necessarily repressed in his role as subordinate. Many studies testify to the deleterious effect which autocratic supervision has on the satisfactions (personal goals) of participants.

The superior's right to monopolize official communication can be particularly damaging to personal satisfactions or goals. As Lewin has pointed out, denial of pertinent information to participants prevents a cognitive structuring of the situation and results in emotionalism, lack of direction, alienation, and conflict. Furthermore, the denial of information, by concealing the relation between activities and the larger group objectives, denies the satisfactions of knowing one is part of a larger, important, co-operative effort. Although the hierarchical role does not *require* the withholding of information, it does condone a certain insensitivity to subordinate needs. Furthermore, the strategic considerations surrounding hierarchical competition and the need to protect the legitimacy of the positions counsel caution in the distribution of information, both to subordinates and to others.

We pointed out above that the currently prevalent concept of organization, the monistic concept, was essentially a formalization of the institution of hierarchy. The monistic concept gives rise to practices and relationships that duplicate childhood to a considerable extent. In monistic theory and somewhat less in practice, each individual in the organization (except the top man) is subordinate to a parentlike figure who instructs, reviews, admonishes, reproves, praises, criticizes, evaluates, supports, rewards, and punishes, thereby duplicating much of the experience of childhood. This denial of adulthood is surely one of the more painful aspects of modern organization. Furthermore, we suspect that performing the role of the parentlike figure would be equally painful for mature, sensitive adults. It may not usually be performed very faithfully.

The most serious impact of the hierarchical system upon the achievement of personal goals within organizations results from its appropriation of the definition of success in our culture. Since the time of the Reformation, success in Western civilization has been interpreted in competitive and individualistic terms of relative social prestige or status. Wealth has long been a dominant symbol of status. As we have shown above, status or social prestige, with all its symbols, including income, had become largely a monopoly of the hierarchy in modern bureaucracy. Bureaucratic hierarchy has inherited the rights and privileges of the early charismatic leader and his retainers, the traditionalistic king and his nobility, and the entrepreneurial owner-manager and his familial proteges. Consequently, to be socially defined as "successful" in our culture, one must proceed up some hierarchy. To have public recognition and esteem, hence self-esteem, one must succeed hierarchically. This situation is painful for the specialist. Even if he is the kind of person who can satisfy his dominance needs by mastering a skill rather than people, he will be denied "success" unless he gives up his specialty and enters hierarchical competition. The converse of the hierarchical appropriation of success is the derogation of intellect, imagination, and skill so prevalent in modern bureaucracy.

· ·

The newer specialties in organizations are usually lumped together conceptually under the name "staff specialist." A number of upsetting relations arise from these new specialties. In the first place, they threaten older specialties with the loss of functions or the addition of new unwanted ones. Especially is this so if the centralizations involved in the new specialties result from the exercise of the hierarchical prerogative to assign duties (create jobs) rather than from the social advance of specialization. Apart from such acts of power, however, the new specialty must achieve social accreditation before it is accepted.

Advancing specialization upsets status expectations as well as vested interests in functions. Specialization, by giving a function to everyone, brings persons of low and high status into interdependent relations, thereby violating the status expectations of the latter.

The "staff" threat to function and status is particularly acute with regard to hierarchical positions low enough down to contain specialist content. In fact, the conflict arising from these new specialties is usually designated as the line (hierarchy) versus staff conflict. Since specialties eventually win legitimacy one way or another, they acquire authority of a nonhierarchical kind which invades the domain of hierarchical authority. In this way there arises a growing discrepancy between expected authority and actual authority which lies at the heart of the line-staff conflict. Mechanisms of hierarchical protection against this threat of specialization are many, but here we wish only to call attention to the universally adopted devices of derogating staff importance ("line is more important than staff") and of attempting to suppress recognition of the unpalatable features of the relation by the use of fictions ("staff only advises; it does not command").

Much conflict in organizations concerns the reality of interdependence (or the need for joint decision). As we pointed out above, part of this conflict is due to differing perceptions of reality between persons in specialist and hierarchical positions. The need for the new specialty, hence the new interdependence, may also be questioned by existing specialists because of fear of loss of function. More important from the standpoint of conflict in organizations is disagreement as to the need for new interdependence which arises when rights (competencies) are allocated in disregard of technical criteria. As pointed out above, one of the rights of hierarchical positions is the right to delegate rights (authority). Thus, it is possible for rights (e.g., the right to review or be consulted) to be distributed in a manner inconsistent with the distribution of ability. It is possible for competencies to be defined in defiance of the needs of specialization.

. . . .

It is likely that newer specialties are more expansionist than old ones, deprived as they are of the full measure of their expected status and function because of lack of full acceptance. If the new centralization (specialization) is an act of hierarchical power rather than a result of the advance of specialization, expansionism probably reflects an attempt to allay the inevitable insecurity associated with an imbalance between authority and ability (the right to be consulted versus the ability to make a contribution). However, expansionism may also reflect simply the attempt by a newer specialty to realize a full measure of function consistent with its technical promise. In this latter case, free interaction between the new and the old will eventually cure the cause of conflict, allowing the new to demonstrate its validity and hence the need for the new interdependence. However, conflict arising from resistance to the interdependence resulting from pure power plays can only be eliminated by a redefinition of jurisdictions to the actual needs of specialization, or by defeatist acceptance of the new jurisdictions. In the latter case, any change in the distribution of political power in the organization (power which comes from the personal support of persons with power) will likely be followed by more or less intense activity seeking to reallocate rights of jurisdiction. In this way, an allocation of rights by arbitrary authority creates an unstable and potentially explosive situation.

A common form of the conflict concerning the reality or need for interdependence is that which sometimes arises over the joint use of means. When centralization is undertaken to allow full employment of the latest specializations in skills or equipment, the minor conflicts from joint use which arise because of some inevitable degree of scarcity are not important and are easily resolved without destroying co-operation. The amount of denial and frustration involved can be shown to be necessary and thus acceptable. When the centralization of means is an act of power, however, frustrations arising from the interdependence cannot be made acceptable because they cannot be demonstrated to be necessary. Attempts to ameliorate the conflict by the permanent, full-time assignment of subunits of means to each client cannot remove the instability in the situation, disclosing as it does the fact that the centralization in question is purely a matter of right, of authority, with none of the requirements of specialization involved. Whenever it is technically possible permanently to assign subunits of means, it is technically possible to decentralize.

To illustrate our point, suppose Miss Brown is the subordinate of Mr. Jones and that she is his stenographer. The organization then decides to centralize stenography by creating a stenographic pool. Miss Brown is transferred to the pool but, to avoid conflict over the joint use of means, she is permanently assigned to Mr. Jones. Her technical relation to Mr. Jones is the same; she is his stenographer. Her authority relationship, however, has been changed. She is now the subordinate of Mrs. Smith, the pool chief, rather than Mr. Jones. The centralization was a pure act of authority. Only authority relations were involved.

We should point out that part of the difficulties which arise from centralization can be traced back to the monocratic character of the hierarchical institution. We have said that activities are frequently centralized to assure full employment of the latest specialization in skills or equipment by concentrating demand for them. If the new specialist could be a member of several organization units instead of one, this centralization of activities would not be necessary. It is held that such multiple membership would violate the principle of "unity of command" and must hence be avoided. The reason it is avoided is that it is incompatible with the institution of hierarchy. It would place the specialist in the subordinate relationship with more than one superior. He would have more than one *boss*. While a person can be placed in a subordinate relation to several nonhierarchical authority positions, and always is so placed in modern bureaucracy, he cannot be placed in a subordinate relationship to more than one boss. The rights of the superordinate role preclude more than one boss. The hierarchical institution is monocratic. Among the many suggestions which Frederick Taylor made, his suggestion for several "functional foremen" for each operator was never taken seriously by management. Such an arrangement would attack the very heart of the institution of hierarchy.

. . . .

The system of specialization requires the interaction of persons whose specialties must be harmonized in order to achieve the organization goal. This interaction is restricted both by the distribution of authority, hierarchical and delegated, and by the groupings formed by the official communication system. The superior's right to be the sole source of influence over subordinates ("unity of command"), his right to be fully appraised of what is going on (supervision), his right to monopolize communication, his right to the loyalty of his subordinates, all restrict free interaction between subordinate specialists of one organization unit and those of another. Reinforcing these restrictions are the demands of the individual's immediate work group (fellow subordinates and possibility his superior) that he share and give effect to their values and perceptions of reality. Although his status grouping may also interfere with communication with a lower-level specialist, it is our belief that this factor is not serious in purely specialist interaction.

Despite these blocks, interaction is technically necessary. And since no formal-unit work group or status strata could contain all the relevant specialties, specialist interaction must take place across formal-unit and status-strata lines. As mentioned above, this necessary interaction carves out specialist channels of communication, and hence channels of influence, of a semi-illegal nature. More important, it leads to the sharing of values and reality perceptions between the specialists — to multiple group membership — and hence, perhaps to divided loyalties, doubts, and guilts. Inter-unit conflict becomes internalized in the individual. All these effects are likely to be reinforced by the specialist's dependence upon specialist lines and channels for personal satisfactions of status and function, unless he is willing to forego his specialty and enter hierarchical competition. Finally, we should point out that the dimensions of the dilemma of specialist interaction are qualified by the importance of the interdependence, by whether the interdependence involves functional necessities or only working convenience (e.g., the clearance of proposed new programs versus the installation of an additional telephone extension).

The bases of intraorganizational conflict can be summarized in a few general propositions, as follows:

1. Conflict is a function of disagreement over the reality of interdependence.
    1.1. Lack of agreement about the reality of interdependence arises from lack of acceptance of specialties.

    Lack of acceptance of specialties results from lack of accreditation of specialties, which, in turn, is a function of
        1.1.1. their newness, or
        1.1.2. the creation of specialties by acts of authority in defiance of technical criteria.
    1.2. Lack of agreement about the reality of interdependence is also a function of differing perceptions of reality. These differing perceptions are a function of position in
        1.2.1. the authority system,
        1.2.2. the status system, and
        1.2.3. the system of person-to-person communication (the group system).

2. Conflict is a function of the degree of disparity between authority (the right to be consulted) and the ability to contribute to goals. This disparity arises from
    2.1. Growing dependence upon specialists (a function of the process of specialization) while hierarchical role definitions change more slowly; and
    2.2. The allocation of rights (delegation) in disregard of the needs of specialization (acts of sheer authority).

3. Conflict is a function of the degree of status violation involved in interaction.
    3.1. Status violation results from advancing specialization and consequent growing interdependence of high- and low-status positions — from positional claims to deference, on the one hand, and the fact of dependence upon specialists, on the other.

4. Conflict is made more or less intense by the relative importance of the interdependence to the success of the organization.

5. Finally, conflict is a function of the lack of shared values and reality perceptions (identifications), which are, in addition to personalities,

    5.1. A function of the lack of spontaneity and freedom in communicative
interaction, which is

        5.1.1. a function of the resistance to penetration from without of the
principal behavior systems — the authority system, the status
system, and the technical system (specialization).

In short, conflict arises from growing inconsistencies between specialist and
hierarchical roles. Whereas there are other bases for conflict, it is likely that they
could be easily managed under a regime of specialist solidarity based upon the
mutual recognition of the need for interdependence.

The conflict between specialist and hierarchical roles has generated mechanisms
of role defense. From the standpoint of the hierarchical role, defense involves
the securing and maintenance of the legitimacy of the role. Here we only wish
to set forth briefly some of the mechanisms of specialist role defense.

We have already mentioned that in order to claim "success," as culturally defined,
the specialist must give up his specialty and enter hierarchical competition. A
person who chooses this course of action must adopt the values of the managerial
group to which he aspires. This "anticipatory socialization" enables such a person
to avoid the worst consequences of specialist-hierarchical conflict. Merton has
pointed out that a specialist not wishing to follow this path may adopt a sort of
schizoid separation of his roles, maintaining his own values privately and relating
himself to the organization solely in his specialist or technical capacity. Thus he
refuses to take any responsibility for the use or nonspecialist consequences of his
advice, regarding such matters as "policy questions" to be handled by the "administrative people." Much specialist training, especially of engineers, contains a
liberal amount of preparation for such a subaltern status.

We have also pointed out that specialists engaged in organization problem
solving consistently evade official prescriptions in order to get the job done, especially in the matter of communication. This evasion of official prescriptions also takes
place in the lower levels of the hierarchy where hierarchical positions contain a good
deal of specialist content, perhaps mostly specialist content.

An increasingly used device of specialist role protection is the formation of local,
state, and national associations of specialists. These associations compensate to
some extent for lack of rights of appeal from hierarchical vetoes by providing a
"free constituency" to which vetoed items may be presented. Although some
professional associations may function as devices of managerial control of specialists
(perhaps some engineering associations have so functioned in the past), it would
seem that most of them severely limit managerial control by specifying just how
their members may be employed in organizations. In short, they are devices for
protecting specialist status and function.

Where a particular skill is concentrated under one or a few employers (that is,
in a specific organization), efforts of the skill group to protect its status and function
are more effective, resulting in distinctive career groups and peculiar "problems of
personnel administration." Examples of such career groups in government organization are: the Forest Service, the Geological Survey, social workers, police,
firemen, school teachers, public health workers. Protective activities of such
groups result in strong attachments to the careers and the organizations through
which they are pursued, emphasis upon objective or proceduralized distribution of
recognition (status), life commitments to the careers, a long-range program for
the whole career, and the like.

Finally, we should mention that pressures for "due process" proceduralized protection of organization employees have specialist rather than hierarchical origins. They originate both in the new specialties of personnel administration and in the employee associations (whether they be called unions or professional societies).

The resolution of conflict in modern organization is made difficult by the fact that conflict is not formally recognized, hence legitimated. To legitimate conflict would be inconsistent with the monocratic nature of hierarchy. It would require formal bargaining procedures. Modern organizations, through the formal hierarchy of authority, seek an "administered consensus." Conflict resolution, therefore, must occur informally by surreptitious and somewhat illegal means. Or else it must be repressed, creating a phony atmosphere of good feeling and superficial harmony.

Toward the New Organizational Theories: Some Notes on Staff*

✤ Robert T. Golembiewski

Organization theory is fast approaching a major reshaping. The burgeoning of the behavioral sciences, most prominently in small-group analysis, erodes the bases of traditional organization theory at a microscopic level: knowledge of group and personality properties sharply reveals the theory's inadequacies. Moreover, a critical literature of long standing complements this challenge to students of organization at a macroscopic level. For example, Stahl has argued that the traditional concept of "staff" as advisor of, and subordinate to, "line" units at all levels "not only *should not be* the case but *is not* and *never has been* the case."

Reprinted from *Midwest Journal of Political Science*, Vol. V, No. 3 (August, 1961), by Robert T. Golembiewski by permission of the Wayne State University Press and the author. Copyright 1961 by Wayne State University Press. Pp. 237–259.

* This title requires explanation. There eventually will be a general *empirical theory* of organization, that is, a statement of what is related to what under various conditions. Such an empirical theory will permit the development of any number of *goal-based*, *empirical theories*. These theories will prescribe the conditions under which various sets of objectives may be attained.

This article points toward the development of new organization theories, both empirical and goal-based empirical. Hence the title above.

In contrast, the literature suffers from the unfortunate emphasis upon *an* organization theory. Indeed, the traditional theory of organization (to be analyzed presently) is often offered as universally valid in both descriptive and prescriptive senses. That is, the traditional organization theory is presented as the general empirical theory. Moreover, the theory is presumed to be the only goal-based empirical theory worth developing. The distinctions between theory-types will be reflected in the analysis. Thus both the descriptive and the prescriptive adequacy of traditional organization theory will be scrutinized here. By way of preview, this theory does not describe reality. Moreover, when the conditions prescribed by the theory do exist, the expected consequences often do not result. The theory-types, and their methodological implications, are considered in more detail in this author's " 'The Group Basis of Politics': Notes on Analysis and Development," *American Political Science Review*, 54 (December, 1960), 962–71.

This paper contributes to this reshaping of organization theory through an examination of the intimate relations between traditional organization theory and the concept of "staff" it supports. The focus is upon the relation of Stahl's position and the revamping of traditional organization theory, which Stahl did not consider. The purpose is to complement what Stahl did, not to indict him for what he did not intend to do.

The burden of this analysis may be abstracted. Three main themes — although they are not considered seriatim — dominate the treatment. The traditional "staff" concept, it will be shown, is a derivative from a general theory of organization whose purportedly empirical propositions inadequately reflect reality. Moreover, the "staff" concept is inadequate for describing relations within and among organizations. Finally, the traditional "staff" concept often does not lead to effective administration even when individuals act in the ways it prescribes. The analysis builds toward these three themes by considering, in order: the skeleton of Stahl's argument; some ideal concepts of "staff"; the traditional "staff" concept as a derivative from a general theory of organization; the method of the general theory of organization and, environmental changes which have undercut the general theory of organization and, thus, the traditional "staff" concept.

The Network of Authority

Stahl recently has argued his thesis that "line" and "staff" are hardly "distinguishable as indicators of power status" in two brief pieces. The following propositions (in Stahl's wording) summarize his thesis:

1. that so-called staff units usually do and must necessarily carry out functions of command;
2. that there are some activities for which there is an inescapable need for organization adherence [which activities the so-called staff units are in the best position to police];
3. that a staff activity is no more a restricted, specialized function than . . . line segments . . .;
4. that staff functions, having to do with *how* things are done more than *what* is done, assume a special importance in the public service;
5. that it is convenient to think of line and staff as "program" functions and "sustaining" functions, respectively, which interlace with each other in a *network;* that the chief executive controls the organization by means of both vertical "program" channels and the horizontal "sustaining" channels; and
6. . . . that conflicts are reconciled and communication facilitated at lower levels in the organization when there is no presumption of unvarying command superiority of line over staff.

Some "Staff" Concepts

Two themes outline this section: (1) that the literature about "staff" is not monolithic, and practice is ever more variegated; but (2) that nevertheless, in terms of central tendencies, a concept has been emphasized which stands in sharp contrast to Stahl's position.

Both themes can be developed by outlining several *ideal styles* of the relations of agencies or individuals performing "sustaining" functions with those performing "program" functions. "Staff" will not be differentiated in terms of the designations commonly assigned to agencies ("general staff," for example) or to individuals ("chief of staff" or "assistant-to," for example). The three styles analyzed, however, will cover the full range of ideal relations of any "sustaining" activity with any "program" activity.

The "colleague" style of "staff," first, implies formal authority independent of — and sometimes superior to — the "line." Consider the German practice of sending direct representatives of headquarters into critical battle areas, not as "line" commanders but as chiefs of staff. These chiefs of staff participated in, and sometimes assumed, command. Their relations with "line" commanders thus were fluid. As one commentator described these relations:

Always the commander commands through the chief and the chief's orders even older subordinate commanders have to follow without murmur. . . . How far the chief can go in issuing orders without the knowledge of his commander is a question that can be decided only between the two and cannot be judged by any outsider.

The concluding sentence is a crucial one. The relations of the "staff" man and the field commander cannot be described simply. They will be determined "only between the two." Moreover, the "colleague" concept of "staff" does not hide the relation of a superior "line" official who is a direct representative of headquarters with a subordinate "line" official in the field. Indeed, the traditional notions of "line" (see the third "staff" concept below) do not apply. For a bargaining situation is implicit in the "colleague" concept. And the traditional "line-staff" distinction permits no such indeterminacy.

The fluidity of the "colleague" concept has this intention: to encourage the active participation in the command function of individuals whose formal positions encourage differing orientations to problem situations. The factors of jurisdiction and pressure of time, for example, would encourage such differing orientations. Jurisdiction-wise, the field commander would tend to emphasize those conditions dominant in his problem area, the "staff" man to be more oriented toward overall policy and strategy. Temporally, the here-and-now would tend to be of most concern to the field commander. A longer-run view would tend to influence the "colleague."

This first concept, then, attempts to provide for the integration of the "part" and the "whole," which is one of the base problems of administration. (In the case of a personnel "staff" service, or similar organization-wide function, the "whole" would be the functional area, the "part" the personnel matters of any administrative unit.) But, significantly, this first concept of "staff" does not attempt to handcuff organizationally either the commander or the "colleague." For, by implication, to do so would result in the inadequate expression of either particularistic or overall considerations.

A second concept of "staff" implies less indeterminacy. This second concept may be called the "alter ego" type. To illustrate the type, the U. S. Army's *Staff Officers' Field Manual* noted that the "staff of a unit consists of the officers *who assist the commander in his exercise of command*." Such assistance is of a quite intimate nature. For the staff officer is enjoined to "live inside the mind of the commanding general, and know what his policies are, even though they have not been announced." This "living inside of" may be reflected, for example, in orders signed by the staff officer "in the name of the commander." Field Marshal Montgomery's *Memoirs* give a precise picture of the relations involved. He articulated his notion of "line-staff" relations in this way:

I appointed de Guingand Chief of Staff . . . ; every order given by him would be regarded as coming from me and would be obeyed instantly.

[The night of the major battle of the African war, I] went to bed early. At 9:40 p.m. the barrage of over 1,000 guns opened, and the Eighth Army went into attack. At that moment I was asleep in my caravan. . . .

[The battle went poorly.] De Guingand rightly issued orders for a conference at my Tactical HQ . . . and then woke me and told me what he had done. I agreed.

The "alter ego" concept of "staff," then, restricts behavior far more than the "colleague" concept. The "alter ego's" orders are to be obeyed, but these orders merely articulate for the commander. There is no provision for the bargaining implied in the "colleague" concept. The "staff" man assumes the personality of the commander, ideally, rather than asserts his own.

Despite the wide usage of these two "staff" concepts and their reputation for getting results, American students of organization — especially in Public Administration — generally have chosen a third concept. It can be characterized as the "neutral and inferior instrument" concept. It is, of course, very familiar. White described it in these terms in his very influential text:

line authorities . . . are the central elements of any administrative system; staff and auxiliary agencies are necessary in a large and complex organization, *but they are secondary*. They serve the line; the line serves the people.

Thus "staff" in this concept is: "outside the lines of command"; "deliberate organization for thought rather than execution"; and "purely advisory." Illustratively, no orders can be issued by the "staff" official who respects the "neutral and inferior instrument" concept of "staff." Nor need such orders be obeyed, *in theory*, were they to be issued. In contrast, the two previous concepts (and especially the "colleague" concept) include ample room for "staff" work inside the lines of command, for execution as well as thought, and for action as well as advice.

The three concepts of "staff," then, cover a broad range of ideal relations. This range of relations may be represented by a funnel. The "colleague" concept is represented by the funnel's wide mouth. It provides broad scope for "staff" behavior. The "alter ego" concept is represented by some cross-sectional area further down the cone of the funnel. And the "neutral and inferior" concept is represented by the narrow tube of the funnel, signifying a very restricted range of sanctioned behaviors. More succinctly, the "colleague" concept is most akin to the position for "staff" recommended by Stahl. The "neutral and inferior instrument" concept, in contrast, is the target of Stahl's criticism.

The three concepts illustrate the variations in "staff" usage. Two cautions, however, must be observed. First, no distinctions are made between "private staffs" and, for example, "staffs" which are themselves complex organizations. For many purposes, such distinctions are crucial. Moreover, second, the aim is simply the outline of possible styles of idealized relations of "program" and "sustaining" functions. Thus the important question of the organizational set-up which would encourage, for example, "colleague"-type relations is not considered.

The "Principles" of Traditional Organization Theory

The explanation of the general choice of the "neutral and inferior instrument" concept by students of organization is a complex problem. The emphasis here is upon a single, but major, explanatory factor: the "staff" concept is merely the protruding tip of the larger body of organization theory which, in general, is reflected in the literature of both business and public administration. This derivative nature of "staff" implies an important point of analytical strategy. It does not suffice to analyze the derivations of a theory. For, even if one of the off-shoots of such an underlying theory is expertly nipped, the theory still remains. And no doubt it will induce a similar derivation in time. Consequently, this analysis will resist the temptation to concentrate upon the interesting difficulties implied by the "neutral and inferior instrument" concept, such as the maintenance of the separation of "service" and "control" which is required by the concept.

There is wide agreement about the properties of the "principles" common to public and business administration. Hundreds of volumes on traditional organization theory emphasize such "principles" as specialization, one-line authority and responsibility, and unity of command. These "principles" — although they do not exhaust the usual lists — are the more central ones of traditional organization theory. And they are also most useful in demonstrating the derivative nature of the "neutral and inferior instrument" concept of "staff." These "principles," in the order listed above, are framed in propositions such as these:

1. Administrative efficiency is increased by specialization of the work process.
2. Administrative efficiency is increased when organization members are arranged in a definite hierarchy of authority from top to bottom and of responsibility from bottom to top, with a single head at the apex and a broad base at the bottom.
3. Administrative efficiency is increased if the unity of command is preserved, that is, if each organization member reports to but one superior.

The "neutral and inferior instrument" concept of "staff" is most consistent with the "principles." Of course, all three ideal concepts of "staff" seem to respect the "principle" of specialization, and little wonder, given its unhappy vagueness. The "principles" of one-line authority and unity of command, however, could be logically at home only with the "neutral and inferior instrument" concept of "staff." Thus "staff" became "purely advisory" and "outside the lines of command." No other concept of "staff" could have avoided so completely any challenge to traditional organization theory.

The molding of the "staff" concept to one-line authority and unity of command received several assists. The apparently greater importance of the "line" functions under the then-existing technology, for example, had this effect. Similarly, an empirically naive but widely professed notion of "popular control" in a democracy provided such an assist in Public Administration. The implicit rationale underlying the central "principles" of one-line authority and unity of command, to develop the point, takes this form: this is a democracy; in a democracy, the people must control the government; but the people elect (quasi-) directly only the chief executive; therefore, the president must control administrative officers. Given the assumption that the "line" should be and/or is fundamentally different from "staff," the convenient alternative was to make "staff" subordinate to the "line." This avoided some embarrassing questions, but posed others.

There also were practical, as well as theoretical, reasons for fitting the "staff" concept to the "principles" of one-line authority and unity of command. These practical reasons encouraged the adoption of the "neutral and inferior instrument" concept in business as well as public administration. Thus one of the embarrassing problems which the traditional "staff" formulation seemed to solve was the acute one of making some peace with patterns of organization which existed before the advent of "staff" aid. These patterns, in sum, were based upon the one-line authority and unity of command of traditional organization theory. The "principles," then, were reinforced by resistance to change. For "staff" units posed a real challenge to the "principles" and to organization practice as well: the purpose of "staff" units was to perform functions "line" officials had performed. The "neutral and inferior instrument" concept at once left the dogma undisturbed and reduced resistance by "line" officials.

Near the turn of this century, to explain, the position of the "line" supervisor was an uncomplicated one. The first-line supervisor, for example, had control, period. He normally hired and fired, scheduled production, set and administered wages, and so on. By 1930, however, many of the foreman's previous functions had passed to "staff" agencies. Thus Personnel, Production Scheduling, Accounting, and the like developed as separate organizational functions. The supervisor no longer controlled, period.

The "neutral and inferior instrument" concept eased the transition. For it seemed to avoid the difficulty implicit in an overt threat to the power of the "line," while meeting the need of rapid and increased specialization attendant on technological advances and growth in the scale of enterprises. This balance is a delicate one. For, after all, the work of the new "staff" had been done by "line" officials, somehow. And the "line" naturally valued their contributions and experience above what often seemed the pretensions of the new specialists. As Dale and Urwick frame this problem and the way in which the traditional "staff" concept seemed to resolve it:

. . . the introduction of many of the forms of specialization in personnel, industrial engineering, research, and so on, to which business is now well accustomed, appeared [absurd and unnatural] to line departmental managers and foremen early in this century. They opposed their introduction lustily, and progressive business leaders who realized the necessity for these innovations if their under-takings were to survive were hard put. . . .

So the fur flew, and harassed chief executives in business after business were driven into a hysteria of assurances that staff specialists were not meant to do what they had manifestly been hired to do. The line managers were solemnly told that the staff men were "purely advisory" and that no one need take their advice if they did not want to. . . .

This explanation provided by the "neutral and inferior instrument" was, to Dale and Urwick, "a glaring example of the irrational."

The alliance — irrational or not — of the "principles" and the "neutral and inferior instrument" concept has proved a stable and lasting one. This lasting alliance constitutes the next explanatory burden. Thus the tendentiousness of both the "principles" and the traditional "staff" concept in the face of massive contradictory evidence will be illustrated. In addition, an attempt will be made to explain this persisting bias in terms of the method of the organization theory which supports the "neutral and inferior instrument" concept of "staff."

The inadequacies of traditional organization theory often have been stressed. This critical literature expresses logical, empirical, and value reservations about the traditional theory. This literature need not and cannot be reviewed here in any detail. We may content ourselves with an overview which focuses upon a limited portion of a single aspect of the case against the "principles," their lack of specificity. Traditional organization theory, to begin, has important logical defects.

The "principles" of specialization and the pair of unity of command and one-line authority, for example, reflect two unreconciled strains of traditional organization theory. As Simon concluded in his classic paper:

What is needed to decide the issue is a principle of administration that would enable one to weigh the relative advantages of the two courses of action. But neither the principle of unity of command nor the principle of specialization is helpful in adjudicating the controversy. They merely contradict each other without indicating any procedure for resolving the contradiction.

Moreover, the "principles" are not well grounded empirically. Value questions are also begged by this empirical footlooseness. To illustrate, the "principles" do not specify the behavioral conditions under which they will apply to man *qua* man, as opposed to man as a mechanical system. This is empirically inelegant. Such empirical specification, existing research demonstrates, will require major revamping of traditional organization theory. This empirical shortcoming also implies a moral insensitivity. For it runs the great risk of obscuring the fact that these behavioral conditions are value-loaded, and must be evaluated in terms other than whether these conditions exist or not.

Similarly, the "principles" are offered as size- and level-universal. That is, they are allegedly applicable to administrative units of all sizes and at all levels. But actually they reflect a low-level preoccupation. The kinship between the "principles" and the organization theory derived by Taylor from his time-and-motion analysis, to explain, often has been emphasized. And it is the case (as one student noted) "that Taylor never went beyond the foreman." The "principles" conveniently, if illegitimately, extrapolated Taylor's low-level working propositions to all organization levels. This extrapolation assumes that which requires study. Consequently, the more levels in an organization to which the "principles" are applied, the less satisfactory the fit with empirical conditions is likely to be. Later analysis will highlight the importance of this point. The aim here is the limited one of demonstrating the lack of specificity of traditional organization theory.

As a result of these (and other) logical, empirical, and value inadequacies, the "principles" have a limited usefulness in both description and prescription. Descriptively, they hardly do justice to the political character of administration — to the dynamic, multi-lateral bargaining situation which exists between organization sub-units. But more of this later.

Prescriptively, it is by no means obvious that effective administration would result if unity of command and one-line authority were to exist. It is usually argued that, whatever the occasional absurdities of unity of command, they are preferable to the certain confusion and inefficiency which result in its absence. This position may be accepted, even though in larger organizations it is highly problematic whether unity of command and one-line authority can exist, let alone lead to the favorable consequences claimed. But it is not clear that some confusion and inefficiency, should they occur, are too high a price to pay for bringing involved interests to bear *directly* on an administrative problem by violating unity of command. If unity of command is respected, for example, long communication chains are required and time is lost. Thus an accountant in Department A cannot receive direct orders from a unit of the Department of Finance. Such an order would have to percolate up through Finance, then across to Department A, and down to the accountant. "Shooting the gap," especially on technical matters, would permit quicker communication with less likelihood of error. Of course, some problems should be allowed to percolate up the hierarchy, when the interests of policy and uniformity demand.

The "neutral and inferior instrument" concept of "staff," in addition, also has been the target of substantial (if infrequent) indictments. Like Stahl, others have argued that the traditional "staff" concept not only should not be the case but is not and never has been the case. Interestingly, for example, Taylor prescribed multiple, or functional, supervision. That is, the various "staff" specialists would control their particular areas of concern on a given job simultaneously, complementing the traditional control of the "line." Uniquely for Taylor's work, however, functional supervision never became widely accepted. Credibly, this was because functional supervision pointedly challenged the "principles" of one-line authority and unity of command. Thus it could not be reconciled with the going organization dogma.

But Taylor was not done with so cleanly. For much of Taylor is patent in the traditional "staff" concept. Indeed, traditional "staff" prescriptions are Taylor's functional supervision *without* formal command responsibility. Moreover, much evidence suggests that multiple supervision will occur in practice, whatever the "staff" concept. Witness, for example, the conflict between the "principle" of specialization (as reflected in the provision of "auxiliary staff" services) and the "principles" of unity of command and one-line authority (which imply the control of the means necessary to perform "program" functions). As Willard Hogan articulated the conflict between "principles":

One of the principal tenets of the practitioners of modern management methods . . . is the centralization of authority. . . . Yet the development of efficient management methods and their application . . . are resulting in a new division of authority and responsibility with resultant cross purposes, and other evils which management methods are designed to eliminate.

The "neutral and inferior instrument" concept of "staff," however, is still a dominant one. Perhaps administrators have been more sensible in practice than the concept requires. But progress on the theoretical level has been slow. This is not due to lack of awareness. Thus Gulick proposed many years ago that, since the "principles" proposed courses of action, it was the course of wisdom that "staff" integrate the "principles" of unity of command and specialization. The course followed, in contrast, was the rational molding of "staff" to unity of command. Similarly, a multi-line theory of organization has not yet appeared, despite the overwhelming evidence which can be marshalled in support of it. As Gaus once argued in outlining a multi-line theory of organization on the president-to-agency level:

Such a theory . . . *is the only one which fits the facts* of contemporary delegation of wide discretionary power by electorates, constitutions, and legislatures to the administrators [who] must, of necessity, determine some part of the purpose and a large part of the means whereby it will be achieved in the modern state.

The Method of the Mother Theory

Given such difficulties with the traditional "staff" concept and the "principles" of traditional organization theory, their persistence may seem surprising. But neither the "principles" nor their "staff" derivative are well suited to "fit the facts." The method underlying them provided unyielding and self-fulfilling support. The critical literature slights the role of method. But it is central.

The centrality of method can be demonstrated by considering the "mother theory" of the traditional "staff" concept. The "principles" of traditional organization theory list the explicit properties of this mother theory. But the mother theory also includes a number of implicit assumptions about the nature of the empirical world. The "principles" are built upon these assumptions. At least the following propositions, to develop the point, are required to make sense of the "principles" of traditional organization theory:

Definition: "Organization" is defined in formal terms of positions and lines of authority and responsibility.

Axiom: The human organism, for organization purposes, is an isolated being with essentially physiological, or mechanical, properties.

Axiom: Management at all levels is supervisory rather than policy-making.

Axiom: Authority is formal, or legal, and derives only from such sources as organization charts, rules and regulations, and the like.

These propositions underlying the traditional organization theory are seldom treated explicitly in the many lists of "principles." But the "principles" logically imply them. To illustrate, consider the "principle" of one-line authority. It logically implies the individual is an isolated being. For, once it is acknowledged that the individual has social affiliations, a cross-pressure condition must be dealt with. Thus a small group may vie with the formal organization for the control of the behavior of a mutual member. One-line authority, to remain unchallenged, must imply isolated man and must avoid the complexity of a cross-pressure condition. Similar analysis could be developed for all of the propositions above, which are logically related.

More than logical consistency, however, is required of an organization theory. Three such desiderata will be considered here, the first briefly, the other two at some length. They involve complex considerations made all the more difficult because of their common confusion in discussions of organization theory.

A first desideratum requires a sensitivity to organization as a moral problem. This evaluation is begged by the broadside that traditional organization theory is "universal." But theories of organization, and there may be many, are all particularistic. That is, they all depend upon the answer to the question: Organization for what? And there are many possible answers to this question. For the propositions of any prescriptive organization theory must be based upon a choice of desired states rather than upon absolute necessity. For example, it might be possible to induce conditions under which man is essentially a physiological being by deadening all but the desired responses through pervasive social training. But the induction of such conditions would be morally reprehensible.

The importance of such moral evaluation of organization theory cannot be overstressed. The emphasis below, however, will be upon two empirical desiderata. This is a strategic retreat. For empirical considerations alone are sufficient to demonstrate the limitations of traditional organization theory and its "staff" derivative.

A second desideratum requires that when the "principles" purport to describe actual relations, their underlying propositions also must coincide essentially with empirical conditions. To the degree that these propositions do not, description will be inadequate. Illustratively, a "society" may emphasize spiritual development and severely limit the extent to which people will consider only (or mostly) their physiological needs. The organization theory of the "principles" would be applicable only to a limited degree under this cultural condition.

A third desideratum requires that, when the conditions prescribed by traditional organization theory do exist, administrative efficiency (however measured) should be higher than when the conditions do not exist. The literature usually neglects the distinction between "principles" as used prescriptively and as used descriptively. Indeed, the "principles" seem to have been meant to apply in both senses. However, the test of the prescriptive usefulness of the "principles" — whether or not they generally describe existing relations — is a crucial one.

The method of traditional organization theory has a profound effect on the degree to which the two empirical desiderata above are met. Thus, whenever a relevant problem arose — e.g., the necessity of legitimating large-scale "staff" aid — the path of solution *in organization theory* has tended to be *through the assumptions* rather than through an analysis of the empirical world.

This characteristic is not necessarily damning. For traditional organization theory and its underlying propositions *were rooted* to a technological, cultural, and methodological environment. That is, the propositions reviewed above and the mother theory did correspond approximately to empirical regularities. And predictions derived from the theory were more accurate for it.

This position can be supported in block-outline. The "principles" reflected with some precision a technology with a low-level bias. For example, the axiom of management as supervisory reflects this bias which fit, more than it did not, the generalized administrative state of affairs. Culturally, also, the "principles" coincided substantially with what appear to have been common notions about authority and its acceptance *per se*. The axiom of authority as formal, for example, assumes that the problem of authority is one of establishing the legitimacy of an order, pure and simple. This is, of course, never the case. But, given a general cultural predisposition to accept directives from acknowledgedly legitimate sources, it will seem to be the case often enough so that one can disregard the exceptions without undue violence to the facts. Methodologically, finally, the formal bias of the "principles" accurately reflected the paucity of knowledge which existed concerning the importance of human behavior. The emphasis was more rationalist than empirical. But, given the support of technology and culture, this methodological inelegance was not crucial.

The method of proceeding through the assumptions of traditional organization theory runs a substantial risk, however. This is the failure to translate changes in environmental conditions into changes in the propositions underlying the theory. The propositions underlying traditional organization theory did not avoid this risk. They proved very resistant to change. Indeed, the theory usually was represented as universal and applicable always and everywhere. This reflects the lack of appreciation of the role environmental factors played in the theory. The presumption also is hardly conducive to change.

The Changing Environment

The degree to which environmental changes have made hollow shells of the propositions underlying traditional organization theory can be suggested in two ways. First, the effect of such changes on the "authority" concept will be outlined. Second, three of the major environmental changes and the ways they have undercut traditional organization theory will be analyzed.

The "authority" concept, first, has been subject to massive technological, cultural, and methodological changes. The increasingly complex *technology* in all areas reduces the efficacy of traditional threat-oriented notions of authority. The point has been demonstrated by dramatic *methodological developments* in the study of human behavior. To illustrate, "learning theory" experiments have demonstrated that, in general, subjects will learn simple tasks more effectively under conditions of threat. But the learning of more complex tasks is inhibited by the same condition.

These methodological developments have great significance. They point up inadequacies in the traditional theory, which always existed, but which are heightened by environmental changes. Thus the "learning theory" experiments demonstrate that the propositions underlying the mother theory do not adequately describe reality. For the individuals in these experiments patently reflect qualities more complex than those implied in the "principles." Moreover, these experiments demonstrate that when the conditions prescribed by the traditional organization theory do exist — high threat in this case — the anticipated consequences often are not forthcoming. A considerable and growing literature — of which but a single fragment is cited above — supports this double-barreled inadequacy of traditional organization theory. The theory's lack of specificity limits its descriptive and prescriptive usefulness.

Massive *cultural* changes complement these technological and methodological developments. The present age seems to have a less general respect for authority. This is, of course, a conclusion that must be offered gingerly. However, much of our social commentary points in this direction. And much of the recent empirical literature of organized life at least demonstrates that authority relations are not as simple as theory usually assumed. The development of unions, the high level of employment, and similar macroscopic trends also would seem to reduce the generalized respect for (or obeisance to) the authority of formal superiors.

Cumulatively, the effects of such environmental changes in the "authority" concept are marked and clear. Janowitz's path-finding study summarizes the forces inducing the emergence of a new concept and also suggests its properties. Both elements — and the implied characteristics of the organization theory which will embody the new "authority" concept — are stressed in this summary of his contribution:

As social demands and organization forms have grown more complex, bureaucratic authority has become generally less direct, arbitrary, and authoritarian. The bases and manifestations of this change [are clear even] in the military establishment, often regarded as the prototype of bureaucracy. The essential change is from an authority system based upon domination to one based upon the techniques of manipulation, brought about by new weapons, the automation of warfare, the demands of technical expertise, and the emphasis upon individual initiative attending changes in warfare. Resistance to such demands and the costs of failure to adjust to the changed environment are [great].

Topically, the effects of the massive changes are reflected in such phenomena as the recent abolition of KP duty in the Air Force.

These environmental changes, in sum, contrast sharply with the low-level bias of the "principles" and the concept of authority consistent with that bias. As compared to earlier times, a higher proportion of administrators operate in highly complex situations. Indeed, a similar effect operates quite far down the organization hierarchy. As in American society, the technology encourages a kind of "middle-class organization" with increasingly greater numbers of trained specialists in comparison to low-level operatives. Instead of the pyramidal hierarchies with which we are most familiar in organizations, many organizations are developing personnel "bulges" at the middle levels. Perforce, administrators must adapt their action to cues from many sources — including the burgeoning specialists — rather than from one superior who is recognized as having authority. Relatedly, a higher proportion of administrators are working under conditions in which creativity and self-reliance — and their concomitant, independence — are more necessary than the ability to execute specific instructions.

Traditional organization theory, more generally, also has been affected by three factors, the main related properties of the "change syndrome" which characterizes the recent history of organization: growth in the *size* of "staff" units; the advancing *level of technology;* and the rapid *pace of technological change.* These changes reduce the descriptive usefulness of the "principles." Moreover, these changes relegate to the pedantic level the question of the prescriptive usefulness of the "principles" and their "staff" derivative. For the administrative world has changed in ways which make it increasingly unlikely that the conditions implied by the "principles" — e.g., a low-level bias of operations — can be approximated closely.

The effect of the increasing size of "staff" units, first, was raised pointedly in the critical evaluations of the core proposals for reorganization of the federal government in 1937 and 1949. These proposals were based upon the traditional organization theory, with provisions for large-scale "staff" for the chief executive and "auxiliary staff" for operating agencies. The traditional rationalizations for such "staff" aid were offered. But their inadequacy was reflected forcefully by the magnitude of the "unit" to which the "principles" were applied. As Finer isolated the crucial issue raised by these proposals: "The paramount question is, whether a multitude of neatly conceived homunculi can ever add up to one man."

The traditional "yes" answer was too pat. For the traditional concept of "staff" became untenable when a complex organization like the Budget Bureau is concerned. One can conceive of small "private staffs" serving a "line" official, most of the time, in the style required by the "neutral and inferior instrument" concept. But when the "staff" is itself a large organization, the concept breaks down. Such organizations have their own interests, their own atmosphere, and their own style of decision-making. These factors tend to fragment the "staff" unit from the "line," whose officials face similar (but often inconsistent) needs in their own units. This is the case even when no empire building is involved. For any administrative unit strives to maintain a sense of potency, if only to increase the chances of controlling and motivating its members. Thus there is no simple driveshaft linking large "staff" units to the "line" executive. Dual- or multi-supervision becomes the order of the day.

The "neutral and inferior instrument" concept of "staff," then, ill suits the changing environment. For the development of the Executive Office of the President over the last decade or so only symbolizes the marked movement into the era of the large "staff" organization, in business as well as public administration.

The level of technology (admittedly a somewhat slippery concept), second, also affects the traditional concept of "staff" and the organization theory from which it derives. The persistence of the "neutral and inferior instrument" concept is wonderful in the same sense that the aristocrats of Chekhov's *The Cherry Orchard* are wonderful. Technology has simply moved out from beneath the concept. A relatively simple technology underlies the subordination of the "staff" to the "line." Thus when Gustavus Adolphus first separated combat from supply, transport, and finance (as "line" and "staff," respectively) there was *some* reason to emphasize the combatant versus the noncombatant nature of the functions and to assign precedence to the former.

There always have been proponents of the thesis that "an army marches on its stomach" (that is, on the contributions of the "staff"). But the point is unavoidable under conditions of a complex technology. To explain, using the military frame of reference, both the combatant and the noncombatant activities are functional differentiations. Both functions are delegated powers from the commander and both are coordinated by him with other functional specialties. Moreover, the assignment of precedence to one of these functional specialties is arbitrary, for their contributions differ basically in terms of time only. Their importance will vary with conditions such as the state of the existing technology. The importance of the functions is not a constant depending only upon the fact that one function follows or precedes the other. Under existing technological conditions, in brief, future wars will be won (or lost) more and more in the laboratory, on the proving ground, and on the training field. Indeed, future wars may be prevented by the "staff" functions. The point also holds for other administrative areas, if sometimes less dramatically so.

Practice in organizations supports this analysis. Increasingly, to illustrate, the importance of "staff" is emphasized, and the necessity of the performance of some command functions by the "staff" also is stressed. Both emphases are patent in this resumé of a recently-held panel on the subject, "Staff: To Advise or Control?"

There is much complaining about the staff concept today because the use of staff is intimately connected with management's growing difficulties in controlling its program. . . .
[Thus the Internal Revenue Service has successfully utilized this technique and has] reduced staff-line conflict: dividing of staff personnel into two groups, one purely advisory and the other empowered to issue directives.

The forces inducing this emphasis upon the "staff" function are mainly two: the increased importance and complexity of many "staff" specialties, which makes "line" reliance on the "staff" for follow-up (sometimes with command power) reasonable, if not necessary; and the probable desire of "staff" officers to increase their control because of the increased importance and complexity of their contributions.

The relative importance of particular "line" and "staff" functions under various technological conditions will not be determined here. The conclusion is more limited: the assignment of "staff" to a subordinate position has no obvious support under conditions of a complex technology. The traditional "staff" concept, in short, is an anachronism.

The orientation toward change, third, also has an important effect on the "neutral and inferior instrument" concept of "staff." If adaptation is valued, there is ample reason not to relegate "staff" to an inferior position in organization theory. For the parity of "staff" with the "line" may act as a stimulus to adaptive behavior. This importance is anchored in what seem to be deeply-rooted orientations toward action characteristic of the "line" function. Thus one "staff" official in a manufacturing concern describes the conflict of his action-orientation with that of "line" supervisors in this way:

The factory supervisors' outlook on things is different. They emphasize today. Yes, they're looking at only the short run. We have to look at things in the long run. We have to see the whole unit. They worry about their individual departments.

The traditional concept of "staff" gives little formal leverage. But "staff" units are likely to perceive — and to monitor solutions of — problems (or "pre-problems") which are long run and organization-wide. The common limited action-perspective of "line" officials, in contrast, limits their effectiveness in the increasingly common burden of organization, the perception and solution of inter-unit, long-run problems. Students of Rickover's battles over the atomic submarine in the U. S. Navy, for example, can provide ready illustration of this point. In addition, Rickover's battle reflects the important underlying influence of the massive assumption of the superiority of the "line" officer over the segregated EDO (Engineering Duty Only). This assumption was a pervasive one, being reflected in every career stage from training onward.

Some balance, in short, between the "line" and "staff" orientations toward action seems desirable under all conditions, save a technological stagnancy at a relatively simple stage of development. Most desirably, the balance should be an easily-shifting one. This is probably too much to expect in any power situation. In any case, the traditional "staff" concept — imposed under conditions which do not correspond to the low-level, static technology implicit in the concept — legitimates a lack of balance and makes organization adaptation sticky.

Some Guides for Theoretical Change

This analysis hardly settles the problems of the "staff" concept. But it does provide some guides which an ultimate solution must respect. These guide lines may be reviewed briefly.

First, changes in the traditional concept of "staff" depend upon the development of organization theory(ies) of greater specificity than is provided by the "principles." The tail, as it were, is attached to a very big dog.

The methodological directions for such an effort, fortunately, need not be developed from scratch. These directions will not permit such mischief as the mere logical wedding of a "staff" concept to an organization theory. For the watchwords of empirical theory — and of the concepts and operations which constitute its vitals — are tentativeness and testing, neither of which characterized traditional organization theory. Nor is it necessary to wait *mañana* for applications of the methodology to provide grist for the mills of theory. Indeed, the natural-science approach to organization phenomena already has yielded quite specific findings which must be built into any satisfactory theory of organization.

Second, the "neutral and inferior instrument" concept of "staff" is inadequate from a number of points of view. Primarily, the concept is a derivative from an inadequate base. The concept does not stand on any substantial proof either of its usefulness or of the degree to which it describes organization relations. Indeed, there is substantial evidence of the mischief of adhering to the concept, as in the matter of adaptation to change. Finally, the traditional concept seems patently out of tune with the modern environment of administration.

Third, the evidence suggests the usefulness of a "colleague" concept of "staff" in many situations, both in *describing* "line-staff" behavior and in *prescribing* the behavior best serving organization purposes.

There is, however, no need to supplant one dogma with another. For there are likely to be significant differences between the functional requirements of various "staff" specialties and the personalities they attract and/or help to develop by training. Compare an accounting office and a research and development (R&D) unit in a manufacturing concern. In terms of their maximum impact upon the organization, the task of the former might be described as relatively "steady-state," the task of the latter as "change-oriented." A traditional pattern of "staff-line" relations might be appropriate, in general, for the accounting office. But such a pattern might limit substantially the R&D impact upon the organization. This would be the case, for example, if most of the work of the R&D unit were discrete problem-solving for the "line," at the "line's" request. This would involve R&D in what is often called "applied," as opposed to "basic," problem-solving. Longer-run problems would go begging.

Fourth, this analysis implies the need for substantial research of a comparative sort. Thus the effects of various "staff" concepts upon effectiveness, satisfaction, and similar variables should be studied. Many knotty research problems, of course, are involved. But the choice of concept of "staff" by logical derivation from an organization theory is a convenience incompatible with a sophisticated theory of organization.

3

Administrative Functions

Aside from the larger theories of organizational behavior, certain functions such as leadership, decision-making, politics, planning and management, can be studied and a better understanding of the administrative process can emerge. Here more limited functions are performed; indeed, decision-making is claimed by its advocates to be at the heart of the administrative process. The functions differ from one agency to another, but these are some of the means by which the organization's goals can be kept in perspective.

These functions are performed in varying degrees throughout the hierarchy of an organization, but the political executives have a particular role to play, and the means by which they are chosen and brought into government may be the first indication of their success or failure.

Administrative Leadership ✤ Don K. Price

One of the classic anecdotes in the apocrypha of Washington tells how the chairman of the board of a great corporation, many years ago, was brought in as a staff member of the White House. When reporters asked how his responsibilities could be distinguished from those of the Secretary of a certain Department, he said, that was easy; unlike the Secretary, he was interested only in policy, not in administration. What, insisted a reporter, was the difference? Well, replied the industrialist, take my company; our board of directors leaves administration to the president; we are interested only in high policy like — well, for example, like the design of a soap wrapper.

This story, of course, is worth cherishing not for its accuracy (not guaranteed) but for its moral. The obvious part of the moral is that men in business often spend their energies on issues less important than those they would deal with in government — which may suggest that the nation could afford to transfer some of their talents to more important public purposes. The less obvious part of the moral is that in

"Administrative Leadership," by Don K. Price, reprinted by permission of the author and the American Academy of Arts and Sciences (280 Newton Street, Brookline Station, Boston, Massachusetts) from *Daedalus*, Vol. 90, No. 4 (Fall, 1961), *Excellence and Leadership in a Democracy*, pp. 750–763. This article also appears in Stephen R. Graubard and Gerald Holton, eds., *Excellence and Leadership in a Democracy* (New York: Columbia University Press, 1962).

government, as in business, high officials may take great satisfaction in dealing efficiently with trivial problems, while the big issues are settled by subordinates, or by accident, or by factional politics, or by default.

For a good many years now we have been informed as to the first of these points. When the Commission on National Goals recently reported to the then President Eisenhower that "the vastly increased demands upon the federal government require at the higher levels more public servants equal in competence and imagination to those in private business and the professions," and suggested that "this involves a drastic increase in their compensation," it was doing little more than repeating what the second Hoover Commission had said soon after Eisenhower took office. But in between, a great many things had happened to change our national attitudes; an administration whose backers at the beginning had looked to it mainly to get government out of competition with business ended by proposing to accept responsibility for inducing economic growth at home and abroad, for producing more physics Ph.D.'s than the Russians did, and for exploring the solar system. It may well be that we are now ready to admit that our government cannot do what we expect of it unless it can claim a larger share of the best administrative ability in the nation. "A great empire and little minds go ill together."

If we come to accept this idea, it will not be merely because the government has grown in size. Even more important are two changes in the kind of things it does, and the way it does them. The first is a change in the degree of specialized competence required to deal with public affairs. This is true of the economic and social as well as the technological aspects of government; in the latter it is only the more obvious. With this change, the technological and scientific corps (in and out of uniform) have begun to exert a more powerful influence on policy. (Who would have dreamed a decade or so ago, when we were holding our annual budget down to thirteen billion, that we would so soon take their word for the need to spend more than twice that much to put a man on the moon!) As a result, the politician may now see in the general administrator, not a bureaucrat who threatens to usurp his policy-making function, but an ally without whose professional help he can never comprehend and control the new social forces.

Second, in the most dynamic sectors of our economy and educational system, we are beginning to change the relation between government and private institutions in much the same way that we changed the relation between the federal government and the states about a quarter of a century earlier. In place of the grants-in-aid that tied the states to Washington in fields like soil conservation and social security, we now have contracts and grants that link Washington with Du Pont in atomic energy, with General Dynamics in the missile program and with the Massachusetts Institute of Technology and the California Institute of Technology in fields ranging from physics to international affairs. We therefore have no longer a system in which all private institutions look apprehensively at the higher bureaucracy as the motive power for immoral government spending, and try to suppress such spending. Indeed, it may now be clear, even to extreme conservatives, that it will require very great authority and administrative strength at the center of our government either to enforce economy against private demands for government spending or to direct that spending in the national interest.

These two changes call on us not merely to get more capable men into government, so as to manage efficiently the policies that politicians have prefabricated. That could be done quite simply by raising salaries and providing other incentives. But there is no point in merely transferring to government the avarice of the private sector without its enterprise, by giving high salaries to men who will not rise to the challenge of big problems. This brings us to the second half of our moral. For our traditional prejudices have not merely made it difficult to get for government a fair share of the top administrative talent, but they have forced the able men now in government careers to concentrate their talents on the interests of particular bureaus or services. And so we have made it almost impossible for the career service to do its main job — which is to look ahead at the great problems that confront the nation, to devise and recommend policies to meet them, and to see that the various departments are effectively coordinated in carrying the decisions of responsible political authorities.

Some of the best career men in government know this quite well, and know what should be done about it. But it is hard for them to do their main job well when our system was set up on the assumption that it ought not to be done at all. We are comparatively good at politics, but then we were born free. At the other end of the spectrum, we are very good indeed at technology and detailed management; no nation is better at getting specific things invented or managed. But the connection between these two aspects of government is weak, and sometimes it is not there at all. This is the crucial blind spot in our political vision.

We hardly notice the gap, perhaps because we have no word for the function that is missing. We have taken the word "administration" from British usage, and it will have to do, but its connotations in Whitehall and in Washington are quite different. The British administrative class hardly manages anything: its job is (under general political control) to make policy and see that the departments are effectively coordinated. Its purpose is to be the corporate custodian of a great tradition, and to adjust it to new political needs.

If we are tempted to comfort ourselves by saying that such a career civil service simply will not fit the American tradition, we ought to forget about the British and look at the career systems we ourselves have created. For, with all their defects — some of which our civil service ought to avoid with the greatest care — the military services and the Foreign Service suggest that, once we decide a career system is worth the cost, we know how to develop it and to train it for the higher functions of policy-making.

We have given up *laissez faire* in any economic issue that we consider of national importance. We are beginning to give it up in education; how many people should be attracted by fellowships into the study of Urdu or microbiology is now acknowledged as a proper matter for Congressional concern. The one field in which we most stubbornly continue our faith in the free play of the market is in the provision of personnel for high administrative positions in government, and this at a time when that type of excellence in government is the key to the success of all our other efforts.

It may be too kind to suggest that this neglect comes from a blind faith in tradition or from absentmindedness. On the face of the matter, it would seem that the system is rigged so that a capable young man, having risen rapidly in government to a position of responsibility for policy, will have to take a private job to protect his family's future.

The main point here is not a very abstruse one. If you talk to a college senior about going into the civil service, you cannot tell him that he will be promoted on the basis of his usefulness to the government as a whole. You are tempted to warn him that, to get ahead, he may have to plan his career in terms of the specialized interest of a single bureau. Happily, there are still men who ignore this counsel of caution, and whose government careers show real dedication to the public service and a breadth of interest that transcends any specialized field in the natural or social sciences or in management. But this is like asking our army to rely on individual heroism or on election by the troops, rather than a system of training and promotion, to develop officers for general staff work.

That, of course, is just what we did do until we saw the importance of the problem. We came to see this only gradually. Today the young man who becomes a military officer knows that the people who decide on his next assignment are instructed to think of it as a step in the purposeful development of his career, in which his rewards for developing as a general officer will be greater than those of any specialty.

There are many important differences between military and civilian administration, but in a rough sense the work of the staff planners and the top command in a military service is like that of central administration in the civil service. Today, in our recognition of the importance of this civilian function, we are not far ahead of where we were in military affairs when President Wilson indignantly ordered the General Staff to stop preparing war plans: we are afraid that such work will usurp the proper function of political leadership.

A half-century ago we had just begun to organize our Army General Staff, in the face of dire predictions that it would lead to a military caste or a dictatorship. Today it is evident that it is possible to develop a professional system for military officers without destroying democratic responsibility: the officer corps of the several services are drawn from a wide variety of civilian universities as well as from the service academies, and the Congressional committees (as well as the President) still maintain a control over military policy that has no counterpart in any other major political system. But the main point is that we recognized in time that we not only needed to have a career system for the officer corps, but that it needed to be headed up in a corporate staff concerned, not with the command of particular divisions or the direction of particular technical services, but with the general policies and strategy of the forces.

It is hard to imagine how we should have survived if we had not developed something like the general staff function in all our military services. The nature of warfare, with its growing complexity, velocity, and lethality, made this function necessary: the new military technology, and the new weapons systems, added immeasurably to the intricacy of military affairs, and to the speed of innovation, and above all to the utterly fatal results of falling behind. If you read the administrative history of the Civil War or the Spanish-American War and compare it with that of the Second World War or the Korean War, the contrast gives a faint idea of the need for general staff work.

Or if your imagination boggles at this comparison, you can try to imagine what the Pentagon would be like if all the staff officers were removed, and their functions were left entirely to part-time consultants from industry, Congressional committee staff members, and political coordinating committees, with a few columnists and commentators taking part occasionally to keep the mixture from being too bureaucratic. This is unthinkable, because everyone understands that the changes in the complexity, velocity, and lethality of our military developments have made a fundamental change in the way in which we must try to keep military matters under democratic control. Political authorities can make decisions on immediate issues only if professional staff officers have worked out acceptable alternative solutions for them, and the most effective use of top political authority may well be to set the professionals to work on issues that have to be faced five or ten years hence — or to develop a system to improve the professional corps so that it can do so.

Political responsibility, in short, depends on having a responsive and well-trained professional corps, and cannot be achieved by keeping it in a state of fragmentation and anarchy. We as a sovereign people are quick to criticize the lack of integration of our military services and their strategic plans, but we would never know of such conflicts if the professional staffs had not prepared the plans and been forced to bring their discrepancies into the open by our civilian political controls. Like any other testy and temperamental sovereign, we resent having our experts bring us hard problems. Perhaps it would be better if they solved them without bothering us. But it would be much worse if they failed to recognize them.

If we are not very worried about the lack of unification of the civilian departments, perhaps it is because they have not been very good about bringing up the issues that we ought not to duck. In the light of the probable developments over the next decade or two, are our agricultural policies as closely coordinated with our plans for industrial development, as our Navy's strategy is with that of our Air Force? I doubt it. Does our planning for the use of radio and television wave lengths take into account our future educational needs? Is someone worrying about the way in which our programs of water conservation relate to the future distribution of our population as it will be affected by our transportation and industrial development and housing policies?

I am not proposing that career administrators have any more authority — but only an opportunity to help bring up the issues that political authority must resolve. Nor am I advocating additional governmental controls — I am only asking whether the extensive controls we already have are being used in a rationally related manner. For if their interrelations are ignored, the waste in our civilian economy will be far greater than could be caused by poor business methods. This is the scale of waste involved not in the mismanagement of logistics, but in civil war. I do not think the metaphor is too strong. President after President has seen the fight between the Army Corps of Engineers and the Reclamation Bureau over the development of water resources; advisory committee after advisory committee has pointed to the waste involved in this competition; but the strife between these two agencies, and their supporters throughout the country representing two sets of interests and two conceptions of policy, has not only kept the President and the Congress from putting a rational single policy into effect, but has destroyed a Presidential staff agency which tried to deal with the question, prevented the development of another, and restricted the staff which the Secretary of the Interior could build up to work on the problem.

Similarly, the political battles of the affected interests have kept our transportation policies mainly in the hands of independent commissions, with little relation to each other or to the President or Congress. Here, too, all recent Presidents have seen the issue; I doubt that any would have been permitted by the Congress even to set up a staff to work on the problem. And without some staff work to bring out the issues clearly, there is no grist for the mills of democracy; as a sovereign people, we do not even effectively know the issues exist, though we may blindly, by governmental action, be determining the economic and social fate of whole industries or regions or metropolitan areas.

If this kind of waste were all that was involved, we could stand it. But there is a graver problem. The basic nature of the relation of military to civilian affairs has changed since World War II. Then, we could still get along with a small peace-time army; then, the term "mobilization" meant that we could wait till after the war began to draft the soldiers and manufacture the munitions. But now, with the possibility of instant long-range destruction, the military cannot be set off in a corner until the shooting starts, when the rest of us can then volunteer for the duration. It has to be interwoven with every aspect of our society, and our future plans. Especially our future plans.

And if the civil government has no future plans of its own, the military will make them. It cannot wait around while civilians squabble about the nature of the regulatory process and government-business relations, when it sees the air space over our major cities cluttered up in a traffic jam of civilian planes that would be fatal in a crisis; it has to become one of the major political stockholders, so to speak, of a new Federal Aviation Agency to replace a Civil Aeronautics Administration. It cannot wait for civilians to settle their arguments about federal control of education or the relation of a potential National Science Foundation to the President; it has to go ahead through military grants to support nine-tenths of the physics research in the major universities in the country. It cannot wait for Congressman Rooney to ease up on the diplomatic allowances or the training funds or any of the other costs of a high-quality career Foreign Service; it can give the military attaché of an embassy or the head of a Military Assistance Advisory Group much more entertainment money than to the ambassador, and the only American official airplanes available in the country, so that the ambassador may entertain and travel by courtesy of his military colleagues.

Any civilian with even a dim sense of our political tradition, when he hears of such cases, is tempted to draw on the mantle of Hampden or Jefferson and wave the banner of civilian supremacy. But this is an irrational reaction. The problem is not caused by any desire of the military to encroach on civilian functions, but by their expansion to fill a vacuum. The vacuum is the absence, on the civilian side, of anything like an adequate career corps to deal with general policies and government-wide interests. In the army, the function of the general staff is to take care of the big general questions; the special staffs and the technical services take care of the specialized and subsidiary and housekeeping problems. On the civilian side, the typical Department head is permitted to have only some special staff units; the real centers of continuing power are in the bureaus, which are the civilian equivalents of the technical services. A civilian general staff would be considered dangerous.

The results are what you would expect. The real old pros are the men who run the bureaus, and a good pro can usually outclass a good amateur. Consequently, the development of civilian policy rather resembles the way I suppose a war would be run if it were left to the technical services and the politicians.

We are still bemused in the United States by the notion that we tolerate the inefficiency of a spoils system because it makes it easier for a new President to come in with a gallant band of amateurs and, at some cost to efficiency, take over the direction of the bureaus. This is wrong on all counts; we do not change many of the real power centers — the leadership of the bureaus — and it would not do any good if we did. The career head of a bureau symbolizes the professional opportunities, and controls the guiding incentives, of his subordinates. Above his post, advancement is possible but risky; there is no system for it, and no chief of a service with a professional interest in developing his men. It is no wonder that the able career people are likely to keep their interests focused on the problems of their own bureaus, and their loyalties engaged in advancing them. This is a sure recipe for seeing to it that the career administrators are interested in the second rather than in the first rank of national problems, or even that they are emotionally engaged in furthering specialized interests at the expense of national interests.

The great failure in our political vision is our not seeing that the main function of the top career administrators is to help develop policy. If the career administrators above the level of the specialized bureaus do not provide strong support for their political superiors in the development of policy, our system of political responsibility suffers. Then the Secretary of a Department can do little but preside over a group of quasi-independent bureaus, while the important potential issues within the Department and between it and the rest of the government will never be brought up for consideration by the President and the Congress. The big issues — at any rate, the biggest — are rarely brought out in the policies which a bureau and its clientele and the related Congressional committees like to put forward for consideration. In particular, in the wide range of problems in which both military and civilian considerations are involved, the advantage in initiative and staff work will rest with the bigger staff battalions of the Pentagon.

If we are to cure this blind spot, we have to give up three prejudices that have come to be accepted as American traditions. The first is the traditional prejudice against hierarchy. We like to think we are against ranks and titles. This works mainly, we may note, with respect to the ranks and titles of other people or in fields we consider unimportant; it does not hold down the number of vice-presidents in any metropolitan bank, or the importance of professorial rank in any university, or the number of general and flag officers; but it does keep us from giving much in the way of rank or status to civilian administrators with broad interests in policy.

We began, during the Federalist period with a rudimentary but respectable corps of career administrators, but the Jacksonian revolution abolished all that. A half-century later, as we began to build up a civil service that would serve the nation rather than the warring parties, we built it from the bottom up, rather than from the top down, as the British had done; we put large numbers in the lower ranks under the merit system in order to deny mass patronage to the bosses, rather than reforming the higher ranks in order to create an effective and responsible system of authority for the President and Congress. Then the organized sciences and some of the professions began to demand that their specialties be exempted from patronage. The dogmas of frontier democracy found it impossible to admit that general administration required any talent that the average citizen could not supply, but such ideas yielded to the special mysteries of the professions and sciences. In an effort to protect their standards against corrupt or ignorant politics, the engineers and doctors and scientists pushed their men up the hierarchy into the jobs at the heads of their bureaus.

The dogmas of frontier democracy would not accept the pretension of general administrative superiority; if anyone was to be given a government job, he ought to be asked to prove his superior fitness for the specific duties of that job. This was not too troublesome at the lower grades; but at the higher, it had two unhappy effects. The first was that administrators, in order to justify a professional and career status for themselves, were forced to develop various aspects of management into specialized techniques. Personnel administration and budgeting, for example, are normal parts of the functions of an administrator, and he may need some people who specialize in them to help him. But we went far beyond that and made them into technical specialties, emphasizing their peculiar mysteries rather than their utility to the central purpose of administration: the development and execution of policy. And then the top political executives, having hardly any other career administrators at hand, had to put too much reliance on the budget officers for the control of policy.

The second bad effect grew out of the first: those who wanted to strengthen the career service emphasized the management specialties because they could be defended as semiscientific and hence non-policy-forming and nonpolitical. Administration became the victim of its own defense mechanism. In the end, this defense was not really persuasive, for the management specialists cannot stay out of policy any more than the admirals or ambassadors can; what is more political than the argument over veterans' preference in personnel administration or over the influence of the budget on military spending? By adopting this defense they perpetuated the dangerous myth that administration is not concerned with policy.

The purpose of a hierarchical pyramid, of course, is to raise to the top the difficult issues that the specialists cannot settle, so that these may be decided by legitimate political authority — in the United States, by the President and the Congress. We still like to think of a President's decision as a lonely act of will at a dramatic instant, just as we like to think of a general's commands as being delivered on horseback, with a wave of the sword. But a decision always requires staff help, to make it and to carry it out, and for that the President cannot rely entirely on any one specialty. On any complex and difficult issue — for example, disarmament — it is impossible for a political executive to make a rational decision merely by taking the well-organized and strongly conflicting positions and programs of different specialized groups and deciding instantaneously among them. If a President, for example, receives staff papers prepared separately by groups of generals, diplomats, and scientists, he probably cannot take immediate action one way or another; all he can do is to determine some guiding principles, and they will be meaningless unless he organizes a system of staff work, involving or controlling all three groups, to work those principles into a program and see that it is carried out. This requires the help of a career service in which the top ranks are the rewards of ability to deal imaginatively with major policy issues in their broadest context — not one of fixed allegiance to the position of a particular bureau or professional service, and not one of devotion to a particular management specialty.

The second prejudice we need to modify is the prejudice against admitting the corporate nature of an administrative service. That prejudice has a sound core: we should not tolerate a closed bureaucracy; we should do all we can to keep the career service flexible in its policy attitudes by a certain amount of interchange at all levels with private careers. But that does not mean that we should not have a system for the policy level of administration that gives some corporate protection to individual careers. We have been improvising a system, but the structure of our institutions is still against it. As the second Hoover Commission said in the best of its reports, "The Civil Service System emphasizes positions, not people. Jobs are classified, ranked, rated, and their compensation determined on the bland assumption that they can always be filled like so many jugs, merely by turning the tap." In short, at a time when the major business corporations and virtually all other major institutions in society (including universities) have come to put great stress on the planned recruitment and training of top talent and on effective long-term tenure, we force the civil service (though not the military services or the Foreign Service) to ignore the elements of continuity and corporate spirit that are essential in order to retain most of the best men it gets.

This tradition that resists the development of a corporate service above the bureau-chief level misleads us most conspicuously in our efforts to coordinate policy. You can bring an outsider in to analyze a scientific problem for you, or a problem in managerial procedure; both can be defined as separate problems, to be solved by a known form of expertise. But the coordination of policy is fundamentally different. It requires not only some understanding of the main substantive aspects of the policy, but also an appreciation of the subtle interconnections of various parts of the government that can come only from years of experience. More than that, it calls for a professional sympathy, a bond of mutual trust based on a common corporate loyalty, between those working in the several departments concerned. This is why we often make no progress toward coordination either by giving additional authority to a political executive or by legislating elaborate structures of interdepartmental coordination. Structure and procedures do not make an organization. After World War II, when we set up a structure of interdepartmental policy committees (such as the NSC), we were imitating the skeleton of British administration without appreciating the function of its central nervous system.

The myth of the Minute Man dies hard. Those of us who are interested in government like to be called to Washington as consultants, or for brief adventurous periods in emergency administration. We cherish the notion that the real ability is outside the career service. We must simply find better ways of bringing it in for one or two years at a time — perhaps by some scheme for supplementing federal salaries for those who are not willing to sacrifice their private incomes temporarily.

But this will not do the main job (however useful it may be as a supplement), again for the reason that we cannot wait for the outbreak of an emergency to call for volunteers as general staff officers. We are already in the middle of the emergency, in one sense; in the other and more awesome sense, if the emergency comes, everything will be too late that has not been started five or ten years before. And the military problem is only the most easily understandable aspect of the many problems that technology has forced on our society.

This brings us to our third traditional prejudice: that government work must not be made as attractive in material rewards as private careers. This might have seemed plausible at one stage of our history: government was not very important in the production of material goods, and government salaries, like relief payments, had to be kept low so as not to reduce the incentive to go into more productive work. But this way of thinking is obsolete, whether you judge the importance of government in terms of sheer military security, or of the hope of building a more humane civilization. Such rational considerations might not prevail against traditional prejudice. But if our logic is weak, our sense of humor is fairly strong, and surely we will soon appreciate the absurdity of holding down the salary of an administrator who runs a government program while at the same time he runs it by contracting with corporations who use government funds to pay higher salaries for less important work. No better incentive could be devised to get administrators to avoid the careers in which they would be responsible for promoting the general interest, and to take jobs which require them to lobby for special interests.

Nevertheless, we cannot solve this problem by higher salaries alone, any more than we can make our affluent society more civilized merely by shifting funds to the public sector. We have invented too many ways in recent years to use public funds for private purposes, for such measures to suffice. A great deal will depend on whether the career administrators who spend those funds are made into a disciplined corps responsive to the public interest, or whether they continue to shape national policy according to their various *déformations professionelles*.

Our foreign-aid and technical-assistance missions, realizing that many under-developed countries fail to progress in specialized fields because they have not learned the arts of administration, complain of the slowness of traditional societies to adapt their governments to modern needs. When we have taught the Asians and Africans how to abandon their traditional prejudices, perhaps we shall be ready to reconsider our own. After all, the British built up their civil service on the principles they had first tried out in the East India Company. It may not be too late for us to learn from the British example and to improve a system whose shortcomings we did not see until we tried to export it.

If we do so, we must surely do the job differently. We should not try to provide the same kind of educational basis for a top civil service, for all our sentimental admiration for the Permanent Secretary who can write Greek verse. The effective theory of the British service was based not on a reverence for the classics but on a determination to get the most capable men by taking them from any field in which they might be studying. "If astrology were taught at our universities," said Macaulay, "the young man who cast nativities best would generally turn out a superior man." This pragmatic approach would lead us in the direction our Civil Service Commission has generally been going, slowly and within the limits of political tolerance, for the past two decades, in recruiting college graduates for government careers on the basis of a solid general education, as well as from the sciences and professions.

When he is recruited, the administrator's training has only begun. From the outset of his career, he will have to learn a twofold job. Its first phase is to deal with the substance of policy. The sciences have swept away the oversimplified notion of the administrator as a complete generalist who needs to know nothing about the content and substance of the policies he administers. More and more we shall be adding men with training in science to our administrative ranks, and those of us who lack it will have to make desperate and belated efforts to comprehend the nature of the impact of science on government and society. That impact is now so great, and science in turn has come to rely so heavily on government policy, that the scientist turned administrator, like the management specialist, will have to acquire an understanding of the complexities of our constitutional system and of the way in which it must bring all techniques into a responsible relation with our political values.

The administrator of the future, for all his concern for policy, can never forget the other aspect of his job, which is to organize and coordinate a complex and dynamic system to carry out policy decisions that are made by others. We are in no danger of establishing an irresponsible bureaucracy, so long as the administrator is kept under the direction of responsible executives, and called to account by an independent Congress. For we do not really want administrative leadership: we want political leadership, which requires a strong administrative underpinning in order to be effective. The professional administrator must try to bridge the great gap between the way the scientists think and work and that of the politicians. He can never enjoy the luxury of the intellectual pride of the former, or the power of the latter. Through his professional skills, he must try to reconcile our technology with our democratic values. In this effort, the purpose of his profession is to carry, with a higher degree of concentrated responsibility, the moral burden that in a free society must be shared by all citizens.

Decision-Making Research: Some Prospects and Limitations ✥ WILLIAM J. GORE

In the past ten years, a good deal has been written and a great deal said in administrative circles about decision-making. The pressures demanding more from administrative leadership may initially have focused attention on decision-making. But the notion that an administrator could become more effective simply by learning how to make decisions has lost some of its luster; one would have expected the vogue of decision-making to have lessened. It might have, if some researchers and theoreticians had not taken up the cause, and if the give-and-take between practitioners trying to improve their effectiveness and researchers seeking to understand more about choice-making had not kept up professional interest in the subject. There are even some indications that as decision-making finds its place among the concepts of administration, it may influence our perspectives toward leadership. Our object in this article is to mark some of the gains and prospects stemming from attempts to use decision-making as a vehicle for understanding.

Mounting pressures on the democratic myth in government and society, and on government itself, as well as the pressures playing directly upon the administrator, have generated widespread recognition of need for new understanding of organizational and administrative processes. In some cases this need manifests itself as the search for yet another technique of management. But in other cases there is a partially articulated idea that something may be wrong with our basic precepts of bureaucratic organization. Such a frame of mind indicates that a new theory of administration is needed.

Decision-making has benefited both those concerned with new techniques and those seeking new theory. However, to be a useful technique, decision-making must be a crucial administrative act that causes or at least triggers important sequences of organizational activity. Since we have often assumed the pivotal role of decision-making in the administrative process, it has been easy to ask a good deal of decision theory. Decisions may be crucial administrative acts, but are not necessarily so; depending on your perspective, decisions are *either causes or consequences* of effective administration. Therefore, decision-making as a managerial technique has real limitations. This leads to the central issue: What are the prospects and limits of decision-making theory?

References to decision-making in our talk and in what we read seem to establish decisions as physical and social facts. Although one knows that decisions are not quite what they are said to be, it is usually inconvenient, even awkward, to stop in the midst of events and determine the source of the difficulty. Research indicates that decision-making is an ubiquitous concept, referring variously to change, to a choice, to a climate of opinion, to a condition of agreement, to communication, or to a vaguely-felt state of affairs which — like ice — melts in the hands of anyone who stops to examine it.

Traditionally, administrative theory is the product of speculative rather than empirical analysis. Gulick and Urwick, for example, sought to erect a formal blueprint for organization as a piece of social machinery. They were not primarily concerned with organization as a matter of personal relationships. Even Chester Barnard — who was immensely sensitive to the interplay of personality and collective image — built his framework from experience rather than systematic analysis. Although it is necessary to rely on the speculative theorist rather than the researcher for the over-all picture, there are differences in what they offer us. The term decision-making is often ambiguous when far removed from the empiricist's orientation toward reality.

Although it is difficult to differentiate the empiricist from the speculative theorist, for each must practice the other's arts, there is a difference in emphasis that touches the root of this ambiguity. Most administrative doctrine in the twentieth century has been designing organizational machinery to transform the democratic myth into effective governmental activity. We have been occupied with perfecting a structure and process of government that manifests responsibility, equality, legality, and rationality in place of the inheritance we rejected in the eighteenth century. Our preoccupation with impartiality and efficiency has led to great emphasis upon crucial administrative acts, such as decision-making, as means to achieving these ends. The assumption seems to have been that decisions made in the open forum of administrative procedure where rationality holds sway (as opposed to the proverbial smoke-filled room) will best realize true democracy.

Research is beginning to show that this is not necessarily true. First, people in organizations undoubtedly need prestige, security, growth, and so on; they satisfy these needs even at the expense of the formally designated decision process. Second, the deep-seated, powerful commitment to rationality in our administrative doctrine denies the efficacy of insight, wisdom, and intuitive understanding, which are universally socially-sanctioned bases of decision in this society. But beyond and underlying both of these is a third assumption; that government in general and policy-making in particular can be managed by men. Partly because an integrated society impinges rather directly upon the individual and partly because of the widespread belief that government should be curbed to serve the individual, we have sought to gain mastery over political and administrative processes. The members of the administrative profession, their friends, associates, and apprentices are unalterably committed to the ideal that government can be managed. In the end, not the elected representative of the people, but the professional public servant, finally bears the burden of public responsibility. In spite of the myth that the legislator decides what should be done and the administrator does it, the administrator picks up the bits and pieces of legislative ideas and attempts to fit them into a coherent program.

As a people, we have sought to balance the individual and the state (in favor of the former) by gaining collective control of the governmental process. More and more the burden of implementing this strategy has fallen on the shoulders of the professional administrator. A doctrine has evolved that specifies in some detail what we seek (responsiveness, efficiency, economy, and so forth) without specifying how it shall be accomplished. Administrators and students of administration struggling with the problem of implementation (for the universal assumption seems to be that the grand strategy is not working satisfactorily because of inept implementation) have sought for the key in morale, training, communication, supervision and supervisory development, incentive schemes of various sorts, and now decision-making. To pit management techniques against the underlying problems of American government, however, is like trying to deal with a serious disease by means of a simple pill and good set of bedside manners. What is needed first is a fully dependable diagnosis of what is probably a major disorder in its early stages. Therefore, our concern should be not with decision-making as a technique but with decision-making as a potential focus for an administrative theory that offers us a more reliable representation of the administrator's dilemma.

Decisions come in a variety of forms. Since they differ in content, in the process through which they are made, and above all in the total impact they have upon the organization, a problem of matching types of decisions and classes of decisional situations arises. There may be no such thing as a generalized skill in making decisions; only skill in handling one or another type of decision. Often the issue is not the candidate's skill in decision-making, but what his skills are in relation to the types of decisions he will most frequently confront. Such issues immediately raise questions for decision theory. What kinds of decisional situations are there, what sorts of decision processes are typically associated with them, and what kinds of managerial skills do these processes call for?

Several classes of decisions have been suggested. "Recurring" and "nonrecurring" are used to separate a class of decisions which are going to be made time after time from those cases that occur once or only once in a while. Confronted with the necessity of setting bail bonds each day the police judge devises a set of criteria by means of which he selects the bond level. Over time these come to reflect the concerns of police officers, attorneys, and other judges as well as his own values. Eventually the recurring decision becomes routine and serves as a monitor, much like a traffic signal, maintaining a balance between streams of organizational behavior that converge about it.

Nonrecurring decisions, on the other hand, such as the decision to create three or four additional traffic judgeships, necessitate a venture into uncharted areas where costly, destructive subfactors may lurk. They almost always pose problems for the administrator because there is not sufficient experience from which to predict possible consequences.

Professor Herbert Simon's classes, programmed and nonprogrammed, deal more satisfactorily with this distinction. In many ways the programmed decision is similar to the recurring decision. Organizations develop routines, like many clerical operations, which become so firmly established that decisions are made almost effortlessly. Routine is not a narrow class, but comprehends both standard operating procedure and such complicated operations as computer programs for the assignment of thousands of units in a branch of the military service. It may embody straightforward or relatively complex sequences of choice-making operations. Any organization must accommodate to many unanticipated situations, but the core of a stable collective enterprise is a repertory of proven, reliable productive activities that move directly toward goals and that are activated, monitored, and terminated by an appropriate set of habituated routine decisions.

When a firm pattern for decision exists (1) the consequences of action (especially negative ones) can be more readily anticipated and because of this a generally favorable balance of benefits and costs can be secured; (2) the most efficient ways of responding have been located through experience making most nonprogrammed activities appear excessively expensive in terms of the time and resources that must be invested to secure a given set of goals; and (3) simply because one is dealing with the familiar and the accepted, programmed decisions are typically accompanied by pleasant or at least tolerable emotional overtones. On the other hand, nonprogrammed decision characteristically amounts to a leap into the unknown accompanied by individual stress that produces considerable discomfort.

For fifty years there have been those, following Fredrick Taylor, who have sought improved ways of making programmed decisions. Their efforts are partly reflected by Scientific Management, then (before and during World War II) Operations Research, and now Management Science. Although only a handful of people are masters of the decisional mechanisms that have been devised through these approaches in the last twenty years, many have heard of linear programming, statistical decision-making, Q-ing theory, and other devices which are powerful tools for making recurring decisions. This has tended to make the nonprogrammable decision somewhat mysterious, the proper object of an intuitive art of leadership that only a gifted few possess. Unfortunately, nonprogrammed decisions are at least as important acts of leadership as are programmed ones.

Until recently nonprogrammed decisions were seen as crucial administrative acts that could never be rationally comprehended. Nonprogrammable decisions have now come under the researchers scrutiny, partly on the basis of the pioneering research of Brunner and other psychologists working on human and non-human thinking, and partly from remarkable advances in computers (especially in computer programming). RAND, Carnegie-Rand, and IBM are all working with problems central to nonprogrammed decision-making. At least as important are efforts in political theory which are, for the first time, assuming something other than a dialectic methodology. From these and other sources are developing conceptual devices rich enough to comprehend significant chunks of the world, penetrating the subtleties involved in an open-ended choice situation; hence powerful enough to indicate a meaningful response. These useful parts must still be fitted into a broad conceptual framework in order to crack this major barrier to increased administrative effectiveness, the nonprogrammed decision.

There are indications that this orienting framework will posit decision-making purely as means. Because we do not know, in the nonprogrammed decision, what parts of an organization, what activities, what costs and benefits, even what timing shall be required — that is, because we are dealing with an unstructured situation — nonprogrammed decision-making tends to range widely, making thousands of bits of information about the organization potentially relevant to a crucial decision. Faced with a mountain of relevant information and hence with the prospect of an impossible task of assessing the situation in one step, the central strategy of nonprogrammed decision-making is to break the major choice into a series of manageable smaller decisions, contingent upon each other.

Viewed from this perspective, decision-making is primarily a means of mounting an appropriate response rather than a dramatic choice between alternatives. For when a problematical stimulus is broken into a half dozen or three dozen or fifty component choices the larger issue is usually overshadowed by the more immediate, more tangible, and more understandable components. It has been suggested that most of us do not, probably cannot, come to grips with major problems until they are translated into smaller, more manageable pieces. However, no one can come to grips with problems of such magnitude as war and peace or economic stability. In a very real sense decision makers dealing with major problems have no course but to muddle through, to use Lindblom's phrase. Simon calls this heuristic problem-solving. Problems which can never be tamed through comprehensive definition, which embody such perfectly balanced value dilemmas that there can never be right answers, are heuristic or not subject to resolution through logic. He suggests that many, perhaps most, of the problems handled by management are of this sort. The implications of this statement could hardly be overstated. Decision-making is not a dramatic, determinative act shaping destiny through setting goals, molding values, and building alliances. Rather, the most crucial kind of decision-making is a catalytic agent by which a number of decision makers seek to muddle through tangled values, inconsistent goals, and mutually neutralizing techniques toward a response that will to some extent insure the continuity of an organization.

In this context the administrator frequently finds himself on the razor's edge between two courses of action, when what he requires is time to evolve a response consistent with the situation. Administrators often carefully avoid raising controversial issues; they commit themselves to action without confronting the broader outlook.

Against the background of these ideas, making decisions is seen as activating decision-making processes that will eventually trigger an organizational response appropriate to the decisional situation. Although it is useful to contrast programmed and nonprogrammed decisions, the pertinent question is when to respond through one or the other. The possibility of error may seem slight on paper; it is in fact an imminent possibility in many, if not most, decisional situations. To make the most appropriate choice of response defining mechanisms the administrator needs a scheme which matches types of decisions and types of decisional situations. The scheme that follows is based upon observation, and though untested, it illustrates the kind of formulation that might be helpful.

We suggest three rather than two classes of decisions. Routine decisions are programmed decisions in their simpler forms. The completely habituated behavior of firemen, in reaction to a fire alarm — in donning protective clothing, moving the trucks out, and dashing to the fire — represents the almost complete routinization of decision-making; only insignificant choices (such as whether to turn at the corner before or just past the fire) are left to be made. The hallmark of the routine decision is the correspondence between the prefabricated response and the response required by the situation. Because any other form of decision is time-consuming, all agencies that deal with crises use a series of integrated routine decisions as their response mechanisms. Police, emergency rooms in hospitals, air search and rescue units, as well as fire departments, rely on routine choices. But the routinized decision is also used generally to set into motion prefabricated patterns of productive activity.

Some productive activities are so stable and so completely patterned that they are activated and coordinated through a chain of routine decisions. These so-called completely programmed operations are typified by the operations in the power engineers' station at a hydroelectric plant where the engineer is employed merely to check upon the instruments monitoring the generators; and in the billing division of a life insurance company where the procedure is so well defined that people make only insignificant choices; and in a grocery store, except where customer satisfaction is involved. Even here ingenious clerks, skilled in interpersonal relations, devise a repertory of responses complete with emotional overtones that fulfill the expectations of most customers. Nurses, service station attendants, receptionists, and members of an older profession do the same thing. Routine decisions are much richer than they may seem at first, for they embody not just the habituation of motor behavior, but of larger behavior components including intellectual and emotional elements as well.

In many cases organized productive activities are so completely routinized that almost all the decisions made — perhaps eighty or ninety per cent — are routine. However, change is so universal in our society that few organizations can survive without constant accommodation. In many cases change comes as undetectable increments in habituated routines. Even participants may be unaware of it. We know very little about incremental change but it is certainly the most painless form of social adjustment.

Since incremental change takes time, it is often necessary to adjust to an anticipated state of affairs. In some cases formal planning procedures will be at hand. In many cases the need for adjustment is so infrequent that no formal procedure exists, but experience in dealing with similar past difficulties provides a precedent. In either case the kinds of decisions that will be involved are of a higher order than the routine decision. But typically they are not so dramatic as a unique, full-scale nonprogrammed decision; these are likely to fall within a readily identifiable zone.

Organizations ordinarily seek to accommodate new situations by adapting behavior to produce specified changes. In most cases, there is little inclination toward dealing with the situation *de novo*. To consider the situation anew, or in a new light, is difficult, and rapidly becomes impossible if too much of the new is incorporated. Looking at new aspects of a situation potentially demands extensive adjustments within the group. When faced with the possibility of change, then, most organizations find themselves seeking to *adapt* existing activities to meet new needs, without disturbing the existing structure of goals.

The adaptive decision is much less a device for triggering and monitoring activity than the routine decision; though it may lead to the initiation of an activity which will meet the new need. The adaptive decision differs from the routine decision in that it focuses upon a problem rather than a task. To this extent it is more a matter of negotiation and development of new understandings than the routine decision. Frequently the latter deal with activities so completely habituated that individual components are not analyzable. In adaptive decisions, dealing with matters of immediate importance, there is considerably more breadth. Frequently the press of circumstances is such that a routine decision is made arbitrarily with the understanding that time will be taken for a leisurely discussion and an adaptive decision later on.

The third class of decisions comprises vehicles for more dramatic, more thoroughgoing change; a change so penetrating that it amounts to an *innovation* rather than an adjustment. Characteristically, the innovative decision picks up where the adaptive leaves off, with a major change in activity and operation which leads to a change in goals, purposes, or policies. A change that penetrates into goals (as opposed to activities) is to some extent unhinging because it raises questions about where the organization should be going that are seldom completely settled anyway. Questions about basic objectives often disturb the inherent equilibrium of an organization, which in turn tends to disorient many people associated with it.

Since only a few painful experiences with innovative decisions will make members of an organization wary of change and eager to accommodate through an adaptive decision, innovative decisions are few in relation to either routine or adaptive decisions. Typically, decision makers become aware of the need for an adaptive decision when some activity handled through a series of routine decisions fails to meet expectation. This leads immediately or eventually to the articulation of the need for adjustment. If only a few are affected, or if other problems of great concern distract the decision-makers or if there is no obvious alternative to the existing state of affairs, the *status quo* may continue for weeks, even months, before anything is done. If, however, some malfunction does violence to values prized by members of an organization, and if there has been a long-standing concern with the problem, a backlog of frustration causing an impulse toward action, then something may be done with dispatch. And the higher the level of frustration the higher the intensity of the impulse for action. However, this reaction runs directly contrary to a larger, more central concern. The energies and resources available in an organization are always limited in comparison with the rewards sought. When the gap between collective aspiration and achievement is increasing the members of an organization generally experience a good deal of stress. Since there is a widespread tendency to assume that basic changes in organizational structure and process will enlarge the gap, there is an almost universal hesitancy to initiate changes likely to influence the organization's productive capacity. Only when the condition of the organization causes deep concern or when there is external evidence and authority on the benefits to be derived from a change, is an innovative decision likely to be initiated.

The innovative decision involves almost exclusively words and ideas, expectations and attitudes. The underlying function of the innovative decision is to induce a climate in which agreement between conflicting centers of power can emerge. In fact, the innovative decision is often little more than an indigenously-sanctioned ritual which embodies synthetic or integrative patterns of interaction. The product of an innovative decision is, therefore, agreement or an inclination toward it, which must be recast into revised patterns of activity through adaptive decisions before they have visible impact upon what an organization does.

These three classes of decision are at once interdependent and independent. Routine decisions activate, channel, and terminate hundreds of units of behavior in such a way that broad goals are implemented through the same activities that meet immediate objects. Since both the conditions under which goals can be realized and the goals themselves are constantly changing, routinized activities must continually be adapted to maintain a satisfactory rate of goal achievement. But since, on a broader field, the objects embodied in goals are changed from time to time, the innovative decision exists. The essential rhythm of organizational adjustment is from routine to adaptive to routine; or from routine to adaptive to innovative and back to adaptive and eventually to routine again.

This theoretical model describes kinds of interrelationships that the administrator needs to be aware of if he is to make decisions that comprehend the full scope of his problems. For example, a formulation such as this indicates that the one crucial question is whether or not an adaptive decision should be reified into an innovative decision or distilled into a new routine. Put this way, the issue is not initially one of right and wrong, health or unhealth but, as was suggested above, whether to effect a full-scale change or a promising adjustment in the *status quo*. We are not suggesting that right and wrong are irrelevant so much as that (1) right and wrong cannot be decided by the administrator; in an open society, they are inherently issues for a larger audience; and (2) that issues of right and wrong are not susceptible to a direct or programmed decision — they must be attacked obliquely through such questions as what form of decision to undertake. The administrator who accepts the burdens of making decisions, as opposed to channeling decision-making processes, is likely to find himself preoccupied with trivia which do not embody the issues in significant degree. Perhaps we can provide some substance to these assertions by identifying some of the conceptions of decision-making developed since World War II.

Professor Simon and his associates at the Carnegie Institute of Technology have developed too many facets of decision-making to be summarized here. One of the general models, from *Organizations*, offers a suggestive conception of the central dynamics of the decision-making process. Labeled a model of adaptive motivated behavior, this conception is built around the dynamic relationships between four concepts; level of operation, expected value of reward, search, and satisfaction. Figure 1 shows these relationships diagramatically. The critical relationships are between level of aspiration and satisfaction (as the level of achievement to which a group aspires rises, its satisfactions with what it is doing falls) and between expected value of reward and satisfaction (the more a group expects and looks for in what it is doing, the more satisfactions will it find in its activities). As increasing satisfactions ease expected reward levels higher, these raised reward levels pull the level of aspiration up with them. And since this lowers the worth of existing satisfactions, it amounts to pushing the level of satisfaction down, with all the subsequent frustration, tension, and possible conflict this involves.

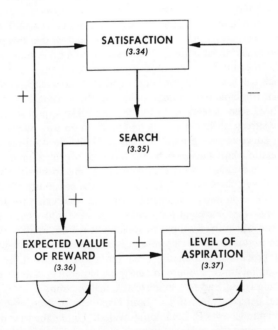

Like all general theoretical formulations, this one is not meant to take account of the myriad factors in a real life situation that influence, often determine, choices which are made. Still, it points out that the dynamics of choice-making are not in the tensions and anxieties associated with selecting one of two alternatives without knowing where either will lead. In the choice-between-alternatives — March and Simon call it mechanistic — model there is the possibility of a one best way, a way which may even be right and rewarding as well. To the researcher such a view is not only over-simplified, it is misguided in a way that often brings vicious pressures to bear upon the decision maker. One who accepts this more complicated view does not expect to find alternatives dramatically different in *the total configuration of their outcomes*. That is, he expects that dramatic leaps upward in satisfaction to have an impact on expected level of reward and consequently upon level of aspiration that soon neutralizes, or more accurately, redistributes the level of satisfaction to a slightly higher balance in the whole system.

Another formulation from *Organizations* further highlights the fluid nature of the factors and forces operating in decision-making. The so-called inducements-contributions postulate is described in terms of the problem of turnover. Assuming that an individual benefits in many ways through his participation in an organization and that he must contribute many things to the organization as a condition of membership, they suggest that the *balance* of inducements and contributions is critical in accounting for turnover. This is not the simple balance of the economist — in the jargon of the theorist, it is not an additive relationship where one compares the sum of inducements and contributions — for it is the apparent sum of each that is important. Since the apparent or perceived sum of inducements increases when there is no possibility of employment elsewhere and since there is a marked increase in the perceived sum of the contributions required of the individual when alternative opportunities are available, the inducements-contributions balance is as much influenced by opportunities outside the organization as by those within it.

March and Simon hold that the inducements-contributions postulate is applicable in a number of other administrative situations. We suggest that this postulate holds in most decision-making situations. The costs of doing one thing are heavily influenced by the possibility (or the absence of the possibility) of doing something less costly which will satisfy the same end. This is, of course, an application of the old and familiar principle of marginal utility; yet the relationships it presents have only recently been seen as relevant to the decision maker's problems.

This cursory survey of Simon's thinking (which in no way reflects the full scope of his efforts) suggests two general attributes of the decision-making situation: (1) In it, the relationship between dynamic forces of organization are such that the bold stroke is usually inappropriate; organizations are so sensitively balanced we must deal with the whole network of forces or face the possibility of self-neutralizing action; and (2) decision maker is dealing with both what exists (or more precisely, what is seen) and what is sought (or what can be read into what might be done). The situation can be reversed simply by looking at it from another perspective. A slight change in posture in these circumstances may result in a different impact upon organizational processes, raising the need for a completely different decisional process. The administrator's failure to detect the imperative embodied in the initial change in posture could lead to administrative malfunction.

Of the several perspectives that have been taken toward decision-making, that of Robert A. Dahl and Charles E. Lindblom is widest. Unlike the view of the administration theorist or even the student of politics, it is a sweeping view that focuses upon a complex institutional process. But this is not the same species of activity as the administrative decision. Where administrative decisions — especially the more important types — are deliberate attempts to implement goals by groups of people familiar with each other and working toward an objective well known to most of them, the decision processes Dahl and Lindblom identify are institutionalized patterns of relationships between large numbers of people who, whether or not they are pursuing a common objective, are participating in a common process, but toward their own ends. Although administrative decision-making characteristically involves a good deal of conflict as well as anxiety, it is essentially a form of cooperative activity, because the success of the participants is tied to the realization of their common enterprise. In the institutional models of Dahl and Lindblom individuals and groups pursue their own diverse ends within the general framework of the institutional process. Success is fragmentary where an individual or group achieves an independent goal primarily through its own efforts. This contrast between two conceptions of decision-making is manifest in several more concrete forms. The participants in the structural administrative decision process have reasonably well defined relationships with each other and social controls which are automatically activated to maintain the balance of power between participants. In the unstructured situation there exists a set of rules of the game that keeps a minimal level of order in the relations between participants — performing a kind of traffic control function — but the participants are not usually linked together in a network of well defined relations. As a result, communication between participants in the structural decisional situation is much higher, its meaning more precise and at the same time rich with overtones, the number and complexity of symbols used being far higher than in the unstructured situation. It follows that the quality of activity is different. Typically, the unstructured decision is carried on within the framework of a formal ritual — a legally prescribed decision point such as a budget determination, a hearing, and the like — while the structured decision is internally specified. Its indigenous patterns may be only partly visible even to participants, and the tone and mood of people dealing with each other here is one of casual intimacy in contrast to the studied postures of participants in formal rituals of decision.

We are used to labeling the structured decision administrative, and the unstructured, policy or political. These terms are not fully consistent with the classes Dahl and Lindblom use, however, for they reach beyond what we usually mean by political. Theirs are policymaking models if policy is used to denote a set of rules of the game played by the dominant political and economic powers. They offer four policy models: the price system, polyarchy, hierarchy, and bargaining. Two of these will give the flavor of the rest.

Under *polyarchy* the tendency toward unilateral control through a hierarchy is almost balanced by a tendency toward dominance by individuals as atomistic members of society. In an intricate balance several kinds of power are neatly distributed between opinion leaders, norm setters, public officials, technicians, clienteles and others in such a way that concerted action is possible on matters of common concern but no one is dominant enough to promote selfish interests at the expense of the majority. This is not so much a model of decision-making as a set of conditions that favor particular types of decisions and provide constraints on others.

By means of *bargaining*, a number of leaders interested in apparently irreconcilable outcomes in the same situation interact within the more general rules set down by society. In this case the relationships are those between equals each of whom has considerable power, intense commitment to his objectives, and some skill in maneuver. Whereas the policy process in the polyarchical setting is likely to be one of swift movement from agency to agency, and from public to public, bargaining is a type of siege between united forces.

The majestic focus of Dahl and Lindblom suggests that a host of policy decisions must be made and remade to sustain society and that these are so difficult in some cases and so crucial in others — so diverse in both cases — that what we require is a policy-making process peculiarly adapted to the circumstances in which it will be carried on. In fact, the main emphasis of *Politics, Economics, and Welfare* is that the prized values of our society may be in jeopardy because we are bargaining away symbols that must remain immutable and committing our price system irrevocably to artifacts unworthy of our sociopolitical heritage.

We have tried to provide glimpses here of some major conceptions of decision-making. Missing is a sketch of statistical decision-making, a refined device for manufacturing programmed decisions. The relations between these forms of decision-making cannot be satisfactorily described at this level. But they do raise some larger issues which deserve mention.

Thirty years of research in social science has provided us with many glimpses into leadership — especially effective leadership. There has been considerable emphasis on the need for flexible, adaptive, opportunistic and, frequently, pragmatic behavior by leaders. Current research in decision-making cuts both deeper and much more finely, and, although it is still only suggestive, this research raises issues of considerable consequence.

Only since World War II have we had adequate tools for the examination of administration. Previous to this our analyses were necessarily dialectical: they involved the manipulation of facts within an elaborate myth system. Two thousand years of this activity had generated a body of doctrine so vast that it had to be considered seriously for its bulk alone. It has allowed us to build great corporations and vast agencies, yet it may have lost much of its utility. We may have gone about as far as we can go, perhaps farther than we should have, with this doctrine.

The body of knowledge already beginning to accumulate from recent research indicates that there is much that should be questioned. Only some of this concerns decision-making. What is happening is that research on decision-making has burst its boundaries and carried us back into the larger area of leadership. One senses that we are on the threshold of an administrative revolution that will dwarf Burnam's *Managerial Revolution.*

The immediate issue is the nature of organization as a mechanism for collective action. At best organizations are inefficient, at worst they spin meaninglessly like a top. Initially, the question was whether or not this could not be remedied by improving decision-making processes. Now it is asked whether the basic nature and structure of organization should not be reconsidered. Much present organization reflects traditional methods without considering what form of collective mechanism is really appropriate to our objects.

All bureaucratic organizations are inconsistent with the basic human motivation to the degree that they attempt to control behavior and channel it into previously defined directions. There is tremendous inefficiency in human activity whenever people are pushed instead of allowed to move under their own power. Although, traditionally, control is necessary, often adequate, and sometimes highly effective, and although our society gives recognition to those who control the most people, there is no reason why social engineers could not perfect a self-energizing system in which individual initiative would displace control, if they were given the central principle. We often talk as if leadership and control were essentially the same. Now we can develop a new concept of leadership upon the basis of fragments of reliable knowledge about man's collective behavior.

As important as the inadequacy of existing leadership patterns as forces supporting motivation is their impact upon the individual. We live in a society dedicated to the primacy of the individual. We hold it a self-evident truth that the individual is more important than the group: that his dignity, his worth, and above all his creativity are the ultimate end of society. Yet we are in the midst of one of those national convulsions of self-evaluation, discovering that according to William H. Whyte, David Riesman, and Vance Packard, we are in fact denying the ultimate worth of the individual. By living in our society, we are all experts on this subject. All of us have seen organizations turn healthy personalities into neurotics and less vigorous ones into jellyfish with barely the minimum essentials of human character. One of the implications of the research mentioned above is that it is no longer so easy to blame some personal inadequacy for these human tragedies. We have broken the strongest souls through the use of sufficiently destructive devices, and we have demonstrated that most healthy organizations clash violently with individual needs at times.

To those who are satisfied with controllership and who are convinced that the organization man represents a suitable level of human achievement the political scientist must raise an additional difficulty. Democracy is on trial around the world. Nationalistic movements everywhere are questioning our commitment to the individual, to freedom, and to self-realization. Using organizational devices that emphasize the group, they are accomplishing wonders; and they are repeating these wonders with amazing regularity. It does no good to say new bicycles or better houses or free books are not worth the price to a man who has never known freedom. He feels no loss. We must create simpler, more effective patterns of leadership that will stimulate effective production and at the same time promote the dignity of the individual. This requires a revolution in leadership patterns.

It seems likely that this administrative revolution will have an impact on the national political scene; for some of our prized political values may be subjected to re-examination. Uniform treatment, for example, is a universally accepted administrative value. Tied to the more general value, equality, and at the same time to administrative regulations and operating procedures this principle frequently stands in the way of reasonable action. The same can be said of many other tenets of administrative doctrine. Some were formulated at a time when corruption was rampant. Others sprang from an agrarian society. Whatever the origins, there is need for a re-examination not only of our administrative doctrine, but of parts of our political philosophy that reinforce ritualistic administration.

It is too early to predict the nature of the new leadership we are looking for. Certainly it will unleash unimagined reservoirs of productive and creative energy. Without doubt it will return to the man who lives and works in a bureaucratic organization a good deal of his dignity and sense of worth. It will most certainly encourage more change, and more rapid change, than we know today. It will substitute creativity for control, self-direction for first-line supervision, and wide participation in decision-making for managerial determination. There will be greater awareness of the full span of an organization's impact (negative as well as positive) and greater emphasis upon long-term goals. Qualitative excellence will be placed before quantitative achievement — although there should be little need for concern with quantitative achievement. The boundaries of organizational concern will rapidly be extended until many agencies that were once antagonists are brought within the circle of protagonists. And denial of self and destruction of one's identity as a personality will no longer be the prime source of adjusting to collective demands upon the individual.

Developments in social science since World War II have provided the tools for re-engineering social organization to suit contemporary needs. What remains is the challenge of creating new patterns of leadership.

The Decision Maker as Innovator

✤ Herbert A. Simon

A properly managed organization can carry on the routine of its day-to-day activity without the constant involvement of its chief executive. His main responsibility to the organization is not for its routine operation but for its modification to meet changing demands and opportunities in its environment.

In a growing society like ours, "adaptation" means something more than mere growth to meet the growth of the society. The chief executive's task is more than this — it is to provide for genuine innovative change in the organization's programs.

What is Innovation?

Most of our activity and most decisions are not innovative, but are governed by "programs" already in existence. There is a distinction between those decisions, on the one hand, that are encountered frequently and repetitively in the daily operations of an organization, and those, on the other hand, that represent novel and nonrecurring problems for the organization.

With the former type we would expect to find, and do find, decision-making governed by standard operating procedures. We would expect operating procedures to have little to say about the latter. We call the former "programmed," the latter "nonprogrammed."

In the situation for which there is no operating program, the task of the executive is to see that one is created. The task is to organize in order to facilitate such innovation and to provide motivation for it.

We can call program-building innovative when two conditions are met: (1) finding the answer to the new problem involves difficult search, problem-solving, and learning activities; (2) the initiation of the new program — the recognition of opportunity or need — comes largely from within the organization as a result of systematic scanning of its environment and sensitivity to problems and challenges.

Innovation, then, is needed at all levels of the administrative hierarchy, but increasingly as we go up to the levels of the bureau, the division, and the department. The main earmarks of innovative administration are initiative in seeking occasions for program-building and vigor in creative problem-solving activity involving search for new solutions.

The point in an executive's career when he moves up to a level at which these innovative responsibilities are critical is an important one. The skills he has drawn on up to this point are no longer sufficient. He must learn new techniques and new ways of approaching his job.

The Processes of Innovation

The classical theory of rational choice is not much help in telling us how to go about making innovative decisions. We need a new theory that captures the salient

Herbert A. Simon, "The Decision Maker As Innovator," in *Concepts and Issues in Administrative Behavior*, by Sidney Mailick & Edward H. Van Ness. © 1962. Reprinted by permission of Prentice-Hall, Inc., Englewood Cliffs, N. J. Pp. 66–69.

features of creative problem solving. We need a description of the decision process that embodies these characteristics of nonprogrammed decision making:

1. Alternatives are not given but must be searched for.
2. A major part of the decision-making task is to discover what consequences will follow each of the alternatives being considered.
3. We are more often concerned with finding an acceptable alternative than with finding the best alternative. The classical theory of decision was concerned with "optimizing," a theory of innovation will be concerned with "satisfying." It can be shown that this change in viewpoint is essential if a satisfactory theory is to be constructed.
4. Problem-solving involves not only search for alternatives, but search for the problems themselves.

Human problem solving and creativity have generally been thought to involve "mysterious" processes — "judgmental," "intuitive," "subconscious," and so forth. Psychological research has recently made great strides toward dispelling the mystery. We now know, with the aid of electronic computers, how to stimulate complex human thought processes. This research has proved that human problem solving — even of quite complex kinds — involves nothing more than complex sequences of simple processes of selective search and evaluation.

Constructing an Environment for Innovation

The major task of the top executive is to create an organizational environment in which these familiar processes of creative problem solving can take place effectively. In doing this, he needs to pay particular attention to two things: his own time budget, and techniques for building innovative activity into the organization structure.

An executive usually starts with a clean slate in a new organization, and gradually accumulates a host of routine "maintenance" activities. He must take steps periodically to free his time from these growing barnacles of programmed activity. Delegation is a continuing process — what is not delegatable this month, because it is important and novel, must and should be delegated next month because it has become routine. Few executives succeed in freeing themselves for nonprogrammed activity unless they give conscious thought to the means of doing it. There is a sort of "Gresham's Law" whereby routine drives out creative thinking. Unless the executive conscientiously allocates time to innovation, he will find ways to fritter away his time by absorbing it in routine.

How can the executive build into his organization the capacity for innovative response to the environment? He can see that the organization is equipped with adequate "radar" facilities for scanning its environment; that it is staffed with individuals and units to carry out the important intelligence functions, and individuals and units to maintain a vigorous long-range planning activity. He can see that the organization possesses, also, adequate technical skills and imagination for the development of new programs in the areas called for.

The nature and competence of an organization's intelligence, planning, and program-development facilities will be a major factor in determining the directions in which the organization will develop and the ways in which it will respond to the environment. The most powerful means the executive possesses for molding the development of his organization is through control over these features of organizational structure, and through the conception of the organization's task — its goals and aspirations — that he provides his associates. Through these means his energy, which is after all only the energy of one man, can be many times amplified through the concerted and creative effort of the entire organization he is directing.

Summary

My observations can be summarized very simply. The main task of the executive is innovation — which involves creative problem-solving activity for him and for his organization. He accomplishes this task by managing his own allocation of attention and effort, and by paying particular attention to the organization's scanning and program-development functions. He contributes to creative innovation throughout the organization by seeing that it has a constantly-revised, clear, simple picture of the world in which it is operating and its goals in that world. Through these processes, he is able to contribute to the organization not merely his energy, but also the means to release in creative ways the energy of others.

A Study of Organizational

Communication Systems ❖ EUGENE WALTON

The overwhelming "fact of life" for modern society is organization. In modern society "no man is an island" and few if any of his needs can be satisfied without his becoming part of, or interacting with, organizations. It seems clear, then, that modern man's major means of expression and influence relative to his environment is in association with organizations of one kind or another.

To the extent that this is true, the factors that account for the TOTAL BEHAVIOR of organizations and how individuals relate to them, become a serious topic for investigation. *It is contended here that the most significant factor accounting for the total behavior of the organization is its communication system, and that the dynamics of the organization can be best understood by understanding its system of communication.*

However the importance of communication in organization, we have insufficient knowledge of the dynamics of the system writ large that clearly explains and accounts for the movement of messages within the organizational environment. We need to know, for example, about why a given bit of information released in the system will move along one path to one destination and not along other paths to other destinations. We need to know more about the characteristics of the movement of various kinds of messages within the system. An overall theory or explanation is sorely lacking. It was the formulation and testing of such a broad, over-all explanation of organizational communication that was the objective of the research project reported here.

"A Study of Organizational Communication Systems," by Eugene Walton from *Personnel Administration* (May-June, 1963), pp. 46–49. Reprinted by permission.

The Suggested Theory

The explanation tested here was dubbed A Magnetic Theory of Organizational Communication. Very simply, the theory hypothesizes that the organization is primarily a communication network, which is dominated by a number of magnetic centers that tend to draw messages unto them. It was further hypothesized that people who draw messages unto them possess one or more of the following:

AUTHORITY, which is the assigned, legal right of command.
POWER, which is the personal capacity to influence.
EXPERTISE, which is the knowledge required by the organization.
SOCIABILITY, which is that quality of character that makes for enjoyable social interactions with others (as seen by others).

The theory suggested that members of the organization initiate contact with these centers in their conscious and unconscious attempts to exert influence. However, it holds, real influence is not exercised by the initiators, but by the skillful and patterned responses of the receivers who occupy the magnetic centers. In essence, it is the decision-making, communicating and motivating of the persons in these magnetic centers that is the real *management* of the organization.

In addition to predicting that such centers existed within organizational communication systems, the persons who occupy these centers were said to differ from those not in such centers in these specific ways:

I. They are more knowledgeable about the kinds of decisions that would be acceptable to the majority of the people in the organizations;

II. They are more satisfied in their over-all positions in the organizations;

III. They feel they have a greater "voice" in the affairs of the organizations;

IV. They are more frequently receivers of "informative" messages, and senders of "action" messages;

V. They experience fewer painful emotional reactions to their communicative interactions with others.

The Research Design

This theory was tested with the following design:

Phase One Questionnaire. Approximately 100 employees of a large government laboratory completed a questionnaire in which they indicated the persons with whom they would *in fact* communicate for a variety of reasons; e.g., to get an official statement of the organization's goals (Authority), to get some "unofficial influence" exerted on behalf of a scheme they were pushing (Power), to get the best all-around explanation of the technical skills required by the organization (Expertise), and if they needed a friendly, sympathetic listener just for "getting something off the chest," or "out of the system" (Sociability). They also gave their "reasons for choice" for each selection. They were given two hypothetical problems and a list of hypothetical solutions and asked to choose the one most acceptable to them personally.

Two-Day Communication Log. About one month after the administration of the Phase One Questionnaire a sample of 30 of the respondents was asked to keep a Two-Day Communication Log. In this log they recorded all their important communications for a two day period. These 30 participants were chosen on the basis of how frequently or infrequently they were chosen as likely communicatees in the Phase One Questionnaire results. Half of the 30 were the most chosen (Centrals) and half were the least chosen (Peripherals).

Phase Two Questionnaire. On the first day following those on which the Communication Logs were kept each Central and Peripheral was interviewed individually on the contents of his log and other attitudes. They were asked which of the hypothetical solutions to the problems in the Phase One Questionnaire was favored by the majority of the people in the survey; they were asked how satisfied they were in their over-all positions in the organization; they were asked how much "voice" they had in organizational affairs; and about each entry in the log they were asked who initiated the contact, whether the initiator's goal was "informative" or "action" in intent, and their emotional reaction to the contact on a pleasant-painful continuum scale.

The Results of the Study

Speaking first to the question as to whether such magnetic centers existed within the organizations' communication systems, we found that on the average 10 to 25 per cent of the organizations' employees were chosen in response to the items on Authority (this usually meant the boss and one other person); from 15 to 40 per cent were chosen for Power (usually the boss and two or three others); from 15 to 40 per cent were chosen for Expertise (usually the boss and two or three others); and from 50 to 80 per cent were chosen for Sociability (which never included the boss and seldom included others who were chosen for Power or Authority, but a host of not previously chosen employees).

Next, looking at the reasons for choice, 55 per cent of the responses to the Authority items correlated with our definition, 29 per cent correlated for Power, 43 per cent correlated for Expertise, and 46 per cent correlated for Sociability. For example, most of the reasons for choosing a person to find out the organization's goals revolved around the fact that "he is the boss," such as

"He is the Department Head and the only one who should make such an official statement."
"No better place to get this information than from the horse's mouth."

A large number of the reasons of choice for "unofficial influence" (Power) were based on the respondent's belief that the communicatee was influential and persuasive, such as those who said

"He has a way of getting what he wants for his group. There must be some powerful influence there."
"He is seen as a key person to block or support schemes."

The responses to the items on Expertise indeed pointed to the perceived knowledge of the communicatee chosen. These reasons for choice included the following:

"I believe he is the best informed man in our area and would be the most helpful person to teach me."
"I have the greatest respect for his technical ability."

Responses to the items on Sociability revolved around the communicatee's friendliness, trustworthiness and good listening habits. These reasons included the following:

"This person does listen and can keep confidential whatever one has confided in her."

"We have been friends for a long time and seem to understand each other's problems."

As for the predicted differences between Centrals and Peripherals of the organizations' communication system, we found that:

I. Centrals were NOT more knowledgeable about the kinds of decisions acceptable to most employees;

II. Centrals did NOT feel more satisfied with their over-all positions in the organization;

III. Centrals DID feel they had a greater voice in the affairs of the organization;

IV. There were no significant differences in the "informative" messages of Centrals and Peripherals, but Centrals DID send a higher proportion of "action" messages;

V. Centrals did NOT experience fewer painful emotional experiences in their communicative contacts.

Conclusions

For Authority, Power and Expertise we concluded that the percentages of the communicatees chosen were sufficiently low to warrant the designation "magnetic center," but that no such case could be made for Sociability (where 80 per cent of the communicatees were chosen). In fact, responses to the Sociability items seemed to have a distinct anti-magnetic characteristic culminating in the complete exclusion of the boss and other power figures from the company of those from whom employees seek sympathetic listening, friendly small talk, etc.

Relative to the psychological consequences of being in or out of a magnetic center, we do not feel that this data supplies us with sufficient proof on which to base any firm conclusion.

As for the concept as a whole, we feel that it provides a useful frame of reference for conceptualizing about organizational communication. More study, it would seem, is needed to add preciseness to the approach and to help fill what is truly an important gap in our information on organizational communication.

The Selection of Federal Political

Executives ❖ DEAN E. MANN

Central to the problem of obtaining intelligent and effective management and policy direction in the federal government are the sources and procedures used in the selection of federal political executives. These executives, occupying positions usually subject to presidential appointment and senatorial confirmation, constitute the "key group in making representative government work within the executive

"The Selection of Federal Political Executives," by Dean E. Mann, reprinted by permission of the author and the American Political Science Association, from *American Political Science Review* (March, 1964), pp. 81–99. This study was originally done under the auspices of the Brookings Institution and the conclusions were based on preliminary figures which are subject to revision on the basis of later work.

branch." Through them the President directs and controls his administration, creates political support, and establishes lines of defense for his political program. Increasing attention has been paid to the selection process in recent years because of frequent reports of extreme difficulty in recruiting able people, inability to retain their services, and allegations that those who have served have proven less than adequate. The problem as broadly stated by the (Jackson) subcommittee on National Policy Machinery of the Senate Committee on Government Operations is: "how to make the quality of appointments of private citizens to national services keep pace with the spiraling complexity and difficulty of foreign policy and defense problems."

The information available on the backgrounds of men who have served as political executives, the duration of their terms, the procedures used in their selection and their reactions to the prospect of government service — in short, the information to substantiate these charges — has hitherto been highly impressionistic, based on inadequate data, out of date, or tinged with ideological preferences. To cite but a few examples, C. Wright Mills characterized the second team of the political directorate in his *Power Elite* on the basis of a relatively brief period at the beginning of the Eisenhower administration, alleging that they were the product of big businessmen fathers, Ivy League colleges, large corporations or big law firms, and country clubs, all of which made them "representative of the corporate rich." In their landmark study of *Federal Administrators*, now twenty-five years old, Macmahon and Millett said that "appointments to assistant secretaryships have been political in most connotations of that word, with little regard for qualifications or the needs of the posts. Few of the occupants of these positions have been conspicuous individuals." One imaginative commentator asserted that the difference between a Roosevelt New Dealer and a Truman Fair Dealer was about thirty pounds; the difference between an Eisenhower and a Kennedy executive was about thirty years and a shift from "gentlemen 'C' boys" to Phi Beta Kappas.

For the present study, several approaches were taken in obtaining information on the process of selecting political executives. First, we secured biographical information on all political executives who had served in the federal government between 1933 and 1961. Using standard biographical sources and information supplied by the federal agencies, we assembled profiles of these executives, including information on place of birth, education, occupation, residence, party affiliation, age at the time of appointment, and length and kind of previous public service. Second, using a modified random sampling procedure we chose 108 cases of appointments during the Truman, Eisenhower, and Kennedy Administrations for an intensive investigation to learn the procedures followed in the recruitment and selection of political executives. Interviews were conducted with the appointees, with the officials chiefly responsible for their appointment — usually the agency heads — and with any others who may have played a role in the selection process. We asked not only about the procedures but also the perspectives and values of each of the participants in the recruitment process, including the appointees themselves. Third, partially as a means of validating the information secured through the case studies, but also to learn more about attitudes toward the recruitment process, interviews were conducted with a wide range of actual and potential participants in the recruitment process. These included White House officers, party officials, members of Congress, interest group officials, career civil servants, and departmental aides. We collected information also on the roles the political executives played in the executive branch and their careers after government service.

Finally, we tried to evaluate their performance and to relate these evaluations to objective factors in their occupational and personal backgrounds. This paper, however, will be devoted to the procedures followed in their selection and an analysis of their backgrounds.

I. Patterns of Recruitment and Selection

The selection of federal political executives is a matter of interest to virtually every major participant in the political struggle, not only to the aspirant himself. The President is interested in staffing his administration with people personally and politically loyal to him, who will at the same time bring competence and support to the programs he espouses. The Secretary often looks for individuals who will similarly serve him, with perhaps greater emphasis on administration and program execution. Party interests tend to center on rewards for support or hopes for future political effort. The goals of senators and congressmen are varied, but often relate to personal interests in particular candidates or to policy commitments. Interest group stakes in administration are almost exclusively programmatic. Each has his own perspective from which to view the process and each uses his influence as he can; but the contest is hardly one of equals.

In general, the agency head is the central figure in the selection process, although his precise role varies from case to case. (See Table I.) In most instances he, or someone he appoints, is directly involved in unearthing eligible candidates and examining their qualifications. In fewer instances, the Secretary may play a more passive role, recognizing a legitimate claim on a particular position by a member of Congress, or the President, or a member of the President's staff. Very frequently, the Secretary plays a vital role in negotiating with interested parties, both inside and outside the government, agreement being arrived at by mutual consent. At the beginning of an administration particularly, the President may fill one or more of the subordinate positions before choosing the agency head, making acceptance of

TABLE I. Principal Participants in Selection of Political Executives*

	Truman		Eisenhower		Kennedy		Total	
	No.	%	No.	%	No.	%	No.	%
1. Secretary — Friends and associates	26	70	27	57	7	30	60	56
2. Secretary — White House Staff	5	14	9	19	10	42	24	22
3. Secretary — Congress	0	0	5	11	3	13	8	7
4. Secretary — Interested Group	2	5	1	2	1	4	4	4
5. President — White House Staff	3	8	2	4	3	13	8	7
6. Secretary — Party Officials	1	3	3	6	—	—	4	4
Total	37	100	47	99	24	102	108	100

* The important criterion in the assignment of these cases to one or another category was the individual's influence in making the decision on an appointment rather than his being the source of the candidate. Clearly the source of a candidate is less significant than the pressures that develop for the appointment of specific candidates.

his action a condition under which the agency head accepts his position. Sometimes an individual opens the campaign in his own behalf. Included in the sample of 108 cases covered in Table I are 17 who actively sought appointments and thus exerted their own pressures on the selecting officers. The self-initiated cases divided nearly equally among the three administrations — seven occurring in the Kennedy administration, five in the Truman and five in the Eisenhower.

Scope of Search. The agency head has the most direct interest in the selection of his subordinates, although his active role may be slight in some cases. It is useful to examine, therefore, the methods he uses in recruiting candidates for a particular position. These range all the way from the consideration only of personal friends and close associates to extended searches among many groups and among individuals whom he does not know personally. And in some instances he allows or is forced to permit others to control every aspect of the recruitment process.

In general there is a tendency for the recruiter to rely most heavily on personally conducted searches among his friends and associates, although some differences were found in the scope of search in the three administrations (Table II). The most notable departure from this pattern was at the beginning of the Kennedy administration when agency heads relied in many instances on candidates supplied by the "Talent Hunt," or when the President directly intervened to place men in whom he had personal confidence or to whom he was politically in debt. Heavy reliance on personal contacts in selecting political executives in the Truman administration is related to a strong tendency to promote men already serving in the federal government to higher positions. With willing men already available within an agency or in another agency, extensive recruiting outside the government appeared to be unnecessary or futile, especially in view of the great resistance to government service in the postwar period.

TABLE II. Agency Heads' Scope of Search for Candidates
for Political Executive Positions*

| | Beginning of Administration | | | | Later in Administration | | | | | |
| | Eisenhower | | Kennedy | | Truman | | Eisenhower | | Total | |
	No.	%	No.	%	No.	%	No.	%	No.	%
Personal search; usually among close friends and associates	7	37	4	19	21	75	10	42	42	46
Extended search; effort to broaden range beyond personal acquaintances	7	37	5	24	3	11	8	33	23	25
Reliance on others to provide candidates	5	26	12	57	4	14	6	25	27	29
Total	19	100	21	100	28	100	24	100	92	100

* Each agency head was counted once in each time period unless the scope of his search changed with different selections, as it occasionally did. This table does not cover the cases in line 5, Table I.

Over two-thirds of the agency heads whose recruiting methods were examined took primary responsibility for finding suitable candidates, either through personal contacts or by a broader search. The remainder allowed or were expected to accept leadership from some other source, although usually reserving the right to object and even veto individuals who were not acceptable to them.

The type of search conducted did not necessarily dictate the type of candidate finally selected, although there was clearly some relationship. The instances where the agency head relinquished control of the process were usually those in which party and interest considerations became paramount in the selection. The criteria for selection tended to be related to geographical representation, party service, or access to some other power-holder in the political system. When the agency head retained control, there was often — although not always — an emphasis on past administrative experience, policy objectives, or substantive knowledge of operations for which an appointee would be responsible on the job. Furthermore, the agency head operated under certain restraints in many departments. Where the clientele groups were powerful, his scope of search tended to be narrow and he tended to lose discretion in choosing among candidates. Where the clientele groups were more numerous, disunited, or had interests which did not entirely parallel agency activities, the discretion of the agency head increased.

To a certain extent, the character of the agency head and his perspective on the process predetermined what process would be followed in recruiting. Those with long experience in electoral politics were often inclined to recognize broader needs of the political system, rather than strictly administrative needs within an agency. They could see wisdom in accepting candidates who wore the *imprimatur* of a particular congressman or an interested group.

Finally, the character of the times was occasionally determinative. A crisis situation, or periods when the attractions of private life are paramount, may lead to reliance on career government employees who are promoted into the ranks of political executives. On the other hand, at the beginning of an administration there may be a tendency to consolidate party gains by granting favors, including high position, to party members and interest group functionaries.

Regardless of the process followed, the specific candidate selected may sometimes be the result of coincidence or desperation. There is no assurance that an extended search for *the* most qualified man necessarily results in finding him or finding him available; and failure to find or get him may lead to the appointment of a man who has little more to commend him than his own enthusiasm.

Criteria of Selection. For the various kinds of political executive posts that must be filled, and for the various kinds of functions which circumstances and agency head expectations may require, quite varying standards must be used in measuring the qualifications of those being considered for appointment. Some recruiters have clear ideas of what they consider are the qualities necessary for successful performance in a job. These may relate to personal skills, to substantive backgrounds, or in some instances only to symbolic values. In other cases, the agency head has only an indefinite notion of "getting the best man" for the job. He looks for successful experience of some sort and tends to attribute success in any line of endeavor to some innate capacity to perform well in all positions, including those in the executive branch. It is not exceptional to find, moreover, that an agency head will begin recruiting with one idea in mind and will end up selecting a person with characteristics quite different from those he originally looked for.

TABLE III. Criteria for Selection of Political Executives

	Beginning of Administration		Later in Administration		Total	
	Eisenhower (Number)	Kennedy (Number)	Truman (Number)	Eisenhower (Number)	No.	%
Expertise in a specific area of responsibility	7	8	3	5	23	21
Expertise plus political factors	1	1	2	3	7	6
General experience in the area of responsibility	3	4	20	12	39	36
General experience plus political factors	8	9	9	3	29	27
Service to the party	2	2	3	3	10	9
Total	21	24	37	26	108	99

The case studies reveal a much greater concern for administrative skill and substantive experience than might be expected. (See Table III.) Membership in the administration party is an almost invariable requirement, but within that context more professional standards are applied. There is usually an implicit assumption that only those who have an orientation on policy similar to that of the President or his agency heads will be seriously considered for an appointment. But for some recruiting officials, policy considerations are of less concern than administrative capacity, substantive acquaintance with specific problem areas, and the political significance of an appointment. The self-promoters and the individuals who appeared on the lists of the Talent Hunt were almost automatically qualified on policy grounds since they were usually sympathetic with the new administration. Obviously however, general sympathy with the new administration did not necessarily mean conformity in policy views on specific issues arising in any particular agency.

The classification of certain appointments as based on "political factors" requires some explanation since all political executive appointments are predicated on some calculation of political advantage, depending on who does the calculating. "Political" criteria were those related primarily to prior political party service or to some party advantage in the future. Seldom were appointments "purely" political, although there were instances of this. Usually, appointments which could be based on compensation for past services could also be justified in some measure on experience and talents which the men brought to the job. Thus, about one-third of all appointments were based on mixed criteria, while less than ten per cent were based solely on political considerations.

The analysis of cases further emphasizes the tendency of agency heads and other recruiters to stress general experience and capacity rather than narrower criteria related to specific activities of an agency. Very often agency heads expressed this preference by saying they were looking for "the best possible man" or a man with "administrative experience" or a man with all of the best personal virtues. This was particularly true of former businessmen agency heads who seldom appeared to compare the specialized private experience of their candidates with the requirements of specific jobs in the government. General business ability and success were accepted as evidence of capacity to perform all sorts of duties in all agencies. It is significant, however, that political considerations tended to play a more active part in appointments based on general administrative ability than in those based on expertise. Presumably, general administrative ability was so common that additional qualifying experience, that is, political experience, was required.

The cases suggest that political and general administrative experience are given the greatest weight in filling the positions of under secretary and deputy. Whether the agency head is looking for an *alter ego* or for an internal administrator, he is generally looking for someone with a broader gauge or perspective than he might look for as the head of one or a group of operating agencies. If he hires a specialist as a deputy, he is liable to lose the deputy to his specialty. Recruiting for the assistant secretary level appears to up-grade technical factors and down-grade political factors in the selection process.

Recruitment at the Beginning of an Administration. At the beginning of an administration the President-elect faces a formidable array of tasks which must be carried out with both dispatch and care. One of the most important of these is to fill the high-level positions with men who are responsible, loyal, and experienced, who will give the proper "image" to his administration and also give him the assistance he needs in policy development and management. The pressures of time are severe and the anticipations of both participants and observers are high. With innumerable candidates to choose from, he must carefully sort out the wheat from the straw.

To assist in this operation, the President gathers about him a corps of trusted aides and personal friends to give him guidance and extend his reach into the many institutions of society with which he may be only dimly acquainted. Thus, at the beginning of his administration President-elect Eisenhower relied on two of his most intimate advisers, Herbert Brownell, who had served as his principal strategist in the 1952 campaign, and General Lucius Clay, a lifelong military associate and personal friend. At a somewhat greater distance, but nevertheless working closely with the President and his chief advisers, were Sherman Adams, who later became the President's principal assistant in the White House, and businessmen such as Sidney Weinberg and Harold Boeschenstein who had long been active in recruitment for government positions. In addition an informal group of Eisenhower supporters had hired McKinsey & Company, a management consulting firm, to study the executive recruitment problem. McKinsey had identified 131 high policy positions which should be filled as quickly as possible, and also prepared a list of thousands of potential candidates for these positions.

At the outset, Brownell and Clay and their assistants were primarily concerned with helping the President select his cabinet officers. President-elect Eisenhower was remarkably quick in making these decisions; his entire Cabinet was selected in less than four weeks. Inevitably in the process of looking for cabinet officers, the searchers were led to consider the qualifications of a great many others whom they eliminated for the top positions but kept in mind for subordinate posts. Little was done about appointments at the sub-cabinet level, however, until the chief positions were filled.

The Eisenhower recruiters looked for individuals who had been active in the 1952 campaign and who were from the liberal wing of the Republican Party. But they recognized the necessity of weighing the competing demands of the Citizens for

Eisenhower and the regular party organization. Campaign activity and political persuasion therefore became important factors. At the same time they undertook an extensive search for men qualified for high executive posts on the basis of their experience and competence in particular lines of endeavor. They made use of their numerous contacts in the business world, the professions, universities, and politics to locate likely candidates.

Through business and professional associations, through boards of directors, and an infinite number of personal ties, these men could drop a net over a large segment of the successful men in America. It was clear that the net was designed to bring in successful businessmen more than any other type. Added to these names were the names of candidates from political sources — members of Congress, national committeemen, state officials, etc. — and the aforementioned McKinsey lists.

Once a cabinet officer or agency head had been selected, Sherman Adams reports, "Eisenhower gave [him] complete responsibility for his department and almost never intervened in the selection of their assistants and other key personnel." Each cabinet member could establish his own criteria for selection, search out his own candidates, and present his preferred choice to the White House for the President's approval. This degree of independence in selecting subordinates was consistent with President Eisenhower's unusual propensity for delegating authority to the point of even accepting views and actions which deviated from his own preferences. He was unwilling to exercise his prerogatives in order to blunt the criticism from congressional sources that they were being short-circuited in the appointment process. Undoubtedly the presidential assistants in the Commodore Hotel pressed such considerations on the new agency heads; but lacking the influential support of the President, there was little they could do to enforce their views.

The beginning of the Kennedy administration offers an unusual opportunity for comparing the characteristics of the recruitment process under conditions of some similarity: pressures of time, use of centralized machinery, and marked interest in the character of the appointments by the public, members of Congress, and other parties with something at stake. But other factors in the situation were different: a president with an entirely different background, a party that had been out of power only eight years but which had to weld together perhaps even more disparate elements than those which composed the Republican Party in 1953.

As soon as victory was assured, while President-elect Kennedy vacationed in Palm Beach and in Georgetown, he and his chief advisers spent the major part of their time talking with prospective candidates and evaluating the qualifications of those who had been recommended or who were recommending themselves. The President-elect took an active role in the early consideration of candidates — consulting with the elders of the Democratic Party, with his chief political aides, and with likely candidates for cabinet positions.

Kennedy and his advisers had two important criteria in mind in settling high-level presidential appointments: recognition of those who deserved appointments on the basis of service to the party; and recognition of the need to obtain the "best talent" to serve in these demanding positions. To make these criteria operative in fact as well as in theory, it was decided to divide the recruitment task between two groups of Kennedy aides, with each group focusing primarily upon one of these two criteria. In the words of one member of the staff, one of these groups sought "deserving people" and "hoped they were bright enough," while the other group reversed this order of priority. Together, these two groups became known popularly as the "Talent Hunt."

Heading up these two operations were the President-elect's brother, Robert, and his brother-in-law, Sargent Shriver. Robert Kennedy worked mainly through the nation-wide network of contacts he had developed during the 1960 campaign, while Shriver drew upon his contacts in the business, professional, and university world. The operation under brother Robert was staffed by the President-elect's campaign and senatorial aides: Lawrence O'Brien, Richard Donohue, and Ralph Dungan. The Shriver operation was primarily in the hands of young lawyers who had also been active in the campaign, such as Adam Yarmolinsky and Harris Wofford. In spite of this informal division of labor, the allocation of responsibilities was hardly distinct. In time, in fact, "everyone got into everyone else's business," as one staff member expressed it.

Of particular interest were the criteria the recruiters tried to use in assessing the candidates' qualifications. Persons suggesting candidates and other respondents were asked to assess the qualifications of the candidates in terms of "judgment," "toughness," "integrity," "ability to work with others," "industry," and "devotion to the principles of the President-elect." The evaluator was also asked to say whether the candidate had a wide or limited acquaintanceship with qualified people in his field of specialty or "only local contacts"; and to estimate whether the candidate's appointment to a high-level government position would enhance the administration's standing "nationally," "in his professional group," "in his state," or "in his community." Under pressure of time, however, the staff members found it increasingly difficult to get careful ratings on candidates on each of these discriminating criteria. Instead, the interviewer was more likely to ask a respondent, "What do you know about this guy?" When all of the evaluated material was gathered together, the staff member added a summary evaluation that included general ratings that ranged from "highly qualified," "qualified," and "some qualifications" on the competence side; and "good Democrat," "politically neutral," "Republican," or "politically disqualified" on the political side.

President-elect Kennedy was relatively slow to announce his first appointments. His first selection, that of G. Mennen Williams as Assistant Secretary of State, indicated both a desire and a will to participate actively in sub-cabinet appointments. It also became known that the President had offered the post of Ambassador to the United Nations to Adlai Stevenson long before Dean Rusk and Chester Bowles were selected as Secretary and Under Secretary. These actions suggested that in cases where he had a direct and compelling interest Kennedy would be willing to make his selections independently of his Secretaries, and expected them to acquiesce in his selections.

In some instances where the President-elect and his chief aides felt themselves inadequately grounded to form a sound judgment both politically and professionally in making selections, they were willing to give a much freer hand to the agency head. But where the appointments required a sensitive balancing, as in the agencies attempting to promote a bipartisan approach, and where the President had a strong commitment to particular policies or political values, he was unwilling to delegate the responsibility. It is clear, for example, that the President-elect and his aides took a much greater interest in the Department of State and the Department of Defense than they did in appointments in the Departments of Labor, Agriculture and Interior.

Within a few days after the appointment of each agency head the Talent Hunt recruiter assigned to that agency met with him and reviewed the list of names in the recruiter's file. At this point the role of the Talent Hunter could follow any of several patterns but almost always along the line of diminished responsibility. In the case of two or three agencies the recruiter was given no further responsibility, the cabinet member preferring to conduct his search by other channels. This was particularly true in agencies whose heads were themselves acutely aware of political considerations and could be relied upon to make selections which would reflect them. In other agencies the Talent Hunt members continued to assist by screening the available candidates and conducting further searches.

In both the Eisenhower and Kennedy preinaugural periods members of Congress were active in suggesting the names and promoting the causes of candidates, often men from their own states. They displayed a wide range of attitudes, however, from those who aggressively sought out the Commodore or Talent Hunt recruiters and the newly appointed agency heads to those who did nothing more than transmit the names of men who had been suggested to them. Their vigor varied also with the qualifications of the individuals in question. Republican senators, in particular, were dissatisfied with the early reception that their candidates received at Republican headquarters, since few of the appointees up to the Eisenhower inauguration appeared to come from the more conservative congressional wing of the party. Congressional leaders met with President-elect Eisenhower and received assurances that their recommendations would be given consideration, although he continued to reserve the right of final choice for himself and his agency heads. Democratic members of Congress voiced little open criticism of the procedures and appointments in the Kennedy administration, although there was occasional private grumbling that clearances had been ignored or wrong choices made. The Kennedy recruiters were more conscious of congressional interests and sensitivities than the Republican recruiters, and generally observed clearance procedures before announcing appointments.

In both administrations the special recruiting groups discontinued their operations after inauguration. Some of the participants themselves received appointments and were distracted by their new duties. Top recruitment responsibilities then shifted to the White House — to Sherman Adams and his assistant Charles Willis in the Eisenhower administration, and to the group of aides President Kennedy brought with him from the Senate. But a large part of the function had already devolved on the departments and agencies, with the White House constituting an important clearance point for anyone who recommended a candidate.

Recruitment During an Administration. The intense concern with appointments that characterizes a new administration fades rapidly a few weeks after Inauguration Day. By summer of the first year practically all of the political executive positions are filled. But with the beginning of the second year of a new administration, the problems of political executive recruitment again begin to assert themselves. Some appointees have committed themselves only for a limited period of time and therefore prepare for departure. A few unfortunate choices are nudged into early resignation. Others, finding new, attractive, and what may appear to be once-in-a-lifetime opportunities resulting from their new visibility, feel compelled to move on. Still others achieve immediate success in public life and are shifted into other positions in the national government or are encouraged to run for elective office. As the departures begin, the agency heads again must devote a fair amount of their valuable time to canvassing potential appointees.

But by now the recruiting environment has changed markedly from the early days of the administration. The central staff operation that produced long lists of eligible candidates for the President-elect's consideration is largely dismantled, although a few vestiges may remain, usually located in the White House office. In any event, the sense of urgency and determination to obtain the best qualified men have diminished. The President is heavily involved in the other responsibilities of his office and usually can concern himself only with the selection of the highest level officers directly responsible to him. Consequently the decentralization of personnel decisions which is apparent at the beginning of an administration becomes even more pronounced as an administration ages.

At the beginning of an administration, the fervor engendered by the political campaign creates an attitude in both political activists and passive supporters which is favorable toward government service. The large majority may not actively promote themselves for political executive positions, but their commitment to the success of the new administration predisposes them to consider favorably the prospect of an appointment. But as time passes those who have not been selected — whether approached or not, whether disappointed or not — turn to their private concerns and give a smaller share of their time and attention to public affairs, particularly those in Washington. They may continue to participate in party councils, contribute money, and cast their votes for the administration, but everyday activities tend to crowd out public issues which seem less pressing and less immediate. Fewer and fewer are actively seeking positions or are "available" when contacted.

Many of those who supported the victorious presidential candidate may have had strong programmatic commitments and looked to the new administration to bring radical changes in existing policies. But as an administration matures it often becomes disappointingly evident that radical changes either are not possible or can be accomplished only with persistent, strenuous efforts. Potential candidates now may make a more realistic assessment of the constraints of the situation, leading to disillusionment about the possibility of major changes. This reduces the receptivity of some potential recruits for the administration.

Finally, as the second year's congressional elections come and go, uncertainty over the future of the administration is apt to mount. The possibility that the President will not be re-elected and his appointees will have to seek other employment tends to reduce ardor for public office. The prospect of coming to Washington for what may turn out to be only a few months or at the most a year or two, when accompanied with heavy financial losses as a consequence of moving, operates to dissuade men from seriously considering political executive service.

These circumstances lead agency heads and other recruiters increasingly to seek their candidates inside the government rather than in private activities. Having encountered difficulty in getting replacements from private life, they become wary of having their offers rejected or their veiled approaches rebuffed. Moreover, with less time to devote to recruitment than they had at the beginning of the administration they have a stronger tendency to take the easier way in filling vacancies. The easiest solution is usually to select replacements from among those who are already in or closely associated with the government. This also makes sense because the agency heads by this are able to make more accurate evaluations of men already serving in the agency than of "unknowns" from outside. They are less dependent on the evaluation of others. With experienced and proven executives on the scene there is a strong tendency to give them preference.

Turnover in the highest echelons of the major agencies also leads to expectations and hopes on the part of subordinates that they will be advanced to the more prestigious and influential positions. Those who have strong public commitments are often ambitious for promotion to positions where they can have a greater impact on policy decisions, where they can share in the emoluments of high office, and where they can gain recognition for their accomplishments. An expectation naturally develops among subordinate officials that successful performance will be rewarded by advancement to higher office when vacancies occur. Failure to be recognized or seriously considered for promotion has been a critical factor in the decisions of some executives to leave the government.

The case studies reveal clearly this pattern of more reliance on government men in recruitment for positions during an administration. In a total of 62 case studies of appointments after the first year of an administration (including all of the Truman administration), 37, or 60 per cent, of the appointees were already in positions in the federal government. For the Truman administration the insider-outsider ratio was 65 to 35 per cent; for the Eisenhower administration it was 52 to 48.

The Truman preference for men already in the government partly reflects the continuity between his administration and the Roosevelt administration. Since the two administrations shared the same party allegiance and avowed generally similar policy orientations, the Truman recruiters felt no strong urgency to seek men outside the government who might introduce new policy viewpoints. Moreover, many Truman executives had had long experience in the government previously and were acquainted with men in their agencies who were considered capable of assuming high level responsibilities. Younger men who had served their apprenticeship during the New Deal and World War II had strong hopes that they might be considered for leading political positions as rewards for their faithful service. Finally, the Truman Administration was faced with widespread public antipathy toward governmental service and a desire by most men to return to or continue in essentially private pursuits. The years subsequent to World War II were probably the most difficult years for recruiting men to public service.

Major differences between administrations show up in the extent to which men with varying kinds of backgrounds rose into the higher ranks of the political executive service during an administration. (See Table IV.) The case studies tend to confirm the view that the Truman administration had a strong inclination to advance men with *careers* in the public service to political executive positions. Often these men had already moved into politically sensitive positions as confidential assistants or personal aides and it was no major step to go on to a presidential appointment. The Eisenhower administration was much more inclined to bring newcomers into the federal government, and subsequently to promote them to still higher political positions.

TABLE IV. Source of Political Executive Appointees During an Administration

	No.	Per Cent of Total	Per Cent under Truman	Per Cent under Eisenhower
Promotion of political appointees	16	26	22	32
Promotion of career officials	15	24	35	8
Transfer of political appointees	6	10	8	12
Appointment of former federal appointees	5	8	11	4
Other appointments	20	32	24	44
Total	62	100	100	100

The Truman administration was particularly notable for its tendency to rely upon men already in the government for its subordinate aides. As indicated above, only nine of the thirty-nine Truman appointees studied were not in the government or had not recently had experience there when appointed. Appointments from outside appeared to be the exception rather than the rule. Many agencies developed what amounted to a tradition of promoting individuals from subpolitical executive positions and from career positions into the political ranks. In such instances the agency head had usually had direct personal contact with the appointee and was able to assess his qualifications for the position to be filled. Many times, the agency head made little effort to consider other possibilities since he was relatively satisfied with those already in the agency. Even with an improved climate for recruitment, Eisenhower executives tended also, after the first year, to recruit from within. Half of the Eisenhower case studies were of men already serving. Often the agency head had been responsible for appointing the individual to his lesser position and had observed closely his performance on the job. There was a much stronger tendency to promote political appointees than career officials, and it was not exceptional to find the promotion principle applying even to appointments at the agency head level. While the failure of some to advance may not necessarily have indicated inadequate performance, it is relatively certain that advancement of others under these conditions did constitute recognition for superior performance.

Variations among Agencies. Both the biographical information and the case studies reveal important differences among agencies in the sources of executives, the style of recruitment, and the criteria used in selection. Although the following generalizations require considerable refinement and qualification, they highlight the variable context of political executive recruitment.

State and Defense: Professionals and Professional Amateurs. In the Departments of State and Defense, the emphasis on previous service and relevant experience is more pronounced than in other agencies. Political executives are chosen for their expertise and sympathy with presidential programs, but previous governmental service — either at the political executive level or below — in these agencies or the military services is the factor that conspicuously distinguishes recruitment in these agencies from the others. The predominance of this kind of appointment suggests that the men who serve in these agencies may be characterized as "professional amateurs," in that they spend a considerable portion of their mature lives within the government or, if in private life, operate in the environment of that policy area. While not professionals in the sense of being committed and dependent on government service as a career, they are nevertheless remarkably well prepared to assume the duties of office.

In our case studies some agency heads and others responsible for recruitment in the Departments of State and Defense showed a measure of deference to party in making appointments, but the strongest opposition to party influence, particularly by the national committees, but also by the White House, was found in these two agencies. Agency officials often tried to suppress knowledge of a probable vacancy, hoping to find a suitable candidate to present to the President before the national committee or the White House staff could propose alternatives. White House and national committee officials testified that they received less cooperation from these two departments than from any other agencies in the government.

The Department of State has developed a practice of balancing appointments between foreign service officers and non-career appointees. Most frequently, foreign service officers are found heading the bureaus with responsibility for policy development and coordination in particular regional areas, and also in some important administrative positions at the secretarial level. Over one-third of all political executive appointees during the Truman, Eisenhower and Kennedy administrations were foreign service officers, the largest percentage appointed during the Eisenhower administration.

Treasury: The Technicians. Recruitment for the Department of the Treasury has been predominantly a search for bankers and lawyers who appear to have specific experiences and skills required for particular functions within the Department. The Treasury political executives included the second highest percentage of businessmen (chiefly bankers) of all domestic agencies and was second only to the Department of Justice in the percentage of lawyers serving in domestic agencies. These two occupations accounted for 78 per cent of all appointments in the Treasury. Furthermore, Treasury had the lowest percentage of political executives whose primary occupation was in the public service.

The appointments at the beginning of both the Eisenhower and Kennedy administrations indicate this emphasis on technical competence. Both Marion Folsom and Stanley Surrey were experts in taxation, Randolph Burgess and Robert Roosa had had long experience in debt management; and Andrew Overby and John Leddy were both intimately acquainted from practical experience in international finance.

These appointments show a marked departure from the pattern of earlier periods. Macmahon and Millett found that three-quarters of the Treasury appointments were accounted for by political considerations, and that few of these were prominent either before or after serving in the Treasury. Nor was there the striking emphasis on technical qualifications in making these earlier appointments.

In recent administrations, Treasury recruitment has been largely conducted by the Secretary himself with the assistance of his chief aides who obtained useful material in evaluating candidates. The secretaries in the Truman, Eisenhower and Kennedy administrations — Snyder, Humphrey, Anderson, and Dillon — all had extensive experience in the business, banking and financial world and could rely on a wide range of contacts to provide them with a supply of candidates. In most instances, it appears that the secretary went directly to individual acquaintances to obtain their services. On occasion, a departing political executive was able to recommend another candidate in his own special area and even assist in getting him to accept.

Justice: Politics and the Law. By the nature of its function as the chief legal agency of the federal government, the chief officers of the Department of Justice are required to be lawyers. It has seldom been enough, however, for an appointee to have only the technical qualification of a legal background or experience in the practice of law. Far more than the State Department, the Defense establishment, or the Treasury, political executives in Justice have had active experience in public affairs, often in elective office. From 1859 through 1938, some 125 men served as assistant attorneys general; nine-tenths of them had held some political office prior to their appointment. In the Roosevelt, Truman and Eisenhower administrations, over 50 per cent of the assistant and deputy attorneys general were serving in the federal government at the time of their appointment. Three out of four in the Truman administration were in that category.

Appointments in the Truman administration were characteristically advancements from lower non-career positions, often on the basis of merit, but it must be recognized that the procedures which brought the appointees into the department initially were usually highly political. Moreover, the political background of the attorneys general made party considerations of more than routine consequence. Partly as a reaction to the low state into which the Department had fallen as a result of scandals at the end of the Truman administration, Eisenhower officials had a greater tendency to recruit outside of governmental and even outside of active political circles, although political considerations still ranked comparatively high.

Post Office: Politicians and Businessmen. No agency has experienced such sharp reversals in the character of the men appointed to political executive positions as the Post Office Department. Traditionally, this Department has been the harbor for deserving party officials. The Postmaster General usually has held a high level post in the party and his appointments, according to Macmahon and Millett, have been "prevailingly political."

In general, Post Office appointees during the Truman administration were Democrats who had performed some service for the party, or who could be expected to do so while in the government and subsequently. The Kennedy administration resumed this pattern of appointment.

In sharp contrast with Democratic practice in recruiting for the Post Office stands the record of the Republicans during the eight-year period of the Eisenhower administration. Although Postmaster General Summerfield followed the traditional route from the chairmanship of the national committee to the Cabinet, at President Eisenhower's insistence he resigned from the national committee upon taking office. Summerfield selected only Republicans as his aides, but he defied tradition in not filling the subordinate posts in the Post Office with individuals whose primary claims were based on partisan political service. Some of the initial appointees, such as Charles Hook, had taken part in the campaign but in no sense could be considered professional politicians. With two exceptions — one a career official in the Department and another a former Civil Service Commissioner with extensive service in the federal government — all of the Summerfield appointees were businessmen. In most instances, they were selected because of some specialty they had developed in their business careers which was considered applicable to Post Office operations.

Interior and Agriculture: Politics, Pressure Groups, and Policy. Of all the major domestic departments or agencies in the national government, Interior and Agriculture are probably the most deeply involved in controversy over public policy. The impact of these policy controversies bears directly on the recruitment of high level executives in these two departments. The department heads are guided by the policy views of the individuals they are considering and the organizations they represent. The recruiters tend to rely on the recommendations of those who have policy viewpoints corresponding with their own. Groups with opposing viewpoints are deliberately avoided in the recruitment effort and seldom given opportunities to pass judgment on the merits of individuals who are under consideration.

The search for executives with acceptable views for policy positions in the Department of Agriculture seems to lead to the interest groups and the party organizations. For a reason not clear, the same problem tends to lead executives in the Department of the Interior either to the bureaucracy or to members of Congress. In no other agency of the federal government did the members of Congress play a more significant role than here. Because the department represents interests located primarily in the West, the western senators and congressmen especially were involved in the selection process.

At least part of the explanation for their role lies in the conflict among the western states over policy and the western sense of proprietorship toward the Interior Department. Representation of a particular area has both a symbolic and a practical value in assuring consideration of its interests in the councils of the department.

Commerce and Labor: Clientele Politics. In recruiting for the Department of Commerce, secretaries since the beginning of the Eisenhower administration have relied almost exclusively on businessmen, with the occasional addition of a lawyer. Of the fifteen men appointed to under secretary and assistant secretary of Commerce in the Eisenhower administration, thirteen were businessmen in private life, one was a lawyer, and another a former member of Congress who had been a lawyer before running for elective office. Similarly, at the beginning of the Kennedy administration all initial selections were of businessmen, although the creation of a new assistant secretary post for science and technology will undoubtedly bring into the Department men with primary backgrounds in the natural sciences who may not have been associated formerly with business. However, the Eisenhower administration placed a heavy reliance on men without previous experience in any level of government. This is understandable, considering that the Republican administration entering in 1953 was the first in 20 years. Nevertheless, the relative lack of public service stands in sharp contrast with many other agencies during the Republican administration whose political executives had had rather extensive service during World War II, the Korean War, in state government, or in federal career positions.

The relationship between the governmental recruiters and the trade unions in the selection of political executives for the Department of Labor was carefully structured, particularly during Democratic administrations. During the Truman administration the chief clientele groups for the Department, the American Federation of Labor and the Congress of Industrial Organizations, tended to receive equal representation in the Department as a kind of gesture toward their equality in the union movement — or else as a measure of prudent neutrality.

The initial selections in the Kennedy administration clearly followed the typical Democratic practice, with one appointee coming from the AFL background, and another from the CIO.

The appointment process during the Eisenhower administration was of a different nature because of the relatively distant relationships between labor and the Republican party. At first, the new Republican administration tried to woo labor through appointments from the labor movement such as Martin Durkin and Lloyd Mashburn. The impasse over one union candidate, however, resulted in a tacit agreement that there would be no attempt to provide direct union representation in the high ranks of the Labor Department. As a result, from 1954 on, the appointees in that Department were men with professional or business backgrounds; some of them had strong political connections. Several had been appointed on a political basis to subordinate positions within the Department, later moving up into secretarial posts.

II. The Background of Political Executives

In this paper it will be possible only to suggest some of the major outlines of the backgrounds of political executives since 1933. In certain respects they represent a broad cross section of American life, far removed from Mills's characterization, but in other respects they constitute a select group, reflecting important special sources from which they have been drawn.

Geographical Background. Political executives were drawn from all sections of the nation, reflecting the population distribution among census regions, although there are natural differences in each administration which are related to voting strength. Both parties drew heavily on the Middle Atlantic states, particularly New York, and then relied on areas of special political advantage — the South for the Democrats and the Midwest for the Republicans. Expected regional emphases in certain departments, notably Interior and Agriculture on the West and Midwest, were very apparent. A strong tendency, however, appears to favor candidates whose primary occupations — distinguished from their legal residence — are in the Washington, D.C. area. This suggests the importance of experience in the federal government and involvement in national affairs as a controlling factor in selection.

Perhaps of even greater long-run consequence is the tendency to prefer men whose backgrounds are urban or metropolitan. While only 59 per cent of the population lived in standard metropolitan statistical areas in 1950, some 90 per cent of the political executives were employed in those areas when appointed. Moreover, when compared with the population residing in such urban places in 1900 — the year nearest to the median year of birth of the subjects in this study — political executives tend to have a much stronger urban background. This background provides a marked contrast with that of senators and perhaps explains some of the conflict between the executive and legislative viewpoints. Don Matthews found that a majority of the senators serving during the years 1947–1957 were born in rural areas.

Education. Political executives far surpass the general population in level of education. Overall, 74 per cent were college graduates and a majority — 57 per cent — had graduate degrees. Less than five per cent had only high school educations. Not unexpectedly, the level of education was higher in each successive administration. In this respect political executives are not markedly different from earlier predecessors in high executive office, or from high-level federal administrators but are well above most other occupational groups in the United States and far above the general population in which only 6 per cent were college graduates in 1950. Differences between Democratic and Republican administrations were very slight and reflected primarily the tendency of Republicans to recruit businessmen who were less likely to have graduate education than men in other professions. Those expecting a greater tendency toward intellectual brilliance in Democratic political executives can find little support here since an equal percentage of executives having Phi Beta Kappa or Sigma Xi memberships were found in the Eisenhower and Kennedy administrations.

According to Mills, attendance at certain "exclusive" schools and colleges marks one as a member of an "elite." Although the evidence lacks complete reliability, apparently at least 9 per cent of political executives attended one of an arbitrarily defined group of eighteen well-known Eastern preparatory schools. In the general population of comparable ages, only 9 per cent attended private secondary schools of any sort including parochial schools. In this respect they were similar to successful business executives and again in contrast with senators who are less likely to attend such schools. Attendance at such schools was much more marked among executives in the foreign affairs and national security agencies than in the domestic agencies.

A similar pattern marks the undergraduate education of political executives. Those who served in the Departments of State and Defense and in the military departments were much more likely to have attended Ivy League colleges such as Harvard, Yale, Princeton, Dartmouth and Cornell than executives who served in the domestic agencies. Of those who served in the security agencies 41 per cent attended these colleges while only 24 per cent in the domestic departments did so and only 19 per cent in the independent agencies. Combined with evidence that will be presented below these patterns of education indicate a common path which executives in these agencies tend to follow, which leads to high government office.

Nevertheless, no university provided undergraduate education for more than 10 per cent of the entire number of executives. The highest was Yale, followed by Harvard, Princeton, Dartmouth, Wisconsin, California at Berkeley, Michigan, Minnesota, North Carolina and Stanford. Twenty-two schools provided undergraduate education for a majority of executives. These same schools figured very prominently in the education of high-level career executives in the federal government and also business executives. Although more political executives come from private universities and colleges than business executives and senators, large percentages of public institutions are represented in the training of political executives.

Religious Preference. The interest in maintaining a balance of religious affiliations among Cabinet officers appears to have little application at the subordinate political executive level, at least in part because of relatively diminished public attention. The expected domination of these positions by members of the Protestant churches was confirmed; 78 per cent of all political executives reported Protestant faiths. Catholics were far better represented in Democratic administrations, as might be expected. Of greater interest is the fact that Catholics were readily able to achieve leadership positions in the executive branch of the government although they are apparently restricted in access to professional ranks in other fields. Twenty per cent of all political executives but only 9 per cent of business executives, and only slightly more of the members of Congress and the uniformed military services, were Catholics. Catholics were best represented in the Departments of Justice, Labor and Post Office, those departments in which political preferment or trade union influence was greatest. In the Post Office in Democratic administrations, of those reporting church membership, 63 per cent were Catholic.

Some significant differences appeared in the representation of the various Protestant churches. Episcopalians were particularly prominent, accounting for 25 per cent of all appointees, although the membership in that Church accounts for only 3 per cent of the total population. Presbyterians were also favored, while Baptists, accounting for 20 per cent of the total population, provided only 6 per cent of the political executives. Episcopalians were particularly prominent in the Treasury Department, the military establishment, and the Department of State, reinforcing the impression of high social status associated with these three departments.

Party Affiliation and Activity. It is hardly surprising to discover that each administration strongly prefers its own partisans in the recruitment of political executives. For ideological reasons, for purposes of rewarding the party faithful, and for welding together the divergent wings of the party, emphasis on party membership is an important factor in the selection process. As Table V shows, each party appointed its

TABLE V. Party Affiliation of Political Executives, by Administration

	Number	Demo-crat (%)	Repub-lican (%)	No Party (%)	Total (%)
Roosevelt	138	88	12	1	101
Truman	166	83	14	4	101
Eisenhower	258	5	73	23	101
Kennedy	103	79	10	12	101

own partisans in an overwhelming percentage of the cases. Democratic administrations were more willing to appoint Republicans than the Eisenhower administration was to appoint Democrats, although the latter administration did appoint a large number of independents. As one might expect, the greatest showing of bipartisanship occurred in the departments concerned with national security and considerably less in the domestic departments. Partisanship might have been expected to be highest at the beginning of an administration, but no significant difference appears in the degree of partisanship from one period of an administration to another.

More intense forms of party activity such as attendance at the national conventions, or large contributions to the campaign war chest did not appear to be important indicators of likely candidates for political executive positions as defined here. Only 14 per cent of the political executives in the four administrations had been delegates at one or both of the national party conventions preceding their appointment. Cabinet officers were most likely to have been delegates; 44 per cent of them had so served during one or both of the two previous conventions. Subordinate executives were considerably less frequent attenders. Not surprisingly, nearly one out of four appointees in the Post Office Department had been delegates while fewer than 10 per cent in the security agencies had attended. Only 13 per cent of all appointees had made reported contributions of over $500 during either of the two campaigns prior to a new President's inauguration. Department heads were the most notable contributors while hardly 10 per cent of subordinate political executives contributed. Departments such as Commerce, Treasury, Defense, and Air Force, that relied primarily on businessmen for their political executives, were most likely to have had executives who made these major contributions.

Occupational Background. Table VI shows the distribution of political executives by their principal occupations. Over the past four administrations the largest source of political executives was among men who had established careers in public service. For the most part, those who became political executives had had careers in non-elective positions and had usually served as subordinate federal officials before their advancement to political executive positions. Often this involved considerable shifting about from position to position or from agency to agency. A good example was Elmer Bennett, under secretary of the Interior in the Eisenhower administration. Beginning his public career as an employee of the War Department in 1942, he

TABLE VI. Principal Occupation of Political Executives, by Administration and Major Occupational Groups

	Num- ber	Busi- ness (%)	Law (%)	Other Pro- fessions[a] (%)	Government*			Other[b] (%)
					Elec- tive (%)	Non- elective (%)	Total (%)	
Persons	789	29	25	11	3	29	32	5
Roosevelt	210	23	26	16	3	30	33	2
Truman	265	23	24	5	2	43	45	4
Eisenhower	293	39	24	9	3	22	25	3
Kennedy	124	20	24	18	4	25	29	10

* All levels of government, including international agencies.

[a] Chiefly education, journalism, engineering and science.

[b] Trade union officials, party officials, farmers and foundation officers.

served successively as a trial attorney for the Federal Trade Commission, as an assistant to Senator Eugene Milliken of Colorado, legislative counsel, assistant to the secretary and solicitor in the Department of the Interior, before his appointment as under secretary. Although trained as a lawyer, his background in fact was that of a public servant.

.   .   .   .

III. Conclusions

Significant changes have occurred both in the character of the process by which political executives are recruited and in the sources relied upon. Far from depending merely on "haphazard political reasons," their selection is increasingly related to some experience factor which qualifies them for office above and beyond the qualifications achieved through party membership or service. Selection appears to depend on the personal confidence of the cabinet officer or the White House aide in the capacity of candidates to perform adequately in dealing with substantive problems of an agency, as well as the significance of the appointment in the total political context. The precise specifications for availability vary markedly with time and agency and even position. Party factors rank high at the beginning of an administration but the numerous instances where they are disregarded even at that period make even such a generalization suspect. Clearly some appointments are "political" in the traditional sense — to placate a wing of the party, to satisfy a group interest, etc. — but these tend to be restricted to positions which are — rightly or wrongly — considered less consequential.

The point of view that political executives are part of a "political directorate" is hardly justified. While tendencies exist in certain departments to recruit from an eastern industrial, financial class, they appear chiefly to reflect the interest such groups have taken in the issues of national security. Thus special qualifications of experience and interest again play important roles in selection decisions. When the appointees to domestic departments are considered it is obvious that the ranks of political executives are representative of a wide range of interests, experience, localities and talents from the more mobile elements of the American population.

❖ 4 ❖

Management Techniques and Innovation

Recent management techniques and processes represent developments in technology and their impact on organization theory and behavior. The rapidly increasing volume of work and the pressures for accurate information upon which management decisions can be made, have greatly stimulated research and experimentation in this area.

The "scientific" tools of management are in the tradition of accounting, budgeting, and work measurement, all of which were designed to improve the management process. Newer developments in the area emphasize quantification, explicitness, and rigor. Increasingly articles published in the field of management claim positive results from the application of one or another of the new techniques. The administrator needs to be familiar with these techniques and to be able to place them in their proper perspective.

The "information revolution" is reflected in the fact that the federal government has about 5,400 computers working compared to ten a decade ago. It is estimated that the federal government is financing about 30 per cent of all the computers in the country, representing approximately $3 billion in total annual cost. Exclusive of military operations and secret uses, the government employs about 1,800 computers and spends almost $1 billion annually on automatic data processing.

Developments in management techniques and processes have their costs as well as their benefits. As Wallace Sayre has pointed out, they have a high obsolescence rate and can become the tool of vested interests or the special guardians of a given technique.

Improving Management Through Continuing Research   ❖ RENSIS LIKERT

An important change is occurring today in the art of management comparable to that occurring in the art of medicine. Both medicine and management are arts since both require decision and action even though the information available to the practitioner is both incomplete and imperfect.

"Improving Management Through Continuing Research," by Rensis Likert, from *Personnel Administration* (September-October, 1963), pp. 37–43. Reprinted by permission.

The art of medicine has long been based on the knowledge acquired by clinicians. Clinical judgment has been the foundation upon which medical practice has been based. During the past decade or two, a new source of knowledge has appeared. Quantitative, systematic research is now coming to be accepted as the soundest foundation upon which to base the art of medicine. Whenever the results from clinical judgment and quantitative research do not agree, the research findings are accepted increasingly as the more valid.

We are witnessing a comparable fundamental change in the art of management. Quantitative, systematic research is beginning to be substituted for practitioner judgment in providing the foundations upon which the art of management is based. This is an important change and will enable management to perform better because the basic concepts underlying managerial processes and procedures are more valid.

I shall not try to present specific research findings in this short paper. Instead, I shall limit myself to general conclusions based on research done by the Institute for Social Research of The University of Michigan and studies by other investigators. The Institute has done over thirty major studies and has collected data from over 50,000 non-supervisory employees and from several thousand supervisors and managers.

I want to stress that while all these research studies provide impressive support for the general conclusions which I shall present, they do not provide absolute proof for them. The conclusions are my interpretations of the data.

I believe that in those broad areas of business management concerned with how best to organize, coordinate, and manage human effort, the results of quantitative research are supplying new concepts more powerful and effective than those which they are replacing. If these basic concepts are found to be applicable to government (a logical supposition since managing people in a government agency is essentially the same process as managing them in a business organization), they will have major implications for public administration.

Management Assumptions

One traditional and central assumption which research is progressively and seriously undermining is the notion that buying a man's time gives the employer control over the employee's behavior. Most organizations base their standard operating procedures upon this assumption. But the plain facts are that the highest producing managers in American industry do not, on the average, believe in its validity nor do they base their managerial behavior upon it. They recognize the great importance of the economic motives, but they seek to harness the economic motives to the non-economic motives so that all these motives reinforce and strengthen one another. High-producing managers have discovered that the non-economic motives which may and sometimes do lead to the restriction of production can equally well be used to encourage production.

Another assumption which research findings are progressively dispelling is the belief that if an organization is to obtain the highest productivity and lowest costs continuously over time, that organization must put direct, hierarchical pressure upon its employees to produce at specified levels. An increasing body of research findings dealing with widely different kinds of work show that high levels of direct, hierarchical pressure for production are more often associated with low rather than high productivity. A high degree of pressure is associated with low productivity. A low degree of pressure is associated with high productivity.

Part of the relationship between pressure and productivity is attributable, no doubt, to the greater attention that management gives to poorly producing units. There is evidence, however, that significant amounts of the causation is in the opposite direction. Data show that when high-producing managers take over a new low-producing department, they do not change their style of leadership. They do not put pressure on these employees for production but may actually reduce it, even though they, themselves, have high performance goals.

There is also evidence that (for periods of two or three years) direct, hierarchical pressure for high or increased productivity does result in impressive increases in productivity. This hierarchical pressure may take many forms, such as manpower cuts, budget cuts, timing jobs, setting standards, and pressing for production levels which meet the standards. The research findings show, however, that such pressure adversely affects the attitudes and loyalties of both supervisory and non-supervisory employees and their confidence and trust in their superiors and in the organization. Pressure seems to cause employee reactions and attitudes to become progressively resentful, hostile and bitter. These unfavorable attitudes lead to greater absence and turnover and to greater pressure on high-producing employees to restrict output. They are a source of more grievances, slowdowns and strikes.

In achieving its impressive, relatively immediate increases in productivity, direct hierarchical pressure liquidates valuable human assets. If the costs of hostile employee reactions, including strikes, were charged (as they should be) against the productivity increases, these increases would often be less impressive and profitable than they are now considered to be.

Although direct, hierarchical pressure for high productivity and low costs has these serious consequences, it does not follow that it is desirable for a manager to have low productivity goals. Quite the contrary! The highest producing managers have higher productivity goals than do other managers, but they do not attempt to achieve high productivity by putting direct, hierarchical pressure on their units.

The principles and procedures used by the highest producing managers provide other new foundations for the art of management. In presenting some of these briefly, I want to remind you again that what I say is *my* interpretation of substantial research findings and is not the last word. We, as yet, do not have sufficient corroborative evidence to establish, beyond all doubt, the validity of all the conclusions.

Principles Based on Research

A most important principle reflected in the behavior of the highest producing managers is *a supportive orientation* toward other members of the organization. Indications of the extent of this supportive behavior can be obtained by asking subordinates such questions as the following:

a. To what extent does your superior try to understand your problems and do something about them?

b. How much is your superior really interested in helping you with your personal and family problems?

c. To what extent is he interested in helping you get the training which will assist you in being promoted?

d. To what extent does your superior try to keep you informed about matters related to your job?

e. How much confidence and trust do you have in your superior?
(1) How much do you feel he has in you?
f. Does your superior ask your opinion when a problem comes up which involves your work?
(1) Does he value your ideas and seek them and endeavor to use them?

A second general principle used by the highest producing managers is *the involvement of subordinates* in decisions affecting them. High-producing managers, in comparison with other managers, involve their subordinates more in work-related decisions and in this process more often use the work group rather than individual employees as the decision-making unit. Work group meetings, either formal or informal, are used more frequently by the highest producing managers than by other managers and the ideas and thinking of the men are taken more seriously and used more fully. This use of group-decision processes develops more loyalty among the men toward each other, more cooperative behavior and greater teamwork, and more commitment to implementing the decisions made and the goals set.

A third general principle of the highest producing managers is that they have *higher performance goals* and greater concern for achieving them than do other managers. As seen by their subordinates, the highest producing managers "pull for the men and the company and not for the company only." These managers establish a reciprocal responsibility. The supportive behavior of these managers and the decision-making processes which they use result in subordinates establishing high performance goals for themselves. High performance goals of the subordinates coupled with their greater loyalty toward each other and toward their superior contribute to high productivity by the work group with a minimum of waste. These work groups accomplish more with less feeling of pressure or strain than do other groups.

The approach used by these highest producing managers to achieve high productivity takes time to pay off. They are trying to establish organizations in which high productivity and low costs are continuous, not a short range, phenomenon. They accomplish this objective by building organizations which, in comparison with others, have better communication, better decision-making based on this better communication, greater capacity to coordinate the efforts of the members of the organization, more favorable and cooperative attitudes, greater identification with the organization and greater concern in achieving the organization's goals. In field experiments involving hundreds of employees, we find it takes at least a year or two for this approach to achieve high levels of productivity and low costs. But once excellent levels of performance are reached they are usually maintained.

Implications for Public Administration

What are the implications of all this for public administration and the operation of the Federal Government? If further research in business establishes beyond doubt the validity of the general conclusions I have briefly described, and if similar research in government yields the same over-all pattern of findings, these results would require substantial changes in some of the major efforts now being pursued to increase productivity and reduce costs in Federal agencies.

There is, in my judgment, sufficient evidence in support of the general conclusions which I have presented to indicate that we should take a hard and questioning look at some of the steps now being taken to reduce the costs of government, and to examine critically the assumptions upon which these steps are based and the evidence supporting these assumptions.

The steps to which I refer are those which involve in one form or another direct, hierarchical pressure on the personnel in agencies to increase their productivity. These include such procedures as across-the-board manpower cuts or budget cuts. These cuts of, say, 2 to 5 per cent are usually made with the expectation that the agency will still perform the same volume of services after the cut as prior to it. Other procedures involve measuring productivity or output, setting standards and pressing to have employees produce at the specified level. Perhaps some of you have experienced such pressures or even applied them.

In making these comments about measuring productivity, I hope I am not misunderstood. I am not suggesting that efforts to measure productivity are undesirable. I hold the opposite point of view most strongly. It is very important to develop sound measurements of productivity, output and costs, and I trust that these efforts will be continued and extended. My concern is focused on how the measurements of productivity are used. My hope is that productivity measurements as they become available will be used in the way the highest producing managers in business and industry use such data and not in the way that the less productive managers use them.

From available research findings, I would expect that direct, hierarchical pressure within the Federal Government will yield, on the average and over the long run, the same pattern of results as it appears to be yielding in business. That is, such pressure will be associated with low, rather than high, productivity. These direct pressure procedures may well yield in government, as in business, appreciable increases in productivity and lowering of costs for about a two year period. Accompanying these favorable productivity changes, however, are likely to be serious adverse changes in the organization. Loyalties will decrease, confidence and trust will decrease, concern for achieving the organization's objectives will decrease, there will be greater pressure to restrict production, absence and turnover will increase, good people will leave the organization, quality of work will slip or be harder to maintain, and hostilities, resentments, unfavorable attitudes will increase.

Such changes in the organization will mean, of course, that the increases in productivity achieved from the direct, hierarchical pressure were obtained at a serious cost to the organization. Substantial human assets of the organization, such as loyalty, confidence and trust, undistorted and efficient communication and high performance goals, are adversely affected. The cost of this liquidation of human assets — perhaps in the form of the dollar costs required to rebuild them — should be charged against the greater productivity obtained by means of the hierarchical pressure. To ignore the substantial dollar costs when an effective organization is "mined" in this way is not sound nor accurate accounting and leads to erroneous conclusions. Until all the legitimate costs are measured and properly charged, all productivity increases cannot be considered actual improvement nor real savings.

If such steps as direct, hierarchical pressure are not likely to yield sustained increases in productivity (in Federal agencies), what alternative courses of action can be recommended? I should like to recommend two:

First, that research be undertaken in governmental agencies to test whether the general conclusions which I have suggested are valid and applicable;

Second, that measurements be taken regularly not only of productivity, output, costs and similar end-result variables but also of all the major variables which need to be measured to obtain accurate information as to an organization's strengths and weaknesses and as to its performance characteristics and capabilities.

Let me elaborate on each point briefly. The civilian payroll of the Federal Government is, I believe, in excess of 14 billion dollars. If a fraction of a per cent of that amount were made available for the kind of research I have been discussing, the applicability to government of the general conclusions emerging from research in business and industry could be tested and validated or modified within a relatively short period of time. Such research would establish far sounder foundations upon which to base the art of public administration than now exists. This would lead to better administration, greater productivity, and lower costs. Based on the results obtained in business organizations when research findings are applied, increases in productivity many times greater than the sums spent on the research could reasonably be expected. I believe that all persons seriously interested in reducing the costs of government should examine carefully the promise which this approach offers.

Using Proper Variables

Turning now to my second recommendation. There are three broad classes of variables that need to be measured if one wishes to have accurate information about an organization. These are the causal variables, the intervening variables and the end-result variables. The *causal* variables are the independent variables such as the structure of the organization and management's policies, decisions, strategies, and behavior. The *intervening* variables reflect the internal state and health of the organization. Examples of the intervening variables of interest here include: the loyalties, attitudes, motivations, performace goals, perceptions, and skills of all members of the organization and the organization's capacity for effective interaction, communication, and decision making. The *end-result* variables are the dependent variables which reflect the results achieved by the organization, such as its productivity, costs, scrap loss, and total output.

All three of these broad classes of variables need to be measured at periodic intervals if one wishes to understand the current state of an organization, its performance capacity, and the character of its current operation. The periodic measurements of these variables, and observations of the changes and trends in them would, for example, actually reveal the consequences of productivity increases when accompanied by the liquidation of some of the human assets. Such information would enable more accurate and hard-headed accounting and avoid the erroneous conclusions often drawn today from short-range trends.

There is an even more important use of the measurements of all three classes of variables. If made regularly available to each administrator or supervisor, these measurements would motivate him to improve his managerial performance and would provide him with powerful resources for enabling him to recognize and diagnose his inadequacies as a manager, to discover what changes he should make in his behavior, and to learn from the measurements whether the corrective steps he has tried to take have actually yielded the improvement he seeks.

This single use of these measurements, particularly the measurements of the causal and intervening variables, in "feedback" processes, coupled with intelligent and supportive coaching, could readily yield improvements in productivity and costs many times greater than the amount which I suggest be spent for research.

The art of public administration plays a key role in our effectiveness as a nation. Improvement in this art, as I have endeavored to show, can be greatly accelerated by building sounder foundations based on rigorous, quantitative research. The encouragement and support of this research offers, in my judgment, the most constructive approach to providing adequate and efficient administration while keeping the costs of government at a minimum. I sincerely hope we will see a substantial increase in the amount of this research conducted both by government agencies themselves and also conducted for them by university and similar research organizations.

Incentive Contracts: Management Strategy of the Department of Defense

✣ HOWARD M. CARLISLE

In 1960 when the Kennedy Administration came into office, two directives were given by the President to his new Secretary of Defense, Robert S. McNamara: (1) develop the necessary defense force without arbitrary budget ceilings, and (2) procure and operate this force at the lowest possible cost.

Responding to these guidelines, Secretary McNamara concluded that a drastic overhaul of the decision making process was needed within the Department of Defense (DOD) and that method had to be developed to improve the utilization of the nation's resources involved in our defense effort. In the attempt to achieve the objective of increasing the effectiveness of the defense industry effort and output, the following major, industry-oriented changes were made by DOD:

(1) Creation of the Defense Supply Agency to centralize procurement management of items common to all of the military services.

(2) Establishment of the Logistics Management Institute, a non-profit corporation devoted to study and problem-solving in a number of logistics fields.

(3) Establishment of the Program Package Plan, which is essentially a budgeting aid whereby costs of developing and operating new weapons are evaluated from a mission-related standpoint and projected five years in advance.

(4) Replacing cost-plus-fixed-fee (CPFF) contracting with contract types which provide more incentive. Under this system, industry would be rewarded heavily (up to 15 per cent) for superior performance and punished (no fee or even a net loss) for inadequate performance based on cost, product performance, reliability quality, and delivery.

This last change involving incentive contracts has had many ramifications which deserve close scrutiny in evaluating the changes and trends in government-industry relationships. To evaluate this impact, it is necessary to appreciate the motives

Reprinted from the *Public Administration Review*, the journal of the American Society for Public Administration, Vol. XXIV, No. 1, 1964, pp. 21–23, 25–27, by permission of the publisher.

behind the strategy which has resulted in this emphasis on incentive contracts and the results which have been achieved and can be anticipated in the future.

In order to fully appreciate the impact of a far-reaching change in defense contracting policies such as this, it is necessary that the importance of the contract in the relationship which exists between the government and private industry be considered. All effort undertaken by a defense firm under an agreement with a federal agency is accomplished through the administrative vehicle of the written contract. In a normal buying and selling situation, an item is purchased by a customer based upon the selling price offered by the selling organization. This type of purchase arrangement is limited in the DOD operations to standard commercial or off-the-shelf items. These are the items which can be purchased as any normal item in a retail store or through a catalog which identifies the specifications and selling price of the article.

Even though off-the-shelf items constitute the majority of procurement actions, only a small portion of the DOD dollars are utilized for procurements of this nature. The greater portion of the dollars are applied to weapon systems which have no, or limited, commercial utilization. The requirements are, therefore, solely to meet the needs of DOD which means that the specifications and performance requirements are established by that organization. All work performed by a contractor must be defined within the written contractual document which is signed and agreed to by both parties. It also contains limitations established by law or by policies of the issuing agency which are incorporated by reference therein.

The contract, therefore, serves as the administrative framework utilized by cognizant government agencies to govern contractor activities. Any change in this framework has a widespread effect on the relationship of buyer and seller; in fact, it affects the whole operation of defense contractors as they are in essence a "captured" industry in a one-buyer market. Contract provisions and stipulations have become so important that the professional status of the "contract administrator" who handles these details has risen to be one of the most important elements in defense contractor management.

Defense contracting since World War II has been governed by the Armed Services Procurement Act of 1947. Prior to this, most procurement was done on a routine "advertise and bid" basis and involved primarily the procurement of goods. During World War II the War Powers Act completely opened the door of procurement practices in order to expedite the war production effort. Most of the previous procurement restrictions were superseded and the President was given virtually a free hand as was the case in most emergency operations.

During the immediate postwar era, one interesting development occurred in relation to contract management which set the stage for a wide variety of changes. The contract, once almost entirely limited to procurement of goods, now became a mechanism for securing a variety of services involving scientific research and development (R & D), policy planning, and management of government facilities. To meet these new requirements, the Armed Services Procurement Act (ASPA) was passed which established the now familiar pattern of fixed price procurement on standard or production items and cost-plus-fixed-fee (CPFF) procurement on research and development efforts. (For an explanation of these contract types with their condition for use, see Figure 1.) This pattern has dominated procurement policy until the incentive emphasis in 1961.

There are many variations of these two standard procurement arrangements recognized by the Armed Services Procurement Regulations, the implementing

DOD regulations for ASPA. These are grouped into three categories — fixed price, cost reimbursement, and special type — for discussion purposes with the characteristics of each enumerated as part of Figure 1. Figure 2 compares the two basic types of incentive contracts, fixed-price incentive (FPI) and cost-plus-incentive-fee (CPIF).

In fiscal year 1951, 78 per cent of the procurements were handled on a fixed price basis and 13 per cent on a cost reimbursement basis. Within the requirements of the Armed Services Procurement Regulations, buying practices became fairly standardized in terms of the types of contractual arrangements which were utilized. However, the advent of the space age and the tremendously large and scientifically complex systems associated with space propulsion tended to change all of this.

Beginning in the early 1950's through the current time period, the trend in aerospace procurement has been to require more and more funds for the development of these intricate scientific weapon systems and to require more limited funds for production. The situation within the airframe industry of limited R & D effort with long production runs has been reversed in the aerospace industry to large development programs with limited follow-on production contracts. Due to the increased size and cost of space vehicles, fewer systems have been developed, even though the dollars allocated for defense spending have increased each year. As the number of new systems has decreased, the number of competing contractors has increased so that the priority for the dollars and the competition to obtain the contracts have become more intense. As a result of these changes in the complexion of the Department of Defense programs, fixed price contracts involved 47 per cent of the procurements in FY1961 compared to 39 per cent for cost reimbursement type contracts.

This marked increase in the utilization of the CPFF type contract caused deep concern to the new chiefs of the Department of Defense when they took over in 1961. The opinion within the Department was that "in CPFF situations there is little inducement to control costs after the contract is made since controlling costs does not affect the amount of profit and there is some evidence that estimates are frequently made unrealistically low as a means of selling the government on a program without undue risk." In order to decrease the cost overruns which were characteristic of most of the early missile and space programs, DOD decided it would be necessary to provide more incentive for the contractors to remain within their original cost estimates. CPFF contracts simply provided "too little incentive to give any real encouragement for cost control and efficiency."

The Importance of Incentives

The provisions of a CPIF contract make the financial incentives much more predominant. Under this type of arrangement where fee is increased as a result of an underrun or decreased as the result of an overrun, the potential profit becomes considerably greater and increases the incentive for rigid program controls and cost reduction. This type of contract strikes at the heart of the profit incentive of private enterprise. In analyzing this impact on the profit motive, DOD representatives estimate that R & D costs under incentive contracts will be 10 per cent lower than they would be under CPFF arrangements.

This is not to say that all non-incentives of a CPFF contract have been eliminated. "Hungry" contractors are still attempting to *buy-in* programs recognizing that they will make no profit on the initial contract, but they will gain the necessary management, technical capability and *current contractor* advantage for subsequent follow-on

FIGURE 1: Contract Types

Fixed Price	Cost-Reimbursement	Special Type
Provides price not subject to adjustment by reason of the cost experience of the contractor in performance of the contract.	Payment to contractor of allowable costs incurred in the performance of the contract. CPFF includes fixed fee negotiated at outset which is unaffected by final actual cost.	Special types to handle peculiar situations not suitable for fixed-price or cost-reimbursement type contracts.
Types: Firm fixed-price. Variations where price is adjusted include fixed-price with escalation, fixed-price incentive, prospective and retroactive redetermination at a stated time during performance or after completion.	Types: Cost contract, cost-sharing, cost-plus-fixed-fee, cost-plus-incentive-fee.	Types: Time and materials (used on occasion for engineering services, repair or maintenance work, work to be performed in emergency situations); labor-hour (same as T&M except materials are not involved).
Features and Conditions for Use: 1. Requires reasonably definite design or performance specifications. 2. Fair and reasonable price based on reliable cost information and competition. 3. Maximum risk on contractor. 4. Greatest profit potential and incentive to reduce cost. 5. Minimum administrative control by government.	Features and Conditions for Use: 1. Difficult to define program and specifications. 2. Accurate cost estimate not assured. 3. Adequate contractor cost accounting system. 4. Minimum risk to contractor. 5. Minimum fee and incentive to control costs. 6. Close surveillance of contractor costs and performance by government personnel.	Features and Conditions for Use: 1. Not possible at time of placing contract to estimate extent or duration of the work or costs. 2. Close government surveillance. 3. Minimum risk to contractor. 4. Minimum fee and incentive to control costs.

FIGURE 2: Comparison of Incentive Type Contracts

	Fixed-Price Incentive (FPI)	Cost-Plus-Incentive-Fee (CPIF)
Types of Targets:	Apply to any one or combination of following: costs, performance goals, schedules.	Same as FPI.
Cost Target:	Establishes target cost. Reimbursed for costs which are negotiated as part of final contract price at end of contract.	Establishes target cost. Reimbursed for allowable actual costs.
Target Fee or Profit:	Establishes target profit. Underrun of costs or exceeding of performance targets increases profit; overrun of costs or failure to meet performance goals decreases profit based on negotiated share arrangement.	Establishes target fee. Underrun of costs or exceeding of performance goals increases fee; overrun of costs or failure to meet performance goals decreases fee based on negotiated share arrangement.
Ceiling Price:	Total dollar amount established above which government will not be liable.	No ceiling price. Government participates in allowable costs on share basis.
Minimum and Maximum Fee:	No such limitations. Government not liable for costs above ceiling price.	Contract establishes minimum and maximum fee ranges.
Risk:	Higher risk due to ceiling price.	Less risk than FPI.
Profit Potential:	Higher potential than CPIF.	Normally lower than FPI.

effort. However, it does tend to minimize the attractiveness of *buying-in* in this manner.

In addition to the cost incentives mentioned above, one of the chief weaknesses of the CPFF contract is the lack of performance incentive. Under a CPFF contract, the "fixed fee" is the same regardless of results. The profit reward is identical whether excellent or poor performance is achieved in terms of meeting schedules and delivering a satisfactory end product.

Incentive contracts provide a distinct advantage over CPFF when performance alone is considered. However, performance incentives are often difficult to apply. Complex questions arise regarding the measurement of performance and the portion of the performance which can be attributed to the contractor under the joint government-contractor technical decision making process which exists on major programs. Also, under the associate contractor concept whereby the government directs several separate contractors in the R & D and production of a weapon system, no one contractor can achieve different performance or schedules without being out of phase with the other associates.

Unfortunately, in many respects, the incentive contracts would have been much more effective several years ago, when the industry was not as much in an over-capacity situation and when competition was not as keen. Under the current situation of fewer programs with more contractors competing, it is likely that some will still resort to underbidding techniques in an effort to gain part of the business. However, in the overall, the experience during the past few years has indicated that most defense contractors have done some belt tightening and are taking a much more hard-headed approach to overhead activities, cost reduction programs, and any other area of effort which might be subject to cost improvement.

The emphasis on effective program and budget control has been markedly increased. This has increased the requirement for capable people and for more effective management systems in these areas. As a result, systems such as the charting technique involved in PERT (Program Evaluation and Review Technique) have been developed. Intense effort is continuing both within government and industry to develop improved systems to handle the complex problems involved in the massive engineering projects representative of the space age.

The Place of the Renegotiation Board

The trend towards incentive contracts has brought many advantages, but it has also focused attention on certain problems and difficulties. It has given rise to some skeptics who warn that the entire positive effect could be overridden by the attitude of buyers or of agencies such as the Renegotiation Board. The prime difficulty with the incentive approach from a practical standpoint is that it requires a firm work statement and detailed definition of effort in order for contractors to effectively evaluate performance incentives and cost estimates. Aerospace programs are characteristically dynamic and changing. If the work to be accomplished is frequently changed, the performance requirements and the costs will be modified with the resulting tendency to lose sight of the incentives.

In the past, contractors have frequently been awarded contracts under which the performance requirements and specifications have been developed as part of the statement of work. The necessity of establishing firm requirements prior to contract award will tend to delay the initiation of major aerospace programs. Such delay is not nearly the problem that was encountered several years ago when each contract extended the state of the art, but it still remains a major difficulty. The rebuttal of DOD officials is that the performance and schedule incentive will more than offset this. Regardless, a much greater burden is placed on the Department of Defense to establish firm requirements prior to the undertaking of new programs. This requirement is extremely difficult to meet due to the rapid change in technology and the lack of firm data available on new or proposed concepts. The inability to meet this requirement will undoubtedly result in extremely complex situations from a contract administration standpoint. It should result in a more difficult administrative job for the government in terms of program and contractor direction, since tighter work statements and contracts will result in the loss of flexibility which has characterized the administration of recent large development programs.

The most frequent complaint of industry in relation to incentive contracting is that if they do perform well and manage to have a cost underrun, the Renegotiation Board will take away any excess profits which they earn. If this is done, the incentive provided by contracts of this nature would be automatically eliminated. As a result, the Department of Defense has been holding hearings with the Renegotiation Board in order to resolve this problem.

Under the Renegotiation Act of 1951, the Renegotiation Board was set up as an independent establishment of the executive branch, based upon the policy that "the sound execution of the national defense program requires the elimination of excessive profits from contracts made with the United States, and from related subcontracts." The problem, of course, arises from defining "excessive profits" in relation to incentive contracts.

No actual satisfactory resolution of this problem has been reached as yet. Since the renegotiation of profits is not a repricing of individual contracts, but of an entire contractors' defense sales for a given year, it makes it difficult to apply special allowances for incentive contracting effort. However, the Renegotiation Board has indicated it will be "taken into consideration" to the degree possible under their regulations. Nonetheless, the Renegotiation Board remains as one of the potential barriers which could limit the effectiveness of the incentive approach.

In relation to incentive contracting, it should also be mentioned that the tendency towards cost effectiveness has also been emphasized by other actions of Secretary McNamara. Programs which have tended to get out of bounds from a cost standpoint have been terminated, and emphasis in contractor selection has been placed on the reasonableness of the estimate and the contractor's prior performance in this regard. Incentive contracting has been the most effective tool in emphasizing the cost improvement drive of DOD but it has been supported by other actions of this nature.

The one last item of concern relates to the attitude of buyers and contractor review boards. In the past, buyers and contractor review boards have established certain percentages of fee as appropriate for CPFF or fixed price contracts. Statutory limitations are actually provided so that R & D type effort cannot be paid fee in excess of 15 per cent, and production type effort cannot be paid fee in excess of 10 per cent. In actuality, the service secretaries involved have an "administrative limitation" of 10 per cent on R & D contracts and 7 per cent production.

In actual practice, the policy of the buyers and the review boards has been to limit these fee percentages to a very narrow range. For instance, most of the CPFF contracts issued since 1960 have been between 6 and 7 per cent. If the buyer and contract review boards assume a similar position on incentive contracts, the tendency would be to negate much of the incentive provided a contractor. For instance, if an attitude is developed that 7 per cent is a reasonable earned fee for CPIF effort, and a contractor on his initial contract underruns or actually earns 10 per cent fee, which the buyer considers to be excessive, it can have a harmful effect on the entire program. Under these circumstances, on a follow-on program, the buyer who ignores the superior performance on the initial contract and attempts to reduce the contractor's anticipated fee to the 7 per cent range, assuming the same superior performance, tends to defeat the objective of the DOD program.

Improved Performance Measurement Needed

The fear has developed that CPFF type thinking will result in forcing CPIF effort into this old pattern. To avoid this, in reviewing the historical costs and fee percentages on prior contracts, buyers must recognize superior performance as such and acknowledge that the higher fee earned was justified. If the higher fee is recognized as unjustifiable and the buyer attempts to "get even" or bring it into line on the next contract, it will make a sham of the philosophy which has been utilized in the push behind incentive contracts. The grass roots philosophies of buyers and pertinent review boards will do much to determine the success of the whole approach.

One of the burdens placed on both industry and government is to provide better measures of performance both in terms of technical effort and cost control. A contractor must be able to show that through superior performance the contract was underran rather than due to an ability to initially fool the buyer through purposely obtaining performance and cost targets which are overstated. PERT and other such systems give promise of supplying more meaningful and measurable cost standards, but other systems and methods must also be developed to better evaluate the total management effort associated with a contract.

There is a tremendous need for improved performance and cost measurements which serve as tools to meaningfully portray the actual program status, and to serve as a vehicle in orienting program managers in government and industry of their joint activities. The burst of technology respresented by the space age has led to an information crisis relative to the data needed to manage tremendously large and scientifically complex projects. Administratively, these programs remain an enigma which has been complicated by the increase in government control. These problems have combined to strain the already involved relationship existing between aerospace firms and federal agencies. Unless better measures of performance are developed, the situation could revert to the battle of wits associated with many ill-defined negotiations in the past. Such a condition would circumvent the advantages offered by incentive contracts and set back the whole McNamara cost-effectiveness program with its promise of joint government-industry gains.

Operations Research Can Help Public Administrators in Decision-Making

❧ Maurice F. Ronayne

There's A Need . . .

Many public administrators today in the world still employ Eighteenth Century management tools to assist them in making Twentieth Century decisions. This is indeed unfortunate, especially since we are now living in an era which treats space exploration as an almost-common thing. Public administrators like their counterparts in business must have the right kind of intelligence to make decisions upon. But . . . they are often frustrated with the vague and incomplete character of the data given to them, which they must utilize to shape life and death policy decisions.

Documentation may often be disjointed . . . sometimes non-existent . . . often badly selected in the first place. Even statistics will show holes through which a herd of bull elephants could be driven. But far worse than all these faults is the deplorable lack of "toughness of mind" to attempt to make more reliable, more valid, and more scientific . . . the public official's job of drafting policy making decisions.

Owing to the complex nature of modern-day affairs on one hand, and to the rapid expansion of all facets of the field of administration, both public and private, not only is it more difficult to determine clearly what decisions must be taken, but decisions made today are more far-reaching and more irrevocable in their consequences than ever before in history.

But one tool, slowly but surely establishing itself as an aid to public administrators, and which offers tremendous promise as a method for obtaining better decision-making capabilities, is Operations Research . . .

History . . .

Operations Research, or "OR" in its abbreviated version, has really been around for some time. But it usually has gone by different names. For example, the use of management games or of simulation techniques, important OR tools, can be traced back to 1872 when the British Army began practicing War Games!

During World War I, inventor Thomas Edison practiced OR. He collected statistics on anti-submarine warfare, developed ideas on sweep-widths for visual search, and applied operational gaming in connection with shipping across the English Channel. Unfortunately, Edison's ideas were too advanced, and most ended up gathering dust in British Admiralty files.

Twenty years later OR became active again when English scientists such as Sir Henry Tizard and colleagues began to work closely with the military to perfect a device to help England defend itself against the Luftwaffe.

Teamwork paid off with radar, making it possible for RAF Spitfires to know

"Operations Research Can Help Public Administrators in Decision-Making," by Maurice F. Ronayne, reprinted by permission of the International Institute of Administrative Sciences from *International Review of Administrative Sciences*, No. 3 (1963), pp. 227–234.

where to fly to engage the enemy. All saving time and precious petrol. . . and above all, Britain!

Later Americans began using OR techniques. Teams of top-drawer scientific researchers with military people pooled disciplines drawn from the life and natural sciences, and mathematics, to resolve problems ranging from the correct placing of "GI" soldier washtubs for cleaning messkits and expediting long chowlines, to picking the optimal number of armed escorts needed for ship convoys without having too little or too much protection against enemy U-boats.

Remarkably enough, through OR analyses, Dr. Glen Camp found out that the real problem was *not* Undersea Welfare, but Overseas Transport! Top-priority emphasis shifted from methods of killing enemy subs to finding different ways of increasing cargo delivered overseas, right in the teeth of even more deadly enemy sub offensives.

OR's capability often to identify the *real* problem rather than the *apparent* one, is one of its most important attributes.

A Few Explanatory Remarks

Operations Research strives to identify the optimal solution, and policy in relation to the total organization. This is perhaps the *key characteristic* of OR. It utilizes scientific techniques to provide management with a quantitative basis for decision-making.

Most often the OR expert will make a mathematical model of a system, connecting to it the certainties and uncertainties in any situation in order to measure and assign relative success rankings to possible solutions. These mathematical models describe the activity under review, and, upon the form of these models, propose alternative solutions to management problems.

Public administrators thus equipped can then make decisions on a rational basis, well aware of the effect that this solution will have on various parts of the organization, but carrying out the decision so that the best interests of the entire organization can be served.

OR is much like a branch of applied sciences. It analyzes facts or complex situations in varied fields, always endeavoring to help the administrator to minimize his resorting to hit-or-miss methods in arriving at decisions, in order to encourage him to base his acts to the fullest extent on the reality of cold, hard facts.

In mathematical terms, this approach narrows down to the general form of an OR model where:

$$E = f(x_i, y_j)$$

Effectiveness (E) of a system is a function (f) of variables that are subject to control (x_i) and variables not subject to it (y_j).

What's In OR For The Public Administrator . . .

Operations Research can help the public administrator to (1) select the best alternatives in a specific problem to yield the best decisions or policies, (2) develop methodologies for making various types of optimum decisions, and, (3) educate others to review systematically all possible alternatives to come up with methods for yielding the best decision.

OR operates best when there are:

— *A large number of controlled variables* . . . Using mathematical techniques OR easily works with large numbers of strategic possibilities and states of nature.

— *A small number of relevant uncontrolled variables* . . . Operations Research methods indentify unknown, but important variables.

— *Relevant measurable variables and good data* . . . Or often provides the necessary problem-solving analysis to relate important variables to one another, to the outcome, and to the payoff measure.

— *Past relationships extending into the future* . . . Mathematical methods can frequently be devised to search for innumerable payoff measures for purposes of applying decision criteria.

One typical problem subject to an OR payoff might be the motor-pool supervisor who wants to know how long it would take for two different brands of tires to wear out on his vehicles. He may decide to get a sample of twelve of each kind and put them on his vehicles. . . . all at the same time. As tires wear out, he jots these facts down.

But . . . is his approach a valid one? How sure is he that the tires are each truly representative of the two manufacturer's products? Maybe one batch was older than the other? How were the vehicles used? Each under similar conditions? These and many other questions must be answered, if the supervisor wants to reach a meaningful conclusion as to which kind of tires to purchase.

This then, is the type of problem the administrator can apply OR to, for best results. It is a tool which helps administration to tie together all parts of any problem into a neat package, so that most effects and implications will be measured, and all costs and tangible benefits fully evaluated.

OR provides Figures, *not* Fancies . . .

Basic OR Techniques . . .

Mathematics and statistics help OR resolve difficult problems. These two disciplines underline the basic OR tool applications.

The general picture of Operations Research shows it composed of several techniques, useful either singularly or in combination. Queuing, Monte Carlo, Simulation, Game Theory, and Linear Programming are the most commonly applied techniques. Here is a description of their characteristics:

Queuing. Developed in the early 1900's by Erlang, an engineer with the Copenhagen Telephone Company, it relies heavily on the use of statistical probability theory as do most OR techniques.

The essential ingredients of queuing include (1) customer, (2) gate or service point, (3) input process, (4) queue discipline, and (5) a service mechanism. An analysis must be made also of (a) waiting time of customers, (b) number of customers in the waiting line, and (c) ratio of waiting time to service time.

Queuing works to reduce waiting time of the customer, number of customers in line, and ratio of waiting-time to service time. It also minimizes costs of the service agency by serving as many customers as possible, with the least number of facilities. This reduces idle facilities, inventory, and manpower.

In capsule form . . . *Service Rate should = Average Rate of Customer Arrivals, recognizing that such arrivals may fluctuate considerably.*

Past experience is analyzed, whenever available, to determine the distribution of random variations, of customer arrivals, orders, paper work flow, trucks, breakdowns, etc. Then, data are converted to probabilities.

Analyzing the random input itself is fundamental to solving a queuing problem. Although the "smoothing" of service times will reduce the congestion in queuing, *the real solution lies in getting better controls over the input* so as to get close to the desired input norm.

Monte Carlo. Uses random sampling to simulate graphically the process being analyzed. Essentially it is a trial-and-error method of repeated calculations to discover the best solution. When a large number of variables is present with inter-relationships too complex to be handled by straight-forward analytical methods, it is especially useful. This technique, particularly relevant to any problem invoking probability theory, best applies when there is no past history on expected happenings. A good example is a queuing problem when the number and time of expected arrivals are completely unknown.

Simulation. Here the model need not have the same physical appearance as the actual system under analysis, but it must resemble it in ways such as the authority and responsibility patterns, the communications network, and the laws and conventions that actually exist.

In reality, the model is an abstraction. It simply duplicates a situation under investigation. No model is the real world! It only possesses what the analyst believes to be the important and pertinent aspects of the original. To get down to brass tacks . . . a model is neither true nor false; either it applies to a certain situation or it does not represent reality. When determining the possible benefit of a mathematical model, one must consider first not only the accuracy inherent in the model itself, but also the necessity to provide this exactness at all!

Game Theory. Concerns itself with the optimal choice of strategies in a competitive situation. Originally introduced by Emile Borel, but more fully developed by mathematician John Von Neumann and economist Oskar Mogenstern to describe competitive economic behavior. Game Theory came about from the study of simple two-man games (for example, coin tossing) with the especial characteristic that one player keeps what the other loses.

Later, Game Theory was applied to far more complex competitive situations with more players capable of providing a strategy of play that could reduce a player's overall loss. This technique also provides for the possibility that "opponents" are bluffing or using a games-theory approach.

To sum up, Game Theory is a mathematical method of picking out the best strategies in situations where people are in conflict. Each person is able to exercise control over some aspects of the game while other aspects are in control of competitors. One person alone can determine the final results of a "game" just as in any regular game of chance. Usually, however, recommended decisions rest more on a strategy of minimizing one's risks rather than maximizing one's goals.

A typical application might be to find out which one among two competing manufacturers, each offering a similar product, will be able to win control over a business market.

Linear Programming. Extremely useful in areas where restrictions on the use of resources make it very difficult to carry out each activity as if it were the only one performed. Linear Programming assumes a linear or straight-line relationship among variables. It only asks that the limits of variation be fairly well defined. Arithmetical computations are simple, but since they are most often used to handle a complex situation with many variables, the volume of computations is usually extensive, and often calls for an electronic computer. Probability plays *no part* in normal Linear Programming, the theory behind the computational routines being that of matrix algebra.

Typical applications may be Inventory Planning, an Improved Product Mix, or an Assignment of Skilled Technicians to repair items as they arrive.

Electronic Computers And OR . . .

A computer's tremendous speed enables it to simulate conditions impossible to study at first hand. Examples include War Games, a flight of a space ship, or the "trying out" of combinations of new engines, transmission, axles and tires for cars of the future.

One Detroit motor executive recently figured that some of the computations made to pinpoint where squeaks were most likely to develop in an automobile would have taken until 2061 A.D. if an electronic computer and OR hadn't been applied.

A Typical OR Application . . .

OR methodologies, backed up with an electronic computer, can work together to solve this problem dealing with the unloading capabilities of a seaport. An optimal situation would provide for sufficient available berths, few ships kept waiting to dock, and berths filled most of the time.

A computer can simulate this problem. Program steps which a computer must answer include: "Is a berth free?," "If yes, is there a ship ready to dock?," "If so, is the tide favorable?," "If all answers are affirmative, how long will the ship take to dock?."

Other variable factors are involved. Vessels of different tonnage differ in their unloading times. Even with a given tonnage the type of cargo affects the unloading time. Personnel problems present trouble too: "Will there be enough men ready in time to unload the boat?," "How many men do we have to have on the payroll at berths of different sizes to be sure that the right number of men will be able to unload the ship?," "How can the right number of men be placed at the dock?," "What are the risks of not getting enough men . . . or, of being any specific number short?," "How many will probably be sick or on vacation?."

If no data are handy to show the detailed effect of these factors, one can assume that there exist frequency distributions of ships handled in varying tonnage ranges and of unloading times achieved in each range. The Monte Carlo method can then be applied to simulate these variations by random-sampling. Coupled with the use of this tool would be the application of Queuing technique to data compiled by Monte Carloing.

Starting from some arbitrary set of conditions with a given number of berths, this model can be run indefinitely on a computer to produce berth-utilization and ship-queuing times after each month's simulated operation. The model, once constructed, can be run repeatedly to try the effects of different numbers of berths. From these data, the administrator can then select the optimal course of action.

The Difference Between Systems Analysis And OR . . .

Basically, the OR Analyst *translates observations into quantitative elements of an abstract mathematical model and then manipulates this model to arrive at an optimal solution.*

Straight systems analysis differs from Operations Research in the fact that OR uses a highly quantitative, often mathematical approach to a problem, which digs below the surface and accepts few conclusions till specific effects can be traced back to clear-cut causes.

An OR man leans heavily on symbolic logic drawn from the scientific disciplines, most often constructing a mathematical model to represent a system. The systems and procedures man usually does not have the habit of mind for applied research as the OR expert has, but instead gravitates naturally towards more empirical formulas. And, most unfortunately, through no fault of his own, the systems man so often becomes overburdened with administrative work or compelled to engage in "fire-fighting", that he has little time to analyze the material available, and falls back on improvisations and "quickie" solutions.

Usually the OR man can work without interruption on his problems. Solitude permits him the luxury of applying his scientific techniques to the fullest on the highly unusual problems he's been assigned to do in the first place!

But . . . an especially valuable partnership can be formed between the OR man and the Systems Analyst. Techniques may not be the same, but they're *supplementary!* When your OR man comes down from his "Ivory Tower" to try out his esoteric formulas, the systems man with his two feet solidly on the ground with his overall knowledge of organization structure, administrative systems, and data processing flow, can not only contribute to the OR man's work, but also help to evaluate it, and when it is okayed, effectively implement the OR recommendations.

OR Limitations . . .

(1) *Mathematical Models.* Models at best are only an *approximation* of real life. Accuracy of the model may be compromised by possible inaccuracies in source data used to set up the model, and by deliberate approximations made during research.

(2) *Intangible Factors.* It is extremely hard to measure important factors as goodwill, human behavior, moral values, human ethics. . . .

(3) *Time.* OR investigations have to have research over long periods of time which makes it ineffective in solving day-to-day operating problems.

(4) *High Costs.* Problem-solving must be limited to only those in which foreseeable gains over costs make it an attractive choice over other analysis techniques. Other problems within its scope must be left out.

(5) *De-Humanization.* OR disregards any individuality and uniqueness among people, completely ignoring out the humanistic approach to administration which has grown tremendously in popularity within recent years.

(6) *Lack of Data.* Many organizations do not have available the data so vital to many OR formulas, nor can data always be successfully simulated.

(7) *Basic Research.* OR men to grow, must not spend all their time on "bits and pieces". They require time for almost completely undirected research . . . a fact of scientific life that not all organizations can afford.

(8) *Sub-Optimization.* There is the problem that the research will become so minute and so precise that the broad systems concept of the organization will be forgotten. It's not easy to locate the right level to optimize at, i.e. to meet the requirement to optimize at a level appropriate to the problem.

Some Problem Areas . . .

To avoid frustration and a sense of complete futility, any OR man hoping to succeed in applying his bag-of-tricks must be alert to possible sources of hostility to his work. Above all, he must be a salesman *par excellence* to get around these organizational roadblocks.

(1) *Different Management Philosophies.* Here the OR man must learn to cope with two types of philosophies, both of them at variance with his own *modus operandi.* There is *old-fashioned intuition* philosophy or the "fly-by-the-seat-of-your-pants" routine still held by many executives who possess complete indifference to all new-fangled management methods. Then, there is the *human relations* approach of getting things done through people by making their working environment as comfortable as possible.

(2) *Communications.* Few public administrators have more than an elementary knowledge of mathematics and for many of them OR terminology is "Greek to them"! OR folks, to succeed must learn to sell their ideas in language which the layman grasps. Too much lingo, OR style, and many an administrator will peg the speaker as too theoretical!

(3) *OR Man's Puff.* Any quackery by an OR man that his tool of management is a panacea for all of an administrator's ills will bring a very acid response from most executives. Too many colleagues have been "burnt" already by overly ambitious OR'ers who have failed to produce after making outlandish claims!

(4) *Naïvety* . . . Unfamiliarity of OR practitioners with public administration practices leads to duplication of approaches already available and needless clashes with existing professions. OR men fresh from stints in military services often fail to realize that the same depth in data availability in the Military is not often the case for civilian government agencies. Others fail to cope with intangible factors of the human stripe. Many times it becomes a case of "fools rushing in where brave men fear to tread." All OR men must spend the necessary time to know as much about their organization and work environment as they can.

How To Get An OR Program Started . . .

Most organizations begin with a team of two or three persons, and, as the work becomes accepted, increase the size of the team. A few worthwhile rules the public administrator can use in directing a new program are:

(1) Make a modest start with a one- or two-man team.

(2) Have the OR'ers work on short-range projects at first that can show immediate successful results.

(3) Don't worry at the beginning about having OR report directly to the director of the organization — an echelon or two below the director won't hurt at the start.

(4) Hitch your OR star to a going concern whenever possible such as the Controller or the Systems, or Industrial Engineering Department.

(5) Be a little modest on putting yourself on record as to what OR can do for the organization. Then you don't have to apologize later for unfulfilled promises!

(6) Don't try to overwhelm senior officials by having your OR experts display all their wares in the first application, unless needed. Only use those tools that will do the job in the simplest way.

(7) Keep the OR people informed at all times of what the intentions of your superiors are . . . first, what they want to know, and secondly, what their goals are . . .

Locating The Right Kind Of Savvy . . .

Who are the Operations Researches?

Some are professional engineers, but mathematicians and statisticians play a prominent part in OR. Next in importance are physical and biological scientists. Economists, and sometimes psychologists, participate in OR studies.

The common-bond has been a background in research, for this experience seems to be the most useful for operations research, probably because these disciplines draw heavily upon theoretical constructs or models.

An operations researcher worth his salt must exercise competence over a wide-range of scientific disciplines. In mathematics, for example, he would have to be on top of probability theory, statistics, calculus, and differential equations.

After picking an OR leader, the public administrator should back him up with individuals thoroughly acquainted with all phases of organizational operations, even assigning one of the systems and procedures experts to work with him. This kind of team-mix stresses a much-needed practical approach rather than a theoretical one.

An OR candidate should have these qualifications:

(1) Fairly mature, with possibly five or more years of professional experience in his fields of training.

(2) Ambition and an appetite for OR work.

(3) A broad-gauge viewpoint of things.

(4) Better-than-average mathematical skill, and the ability to show results in quantitative form.

(5) Ability to establish rapport, or to be at ease, with those with whom he works and to convince them that he knows what he is doing.

(6) Forcefulness and clarity in expressing himself in writing or in speech, in order to "sell the ideas."

(7) Resourcefulness to work independently and with a minimal amount of support.

(8) Willingness to go anywhere at any time, and to do anything ethical.

(9) And, *imagination* — perhaps *the most desirable attribute* needed in an OR expert.

Positioning OR In The Organization . . .

Most staff functions feel that they're big and important enough to report directly to the senior official of the organization. A few do!

But with OR, the trend in government is for this function to report to the director or perhaps deputy director of an organization.

It's not absolutely necessary to have your own OR group report to the organization director. What is important is that the function has (1) a sponsor or "a friend in court", and (2) a position in the hierarchy to allow it to have ready access to the data which will enable it to look at problems in their full dimensions.

If is very essential that the OR function reports sufficiently high enough in the organization so that its status lends it enough backing and prestige, so that it can investigate problems and collect data across functional lines with a minimal amount of bureaucratic interference.

How To Organize For An OR Study . . .

Before an OR study is even begun, a feasibility study should be made to decide whether or not to apply Operations Research techniques at *all!*

Senior officials should make this determination based on facts gathered by personnel other than OR experts. Systems and procedures analysts can be most helpful. This approach will serve as a safeguard against using expensive OR techniques to solve problems which can be worked out utilizing less complex and expensive methods.

Of course, the main difficulty in the solution of any problem is its *identification*. However, once identified, a task force can begin to work on its final solution.

Perhaps the best OR team combination consists of personnel from different specialized fields in the sciences with no set pattern of representation or specific methodology to be used. It is here that the use of systems analysts as team members can help to expand the team's knowledge of the intimate operations of various components of the organization.

For example, it was slow progress for one OR team from Johns Hopkins University, which was making a study of the operations of a Baltimore hospital, until it added a systems man to the team. The final report stated that "No other single administrative step has done more to aid the initial efforts of the research group."

Digging For The Facts . . .

When an OR man analyzes a system he asks these basic questions:

(1) Is the present system necessary?
(2) Can it be improved?
(3) What will future needs be?
(4) Of the available alternative systems, which will fit needs now and in the future?

Selling The OR Proposals . . .

One word of warning. — A public administrator should never let the OR men get so wrapped up in their trade jargon that their reports read something like Einstein's Theory on Relativity. For example, one recent report submitted to senior officers of a government department read:

We don't recommend using a Second-Degree Parabolic Function as it tends to curve too much and becomes highly volatile . . . and especially dangerous when extrapolated too far.

What this meant in Plain English was simply that while a certain trend is all right for a five-quarter forecast, it becomes highly suspect when used to predict events far into the future.

Public administrators would like answers in easy-to-understand layman's language to cover these main points:

(1) How specific is the plan of action?
(2) To what degree is the certainty of the outcome?
(3) Can a decision favoring the recommended course of action be reversed without any loss whatever?
(4) How permanent will the solution be?
(5) Can the recommendation be used again, or in other similar problem areas?

OR reports, if written skillfully, present conclusions which should be self-evident. They should be written *for* the administrator rather than *to* him.

The Pluses Of OR . . .

OR today has already been accepted by many private business organizations as an important management tool. Around the world OR in private industry is being utilized for such applications as (1) locating the optimal path of flight for jets for Swissair in order to cut fuel consumption costs; (2) the minimum amount of life insurance for which a patient need not take a costly medical examination . . . being worked out for a Zurich firm; (3) the problem of mathematically describing and solving the transportation needs of Vienna; (4) in a Duisburg, West German, steel plant, the finding of the optimal sizes of iron sheets according to consumer demand so as to minimize waste because of cutting; and (5) in Munich, for Siemens, a manufacturer of electrical appliances, the use of OR-computer techniques to schedule delivery of hundreds of thousands of electronic parts to customers.

With each passing day, public administrators find more and more applications for OR. Not so long ago, the United States Department of the Navy used OR techniques to assign medical interns. Until OR, interns were often assigned to locations not always in attune with their original choices. OR techniques enabled Navy to allocate medical interns to at least one of the five hospitals to which they requested to be assigned. Highest ranking interns received billets to hospitals high on their selection list. As a result, over-all morale was greatly improved in this critically short field of occupational skills.

Federal agencies in the United States as the National Bureau of Standards and the National Capital Transportation Agency have applied OR to resolving traffic transportation problems. Also, the Department of Agriculture has begun employing OR techniques to resolve personnel management problems.

Finis

The public administrator has the responsibility of recognizing the kind of problems which can be solved by OR. With this knowledge he can delegate to specialists the work of solving these problems more effectively. And — if he doesn't understand OR right now — then he should begin learning about OR as soon as he can.

In his position as an official of the organization the public administrator must explain to those who have the responsibility for Operations Research practices, what the objective is and what must be known in order to realize it.

It's up to the public administrator to give his specialists the maximum amount of information about the direction in which his own thoughts are moving and what is in the back of his mind. On the basis of these details the OR workers can then plan their work with complete scientific and technical detachment. If confidence and frankness do not exist between the public administrator and his OR staff, any work done will be hobbled from the start.

Final responsibility for decision-making cannot be delegated to anyone by the public administrator. Final responsibility for results remains with him. And that's the way it should be. No matter how extensively the data provided by OR analysis, few policy decisions can ever be made without the application of experienced judgment. OR simply provides a quantitative basis to narrow the range of intuition that the public administrator would otherwise have to fall back on for his decision-making.

With OR, decisions rely on Facts — *not* Fancies . . . It's time for OR to take its rightful place as an important tool of management for the public administrator to use to make him a more effective decision-maker.

PERT Controls Budget Preparation

✤ RICHARD P. WAHL

Pert (Program Evaluation and Review Technique) was utilized by the Fairfax County Budget and Research Division last year as a guide for the preparation of the 1964 budget documents. The results were very rewarding.

The Problem

In prior years, the Budget Division has experienced the usual production problem which often faces any budget office: chronic overtime. Factors which contributed to this problem were *omissions* in final summary schedules, *parallel preparation of dependent sections* of the budget, and, most important, *underestimation* of time required to complete various parts of the whole.

These difficulties did not result in production failures. The documents were published as required and were good, meaningful, and useful. But the road to completion was a rough one, and the trip was exhausting.

Prior to the 1964 budget cycle, the Budget Division had an additional problem. Much of its staff had changed, and the new employees were inexperienced. Moreover, management had determined to produce the budget documents in a shorter period of time than had previously been allotted.

In an effort to improve the internal operations of the office, the Budget Division decided to implement the PERT technique. Particular emphasis was given to program planning. This emphasis was extremely beneficial.

Results

What results did Fairfax County derive from the utilization of PERT techniques?

First, by giving careful attention to the program planning stage, it was possible to develop accurate time estimates. This was because each activity of the entire program was analyzed in detail, and therefore *all* of the many minor parts of the entire program were judiciously considered. It is apparent now that the improvement in time estimates was due almost entirely to the fact that *all* of the activities were considered.

It was possible to adhere to the established schedule. Previously, there was one deadline — publication date. With PERT, many deadlines were developed, and it was possible, therefore, to measure progress during the entire work cycle. Reference to the PERT charts enabled the staff to determine whether the events noted were being completed on schedule. If not, overtime was authorized immediately to put the program back on schedule. Overtime was used when needed, not concentrated in a furious flurry at deadline time. Although overtime was authorized from time to time throughout the entire cycle, the amounts were small and added up to less than had been required in previous years.

"PERT Controls Budget Preparation," by Richard P. Wahl, reprinted by permission of the International City Managers Association from *Public Management* (February, 1964), pp. 29–33.

Periodic review of progress has a two-fold result: (1) trouble spots are discovered early; (2) corrective management action is prescribed early. In Fairfax County some problem areas were detected as much as one month earlier than had been the experience in previous years.

The effect of PERT on the new staff was astonishing. A new, inexperienced staff actually required less direct supervision than had been the previous experienced. The PERT charts were available to the staff, and it was easy for them to determine which events had been accomplished and which events were next scheduled for completion. The staff was able to act independently through many phases of the work without the problems of omission or parallel preparation cropping up. The staff followed the charts — the charts prevented omissions; the charts kept the work flowing in a smooth, orderly, logical fashion.

The network charts used by Fairfax County showed management which events had been completed, and they also showed management by whom the events had been completed. Therefore, management was able not only to prescribe corrective action when necessary but also to have a complete measure of individual productivity. Similarly the members of the work force were able to measure their own output in relation to the group. The experience of the Fairfax County staff was such that the less productive members strove to improve output, and the more productive members strove to maintain their position of excellence. It was not an expected result, but the PERT charts introduced a very desirable atmosphere of constructive competition.

Fairfax County considers its PERT charts for the 1964 budget cycle to be a "minimum procedures manual." The events, activities, and work flow have been documented: to be sure, the documentation lacks narrative explanation, but the essentials are available for reference. In fact, the PERT charts will be used as the prime basis for developing a formal procedures manual.

Finally, the PERT charts provide a complete history of what happened. They have provided a wealth of information which was useful during the program planning phase of the 1965 budget cycle. Areas which were trouble spots last year were very carefully analyzed this year. The new revised PERT charts which are now being used are expected to be better tools than last year's.

What Is PERT?

PERT was the selected tool for success. What is the nature of this tool? PERT is a technique of logically presenting an illustrated statement of a job to be done. It involves preparation of detailed documentation of the various parts of a job. The principles are simple and involve three phases: (1) program planning, (2) periodic evaluation of progress, and (3) management action.

First, the objectives of the program must be defined. What is to be done? Second, it is necessary to state how the program is to be accomplished. It is absolutely essential to begin the program planning phase of the PERT system well in advance of the time when work is actually begun. To develop a logical arrangement of steps, PERT uses three basic planning elements: events, activities, and networks.

Events. These are occurrences or results. They represent measurable points of progress. Events are described by such words as complete, issue, begin, approve.

Activities. These are actions. They are described by such words as design, develop, prepare, transmit. Three types of activities are considered: (1) tasks involving the work of people, (2) information being transmitted, and (3) constraints imposed on the completion of other events in other parts of the total plan. A constraint serves the purpose of informing the work force that event B cannot be completed until event A is complete. Also, work cannot be started on events following B until A is complete.

Networks. These are illustrations which show the logical path or flow of work to be accomplished. A network drawing shows the interrelation of the events and activities, the direction of work flow, and the timetable upon which the work is scheduled. The network drawing may also include provisions for showing that work has been completed, and by whom. (Portions of the Fairfax County network chart are shown in the illustration below.)

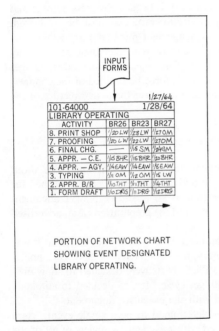

PORTION OF NETWORK CHART
SHOWING EVENT DESIGNATED
LIBRARY OPERATING.

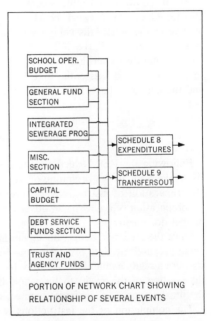

PORTION OF NETWORK CHART SHOWING
RELATIONSHIP OF SEVERAL EVENTS

Portion of Network Chart, Fairfax County, Virginia

The network is first drawn to indicate the events, activities, and work flow. The timetable aspects are not initially considered. After the network is drawn, it must be analyzed and reviewed to ensure that it depicts a logical representation of the work project. If necessary, corrections or changes must be introduced and the network chart revised so that it really reflects the way in which the work project will be accomplished.

Timetable. Having illustrated the job, the time-estimating portion of the program planning phase begins. In turn, each activity is analyzed and a time estimate is assigned. PERT uses three estimates: optimistic time, most likely time, and pessimistic time. Estimates should not consider the possibility of overtime and should be based on the standard work week.

Using the three estimates, the predicted time is then computed. Predicted time is developed by adding the optimistic time, plus four times the most likely time, plus the pessimistic time, and then dividing this sum by six. Predicted times for each activity are used in developing the timetable or schedule.

The timetable should be developed by first determining the final completion date for the entire work project. Working backwards from this date, the predicted times for each activity must be subtracted from the final completion date. Thus, scheduled completion dates for all the intermediate events can be established.

Working backwards in this fashion, it may become apparent that there is not sufficient time available for certain events to be completed on schedule. When this happens, management must make provisions to shorten the predicted time for the affected activities. This may be done by allowing for scheduled overtime, increasing manpower, or reducing the workload by revising the requirements of the activity.

At this point, the schedule is complete, and work is begun. Progress is measured and noted on the network chart, and periodically progress must be evaluated. Whenever the work falls behind schedule, management must step in to take corrective action. Similarly, if the work gets ahead of schedule, management may wish to modify the program. In any case, when management introduces changes to the program, it is essential that the entire work force be notified of the changes, and the network charts must be kept up to date to reflect the actual picture of the program.

Fairfax County Procedure

Following the PERT rules, the staff entered the program planning stage about six weeks prior to the beginning of work. Program objectives were established for (1) preparation of instructions, (2) preparation of an executive budget document (3) preparation of a newspaper advertisement, and (4) preparation of an advertised budget document.

Since the executive budget document had been developed to the point that it was being prepared on data processing machinery, the documentation and work analysis were already available. Therefore the PERT charts were designed to show only the relation of this event to the whole budget cycle. It was decided to eliminate the illustration of the activities connected with the executive document.

The completion of the instructions was determined to be a single event. As a basis for developing the activities associated with this event, a review of all of the forms to be used by the submitting agencies was instituted. This review enabled the staff to estimate the time required to write instructions concerning each form. Also, the staff estimated the time required to prepare a "sample agency budget" which was presented on facsimiles of the forms involved.

The major effort, then, with regard to PERT development was devoted to the definition of the newspaper advertisement and the advertised document. Analysis showed that the newspaper advertisement was actually a shorthand version of the advertised document, and therefore program planning was concentrated on the analysis of the advertised budget document itself.

A starting point for analysis was determined to be a review of the table of contents of the previous budget. This review revealed that each entry in the table of contents logically presented itself as an event: the completion of each entry became a measurable point of progress. Constraints on various events were determined by further analyzing the table of contents entries. For example, it became obvious that "Part I, Summary Schedules and Charts, All Funds" was a series of events related to the completion of almost all the other events associated with the entire budget.

Similarly, "Part II, Summary Schedules and Charts, The General Fund" was constrained, in part, to the completion of "Part III, Detailed Budgets, The General Fund." However, other parts of the document were seen to be composed of events which were entirely independent of any other event. Thus it was possible to determine which events could be processed in parallel without fear of later facing the problem of omissions. For example, work could be carried out on "Part VIII, Trust and Agency Funds" simultaneously with work on "Part V, Integrated Sewerage Program and Sanitation Funds."

This kind of analysis enabled the staff to develop a network chart which had the effect of constraining the activities when they were dependent on each other but allowed the staff to compress the calendar schedule where parallel activities could be permitted.

Pursuing the analysis further, the various activities involved with the completion of a particular event were isolated and named. As an example, an event designated "Schedule 13 — County Library Operating" was seen to consist of three activities: (1) completion of a Fund Statement, Form BR 27, (2) completion of a Performance Data Sheet, Form BR 26, and (3) completion of a Summary and Narrative Sheet, Form BR 23.

Final analysis then related the individual steps which had to be performed by the staff to accomplish the various activities. All of the input forms from the submitting agencies were reviewed; time was set aside for manual preparation of the staff-prepared forms, and the typing, proofreading, and checking associated therewith; and time was allotted to the investigative procedures which the staff could expect to perform.

Although the foregoing may appear to be extremely complicated, detailed, and very time-consuming, it was not actually so. This is because the analysis showed that there were a great many similar, indeed identical, activities associated with many of the events. Thus an analysis of one event often provided the staff with a guide for another event. Therefore the only planning involved for a great number of events was to make the time estimates according to a "model" analysis of those events.

The network chart prepared by the staff was drawn so that it could be viewed from a distance and thus both the staff and management could quickly ascertain the total picture of work in progress. In all, this network chart reflected the logical relation of over 1,200 activities associated with the development of the work program. One year's experience has shown that such a network chart is a most practical and easy-to-use guide. The chart was referred to constantly by both the staff and management.

At the outset, it was debated as to whether space should be provided for the staff to post their initials to signify that an activity had been completed. Experience shows that this feature is most desirable. By requiring the staff to go up to the chart to post progress, one builds into the system an automatic review process. Each member of the staff can see what is happening, and daily his contributions to the total effort are displayed for all to see.

Conclusion

The utilization of the PERT technique as a guide in the preparation of Fairfax County's 1964 budget was a sound management decision. The results were rewarding, and the task was accomplished better than ever before. The product was accurate and completed on schedule, but the effort was ordered, measured, and precise. The workflow was leveled over the period, and crises were minimized.

PERT provided a number of benefits: measurable progress, adherence to schedule, reduced overtime, elimination of omission, reduced elapsed time, *esprit de corps*, a wealth of historical information, and a "minimum procedures manual."

However, all of these benefits are related to something which PERT imposes which may often be what is most needed in any organization: *discipline*. The requirements of the PERT technique are such that the work and workers both become disciplined. The efforts become orderly, logical, precise. The planning is careful and complete, the requirements are clearly documented, progress is methodically measured and reviewed, corrective action is provided if necessary and when necessary, and the total effort is kept in clear perspective.

Policy Decisions and EDP Systems in the Federal Government ❖ Frank W. Reilly

The last ten years have witnessed the expansion of electronic data processing technology from a few digital computers and a handful of people to more than 10,000 digital computing systems and hundreds of thousands of trained personnel. The federal government started the "electronic rush" of the fifties with installation of the first two general purpose computers and ended the decade with nearly 1,000. Direct EDP employment in government rose from less than a hundred in 1951 to more than 34,000 today. Federal EDP costs totaled $497 million in 1961 and all projections foresee continued increases in all cost areas. However intriguing these statistics are, the real importance of this tremendous growth is found in what government agencies have done with these quantities of men, equipment, and dollars.

Applications: Administration, Program Area, and Scientific and Engineering

An analysis of government EDP applications (excluding tactical military) reveals three broad categories: administrative activities, program areas, and scientific and engineering applications.

The two most popular administrative applications for computers have been payroll and logistics. There is hardly a self-respecting federal agency that does not have its payroll on a computer or else has firm plans to put it on. Generally these have been rather straight-forward payroll computations without integrated personnel, budgeting, and cost accounting programs. In the logistical and supply areas, data processing systems have provided singular benefits by improving inventory control practices, insuring planned procurement, and making possible a common cataloging for all government agencies.

Reprinted from the *Public Administration Review*, the journal of the American Society for Public Administration, Vol. XXII, No. 3, 1962, pp. 130–133, by permission of the publisher.

Probably the best known federal data processing activities are in some of the major program areas. Census enumeration and demographic analysis, Social Security record-keeping, and Treasury check disbursement and reconciliation are examples of EDP in large-scale clerical operations. The Labor Department relies on computers to handle all its statistics as does the Veterans Administration to operate its large insurance activity.

The scientific applications which have occurred in this first decade range from the spectacular to the prosaic. Rocketry and space exploration have relied upon digital computers for design, test simulation, and operation of their systems to an extent incomprehensible to most of us. Can anyone conceive of a missile shot or a space probe happening without the use of the most sophisticated data processing systems? The research and development of nuclear energy is another program literally dependent on EDP. Weather forecasting may be more prosaic than space shots, but what if they learn how to modify climates? The earth sciences are using EDP in areas of hydrology, geology, and geodesy. Much of this information is useful in applied fields such as highway engineering. The life sciences are just beginning to use EDP in dynamic situations. They have tended toward reliance upon brute force statistical analysis for their problem solving in the past.

The First Decade's Experience

I can very glibly sum up our first decade of experience by saying that administrative and scientific applications have been mostly single shot approaches which have been limited to a restricted sphere of work, be it payroll, cut and fill highway computations, or an epidemiological statistical survey. The use of EDP in program areas has tended to be broader in concept and context since this type of application must be concerned with the total effect upon an agency's functional performance.

From all of this, we have learned a great deal — we have learned how to use machines; we have trained a large number of people (for industry to hire); and we have sold most of our bosses in both the executive and legislative branches on the importance of EDP. But when the historians look back upon this first decade, I think they will note as our greatest achievement the development of the systems concept; the realization that no problem is an "island unto itself," but that most activities are related to one or more programs in a particular agency, in a particular substantive field within the government, or even within a society.

The Second Decade of EDP

As we begin the next decade, we know that the number of digital computing systems, personnel, and costs are likely to triple by 1971. When I look at my own agency, the Post Office Department, and see the extensive areas where EDP can serve management and more importantly our employees and the postal patron, I am overwhelmed by the enormity of the job that lies before us. In this second ten years, I believe the big emphasis is going to be on the broad technology of systems data processing rather than just the digital computer.

Source data automation, particularly character scanning, is going to be *very* big. Our primitive information retrieval systems will progress both in terms of electronic machines and the science of knowing what data to store, how to index it, and how and when to retrieve it. Data transmission has begun a growth curve which the president of AT&T predicts will result in 1970 data transmission revenues equal to its voice transmission income. Source data automation devices will talk to computers, computers will talk to other computers, and we will probably end the decade with a case of *datarrhea* just as we began it with printed logorrhea on tab sheets. Our main hope in avoiding this "bit" verbosity and designing systems rationally and intelligently is the use of simulation techniques. If operations research was the magic word in the fifties (and a word which never became flesh), then simulation promises to provide answers to problems before the problems actually occur. I believe all major integrated systems of the future, be they military, scientific, program, or administrative, will be designed and tested through the use of these model building-solution approximation techniques. They promise to help us better analyze our problems, to test the solutions we propose, and to determine optimum design features.

"Organism Management"

I believe the 1960's will be characterized by total management information systems, or what I call *Organism Management*. I would define this as relating pertinent data from all components of an organism into a system which provides management with decision-capable information. In this context *Organism* can be conceived as broadly as you desire. It can be a function within one organization, it can be a series of functions within the same organization, it can be the relationships of all of these functions within this organization to another organization, or finally it can be the interrelationships of functions between organizations both private and public. However, this description is too pedantic. If I relate its possible use, the term should have more meaning.

I mentioned earlier that the use of EDP in medical applications has just begun. This area of investigation promises many benefits to mankind. For example, we know that doctors using computers for electrocardiogram analysis can detect certain heart abnormalities with greater proficiency than the average physician. Other bodily functions lend themselves to physical and chemical measurement and analysis, including brain waves, the respiratory system, blood pressure, and temperature systems. As scientists develop the ability to collate the "soft" data, or the patient's history and symptoms, with this more objective data, their techniques will provide physicians with the means to do a better job of diagnosing the *total* patient. This then is an example of *Organism Management*. Now if Medical Science can devise a system for an individual patient, then it is logical to assume that medical information systems will eventually include clinical management of a patient throughout his hospital stay by the means or the use of patient data automation systems. The clinical data can also be accumulated by information storage and retrieval techniques for research purposes. Paralleling this will be the use of data processing systems for all the administrative activities of a hospital, including admissions, accounting, dietetics, procurement, and supply. All areas of medicine — research, clinical, and administrative — appear to be adaptable to electronic data processing systems.

Natural Resources Illustration

I have given *Organism Management* a biological and medical context in recognition of the usual meaning of the term organism. Now I would like to cite an example of its application in the possible management of an extensive federal program, natural resources.

The 1948 Hoover Commission strongly recommended the creation of a Department of Natural Resources. The intervening fourteen years have not brought this recommendation much closer to fruition. I like to think we may arrive at a stage in the near future where the use of electronic data processing will make such a department not only possible, but really desirable. Let me illustrate what could be done for one kind of a natural resource to buttress my argument.

Water is one of our most precious resources. Without diversion of distant rivers, Arizona and Southern California would be sparsely populated winter spas. Water first occurs in rainfall which the Weather Bureau predicts with greater accuracy daily. Perhaps man may eventually influence climate and cause precipitation where needed through a better understanding of the weather phenomena via simulation techniques. Once rain occurs, it falls to the jurisdiction of a number of government agencies. The Corps of Engineers controls it to prevent floods and generate electric power. The Interior Department has many water responsibilities, including surface and ground water analysis and research by the Geological Survey; irrigation, recreation, and flood control by the Bureau of Reclamation; and power production by Reclamation, Bonneville Power Administration, and South Eastern Power Administration. Various bureaus in the Agriculture Department also are vitally concerned with water: the Forest Service for trees and pastures, Commodity Stabilization Service for crop planning and marketing, and the Soil Conservation Service for soil protection.

From the time water occurs as a rain prediction by the Weather Bureau until it is consumed by its various users, it comes under the jurisdiction of the Commerce Department, the Department of Defence, the Department of Interior, and the Agriculture Department, just to mention some of the major agencies involved. Certainly, an integrated water source data system would provide a common base for all these agencies to pursue a cohesive water development program. This involves more than just the simple matter of avoiding duplicate effort in data accumulation. What the national water program requires is a network analysis which can simulate the total effect of the occurrence and use of this resource. The design of this data processing system would be the beginning of *Organism Management* in natural resources. This could lead top management in government to seriously look at the recommendations to form the Department of Natural Resources. We need better organization of our resource activities than the present arrangement of conflicting and overlapping functions performed by various bureaus and agencies. The present disorganization has proliferated into counterpart creations in state and local government. Whatever improvements occur at the Federal level should have corresponding responses throughout our governmental structure.

The Challenge to Management

Similar examples for other major nationwide activities could be cited, but I trust my point has been made. I would like to conclude by quoting an excerpt from an article by F. T. McClure in the March 9, 1962, issue of *Science Magazine* entitled "Rockets, Resonance, and Physical Chemistry":

It seems to me that if anything characterizes our times it is the necessity of facing the problems which arise in closely coupled systems. Systems may be broken into components which may be studied independently. Yet the system may exhibit behavior which is by no means the simple sum of the behaviors of the components.

The components acting in unison produce phenomena which might not have been expected from studies of them individually.

Integrated machine data processing systems are frequently cited as models of a well-designed EDP system. This is not the criteria for a closely coupled system. The mere physical connection of automatic source data devices via data transmission to a digital computer and its hi-speed printer may only produce what has been called "instant inefficiency." The challenge to management in the federal government is to free itself of preconceptions at the policy level *before* calling in the data processing fraternity to design these advanced systems. An illustration of such a policy determination would be the deceptively simple decision to cycle check payment days for large disbursing programs (e.g., Social Security and Veterans Administration). Converting from a once monthly payment date to a twenty-day payment frequency can immediately save millions of dollars in interest just by reducing the cash balance required for any one day. In addition, this system makes for more even check preparation work load by Treasury and it helps the Post Office Department flatten the mail peak at the first of the month. Conversely, the Natural Resource Program is an example of systems change of great complexity and extensive consequence. But the significant fact in both cases is the need to look at the whole function and not just a part of it. Successful EDP in this decade will be a result of the skillful use and our technical resources by perceptive and courageous management.

5

Personnel Administration

The development of a "neutral" career service to insure competence and expertise was the objective of early civil service advocates and still remains in the minds of some as the ultimate objective of a career merit system. In order to maintain the system, appointment was to be based on merit rather than on political spoils, employees were to have tenure or security in their jobs, and were to refrain from participation in partisan political activity.

Like the rest of society, government has changed and become more complex. The clerical and custodial jobs which once occupied most members of the civil service now form only a small part of their work. Government now employs persons from almost every known profession, occupation, and field of specialization, and their various duties are no longer so plain and simple than men of intelligence can quickly learn to perform them without previous background and training.

Personnel administration has followed a pattern of decentralization. The Civil Service Commission, once regarded as a bulwark against assault on the merit system, now assists the agencies to administer their own personnel programs. Personnel administration is now regarded as part of line management, and the Civil Service Commission functions as a major staff agency to assist and guide the agencies in the personnel and related fields.

Personnel administration in recent years has placed emphasis on the employee as an individual, a member of a work group, and as one employed in an organization that can be regarded as a social institution. Increasing numbers of employees have affiliated with employee organizations the better to be able to deal with management and to maintain some independent bargaining power of their own.

Government faces the problem of recruiting and holding capable and skilled people in the public service. The professional satisfaction and rewards which a government career system can offer, in comparison to other alternatives in society, are indicators of the kind of civil servants government will have to work with.

Civil Service and Managing Work:
Some Unintended Consequences

✤ ROBERT T. GOLEMBIEWSKI

Nature seldom allows us to get what we wish without paying her price. This truism is commonly illustrated by the delicate balance in animal life which often cannot be disturbed to satisfy man's wants (e.g., for fox hunting) without demanding of man in return (e.g., by increases in the rabbit population and in crop damage).

The several civil service systems in this country also illustrate this bittersweet combination of intended and unintended consequences. The argument here will not go to the extreme of one observer, in whose judgment the United States Civil Service Commission was the single greatest obstacle to the successful waging of World War II. Rather, the focus here will be upon several characteristics of our civil service systems that have as presumably unintended consequences an increase in the burdens of managing work. For the most part, the analysis of management problems will derive from the research literature dealing with behavior in organizations, a field of study presently seething with activity.

I. The Goal-Matrix of Our Civil
Service Movement

The nature of these unintended consequences is suggested by the matrix of goals, or purposes, underlying our civil service movement. The primary goal, of course, was the separation of the management of public work from party patronage. Within this overriding goal, Sayre has noted three early subsidiary purposes of our public personnel systems:

1. the guarantee of equal treatment of all employees and all applicants for employment;
2. the application of the logic (or theory) and methods of "scientific management"; and
3. the development of a public career service.

These goals define the field of my present effort. Detailed analysis later will demonstrate the significance for the management of work of the unintended consequences which derive from the ways adopted to achieve these purposes. I take this opportunity to suggest the general nature of these consequences.

Consider first the general tethers on the management of work implicit in the historical pursuit of the three purposes listed. The guarantee of equal treatment, to begin with, has never quite made peace with the managerially convenient notion that unequal contributions demand unequal reward. To take a recent and characteristic example, the teachers' union in Illinois has lately expressed violent opposition to a proposal for merit pay increases based upon performance. This opposition

"Civil Service and Managing Work: Some Unintended Consequences," by Robert T. Golembiewski, reprinted by permission of the author and the American Political Science Association from *American Political Science Review* (December, 1962), pp. 961–973.

goes deeper than the convenience of seniority or of hours of graduate study as objective criteria for pay increases and far deeper than the blatant protectionism of hacks. However lofty the motives, their effect is clear. In practice, the struggle toward the "equal treatment" goal virtually forced public personnel systems into a monumental preoccupation with technique and mechanics. As Sayre concluded:

Its main effect has been to move personnel administration, in the words of Gordon Clapp, "into the cold objective atmosphere of tests, scores, weighted indices, and split-digit rankings" so completely that "these technical trappings have become symbols of the merit system."

The management of work pays a stiff price for such technical elegance. Work is notoriously insensitive to such easy capture, and the most subtly contrived managerial rewards and punishments might be frustrated by an awkward distribution of test scores. Moreover, these technical trappings put powerful weapons into the hands of "staff" people. That more than one "line" manager has been stymied by one of these "split-digit rankings" without accepting the results as divinely ordained, moreover, does nothing to lessen the often intense jurisdictional tugs-of-war encouraged by the traditional "line-staff" distinction. These tensions are apt to be increased by the time lag inherent in centralized administrative systems, and public personnel systems are usually operated centrally.

The logic and methods of "scientific management," second, tended to condemn managers to a treadmill even as it aided them. Scientific management was imported from the "practical" world of business where its impact was enormous. But the impact was not one-way. Thus there is no denying the useful revolution in viewing work that the methods of scientific management sparked. However, as recent research particularly demonstrates, the assumptions in the logic (or theory) of scientific management concerning man and his work were mechanistic caricatures. Consequently, the manager tended to be less effective in direct relation to the degree that he patterned his behavior on the logic of the approach. That is, the reasonable methods of scientific management often were guided by an inadequate theory. Consequently, the usefulness of engineering a task with the methods of scientific management must be differentiated sharply from the usefulness of organizing a task's component sequential steps in terms of the theory of scientific management.

The establishment of a public career service, third, also tended to have unintended and unfavorable consequences which counterbalanced the favorable and intended consequences. As Sayre put it,

Stated in its most positive terms, this objective represents an effort to provide the conditions of work which will attract and hold a public service of optimum talents. In its negative aspects, the goal has been translated into an elaborate system of protectionism. In the area of methodology the negative connotations have slowly but surely won the dominant position. . . .

Such protectionism, of course, often would bind the manager severely even as it safeguarded him (and his subordinates) from arbitrary removal.

In sum, then, striving toward the purposes of the civil service movement had its general costs. Three more specific sets of restrictions that burden the management of work in our civil service systems will concern us presently.

These costs of our civil service systems, however, must be kept in perspective. Today we can profit from hindsight and a sophisticated research literature. The efforts to achieve the separation of the civil service from patronage, in contrast, came before enough was known about the conceptual and operational problems of the description of organization, personality, or "position" to preclude an uncomplicated Tinker Toy approach to all three of these elements of personnel administration. That is, simple assumptions took the place of an understanding of empirical phenomena which were at least more complex and often essentially different from the assumptions.

Consequently, the early approach to public personnel administration is understandable, if inadequate. The compulsions of life could not wait on the scientific explanation of the universe. However, necessity should not be suffered to be a virtue, lest the original simplistic assumptions become too deeply buried under a specialized literature. Students of public personnel administration, fortunately, have done considerable self-critical work of late. The determined, if preliminary, efforts since World War II to outgrow its early biases are a leading feature of the reorientation currently underway in public administration.

II. Supervisory Power and Civil Service

Perhaps the most rewarding clue to supervisory effectiveness in recent research exploits the "power" concept. "Power" refers, in general, to the ability to control the job environment. Getting recommendations for promotion accepted, for example, indicates that a supervisor has relatively high power. "Power" thus conceptually complements "authority," which refers to the degree to which the formal organization legitimates a supervisor's control of the job environment. Typically, all supervisors at the same level monitoring similar operations have similar authority; and typically, these supervisors will differ in their power.

Power seems to be related to effective supervisory performance, whether it is exercised upwards, as influence with superiors, or downwards, as control of the specific job site. Pelz, for example, studied some fifty measures of supervisory practices and attitudes without finding any marked correlations with employee morale and attitudes. When the influence of a supervisor with his superior was specified, however, rather sharp differences were observed. High supervisory power was associated with effective performance. Consequently, as Likert concluded, a supervisor must be an effective subordinate as well as an effective superior. Otherwise, reasonably, a supervisor cannot be expected to influence his subordinates consistently.

Similarly, power expressed as control of the job site is associated with effective performance. Likert provides much supporting data. A comparison between the top third and the bottom third of departments (ranked in terms of productivity) is particularly relevant here. Personnel in the "top" departments, in contrast with the "bottom" departments, uniformly attributed greater influence over "what goes on in your department" to these four sources: higher management; plant management; department manager; and the workers themselves. Moreover, the "top" departments also desired that greater influence be exercised by all four sources than did the "bottom" departments. Significantly, the greatest differences between the "top" and "bottom" departments are in the power attributed to department managers (their primary supervisors) and in the power the men desired that department managers exercise. These are reasonable results. A low-power supervisor has little leverage for motivating his men *via* his control over the job site. That is, the men have little reason to take him seriously.

If the reasons for the importance of supervisory power to effective performance seem clear enough, our civil service systems do little to ease the burdens of managing work *via* increases in supervisory power. This is particularly lamentable because much evidence suggests that the "power" variable may be influenced substantially by the design of the job, by the organization structure (of which more later), and by training. The supervisor's personality, in short, does not appear to be the crucial (or major) factor in determining power.

Although only empirical research can establish the point definitely, there seems ample evidence of this failure of civil service systems to respond to the need to facilitate the management of work by increasing supervisory power. On the broadest level, the first and third primary goals of the civil service movement certainly do not encourage supervisory power; and (as will be demonstrated) the application of the logic and methods of scientific management has the same effect.

To become more specific, these limitations on supervisory power have many practical impacts. For example, first-line supervisors seem to have less control over hiring and firing than their counterparts in business. The difficulty in business organizations of firing or reductions-in-force need not be underplayed, but the elaborate review procedures and the novel "bumping" arrangements often found in our civil service systems probably admit of less flexibility in public agencies even on the part of officials at relatively high organizational levels. Raw turnover ratios seem to support this position. Similarly, the emphasis upon seniority in promotions and pay increases in the public service plus the failures of supervisory rating of employee performance — both common in our civil service systems — suggest that the environment in public agencies has not been conducive to the general heightening of supervisory power.

. . . .

III. Job Design and Civil Service

Similarly, our civil service systems tend to limit the potential for increasing managerial effectiveness implicit in job design. The second primary goal noted above is the chief culprit, with strong support from the goal of "equal treatment." Their interaction in increasing managerial burdens can be illustrated in two ways, by considering specific job content, and by considering the place of the job in the broad organization structure.

In its doctrine about simplifying job content, particularly, the logic of scientific management makes difficulties for managing work effectively. As in industry, at low organization levels, the process of routinization often has been carried too far in the public service. The effects of "job enlargement" on employee performance, at least in business concerns, suggest the contribution to effective management that may be gained by adding content to a worker's responsibilities. This may be accomplished by increasing the scope of jobs or by rotating individuals through several jobs. The crucial factor does not seem to be the number of task-elements given to an individual or the complexity of these elements. Patently, a job could become too complex. Rather, the significant point seems to be that various techniques of job enlargement, when they work, work because they increase the worker's control over his job environment. Hence the success of plans for increasing the employee's control over factors which are not in his flow of work, such as that often called "bottom-up management."

The effects of "job enlargement" may be explained in terms of the earlier analysis. In Likert's study, as already noted, employees in high-producing units felt that they themselves exercised and desired more power over their work than did individuals in low-producing units. This is consistent with the favorable effects on output commonly reported in the "job enlargement" literature, while it suggests an apparent paradox. Note that Hi-Pro units ranked themselves *and* three levels of supervisors as higher on "power" than did Lo-Pro units. This might seem curious, but only if one assumes that there is only so much "power" to be had, so that what superiors gain subordinates must lose. The fact seems to be, on the contrary, that a high-power supervisor can afford to (and usually does) allow his subordinates to exercise greater power also. A low-power supervisor is in such an insecure position that he can seldom bring himself to be so generous. The real paradox, then, is that the apparently most straightforward way of adding to one's power is often the most direct way of reducing it. The common mechanical conceptions of organized activity implicit in scientific management discourage such thinking.

The often marked consequences of job enlargement may be illustrated briefly. Machine operations in an industrial concern, for example, had been plagued by an array of difficulties: productivity and quality were falling; and tension between operators and inspectors was growing. The crucial factor was that the tool in this particular operation, when dulled to a certain point, would suddenly begin producing pieces which did not meet specifications. Inspectors were not always able to spot such sudden deteriorations in the product quickly, and operators (inspection not being *their* job) did not always cease work even when the quality was obviously unacceptable. Inspection reports helped little when they did come, the operators marking them down as "ancient history." The solution was easy. Simple gauges were given to operators to make periodic checks on their production, and the operators were allowed to decide when it was necessary to resharpen their cutting tools. The consequences: runs of defective products became shorter and less frequent; the nagging tension between inspectors and operators was reduced; and output zoomed.

Examples need not be confined to industrial operations. In a paperwork operation, similarly, a rather simple change increased output by 30 per cent and reduced employee turnover by 70 per cent.

Although the design of the job could be an important means of reducing the problems of managing work, however, our civil service systems do not encourage the exploitation of such techniques as job enlargement. Consider only one feature which has an inhibiting effect, the very detailed job descriptions common in the public service. That these are an important part of the mechanisms for guaranteeing equal treatment of employees and for developing a career service does little to encourage flexibility in job design. Employee unions and the civil service commission staff can make much of these job descriptions, even in cases in which employees solidly favor changes of a job-enlargement sort. The difficulty is not necessarily avoided by job descriptions which conclude: "or other duties the supervisor may designate." Custom, employee unions, and an overprotective civil service commission can void such open-end descriptions.

Perhaps, however, this leans too heavily on personal (and limited) experience. Some administrators no doubt pay little attention to detailed job descriptions, except for such purposes as convincing the civil service commission that an individual deserves a multi-step promotion. And it may be argued that the significant point is not whether detailed job descriptions exist, but whether strong employee unions exist. Even in such cases, however, the detailed job description is part of the institutional framework within which management and union must function.

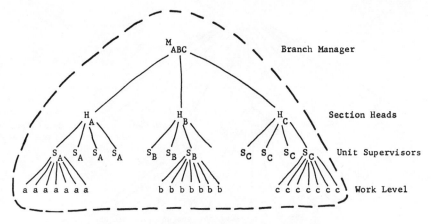

**Figure 1A: Functional (Process)
Organization with Narrow Span of Control**

In determining the place of the job in the broad organizational pattern, our civil service systems also increase the problems of managing work. Consider two characteristics which tend to dominate patterns of organization in the public service, a limited span of control and organization by function or (at lower levels) by process. These characteristics largely derive from the impact of scientific management upon public personnel administration. Analysis of these two characteristics is particularly useful because it demonstrates, among other features, their tendency to reduce supervisory power.

The analysis of these two characteristics is facilitated by some simplified graphics. Figure 1A presents the orthodox organization of functions (or processes) A, B, C — which may be taken to be any components whose integration is required to perform some administrative task — under the condition of a limited span of control. Figure 1B presents the more unorthodox organization by product (or discrete sub-assembly), which permits a far broader span of control.

The functional model, with modest reservations, can be considered *the* pattern for government organizing. This does not do full justice to the diversity of actual organizational arrangements, admittedly. Various factors — size, pressure of work, geography, and the like — have encouraged significant deviations from the functional model. Thus the Justice Department long ago surrendered the fancy of having every government lawyer in the department. The functional model, however, is commonly encountered in practice and it is certainly the most commonly prescribed model in the literature, as in the Hoover Commission's *Report on the General Management of the Executive Branch.*

The following contrast of the functional model with the product model, then, requires that two points be kept in mind. First, the functional model does not guide all public organizing, but it is nonetheless influential. Second, the product model will not always be a feasible alternative, although it often will be. The contrast, that is, has much to recommend it, although hardly everything. Thus, although the analysis may have an either-or flavor, many other factors would serve to soften the contrast in practice and would guide the choice in specific cases of the functional model, the product model, or combinations of the two.

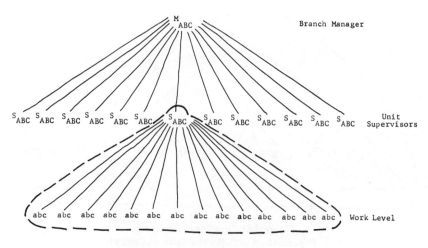

**Figure 1B: (Discrete Sub-Assembly)
Organization with Broad Span of Control**

These simple variations in the organization of jobs in larger structures can have profound consequences for the management of work. In general, the type of structure common in most public agencies (see Figure 1A) incurs substantial costs avoided by the less familiar structure in Figure 1B. These costs derive from three features associated with these two patterns of structure: job enlargement; the size of the "managerial entity"; and supervisory power.

First, to point up the obvious, Figure 1B is based upon job enlargement at all levels. Each employee at the work-level in Figure 1B performs all three components of the task, and each supervisor's responsibilities encompass all three. Figure 1A's emphasis upon routinization limits the scope, and perhaps thereby the effectiveness of the management of work. Of course, there are some limits on the functions or processes (A, B, C, . . .) that may be strung together. In general, however, the limits seem to be very broad indeed.

Second, the "managerial entity" is vastly larger in Figure 1A than in Figure 1B. The size of the managerial entity can have profound consequences. It may appear, for instance, that the structure in Figure 1B puts too much strain on the capacities of management, because of the apparently greater demands it imposes upon the supervisors. In reality, however, structures such as that in Figure 1A often imply greater (and different) demands upon management talent. Figure 1B structures reduce in significant ways the management burden carried by M_{ABC} and the supervisors as well. The difficulties faced by M_{ABC} in structures like that in Figure 1A cause considerable problems for supervisors, for example, by tending to reduce their supervisory power. Many of the problems associated with sizeable organizations, more generally, derive not from the aggregate size of the organization, but from the size of its component managerial entities. Thus the manager in our hypothetical organization in Figure 1A directs the work of 99 employees and encounters the difficulties to be enumerated below; the manager in Figure 1B oversees the work of 195 employees, yet significant problems facing the management of work are reduced.

The "managerial entity" concept warrants further analysis. Worthy defines it in these terms:

The administrative unit can be no smaller than that portion of the organization falling within the jurisdiction of an individual who controls enough elements of the total process to make effective decisions regarding the total process.

A high-level managerial entity might be organized around some total product, for example, water resource development in the Kings River Valley. The processing by each of several competing teams of all categories of mail received by the Government Printing Office, with each team handling all correspondence from writers whose names begin with designated letters of the alphabet, illustrates the kind of discrete sub-assembly around which a low-level managerial entity might be organized.

At whatever level of organization, then, a "managerial entity" contains that parcel of process-components necessary for the performance of some discrete task. The areas enclosed by the heavy dotted lines in the two figures above symbolize "managerial entities." Interpretively, any S_{ABC} in Figure 1B can "get all the way around" our hypothetical administrative task. In Figure 1A, in contrast, only M_{ABC} can do this job. M_{ABC} in Figure 1A has a managerial entity which contains 100 individuals; that of S_{ABC} contains only 15.

Many of the problems in sizeable organizations derive from the failure to restrict the size of the organization's managerial entities. Haire's analogy seems apt in this connection. He suggested the mushrooming problems caused by the growth in the size of organizations *via* the "square-cube law" applied to the story of Jack and the Beanstalk:

... Jack had nothing to fear from the Giant. If he were, as he is pictured, ten times as large as a man and proportioned like one, Jack was perfectly safe. The Giant's mass would be 10^3 or a thousand times a man's, because he was ten times as big in every dimension. However, the cross section of his leg bones would have increased in only two dimensions, and they would be 10^2 or a hundred times as big as a man's. A human bone simply will not support ten times its normal load, and the Giant, in walking, would break his legs and be helpless.

In a similar way, arithmetic increases in the size of the managerial entity seem to generate exponential increases in the problems of the management of work. Meeting these increases in size within the framework of the type of organization structure in Figure 1A does nothing to reduce these difficulties.

This general position can be elaborated. The size of the managerial entity, in sum, is likely to affect such significant features of administration as: the time lag between the perception of a problem and action on it, which influences supervisory power; the style of supervision; the measurement and the motivation of performance; and the training of subordinates.

Patently, first, decisions will tend to be pushed upward in an organization such as that in Figure 1A; for only M_{ABC} oversees all of the components which require integration. As a result, delegation to supervisors is all but restricted to routine matters, that is, those which involve the single component supervised by any supervisor and only that component.

The separation of decision-making from the action level often has significant costs. Overloading upper levels may make time-pressure a very serious factor, the more so if the stakes are high. A shutdown in any of the sections in Figure 1A might cause output to drop as low as zero. The manager, then, is under great pressure to assure that A, B, and C are integrated, and he is likely to exert that pressure downward. This does not encourage upward communication, in turn, which is difficult enough in the "tall" organization described in Figure 1A. (Notice that Figure 1B, with 69 per cent more people, has one less organization level than Figure 1A.) The efforts of the manager to fight the daily battle of integration of the components of his operation and to get the information required for his job, finally, will tend to undercut any efforts by the supervisors to gain high power. The common development of large "staff" units complements this tendency.

In contrast, decisions in Figure 1B organizations would strongly tend to be forced down to the action level, and certainly at least to the level of S_{ABC}. Indeed, M_{ABC} may have no other reasonable alternative, given his broad span of control. Upward communication and supervisory power often will be affected favorably. M_{ABC}, consequently, should be freed from the unremitting pressure of integration implicit in a Figure 1A structure. Downtime at any work station, for example, will not cause difficulty throughout the managerial entity. Output would fall at most by $1/N$. The manager therefore could devote himself to motivating superior performance, to training and counseling, and the like, rather than attempting to eliminate the possibility of error.

These comments on decision-making, second, suggest that the two types of structures encourage different styles of supervision. The structure in Figure 1A encourages "close supervision," i.e., detailed instructions, persistent attempts to direct and observe performance, and the like. The limited span of control, of course, permits this, and the pressure for the integration of the task components may force it. The structure in Figure 1B encourages "general supervision," i.e., monitoring performance in terms of results with considerable freedom for the employee so long as he is performing up to standard. Close supervision of janitors, for example, would require such directions as: "You will sweep from left to right, forty strokes per minute," and correspondingly close checks on performance. General supervision, in contrast, would assume competence and give such instructions as: "Sweep the floors in such time that you are able to get your other work done and so that the floor will reflect x units of light from a refractometer." The refractometer provides the check on performance. Acknowledgedly, this goes a little far. All of the components of general supervision are there, however, especially the measure of performance.

. . . .

IV. Job Description and Civil Service

It says worlds, while it avoids an enormous complexity, to note that our civil service systems typically are based upon a duties classification, as opposed to a rank classification. Public personnel specialists have gone in for a duties classification with a sometimes uncritical zeal. As Nigro explains:

In a duties classification, the beginning point is a detailed analysis of the tasks required in the individual position. In fact, the tendency in the United States has been to make fairly minute investigations of job content.

The emphasis need not be exaggerated, for the specialists have providently refrained from stressing the content of all jobs. The handling of secretarial positions — whose importance is usually measured by secretaries and bosses in terms of what the boss does rather than what the secretary does — is perhaps the most striking illustration of what has been called the "realistic" approach to classification.

But the bias of job description in this country has not moved very far from the classic expression it was given, for example, in the 1932 classification plan for Philadelphia. Nigro called this "one of the best books of specifications on record." It listed twenty individual classes of clerks, for each of which specifications had been developed. Specifications also were stated for thirty additional classes of principal and chief clerks in the various city departments.

The inspirations for this emphasis on job description in our public personnel systems seem clear enough. The logic and methods of scientific management — — which encouraged the view of organization as a "delicate mechanism" of gear-like "positions" whose driveshaft was the line of command — clearly had their influence. Moreover, position classification provides the bases for equal treatment, general formal policies and procedures regarding recruitment, salary, promotions, and the like. Finally, position classification encourages the attempt to group similar jobs into a reasonable number of classes, sub-classes, and so on. This provided a ladder-like framework upon which a permanent career service could be built.

Despite its contribution to achieving the goals of our civil service movement, the American approach to job description has its unintended costs. Some obvious costs will be considered immediately; subsequent analysis will consider one less obvious set of costs in some detail.

Since one product of position classification was to be a manageable number of classes, first, this required a procrustean neglect of distinguishing job character-istics. The position approach, second, became the victim of its own imprecise terms. Consider the common observation that the "position" is the "universal building block of all organizations." The observation has a certain validity, since all organizations contain positions. It tended to mislead the unwary, however, into supposing that "organization" is only a set of positions. The temptation to think of organization as some massive mechanical structure of positions linked by lines of authority was strong, since it apparently served to simplify the problems of personnel work.

The emphasis upon a duties classification, third, implies a substantial rigidity. Consider the difficulties of dealing with the many positions which have a kind of life cycle, with stages that impose varying demands on the incumbent. Developing an administrative role may be a very delicate task, while playing the role thereafter may be child's play. This phenomenon is difficult to accommodate within the framework of most of our public personnel systems. Some adaptations may be made quickly enough. But often it is necessary to waste a "big" man on a job too small for him or to give a "small" man a job too big for him. Similarly, the emphasis upon a duties classification makes it difficult to utilize positions for training purposes without the stretching of a point or two by the position analyst. The traditional question — What does the incumbent do? — is not appropriate for such positions, for he may, in fact, contribute little toward immediate task performance.

The abortive struggles toward a Senior Civil Service, and then a Career Executive Program, for the federal government, reflect the tenacity of the grip of these two types of inflexibilities. For it was intended that the highly mobile and select corps of administrators in such programs would be used in both of the ways alluded to above, that is, as experienced "firefighters" and as trainees getting the "big picture." The rank-in-job bias in our civil service systems played not a little part in the lack of action.

Fourth and finally, the approach *via* a duties classification taken in this country is not the only available one. Indeed, in public administration, it appears that only

Canada and Brazil follow our example closely. Many personnel systems — public and business — emphasize broad and general classes rather than narrow and detailed ones.

. . . .

The question remains, what is significant in describing a task? It is a disarming question. Existing research does not suggest that it has an obvious or an uncomplicated answer. Factor analysis, a sophisticated mathematical technique, perhaps offers the most hope of developing a set of dimensions which will permit us to describe jobs precisely. A technical discussion of factor analysis hardly can be attempted here. In general, however, the technique permits an initial judgment as to the number of independent dimensions necessary to account for the variation in some batch of scores (e.g., in rankings by several analysts of jobs in terms of the discretion they require incumbents to exercise). The technique has been utilized, for example, to isolate the various kinds of intellectual abilities measured by intelligence tests. There is no way to solve such problems *a priori*. Factor analysis, in sum, might well complement and direct the enormous amount of observation that normally goes into developing a duties classification and into keeping it current.

Applications of factor analysis to job description suggest the problems which must be met. The technique, for example, has been applied to the ratings of a very large number of characteristics of various jobs. Existing results do not suggest that a synthesis is imminent. A simple manual task, for example, required only a few factors to describe it in one study. Another factor analysis of more complex tasks isolated twenty-three factors. Yet only seven factors were considered necessary to describe the 4,000 jobs listed by the U. S. Employment Service. Thus existing work does not suggest a clear pattern. To further complicate matters, there seem to be "families" of tasks for which individual sets of factor dimensions probably must be developed.

Despite the inconclusiveness of such factor analytical work, two points seem clear. First, the dimensions isolated thus far do not closely resemble the guidelines implicit in much classification work. In fact, the factors need not have any obvious connection with "commonsense" notions. Second, the isolation of such factors is only the initial step. Factor analysis provides a rough map of those things which are important descriptively. Successful prediction, however, is the crucial test. Such validatory work might take such a form: If the task has dimensions a and d, individuals with such-and-such training, proficiency, attitudes, and personality will prove to be high producers.

Even this preliminary factorial work has clear implications for our public personnel systems. Duties classification will have limited usefulness to the degree that task dimensions are not developed and the validatory work referred to above is not undertaken. The interim question of whether the pursuit of precision about characteristics — which may or may not be functionally important in describing the task — is worthwhile probably must remain open. The answer is not obviously in the affirmative. A fundamental reevaluation of the common approach to job description in this country seems required, while we await the scientific explanation which will permit great precision. It would seem useful to attempt to test whether general classification provides savings beyond the reach of the detailed classification.

If detail there must be in job description, many factors could fruitfully be included in the usual duties classification. One such is the style of supervision.

Different jobs seem compatible with different styles of supervision. On the available evidence, general statements under this head must be tentative, largely because we know so little about the dimensions along which tasks differ. An example, however, may be hazarded. Provisionally, jobs may be conceived as differing in the degrees to which their performance is programmed and to which their successful performance requires interpersonal cooperation. When a task is unprogrammed and requires high interpersonal cooperation, a permissive supervisory style has seemed most appropriate for those subjects tested. An authoritarian supervisory style will cause the least socio-emotional dislocation on tasks which are highly programmed and require little interpersonal cooperation. These are general relations, indeed, and require much specification of intervening conditions. Similarly, individuals with differing personality characteristics tend to perform most effectively under different supervisory styles. Meeting the needs of employees *via* an appropriate supervisory style probably would serve to increase the power of supervisors, or at least to provide supervisors with a favorable environment in which to seek high power.

The specification of such factors as the supervisory style congenial to a job is particularly important because the logic of scientific management encourages the choice of a generally inappropriate style. Thus close supervision — which is consistent with this theory — seems to be associated with high output in only a minority of cases, as already noted. If one had to make a choice between the two types of supervision, then, it is not crystal clear that one would be well advised to obey the logic of scientific management.

This analysis can be extended. Close supervision, patently, is encouraged by a structure such as that in Figure 1A. Supervisory pressure would seem to be most directly applicable in this model, which in turn might suggest high supervisory power. Things, however, do not seem to happen this way often. Likert reports that the more "unreasonable pressure" reportedly exerted by a supervisor, the less the power attributed to that supervisor. Moreover, evidence suggests that greater supervisory pressure serves to isolate the supervisor from his men by increasing the danger of communication. In addition, pressure seems inversely related to output. For example, ten of eleven departments in Likert's study which reported little outside pressure to control the pace of work were above-average producers. Nine of ten departments reporting great pressure were below-average producers. Reasonably, then, job descriptions might well profit from the specification of such job-relevant factors as the style of supervision.

This discussion of two approaches to job description — through those factors normally included, and through those factors which are often neglected — permits of simple summary. There seem to be very substantial costs of commission and omission in the job descriptions common in our civil service systems. These costs complicate the management of work, however nicely the systems fit the three core goals underlying the American approach to public personnel administration.

V. Summary

Our federal Civil Service Commission has been accustomed to serve more than one master. As one commentator noted:

"For whom does the Civil Service Commission work?" We used to reply, "Well, we think it works first for its congressional committees, second for the status employees, third for the American Legion in support of veterans' preference laws, fourth for civil service employees' unions, and possibly fifth for the President." Since the end of World War II, the President has moved up in this list but it is difficult to tell just how far.

The analysis above, in essence, argues that yet another master requires service, the development of a work environment within which a professional manager can do his most effective job. Substantial revisions in traditional thinking and technique about our civil service systems will be required to that end.

A Critical Look at the Hatch Act

HENRY ROSE

Political activity by public employees was a matter of official concern in the federal government long before the Hatch Political Activities Act; in 1907 President Roosevelt ordered Civil Service Rule I amended to provide that persons "in the competitive classified service, while retaining the right to vote as they please and to express privately their opinions on all political subjects, shall take no active part in political management or in political campaigns." During the next thirty-three years the Civil Service Commission applied this general rule to particular cases, thereby building up a body of case law of over three thousand decisions. At irregular intervals during that period, the Commission published a pamphlet which contained a brief and concededly incomplete summary of the activities previously found to violate rule I. The pamphlet was widely distributed among the employees affected, and was used by the Commission as a basis for rendering decisions in individual cases and for responding to requests for advice.

Rule I applied only to those federal employees who were in the "classified," also called "competitive," civil service, a category of employees who enjoy a measure of job protection. In 1939 there were 953,891 federal employees, of whom only sixty-nine per cent were in the "classified" civil service and thereby subject to rule I. A principal legislative purpose of the 1939 installment of the Hatch Act was to extend the proscription of rule I to most of the other thirty-one per cent; the 1940 installment had as its major purpose a further extension of coverage to state and local government employees who worked on federally financed programs. The 1940 amendments also included section 15, which states:

> The provisions of this Act which prohibit persons to whom such provisions apply from taking any active part in political management or in political campaigns shall be deemed to prohibit the same activities on the part of such persons as the United States Civil Service Commission has heretofore determined are at the time this section takes effect prohibited on the part of employees in the classified civil service of the United States by the provisions of the civil-service rules prohibiting such employees from taking any active part in political management or in political campaigns.

"A Critical Look at the Hatch Act," by Henry Rose, *Harvard Law Review* (January, 1962), pp. 510–526. Copyright © 1962 by The Harvard Law Review Association.

To date, neither the Commission nor the courts have found it necessary to discuss in depth the construction of section 15. Two questions arise: (1) Exactly what is incorporated by that section, i.e., what is the referent? Does it give the force of statutory law to each of the thousands of individual prohibitions represented by the pre-1940 determinations of the Commission? Or does the section give statutory force to the Commission's summary of those determinations? Is the phrase "active part in political management or in political campaigns" meant to be coextensive with the pre-1940 determinations of the Civil Service Commission? That is, does section 15 refer to the prior determinations exclusively? Or does the section adopt by reference those prior determinations as a base, leaving the Commission to interpret the general prohibitory language to include activities not previously determined to be violative?

The latter question is answered with unusual clarity by the legislative history of section 15. The wording of section 15 in the amendatory bill which was the basis for most of the 1940 debate in the Senate was entirely different from the language finally enacted. The earlier section 15 read as follows:

The United States Civil Service Commission is hereby authorized and directed to promulgate, as soon as practicable, rules or regulations defining, for the purpose of this Act, the term "active part in political management or in political campaigns." After the promulgation of such rules or regulations, the term "active part in political management or in political campaigns," as used in this Act shall have the meaning ascribed to it by such rules or regulations. The Commission is authorized to amend such rules or regulations from time to time as it deems necessary.

The opposition in the Senate to such a broad delegation of authority to the Civil Service Commission was strong and persistent. After almost two weeks of debate on the entire bill, Senator Hatch proposed to substitute the present language of section 15. The change was obviously a substantial one and was intended to undercut this opposition. He introduced the proposal with the remark that "all the substitute does is to prescribe in the law itself that the present prohibitions . . . shall be the political activities prohibited by the Act; that it shall be limited to those interpretations . . . ." He then concluded that this would do away with the delegation-of-power question. At another point in the debate on the substitute section 15, he said: "[I]t seemed to me to be very wise not to give the Commission any more power to interpret further in the future." That he was successful in conveying his concept of the impact of section 15 was evidenced by the remarks of Senator Brown, who was opposed to the bill and to section 15 in particular, when he said: "We are asked to fix into hard and fast statute law every interpretation which has heretofore been made. . . . In other words, there could be no building up of a body of judicial interpretations which might hereafter change."

Although it is thus clear that Congress adopted by reference specific, existing prohibitions, not subject to change, there has been some confusion whether the statutory referent was the administrative determinations under rule I or the Commission's summary of them in *Pamphlet 20*. The debates show that some senators apparently thought that the Civil Service Commission had a set of rules and regulations spelling out in detail the prohibited political activities until Senator Hatch informed his colleagues, during the last phase of the debate on section 15, that "there is but one rule of the Civil Service Commission . . . [which] is almost the exact language of the pending bill and the exact language of the law that was passed [the prior year]. . . . Under that rule, which has been in existence for more than 50 years, the Civil Service Commission has made certain definite findings that this thing is political activity within the meaning of the rule, or that something else is not . . . ." And it was at this point that the referent was seemingly made explicit, for Senator Brown asked Senator Hatch whether "section 15 relates to the interpretation of the rule . . . ," to which the latter replied, "Yes. . . . [W]e are writing into the statute the interpretation of it."

Because the section 15 substitute was proposed by Senator Hatch and adopted by the Senate on the same day, without prior announcement that the particular proposal would be made, there was very little opportunity for members of the Senate to investigate and find out what was being incorporated by the section's reference. When Senator Brown protested that "before we make those interpretations in effect the statute law . . . we ought to have those interpretations . . . before us . . . ," the majority leader, Senator Barkley, expressed confidence that Senator Hatch had read "as many interpretations . . . as there have been cases before the Civil Service Commission upon which it had to pass," and argued that separate consideration of each Commission interpretation would unduly delay a vote on the bill. Shortly thereafter, the Senate approved the substituted section 15, but not before there was an accumulation of convincing evidence of a congressional purpose to adopt thereby the individual pre-Hatch Act Commission determinations, rather than the pamphlet summary.

It is possible of course that had Congress investigated in a responsible manner, it might still have voted as it did — but it is highly unlikely that it would have endorsed every one of the three thousand decisions. For example, would Congress knowingly have approved a proscription on writing an isolated letter to a newspaper on a political subject? Or would Congress have assented to the Commission's decision in *Archie B. Cole?* Mr. Cole was a rural mailcarrier who also happened to be a member of the Watch Tower Bible and Tract Society, better known as Jehovah's Witnesses. The evidence of Cole's "political activity" was

that he is a member of the faith or doctrine taught by the Watch Tower Bible and Tract Society, which is vigorously opposed to war . . . that meetings of the Society have been held in the carrier's home . . . that the literature published by the Society is devoted in a large part to vigorous criticism of our governments, statesmen, financiers, etc., as well as other governments, and the churches and clergy in general.

When Cole realized that he was in danger of losing his job (this was in the depression year of 1932), he promised to mend his ways and withdraw from such activities — but the Civil Service Commission sternly concluded "that Mr. Cole's participation in meetings, circulation of literature and other activities in connection with a society antagonistic to governmental policy is sufficient evidence of his unfitness for government employment to warrant his dismissal from the service" for political activity. Accordingly, the Commission recommended that he be removed, and the Post Office Department promptly dismissed him, though there was no evidence that his activities as a member of the Society interfered with performance of his duties.

Happily, no Hatch Act case has invoked the rule of the *Cole* case. It is even probable that during the past two decades the Commission has been as unaware of the *Cole* case as was the Congress in 1940, for no hint of the case appears in any Commission publication and the decision itself is buried in the raw file in a dusty storage cabinet. Thus, it appears that the Commission's blissful ignorance or disregard of the *Cole* rule has prevented the application of an outrageous and apparently unconstitutional rule.

By resorting to the hastily improvised incorporation-by-reference device in order to avoid either delegating the job or undertaking itself the onerous task of defining ambiguous key language, Congress unintentionally cast its net too far with the result that the statute proscribes conduct not within the legislative purpose, as in the *Cole* case. Conversely, some conduct of the general type Congress was seeking to halt fell outside of that carelessly cast net, as the following illustration shows. After a change of administration in Idaho, officials of the state's highway department allegedly discharged subordinate employees because their political allegiance was not to the party in power. Although a principal goal of the Hatch Act was to protect rank-and-file government employees from being pressured to engage in involuntary political activity, the Commission responded to the complainant that it was unable to do anything. It was helpless, in spite of the allegations of such flagrant political conduct by the Idaho officials, because such acts have

. . . never been considered to be contrary to and punishable under the particular provision of the rules specifically referred to by Congress in Section 15. . . . Accordingly, on the basis of its precedent decisions which have in effect been written into the law by Section 15, the Commission must hold that the activities described in your complaint do not constitute "political management" within the meaning of the Hatch Act. On this basis the Commission can take no further action on your complaint.

The Commission has often recognized that it is bound by its pre-1940 administrative determinations. In *David B. Smith*, it stated: "It is established by determination of the Commission prior to enactment of Section 15 of the Hatch Act, that circulation of a political petition . . . comes within the prohibition . . . and that Section 15 precludes us from making any change in those determinations." In another case involving a finding that service on a political committee violated the act, the Commission remarked, "even if we were inclined to re-examine the question, it would be beyond our authority to do so. By Section 15 . . . Congress has adopted that rule. The Commission is as little able to change that, as it is to change any other enactment of Congress." And the Commission's Chief Hearing Examiner has concluded that

. . . if in Sections 9 and 12 of the Hatch Act Congress had simply prohibited those subject thereto from taking "any active part in political campaigns," there always would have remained an opportunity for logically reasoned conflicting arguments as to what falls within the scope of the prohibition. But Sec. 15 of the Hatch Act makes for inflexibility in interpretation, establishing what may be considered a mandatory principle of *stare decisis*.

The Commission's administration of the Hatch Act has not, however, adhered to its pre-1940 determinations as uniformly as the preceding quotation might suggest. It has implied at times that the summaries of decisions in *Pamphlet 20* and not the specific decisions themselves were given statutory force in section 15. In those cases where it feels called upon to cite authority for the proposition that certain conduct constitutes a violation of the Hatch Act, the Commission typically quotes from some portion of those summary pages in *Pamphlet 20*; sometimes a reference to section 15 is added, with the implication that the text of those few pages in the pamphlet have been given the force of statute. Individual pre-1940 cases are almost never cited; the Commission feels that *Pamphlet 20* "is an authoritative summary of its rulings (given the force of statutory law by section 15 of the Hatch Act) on what constitutes prohibited political activity."

In *Herbert S. Reed*, respondent was charged with executing "the affidavits of a 'qualified elector' to two nominating petitions" though he had not circulated them. In its decision the Commission announced that "an examination has been made of decisions rendered prior to July 20, 1940 (effective date of Hatch Act Section 15 . . .), which relate to political petitions. None is found is which a person was charged with executing a 'qualified elector's affidavit' and nothing more." If the Commission has no power to make additions to the list of prohibited activities, should not that be the end of the matter? Not in the view of the Commission, for it added, immediately after the above statement, "That still does not necessarily mean that Mr. Reed's role of affiant was not a violation." Because, the Commission went on,

It can not be expected that for every case there will be an exact factual prototype. Decisions must be made according to authoritative determinations by the Commission *in which the controlling principles are the same*. Summarizing in broad terms what the Commission's determinations have sought to effect, Form 1236 [*Pamphlet* 20] has said:

12. *In general.* — In brief it may be said that the law is designed to prevent those subject to it from assuming general political leadership or from becoming prominently identified with any political movement, party, or faction, or with the success or failure of any candidate for election to public office.

We, therefore measure the instant case by that standard.

This kind of reasoning can be explained by two theories — both erroneous. It may proceed from the view that the Commission, although bound by section 15 to continue to hold violative those activities which were found to be prohibited prior to 1940, may add new activities to the prohibited list. Or the reasoning may be based on the view that when section 15 says the pre-1940 decisions are binding, it refers not to the individual decisions, but rather to the relatively few general principles culled from the Commission's analysis and synthesis of those thousands of decisions. By this theory the Commission applies to particular cases general principles which it has itself formulated. The latter theory appears to have been the one underlying the reasoning of the Commission in the *Reed* case. Note the anomalous result of such reasoning: Whereas Congress was unwilling to authorize the Commission further to interpret "active part in political management or political campaigns," the Commission arrogated to itself the power to interpret and apply the much broader and vaguer interdiction used in the *Reed* case. Either of these theories amounts to the rewriting of the act by the Commission. Congress debated at length a proposal to delegate to the Commission authority to define the specific activities to be prohibited under the act, and, in the face of opposition, that proposal was dramatically abandoned in the closing phase of the debate.

The *Reed* case is unusual in that the accompanying opinion makes an attempt to reconcile section 15 with the Commission's practice, so that the Commission's misreading of the act is demonstrable. More often, the cases reflect a lack of awareness of or an indifference to the congressional definition of "active part in political management or in political campaigns." In decision after decision, the Commission has ignored the statutory definition, i.e., section 15 and its referents. Of course it may be argued that an administrative agency does not require specific authorization to interpret and apply general prohibitory language in a statute which it enforces. Such power may be implied from the assignment of the enforcement function to the agency. However, it is clearly within the power of the Congress to limit the interpretative discretion of an agency.

The significance of the Commission's reliance upon *Pamphlet 20* depends on the accuracy of its summary of pre-1940 decisions. It is questionable whether a body of case law made up of thousands of decisions covering a wide variety of offenses can ever be accurately summarized in less than seven pages. Such a summary may be adequate for the general orientation of a new employee, but it is of doubtful value as a basic legal text. Furthermore, once such a summary was made after 1940, if accurate, it would require no modifications thereafter. However, over the years since 1940, modifications have been made in that summary. In addition, it is noteworthy that the portion of the pamphlet "devoted to a discussion of activities that, prior to enactment of section 15 of the Hatch Act . . . the Civil Service Commission had determined to be activities prohibited by the civil-service rules" contains material which clearly is not part of such "discussion." For example, it contains quotations from other statutory provisions and references to opinions of the United States Attorney General. Moreover, the text is liberally sprinkled with what employees "may" or "may not" do politically (although at other points, it states that the "Commission has held" various activities prohibited or permitted). At one point in the 1958 edition, employees are gratuitously warned that "it is regarded as contrary to the spirit of the law for a public servant to make a partisan display of any kind while on duty conducting the public business." Thus the "authoritative summary" does not warrant its characterization as such, and leaves the reader with insufficient guidance as to where authoritative summarizing leaves off and editorializing begins.

Although the Civil Service Commission generally uses the pamphlet as an authoritative listing of what specific political activity is prohibited, it has recognized on a few occasions that it is not safe to rely solely upon the pamphlet. It has cautioned that *Pamphlet 20*'s "general rules should be taken as of general and *prima facie* application, but not necessarily as without any possible exception." The Commission has not, however, enabled the bar or the regulated employees to determine what these exceptions might be or to contest a determination that none exists. There are no regular reports of the Commission's decisions. The pre-1940 decisions are not even available to the public. Copies of particular post-1940 decisions, under the Hatch Act, may be obtained from the Commission upon request. But since no adequate digest or topical index is available, it is unlikely that anyone would know which of the decisions, arranged by docket numbers — roughly a chronological order — should be requested. The expense of personally checking the approximately 350 formal decisions under the act would usually be prohibitive, especially since there is no bar specialized in Hatch Act proceedings and the average client has quite limited resources. The unavailability of administrative decisions is all the more regrettable in view of the small number of judicial decisions that have involved the act. The result is that *Pamphlet 20* is the principal source of guidance, not only to the regulated employees but also to both their lawyers and the Commission, in determining what is prohibited political activity.

Many of the decisions that are available may be less than enlightening; and since 1953 the Commission has followed a policy which largely relieves it even of the burden of preparing an opinion to support its decisions in Hatch Act cases involving federal employees. Since that date the Commission has explained with full opinion approximately one decision per year among its federal cases. The Commission disposes of the bulk of these cases by letters to the respondents or their attorneys with little or no explanation, a practice which flies in the face of good adjudicatory practice. Even in the cases where the Commission has issued opinions, they have been anonymous; it has not followed the practice, recommended recently by

President Kennedy, of assigning to "individual agency members the responsibility of being individually responsible for the formulation of the rationale underlying important agency decisions . . . ."

If the present regulatory scheme is to be continued, it is incumbent on the Government to make available in usable form all Commission determinations relating to political activity, whether made before or after passage of the Hatch Act. The persons subject to political-activity restrictions and their attorneys should have these available for whatever guidance they offer for predicting the legitimacy of future conduct. And if it is necessary for a democratic society to curtail the political liberties of some of its citizens, the necessity should be fully stated. Where political appointees administer restrictions on the political activities of millions of their fellow citizens, great effort should be made to avoid not only the possibility of partisan regulation, but also the appearance of it. Disclosure of decisions together with the Commission's reasoning would require it to give more attention to the consistency of its action with the law and would tend to dispel perhaps unwarranted suspicions. It would also provide Congress with a more adequate basis for review of national policy in this area of regulation.

The freezing of precedent decisions into doctrinaire rules to control decision of future cases is at odds with our adjudicatory tradition, is unsound, and is unworkable. The attempt of Congress to establish such a rigid precedent system by section 15 was doomed from the start — and the experience under the act lends additional support to Professor Llewellyn's observation that even where there is "deliberated determination to plant feet flat 'upon the ancient ways' movement and change still creep up on the blind side of the stagnators." It is time to acknowledge the failure of this attempt. The road to a fair balance of competing interests cannot be navigated with only a rear view mirror.

But providing administrative flexibility is not enough; it should be accompanied by fresh legislation based on a reappraisal of national policy regarding political behavior of public employees. Repeal of section 15 would legitimatize a measure of discretion in the Commission, but probably would not significantly affect the course of current decisions; after all, section 15 carried forward prior Commission policies. And it will be recalled that the adoption by reference was a substitute for undertaking or delegating the task of defining the activities to be proscribed. Thus, the removal of that prop should be coupled with a new look at the problem it was used to avoid. Ostensibly, the Hatch Act was primarily aimed at protecting public employees from pressures to engage in involuntary political activity. Yet the overwhelming majority of Hatch Act cases in recent years contain no suggestion of involuntary political activity. Indeed, it should be reconsidered whether the protection of public employees from involuntary political service requires the prohibition of any voluntary political activities. Consideration might also be given to whether the same restrictions should apply inflexibly to all covered employees, or whether the stringency of such restrictions should vary with the employee's governmental function, his contact with the general public, the degree of his job security, or other factors.

Even a much narrower inquiry by Congress could be useful, if it resulted in greater clarity as to the political-activity restrictions. A most unfortunate result of the present vagueness of the act is that because doubt as to the permissibility of a kind of political activity continues, an inestimable quantum of voluntary and desirable political participation goes undone, though it may be determined at a later date that such acts are permissible.

Judicial Review and the Removal of
Federal Employees ✤ CORNELIUS J. MURPHY

During calendar year 1959, over forty-eight thousand federal civilian employees were either discharged from government service or separated for other administrative reasons. Because of the difficulty in obtaining judicial review of these actions, their legality will, in many cases, go unchallenged. It is the purpose of this article to reexamine the reasons why review is so limited and to suggest some means by which the end of justice can be better approximated.

The federal courts have been traditionally without power to review the removal of federal employees, except where there has been a violation of applicable statutes and regulations, or where there has been a manifest abuse of discretion. With this there can be little quarrel, such as approach to the problem reconciles the requirements of justice with the necessity that governmental operations be free of undue interference. The difficulty lies with the availability of a court to which an employee may turn for redress if his removal were procedurally defective or arbitrary.

It is repeatedly held that only the District Court for the District of Columbia has the power to order reinstatement of an illegally removed or separated federal civilian employee, reinstatement being achieved, theoretically at least, through the exercise of the power to issue original writs of mandamus.

In lieu of a petition for writ of mandamus, the adversely affected employee may sue, in the United States Court of Claims, for damages sustained as a result of the removal. This is, of course, a money judgment, and does not affect a reinstatement.

Both courts are located within the District of Columbia.

I. Geographical Distribution of Federal
Civilian Employees

In pre-war America, the predominant geographic concentration of federal employees was in the metropolitan Washington, D.C. area. For example, in 1939 126,000 people were employed there, more than the number employed in any of the States. Wartime America considerably changed this geographic distribution. Of the more than two million persons employed by the federal government in continental United States during calendar year 1960, only slightly more than 168,000 worked in metropolitan Washington, which was less than the number employed in California, where over 239,000 were employed, and New York with over 179,000, and Pennsylvania having in excess of 130,000 federal employees. More significantly, of 11,800 employees discharged during 1960, only 688 worked in the Washington area; of 19,000 separations for reduction in force, only 425 worked there.

Statistics such as these show the remoteness, for a substantial number of adversely affected employees, of the District Court for the District of Columbia and the Court of Claims. It is an obvious hardship for one living and working in California, or Texas, or even New York, for that matter, to go to the trouble and expense of

"Judicial Review and the Removal of Federal Employees," by Cornelius J. Murphy, reprinted by permission of the Federal Bar Association from *Federal Bar Journal*, (Winter, 1962), pp. 25-31.

prosecuting a suit in the District of Columbia. It is in the light of these statistics that the reasons precluding review in the District Courts located within the several states should be re-examined.

II. Mandamus

Ex parte Sawyer was the landmark case from which the courts evolved the rule that mandamus was the proper remedy for a federal employee either threatened with discharge or actually removed. In *Sawyer,* a municipal judge named Parsons in Lincoln, Nebraska, threatened with discharge by the Mayor and Councilmen of that City, obtained a restraining order from the Federal Circuit Court. Disregarding the order, the officials removed Parsons and made a new appointment. Contempt proceedings followed and the officials were imprisoned. They filed a petition for habeas corpus challenging the jurisdiction of the circuit court to issue the restraining order. In sustaining the petition, the Supreme Court, speaking through Mr. Justice Gray said:

. . . It is well settled that a court of equity has no jurisdiction over the appointment and removal of public officers, . . . The jurisdiction to determine the title to a public office belongs exclusively to the courts of law, and is exercised by *certiorari,* error or appeal, or by *mandamus,* prohibition, quo warranto, . . . according to the circumstances of the case, and the mode of procedure established by the common law or by statute.

In view of the rule that only the District Court for the District of Columbia had jurisdiction to entertain original petitions in the nature of mandamus, jurisdiction to determine the legality of removal of federal employees has been confined to that court. A careful reading of the *Sawyer* opinion shows, however, that the court was concerned with equitable interference prior to removal, as distinguished from an equitable remedy of reinstatement following the discharge. This is clear from the dissent of Chief Justice Waite:

I am not prepared to decide that an officer of a municipal government cannot, under any circumstances, apply to a court of chancery to restrain the municipal authorities from proceeding to remove him from his office without the authority of law. There may be cases, in my opinion, when the tardy remedies of *quo warranto, certiorari,* and other like writs will be entirely inadequate. I can easily conceive of circumstances under which a removal, even for a short period, will be productive of irremediable mischief.

Some courts have not interfered, on the theory that only if a clear violation of the employee's statutory rights is alleged, may the court intervene prior to a final administrative action, but the wisdom of such a practice is indeed dubious. A more pertinent inquiry should be: Following adverse administrative action and exhaustion of administrative remedies, can the district courts afford any relief if the action is shown to be wrongful? A strong argument can be made that the district courts, through their inherent power to issue mandatory injunctions, can afford relief by ordering, in an appropriate case, the reinstatement of a wrongfully affected employee. The equivalence of mandatory injunction and mandamus has long been established, and it has been held that a mandatory injunction may issue if mandamus is not available. In *Delaware and Hudson R. Corporation v. Williams,* the Court stated the rule: "Although in many instances a writ of mandamus will not issue, the courts are authorized to compel action through injunction when and if the facts warrant it." It is discouraging to see courts, faced with petitions by aggrieved federal employees, recognize the equivalence and then refuse to take jurisdiction.

III. The Administrative Procedure Act

Another argument favoring jurisdiction is that, in view of the abolition of the writ of mandamus by Rule 81(b) of the Federal Rules, the subsequent passage of the Administrative Procedure Act, making the form of judicial review include mandatory injunctions, was sufficient to confer jurisdiction to hear these suits upon all district courts. The theory that jurisdiction exists under the A.P.A. is supported by respectable authority but has found little support in the courts. Yet the act clearly provides that "any person suffering legal wrong because of any agency action . . . shall be entitled to judicial review thereof." Review is not limited to situations in which express provision is made therefor by statute but extends to . . . "every final agency action for which there is no other adequate remedy in any court . . ." Courts which deny that jurisdiction exists under the act seize upon the limitation that review is not available where the "agency action is by law committed to agency discretion." Yet, the Supreme Court has made it clear that it will not allow arbitrary actions affecting personal rights. In reviewing the legality of action by the Secretary of the Army in issuing a discharge certificate in form other than honorable, it expressly rejected the argument that the matter was not reviewable because committed to "agency discretion." If the Secretary of the Army exceeds his powers ". . . his action would not constitute exercises of his administrative discretion, and in such circumstances . . . judicial relief from this illegality would be available . . . ." The same reasoning should apply to personnel actions. This has been the theoretical position with respect to dismissal of federal employees, that in some cases arbitrary or ultra vires action is reviewable. The "discretion" reservation is particularly unfortunate because of its vagueness. It should properly apply, in cases of application of broad principles to particular cases, where the complexity of the problem involved requires the use of informed judgment or administrative expertise.

A reading of the act as a whole should lead to the same conclusion, as other questions of doubt should be resolved in favor of the existence of jurisdiction. For example, the statutory definition of "agency" lists several exclusions, none of which apply to personnel boards. It is true that standards for agency adjudications are specifically held to be inapplicable where there is involved "the selection or tenure of an officer of the United States." But that refers only to hearing requirements and does not in any way have reference to the availability of review of an administrative *decision*. The same is true with rule-making requirements which do not apply to personnel matters. It is, in fact, a more plausible interpretation of the act, that in view of its failure to exclude matters involving personnel from the definition of agency, that Congress intended to permit the review of these decisions. If such is the case, refusal to accept jurisdiction because of procedural anachronisms is not justifiable. Furthermore, in view of the substantial inequities involved under the present procedure, refusal to construe the Act as conferring jurisdiction seems unnecessarily conservative, since the act was intended to make review more available than it had been prior to its passage.

IV. Declaratory Relief

The development of the theory that district courts, other than that of the District of Columbia, are without jurisdiction to entertain original petitions in the nature of mandamus has led to the additional restriction that they are also without power to entertain petitions by federal employees for declaratory judgments as to the legality of the questioned administrative action. But the Declaratory Judgments

Act specifically provides for such judgments regardless of availability of future relief. Furthermore, the Federal Rules encourage its use in appropriate circumstances if some useful purpose will be served thereby. It is important to note in this connection that it is possible, if the court finds that the employee's rights were violated, for courts in the District of Columbia at least, to issue a declaratory judgment to that effect, and retain jurisdiction until the employee is restored to his position. This is explained in *Borak v. Biddle*.

. . . It is enough for appellant's purposes, at least for the time being, that a declaratory judgment should be made by the district court establishing his right, prior to dismissal, to notice and the sort of hearing provided by the statute. But the district court should retain jurisdiction of the cause so that, if at the end of ninety days . . . appellant (is not) restored to office, a writ may issue.

Sufficient "comity" probably exists between the governmental agencies and the various district courts so that any declaratory judgment of the courts with respect to employee's rights would be respected.

V. The Indispensable Party

The case of *Blackmar v. Guerre* is considered authority for the proposition that a suit by a federal employee, seeking to review administrative action of a local official is not maintainable unless the superior officer or the agency entering final administrative appellate action is made a party defendant. In *Blackmar*, a Veterans Administration employee working in Louisiana was fired by a local official. He appealed the dismissal to a Regional Civil Service Board, which reversed and ordered reinstatement. The Veterans Administration then appealed to the Civil Service Commission in Washington which reversed the Regional Board and affirmed the original decision. The employee commenced suit in Federal District Court in Louisiana, naming Guerre, the local official who fired him and the Commission as defendants. He sought to set aside the original discharge and the Commission's action in reversing the Regional Board. He also prayed for a judgment declaring that he was entitled to an order from the Commission directing his reinstatement. Service on the Commission was attempted by serving the United States attorney and the regional director in Louisiana, and mailing copies of the complaint to the Commission in Washington. The action was dismissed as to the Commission for lack of jurisdiction over the person of the Commissioners. The Circuit Court affirmed. On certiorari to the U. S. Supreme Court, the affirmance was upheld. In the course of the opinion, the Court said of Guerre: "It is obvious that no relief can be granted against him." Despite severe criticism, *Blackmar* has been interpreted by the lower courts as requiring dismissal of an action where the superior officer of the department entering final agency action is not made a party, with little attention given to the importance of the distinction between the review of decisions made by a superior officer and those made by a subordinate.

VI. The Doctrine of Pedreiro v. Shaughnessy

Three years after *Blackmar*, the Supreme Court decided *Pedreiro v. Shaughnessy*. It concerned an attempt by an alien to have a deportation order declared void in a suit brought in the District Court for the Southern District of New York, against the Commissioner who had issued the order. The defendant District Commissioner had full power to issue the order. Prior to commencing suit, petitioner had exhausted his administrative remedies. A motion to dismiss on the grounds that the Attorney General was an indispensible party was granted. On appeal, the Second Circuit reversed. The Supreme Court affirmed. In the opinion, the following important language appears:

We also reject the government's contention that the Commissioner of Immigration and Naturalization is an indispenable party to an action for declaratory relief of this kind. District directors are authorized by regulations to issue warrants of deportation, . . . The regulations purport to make these decisions of the district director final. It seems highly appropriate, therefore, that the district director charged with enforcement of a deportation order should represent the government's interest . . . Undoubtedly the government's defense can be adequately presented by the district director who is under the supervision of the commissioner . . . Our former cases have established a policy under which indispensability of parties is determined on practical considerations.

Professor Davis enthusiastically favors the view expressed in the above quote:

This ground for decision is both entirely new and entirely sound. It should become the foundation for future law. The beauty of the Pedreiro opinion is the emphasis on the practicalities of venue and geography and the complete absence of purported reliance upon such unworkable distinctions as those between action and inaction and between action of a subordinate and action of a superior through a subordinate.

Pedreiro has been well received in certain circumstances, but has been strictly interpreted in employee actions to require proof that the challenged official has the power to afford the relief requested. While in many situations reinstatement power actually exists, the employee's day in court should not turn on such distinctions. For it is well established that the Court can order a subordinate official to disobey his superior, although the subordinate normally is not empowered with authority to be disobedient. Further, such distinctions run against a basic tenet of our jurisprudence that the party who acts is the one who must account for the results. The courts also fail to see finality in action by the local official where the same in subject to administrative review. While there is some basis for this in veterans' appeals to the Civil Service Commission, there are other situations where the "appeal," so-called, does not include a formal hearing and results in a cursory confirmation of lower officials decisions. Also overlooked is the Administrative Procedure Act's provision providing for review of agency action regardless of administrative appellate procedures. Finally, little consideration is given to the policy of the Federal Rules which makes joinder of parties defendant dependent on practical considerations.

VII. Conclusion

It would not take much equitable ingenuity to substitute mandatory injunction for mandamus, to enter declaratory judgments of rights to employment in the belief that sufficient comity exists between the judiciary and the executive to make them worthwhile, and to subject the indispensable party doctrine to practicability and convenience. The present judicial timidity in this area is perhaps grounded on the belief that to permit such suits in the federal courts would be an unwarranted intrusion on the doctrine of separateness and independent status of the executive branch. But there is no doubt that a cause of action exists within the area of procedure and good faith discretion, so that the issue is unreal. Perhaps the reluctance has its foundation in a belief that to permit suits in the districts where the action took place would unduly interfere with internal management of the government. Yet the results would be chaotic if the fifteen thousand employees discharged in 1959 all brought petitions in the District Court for the District of Columbia. It may well be that the proper solution would depend in part upon a venue statute as is the practice in some States. Whatever the result, the problem deserves more attention than it presently receives.

New Dimensions in Employee-Management Relations in the Federal Civil Service*

❖ MAURICE E. O'DONNELL

The traditional approach to labor-management relations in the federal civil service was essentially conservative. The right of employees to organize was recognized, but only in neutral terms that no real encouragement was given to such organizations. Critics argued that the labor-management relations policies of the federal government did not square with developments in human and industrial relations. The federal government, in effect, refused to grant to its own employees the rights of collective bargaining which it guaranteed to many employees through their unions in the private sector of the economy.

Defenders of the status quo in government, mostly managerial and personnel officers, argued that the sovereign nature of the state prevented it from entering into meaningful collective bargaining agreements with its employees. They further pointed out that the decisions concerning wages, hours, and working conditions were made by the Congress and that employees had already been granted collective bargaining privileges in keeping with the legal requirements and the peculiar relationship which must exist between the government and its employees.

The first organizations of public employees appeared among the skilled and semi-skilled workers such as printers, machinists, carpenters, and other craftsmen. The first strictly public service unions began in the postal service when in the 1880's and 1890's letter carriers, post office clerks, rural carriers, and railway mail clerks set up their organizations. The dominant postal unions which emerged were the National Association of Letter Carriers, the United Federation of Post Office Clerks, and the National Federation of Rural Letter Carriers. The first of these organizations affiliated with the American Federation of Labor. The Lloyd-LaFolette Act of 1912 gave postal employees, and by interpretation all federal employees, the right to associate and to deal with the Congress.

Outside the Post Office Department employee organization development lagged behind and developed after World War I and during the depression of the 1930's.

The National Federation of Federal Employees and the American Federation of Government Employees were designed to provide general coverage crossing agency lines in recruiting membership.

Over the years employee organizations labored to improve working conditions and personnel practices. They sought to influence the Congress and to get support for measures such as the Classification Act of 1923, retirement act improvements, and periodic pay increases.

Beginning in 1949, and in each succeeding session of Congress, a bill sponsored by Representative George M. Rhodes of Pennsylvania and Senator Olin D. Johnston of South Carolina was introduced to provide for statutory recognition of organizations of postal and federal employees. Although the bill was never voted on in either house, it was supported by the national headquarters of the AFL-CIO and their affiliated unions, representing a substantial number of government employees, and by most independent national unions.

After the election of President John F. Kennedy in 1960, who had received heavy support from big labor, many felt the administration would push the Rhodes-Johnston Bill and that its enactment would spur the organization of white collar workers in government and thus spread organization to the rest of society. Instead the new administration appointed a Task Force on July 22, 1961, to examine employee-management relations in the federal government and to make recommendations to the President.

The President's Task Force

Upon establishing the Task Force the President stated his belief that "the participation of Federal employees in the formulation and implementation of employee policies and procedures affecting them contributes to the effective conduct of the public business."

The Task Force was headed by the then Secretary of Labor, Arthur Goldberg; other members were Defense Secretary McNamara, Postmaster General Day, Budget Director Bell, White House Counsel Sorensen, and Civil Service Commission Chairman Macy. Clearly, it was made up of top-level appointees who were not specialists in the personnel field, and the influence of the Labor Department through Secretary Goldberg was the dominant influence.

Studies by the Task Force found that 33 per cent of all federal employees, approximately 762,000 persons, including 489,224 in the Post Office Department, belonged to employee organizations. This percentage matched closely the national proportion of organized workers in non-agricultural areas exclusive of federal employment, which was 32.4 per cent in 1960. It was a proportion half again as great as that of the total labor force in which 23.3 per cent of the workers were organized.

The personnel practices of some fifty-seven departments and agencies were studied by the Task Force, which found that twenty-two did not have any stated labor relations policy. Eleven other agencies simply provided that employees had the right to join, or not to join, legitimate employee organizations. Twenty-one of the departments and agencies had patterned their employee relations policies on a guide prepared by the Federal Personnel Council, an advisory group of federal personnel officers. These policies, in general, established the right of employees to belong to legal employee organizations; to express management's desire to encourage discussion with employee organizations; and to specify certain services which could be provided to employee organizations. It was noted that the Department of the

Interior was alone among the departments in providing a comprehensive code of labor relations procedures.

Membership in employee organizations was found to be greatest among craftsmen and other blue collar workers. Government corporations, such as the Tennessee Valley Authority, had a heavy trade union membership. Among the Cabinet departments, membership in employee organizations ranged from the Post Office, with 84 per cent of a total of 582,427 employees, to the State Department, which had eleven members.

The more the work of a governmental agency resembled work in private industry the more government employees were organized; indeed, their relations with management were often similar to those in private enterprise. In the Tennessee Valley Authority and in various units of the Interior Department, close to full-scale collective bargaining had been going on for some years. The Task Force found, for the most part, however, that employee organizations in the federal service were given only limited recognition and that employee organizations were capable of contributing more to the effective conduct of the public business than had previously been the case.

Executive Order 10988

Based on the recommendations of his Task Force, President Kennedy issued Executive Order 10988 on January 17, 1962, entitled, "Employee-Management Cooperation in the Federal Civil Service." In effect the civil service was given a labor-management relations policy which recognized employee associations and gave them a role in dealing with management.

The Executive Order provided for three kinds of recognition of employee organizations: (1) informal, (2) formal, and (3) exclusive. Informal recognition is given to an employee group that does not have a sufficient number of members "within a unit defined by the agency" to gain formal or exclusive recognition. Under such recognition management is not obligated to engage in advance consultation with representatives of the organization before making personnel policy decisions.

To be granted formal recognition an employee organization must have at least 10 per cent of the workers in the unit. Management is bound to consult regularly with such employee organizations on the "formulation and implementation of personnel policies and practices."

Whenever a majority of employees in any federal activity selects a given organization to represent them, that organization must be recognized as the exclusive representative of all its employees, with power to enter into negotiations leading to formal agreements on any matter under management's control which affect working conditions. Exceptions to exclusive recognition are organizations which include in their membership any "managerial executive," members performing federal work, and supervisory personnel who supervise and evaluate the performance of employees in the organization. Organizations with professional and non-professional employees are not given exclusive recognition unless a majority of the professional employees vote to be included in such an employee organization.

The Executive Order permits agreements to be concluded between government and employee organizations which cover grievances, personnel policies and practices, and "other matters affecting general working conditions of employees in the unit." If laws, regulations, or administrative policies limit an agency's discretion it cannot negotiate with employee organizations on such matters. Since pay, hours, and fringe benefits of most federal classified employees are prescribed by law, these areas are not subject to negotiation with employee organizations. The areas open for negotiations are "working conditions, promotion standards, grievance procedures, safety, transfers, demotions, reductions in force, and other matters consistent with merit system principles."

In summary, the Executive Order formalized practices already existing in some agencies; gave employee organizations limited rights, and required management to recognize these rights; strengthened grievance procedures; created a central labor-management policy with uniform rules for all agencies; and defined lines of management authority and responsibility within agencies and between agencies and the Civil Service Commission.

Developments Under the Executive Order

By the end of 1964, federal departments and agencies had negotiated 205 agreements covering more than 600,000 of the government's 2.5 million employees. Personnel covered by the agreements were represented by thirty-five employee organizations, two thirds of which were affiliated with the AFL-CIO.

The most significant agreements were those involving the highly organized postal employees, covering their working conditions, grievances, and appeals. These employees accounted for about 75 per cent of total worker coverage under all agreements. Next to postal workers, the agreements involving federal blue collar workers were more far-reaching than those involving federal classified (white collar) employees. The largest federal employee union, exclusive of the postal unions, was the American Federation of Government Employees (AFL-CIO), which represented 55,000 workers under 108 contracts.

The 205 agreements were negotiated with twenty-one federal departments and agencies. More than half of these were with the Defense Department and applied to more than 80,000 workers. Other federal agencies negotiating ten or more agreements were the Veterans Administration, 29; General Services Administration, 21; Interior, 14; and Health, Education and Welfare, 10. Several large agencies with predominantly white collar employees had no agreements or very little coverage under any agreements.

Nearly half of the 205 bargaining agreements had 150 or fewer employees, and these totaled about 6000 employees. About 510,000 were in six bargaining units with 5000 workers or more. About half of the agreements were concerned with grievance procedures, and four out of five of the agreements dealt with such matters as safety, training, labor-management cooperation, and the union's right to be notified when an adverse action is to be taken against an employee.

About half the agreements covering wage-board (blue collar) employees referred to wage surveys designed to determine the prevailing rates of pay for comparable industry work in the area. Union representatives, as a rule, were allowed to participate in area wage surveys, and in some agreements could request new wage surveys or appeal the findings of wage boards.

In 1965 the Civil Service Commission took action to expedite union-agency agreements by permitting advisory arbitration of government employee appeals from adverse actions such as firings and demotions. Provision is made for an outside arbitrator to hear the evidence in each case and make a decision which is not binding on the agency.

In cases of advisory arbitration involving bargaining impasses between agencies and unions on working conditions, personnel policies, and unit recognition under the Executive Order, agencies have followed the decision of the arbitrator. In cases of employee appeals, such arbitration can only be negotiated in cases where unions have exclusive recognition in an agency unit. The Executive Order bans any agreement or decision that would be contrary to civil service regulations.

The Future Under the Executive Order

The existence of the Executive Order has not unionized the government service. Especially among classified employees (white collar) the growth in union affiliation has been slow. Overall membership in unions has grown but not at a dramatic rate. The extension of the voluntary dues checkoff privilege to government employees has helped to stabilize membership in the employee organizations.

The extent of exclusive recognition has been small. In the first six months after the Order went into effect, exclusive recognition was granted to employee organizations at only sixty-one representation units. Only as gains are made at this level can there be effective bargaining from the employee organization's point of view.

Experience should, in time, begin to settle questions of representation and what "unfair labor practices" are. Most agencies have implemented their directives in this area by suggesting that only "personnel practices and policies" are subjects for negotiation, not general management decisions. There still remains the role of employee organizations exercising a significant influence in bringing about management improvements and employee reactions to management decisions.

Those employee organizations which are strong and aggressive and grow as exclusive representatives will force out those which are less successful in gaining this prestige. New organizations, especially those representing "professional" employees, have been given a stimulus to grow and to obtain recognition as representatives of employees in their particular areas of interest. New organizations must accommodate those managerial and professional personnel who are restricted from active participation in unions of rank-and-file employees. Some organizations have tried to attract membership from other employee organizations.

In the spring of 1965 Representative James Morrison of Louisiana introduced legislation to give government employee unions the same collective bargaining rights that industrial unions have under the National Labor Relations Act. The bill provides for an Employee-Management Cooperation Board consisting of three members, appointed for five-year terms by the President with Senate confirmation, to settle disputes and impasses between unions and management, as well as employee appeals and grievances. Mr. Morrison pointed out that, "Government employees cannot have the right to strike . . . but there is no reason that they should not have the same rights that government guarantees private industry employees."

The federal government was once regarded as a "model employer," and union leaders want to restore that position. In government it is more difficult to define clear boundaries between management and labor, but employee organization influence is still restricted to those sections of the service where unionization represents a response to real needs.

The Several Worlds of the Administrator

❖ W. LLOYD WARNER, PAUL P. VAN RIPER,
NORMAN H. MARTIN, AND ORVIS F. COLLINS

Variations in Style

Although the men making up the federal service display a rather remarkable similarity in psychological makeup, variations may be observed. Differences in social background, age, and position within the executive hierarchy produce variations in their psychology. The conditions of their service, whether political or civil, point up differences.

Yet these are variations in style — differences in degree rather than in kind — for there is more similarity than difference, more homogeneity than heterogeneity.

In general, the *career civil service executive* possesses psychological characteristics that may be described thus: he possesses lofty aspirations, the majority of which stem from external influences, from heroic figures or models, and from demands made upon him by the system and by his role as a career man.

Achievement orientation is strong. For the most part he achieves in a good way by direct action and mobilization of inner resources, by using assistance from his environment, by internalization of the press to achieve so that such influence from the external environment becomes an integral part of his ego-ideal. In other instances, lofty ideals are scaled to realistic proportions.

Yet the career civil service executive frequently experiences feelings of inadequacy and lack of insight into the means to be used to realize his lofty aspirations. In the majority of cases he overcomes these feelings of inadequacy in the ways we have indicated above; in the remainder he responds with feelings of hostility which in most instances take a hidden form such as resentment, or failing in tasks of "going it alone," or movement into fantasy and the realm of "magical" solutions.

Intimately part of a large and complex system of affiliation and connection, he is entangled in the dilemma of striving for independence and severing ties of affiliation and dependency, yet retaining such ties and support. In the push and pull of these emotional needs, he is able to find resolution at times by making the emotional break and asserting his independence, when he may feel emotionally positive in his freedom or retain feelings of guilt and loss.

The *political appointee* is very similar — he is of the same mold, although the shadings are not quite so vivid. He too possesses lofty aspirations but not to the same degree of intensity or commitment, for he is not certain they are worth the hard work and self-sacrifice. Sometimes he is concerned with his ability to attain these high objectives. If they should prove to be too high or unrealistic, he gives them up. Uncertainty, fear of failure, and doubt of capacity mark the political appointee to a much greater extent than the career civil service executive.

The issue of dependence-independence is also crucial to the political executive. He tries to break ties of emotional support and nurturance. Although he is often

"The Several Worlds of the Administrator," by W. Lloyd Warner, Paul P. Van Riper, Norman H. Martin, and Orvis F. Collins, from *The American Federal Executive*, (New Haven, Yale University Press, 1963), pp. 195–202. Reprinted by permission.

able to do so successfully, in a large proportion of cases this brings with it sorrow and more doubt. Often he completely rejects any major dependency ties, but sometimes a strong residue of hostility is retained. He wishes to be independent, but he finds it difficult. Relationships with authority are good; advice is sought, received, and acted upon with good resolution.

Although there is variation in degree and intensity, on the whole the career civil service executive and the political executive are similar psychologically. The career civil service executive most consistently and most intensely displays a lofty aspiration drive. He is committed to high achievement goals in a very genuine sense. While these ideals are primarily derived from external influences and from exemplary figures, in considerable measure he internalizes these pressures so that they become an integral part of his being.

The political executive is somewhat less committed and does not aspire to the same lofty heights. Further, the source of motivation for him is more internal, flowing directly from fundamental personality characteristics.

A second-order contrast between these two groups exists within the notion of self. The political appointee appears to be less certain of his capacities; he doubts that it is worth the effort. And while neither group could be characterized as possessing a strong sense of self-identity and self-confidence, the career civil service executive appears to possess these feelings to a greater extent. Assuming this to be so, it may well be that the individual turns to the environment for cues and direction, for emotional support and affiliation. Both groups of men have strong tendencies to identify with the system, with authority, and with structure. A sanctification of power seems to occur; the system can do no wrong or — always the crucial doubt — can it? This is a response to real or imagined weakness, but it is also an indication of the mobility drive of these men to identify with those higher in authority.

The system of authority is viewed largely in a very positive sense by both groups. Supportive, directive, and "sympathetic," it provides a definite structure within which they can adjust and carry out responsibility. Thus both characteristically defer, receive advice and direction, and move on.

Both groups are commonly more concerned with the external than with the internal. In Fromm's words, they are "afraid to fail and anxious to please." Generally lacking is any cold disdain of close emotional tie; the objective manipulator of the scene, the active protestant, or the revolutionist is not a member of these two groups. Both sincerely respect and follow the conventional values as these relate to them as persons. If they sometimes react with hostility, it is largely covert, rarely expressed outwardly.

Emotional relationships with environment and especially with the handling of close relationships with others clearly constitute one of the most difficult issues for both classes of federal executive. Here is the problem of handling dependency. Thoroughly imbued with conventional values, the federal executive, we infer, is clearly aware of the image of the American male as masculine, assertive, and independent. He wishes to fit this image, but he is never the purely independent type; he has strong needs for affiliation. And herein is the problem — the problem seen almost equally with all groups of federal executives under study. Both political and civil service executives have difficulty resolving the issue. Perhaps the political executive most frequently makes the break and asserts his independence. For the majority, however, there is no resolution. The desire is there, yet it is difficult.

Among the *mobile* and the *nonmobile* there tends to be homogeneity rather than heterogeneity; differences are a matter of degree. The socially mobile executive tends to seek autonomy, in rather definite contrast to his nonmobile counterpart who is more inclined to be concerned with achievement. Coming from a social background higher than his more mobile associate, the nonmobile executive tends to accept the social structure, the status system, and his place within it and focuses his attention upon performance and achievement within the system.

The mobile executive, on the other hand, is more inclined to resist structure and authority. Seeking to go his own way and be autonomous, he strives for self-determination rather than achievement. Probably here, more than in any other psychological dimension observed, is a significant differentiation between the mobile and the socially stable federal executive.

Yet in this drive for autonomy, and this is particularly the case in situations wherein authority is present, the mobile executive is more inclined to passively submit to environmental demands. Although he frequently utilizes this environment as a supporting mechanism, he tends not to interact actively and mold his surroundings to fit his needs, at least not to the same degree as his nonmobile counterpart.

The nonmobile executive tends to relate more actively to his environment, to utilize it so that it serves his needs for achievement. This may be observed most clearly in his relationships with the structure of authority and with authority figures. For him the environment is also supportive, upholding, sustaining, and guiding him.

In coping with problems psychologically, however, there is little difference between mobile and nonmobile executives as to whether good or bad outcomes are expected by them. That is to say, mobility is not a particularly significant determinant of capacity to reach resolution of psychological issues.

When we turn to the problem of achieving emotional independence, however, differences again can be noted. In this area, the mobile executive resolves the issue more favorably than does the nonmobile. It appears that the executive who has not risen from a lower social background is tied with closer emotional ties to others and to the structure than is the socially mobile executive. Consequently he tends to be more dependent, seeks to retain ties. This is not to say, however, that either the mobile or the nonmobile federal executive should be characterized as possessing strongly independent personalities. Both veer toward dependency.

One of the more striking differences to be observed in comparing *older* and *younger executives* centers on the rather strong tendency of the older executive to seek autonomy. This drive is heightened in situations in which direction by authority is inherent, in situations tightly controlled by higher levels. Self-determination then becomes a concern of first-order importance. Yet in pursuing autonomy his ways of coping with the situation and with authority tend to be passive. He does not move directly in terms of actively engaging and dealing with authority, but he strives for autonomy covertly or at the level of fantasy. As a result, the older executive does not often satisfactorily resolve such problems; they remain with him.

The younger federal executive, in contrast, is more directed toward achievement. He accepts the restrictions of large organization, the many directives, and the need for coordination and cooperation. And given this acceptance he orients himself toward achievement rather than autonomy; he does not fight the system.

Being more concerned about autonomy, the older executive tends to be implicated to a high degree in the issue of emotional independence. While both older and younger men experience difficulty in resolving the problem of dependency, the older does so more often and to a greater extent. He may wish to assert himself and sever ties of affiliation but he has considerable difficulty, as though his full development were contingent upon his relationship with others and that to break such ties would threaten his integrity. Not being able to cope with such a break, he tends to remain dependent or not resolve one way or the other.

The younger federal executives, on the other hand, although they retain strong emotional feelings, more frequently do make the break and function in a self-contained way. It appears that many of these younger men are deeply dissatisfied with their self-image. Possessing lofty ideals and high levels of aspiration, they are drawn to the service and to the system of authority and structure in search of a more successful self-identity. Identifying with the system which they firmly believe to be right and good, the younger executives seek the advice and support of the system. They utilize it as they see fit and move on their own. This is not a passive reaction but an active interaction with the system and individuals and culture.

This same system of authority and structure tends to be differently regarded by the older man. He depends upon it, yet he rejects it. He does not seek its advice and direction in the same positive way as does the younger; or if he does, he does not feel capable of acting upon it or receiving support. There is more resistance, more negative reaction, more hostility, and less identification. He needs, yet rejects.

It would seem as though the older federal executive reflects the same general mode of reaction and behavior as does the older person in all walks of life in our society. His ideals tend to be less elevated in character. He is prone to be less ambitious or more realistic and less romantic than his younger associates. Regarding his capacity to achieve, he entertains more doubt. As he grows older, he has less time to attain the dreams he once held. With increasing age, many are inclined to resist the system more and more — to attribute to the system lack of success if that be the case.

The younger, in contradistinction, still has time to realize his aspirations. He seeks to achieve; he still has confidence in his abilities and can effectively relate to the system and utilize it.

Undoubtedly the differentiation is overdrawn. Many older executives clearly possess effective psychological mechanisms of adjustment; many relate effectively to the governmental system and their role within it; many strive for achievement or autonomy with great success. We point out, however, what is a quite clear variable of differentiation among federal executives — the element of age. Here, as is frequently observed in society at large, aging brings increasing vulnerability.

The Federal Executive by Grade Classification

Executives in our sample were all drawn from the upper levels of the federal hierarchy — General Schedule grade levels 14 through 18 and above. The research question asked was, "What psychological differences, if any, may be observed to exist in individuals occupying positions among these top levels? Is there greater similarity or difference?"

On the basis of their general role in the "top management" of the government, it could be predicted that a core or basic personality pattern could be isolated. On the other hand, some fairly well-defined differences in environment among these levels probably exist and consequent variation in psychological characteristics.

Our findings indicate a much stronger tendency toward similarity than difference. It appears that the role of a "government man" exerts a considerably stronger influence than the executive role per se. That is to say, the differential demands made at the highest executive levels, compared with lower levels, are not of such magnitude as to attract or mold a significantly different personality type. In general, the same type of individual is found at the top grade as at the relatively lower levels of top management in the government service.

Differences here are of the order of magnitude of "slightly less" or "slightly more." Thus as one ascends the hierarchy of federal executives, achievement tends to become an issue of more and more relevance. Conversely, autonomy is the psychological issue found with increasing frequency as observation proceeds from higher to lower levels, but it is present at all levels. This is especially noted if authority is present when lower levels appear to push very hard for autonomy.

All levels tend to be more passive (as, for example, compared with business executives) than active in their relationships with the environment. Little real differentiation is to be found between grades. Acted upon rather than acting, they are all in considerable measure sharply affected by outside forces. The majority are not self-assertive and do not typically demand recognition of their own thinking and needs; they adjust to environmental demands.

However, in direct dealings with associates, superiors, and subordinates within the structure of government active and effective coping mechanisms increase with executive level. There is a greater tendency for individuals in top positions to view the environment as supportive — to utilize it, to receive counsel and guidance, and to cooperate with it. This is of course consistent with, and directly related to, our earlier point that lower levels are more concerned with the issue of autonomy and higher levels with the issue of achievement.

It is perhaps in the issue of emotional dependency that the clearest difference in executive levels may be noted. On the whole, lower levels strive for emotional independence and succeed in making the break with greater frequency than do their higher level associates. It would appear that higher levels are more emotionally tied to the structure, to their informal groups, and to the system than are those who occupy relatively lower positions.

One last point remains to be made with respect to differences among executive levels. The ability to arrive at satisfactory resolution of psychological issues tends to increase with higher executive level; lower levels have more of a problem. Indeed, executive position or level within the hierarchy appears to be one of the best indices for predicting capacity to produce good resolution. Perhaps this is because the men in lower positions are striving more for autonomy, a goal that would be exceedingly difficult to realize in as persuasive a structure as the federal government; perhaps it is because those at higher levels tend more actively to relate to the structure and see it as a support rather than a hindrance.

At lower levels, our observation of the psychological data indicate a much greater tendency to engage in resentment and ineffective resistance. Here there would be more feelings of inadequacy, and fear of rejection, reprimand, and hostility. One seeks for self-determination, but the way is not clear.

It may now be fruitful to summarize what has been said. With decreasing executive level, lower social class origins and older age, there is an increasing tendency to seek autonomy. Thus, at one extreme, the younger, nonmobile, top executive presents the achievement issue 70 per cent of the time; at the other, the older, mobile, GS levels 14 through 16 or equivalent, present the autonomy problem 77 per cent of the time. An individual in the former group is most likely to perceive himself as an achievement-oriented person undisturbed by conflicting pressures from the outer world or by unresolved internal doubts. He tends to know what he wants and the primary question for him is what, if anything, he will do to win his objective and what, if anything, will result from his efforts. The basic question here is, "Is it worth it?"

Since the more mobile, the older, and those occupying lower levels are more concerned with autonomy, they feel pressure from the outer world and specifically from the structure of which they are members. In this world of pressure, they question the extent of their own motivation toward success and mastery; they question their capacities. Thus it is the socially stable, younger, high-level executive who relates most easily and well to the authority structure and to the total system. It is this group who are most prone to view the governmental complex as supportive and who blend their own personalities to it in the most active manner. And it is this group who are most capable of achieving a psychologically adequate resolution of the problems of achievement, autonomy, and emotional independence.

The nonmobile, younger man who occupies higher position seems to be best able to cope with the independence-dependence issue. Either he is able to achieve emotional independence or he is happily dependent. In either event, he adjusts. The older, lower-level executive is more apt still to be emotionally involved and unable to resolve this problem.

We thus observe the federal executive, the basic form of his personality, and how the general diversifies into several types or styles. One such style emerges in the form of an individual intensely committed to high achievement who is uncertain of goals and lacks the coping mechanisms to resolve the many issues deriving from role and environment. Still another resists the structure of authority and its many directives. Either covertly hostile or undermining, he nonetheless cannot break dependency ties and is caught. Here too is the conformist. Deferring to the system, his own needs are subservient to external pressure. Here is the "organization man."

The personality structure we have here portrayed, nevertheless, in both its general form and variations, fits the role defined by a vast, large-scale organization — even though some of the individuals currently filling governmental roles appear to be out of phase.

There is in the federal executive much of the universal. We see in the personalities sketched in these pages much of what is seen in man in general — the same feelings of inadequacy, the same uncertainty, the same desire for guidance and social ties, the same deference to authority. We see the same tendency to rebel against authority to be self-determining, and to realize independence. We see the same ambivalence, the same clash of needs.

He is not different, yet he is. A particular constellation of psychological characteristics draws him to the federal service; a particular role permitting the gratification of both dependency feelings and a drive for autonomy exists within that structure. In this sense, personality and role are functional — one fits the other. For here is a body of men in the Sunday dress of common men. Possessing deals which raise them above that level, possessing a strong and lofty sense of values, they identify with national purpose. They raise themselves literally by their bootstraps. They feel, in a sense, men of destiny.

✤ 6 ✤

Financial Administration

Financial administration reflects the growth and expansion of governmental functions. Here in this process the financial resources must be set and then distributed to various areas and functions. Financial administration becomes, therefore, an important part of the political process by means of which financial resources are translated into human resources.

The President's budget message is much more than a statement of proposed expenditures; it is an important political document which reflects the goals and aspirations of an administration. The development of the executive budget process, centered in the Bureau of the Budget, has given the President far-reaching controls over the various agencies since the budgetary process determines in the first instance the financial resources that will be made available for various programs.

Reformers sought to make the budgetary process more efficient and to take "politics" out of budgetary administration. Reforms or changes in the process do not stop at one point but, like a chain reaction, they influence the whole political process. The shifting weights of political influence among the Executive, Congress, agencies, and interest groups are reflected in the decisions which are finally made.

Portions of the President's Budget Message, 1966

To the Congress of the United States:

I am presenting to you today the budget of the United States for the fiscal year 1966.

A budget is a plan of action. It defines our goals, charts our courses, and outlines our expectations. It reflects hard decisions and difficult choices. This budget is no exception.

It is a budget of priorities. It provides for what we must do, but not for all we would like to do.

"Portions of the President's Budget Message," from *The Budget In Brief: Fiscal Year 1966*, (Washington D.C., Government Printing Office, 1965), pp. 59–69.

It is a budget of both opportunity and sacrifice. It begins to grasp the opportunities of the Great Society. It is restrained by the sacrifices we must continue to make in order to keep our defenses strong and flexible.

This budget provides reasonably for our needs. It is not extravagant. Neither is it miserly.

It stands on five basic principles:

• Government fiscal policies must promote national strength, economic progress, and individual opportunity.

• Our tax system must continue to be made less burdensome, more equitable, and more conducive to continued economic expansion.

• The Great Society must be a *bold* society. It must not fear to meet new challenges. It must not fail to seize new opportunities.

• The Great Society must be a *compassionate* society. It must always be responsive to human needs.

• The Great Society must be an *efficient* society. Less urgent programs must give way to make room for higher priority needs. And each program, old and new, must be conducted with maximum efficiency, economy, and productivity.

The major features of the 1966 budget translate these principles into action.

First, excise taxes are substantially reduced. Social security benefits, including hospital insurance, are increased. These are combined with other expenditure increases to yield an overall fiscal policy designed to maintain our steady economic expansion.

Second, the budget supports a massive defense establishment of steadily growing power, within reduced outlays.

Third, our international and space programs are being advanced at a satisfactory rate, but with smaller increases than in earlier years.

Fourth, expanded programs and higher expenditures are proposed to:

• Provide better and more education for our children.

• Extend the war against poverty.

• Promote advances in the nation's health.

• Improve conditions in the urban areas where most of us live.

• Help the Appalachian region lift itself out of its present depressed condition.

• Strengthen our social security protection.

• Increase economic opportunities in rural communities.

• Encourage sound use of our natural resources.

• Conserve natural beauty in our land.

Fifth, a large part of the funds for needed program expansion has come from savings, reductions, and economies in other parts of the budget.

Fiscal Policy

This budget recognizes that a growing economy is needed to promote national strength and progress. It is also needed to move us toward a balanced budget. When the economy slows down, federal revenues fall and spending tends to increase. The result is larger, not smaller, budget deficits.

Nearly four years ago, this nation began its fourth postwar economic expansion. With the help of last year's income tax reduction — the largest and most comprehensive ever enacted — this expansion has already outlasted each of the previous three postwar recoveries.

During the past four years, the nation's real output of goods and services — the gross national product — has grown at an average rate of about 5 per cent per year.

New highs have been achieved in employment, income, and profits. Unemployment has been reduced. Price stability has been maintained.

This is a creditable record of achievement. And we look forward to continued growth in the year ahead. The nation's output in calendar year 1965 is expected to reach $660 billion, plus or minus $5 billion.

Nevertheless, we must keep in mind that our economy is still producing at a level well below its potential. Nearly 4 million people are out of work. The unemployment rate is still nearly 5 per cent. Plants and machines are standing idle while human wants and needs go unmet. An estimated 35 million people continue to live in poverty.

We cannot substitute last year's achievements for next year's goals; nor can we meet next year's challenge with last year's budget.

The revenue and expenditure proposals presented in the 1966 budget are carefully designed to promote continued economic expansion and improved economic opportunities.

This budget takes into account the need to reduce the nation's balance of payments deficit. During the last calendar year, the deficit showed a significant decline. To help insure continued improvement, I will intensify efforts to carry out federal activities with the least possible burden on our balance of payments.

Budget Summary

Administrative budget.—In preparing this budget, I have applied exacting tests of efficiency and necessity to all proposed expenditures. As a result, total administrative budget expenditures are being held to $99.7 billion in 1966. Although expenditures will rise by a relatively small amount, they will decline as a percent of the gross national product — to less than 15 per cent, the lowest ratio achieved in 15 years.

Administrative budget receipts are expected to increase in 1966 to $94.4 billion. This is $3.2 billion over the estimated level for 1965. This increase reflects the economic growth anticipated in calendar year 1965. It also takes into account the revenue losses from proposed excise tax changes and from the second stage of income tax cuts enacted last year.

The resulting 1966 administrative budget deficit of $5.3 billion is $1 billion lower than the 1965 deficit, marking continued progress toward a balanced budget.

As our population increases, as science and technology change our methods of doing things, as our wants multiply with the growth in our incomes, and as urbanization creates new problems, there is growing need for more public and private services. It is evident that unless defense needs should decline substantially, government expenditures will continue to rise over the long run.

At the same time, we have good reason to expect that government expenditures in the years ahead will grow more slowly than the gross national product, so that the ratio of federal spending to our total output will continue to decline.

The expenditures proposed in this budget reflect a careful balancing of national goals against budgetary costs. The budget I now present will, in my judgment, carry out the responsibilities of the federal government efficiently and wisely. It was constructed on that basis alone.

My budgets for both 1965 and 1966 have provided for major increases in areas of high national priority — particularly education, health, aid to the needy, housing, and the war on poverty. Also, for these two consecutive years, careful pruning of less urgent programs and vigorous cost reduction efforts have, on balance, resulted in lower expenditures in other major sectors of the budget. The application of these strict policies of priority and frugality is evident in the modest growth in administrative budget expenditures.

The Changing Federal Budget
(Fiscal years. In billions)

Description	Administrative budget expenditures				
	1964 actual	Change, 1964 to 1965	1965 estimate	Change, 1965 to 1966	1966 estimate
National defense and space	$58.4	−$1.3	$57.1	−$0.4	$56.7
Interest	10.8	+.5	11.3	+.3	11.6
Health, labor, education, housing and community development, economic opportunity program, and aid to the needy	6.7	+.7	7.4	+3.6	11.0
All other	21.8	−.1	21.7	−1.3	20.4
Total, administrative budget	97.7	−.2	97.5	+2.2	99.7

Consolidated cash statement. — The administrative budget is based on a definition of federal spending which excludes such important federal activities as social security and highway construction that are financed through trust funds. A more comprehensive measure of the government's finances is the consolidated cash budget which covers all of the government's programs.

On the consolidated cash basis, total payments to the public are estimated at $127.4 billion in 1966. Total receipts from the public are estimated at $123.5 billion, resulting in a net excess of payments of $3.9 billion. The estimated increase of $6.0 billion in cash payments in 1966 over 1965 is mostly in trust funds which are financed by special taxes.

About $9.5 billion of the nondefense payments recommended in this budget — almost 2½ times the size of the entire cash deficit — represent an investment in physical and financial assets which will provide benefits to the nation for many years to come. These payments are made for federal civil public works, equipment, and loans as well as for highways, hospitals, and other state, local, and private assets.

Federal sector, national income accounts. Another measure of federal finance which includes trust funds emphasizes the direct impact of government fiscal activities on the economy. This measure is based on the national income accounts. Under this concept, federal fiscal data are estimated on an accrual rather than a cash basis. Purely financial transactions — such as loans — which do not *directly* affect production or income are excluded. On this basis, the deficit for 1966 is estimated at $6.0 billion.

Federal expenditures as measured by the national income accounts are estimated to rise by $6.0 billion in 1966. This increase — covering both purchases of goods and services and other types of payments — will provide a strong stimulus for continued economic growth.

Federal Revenues

The Revenue Act of 1964 has played a major role in widening and strengthening our prosperity. At the beginning of this month, the second stage of the rate reductions provided under the Act became effective. In total, last year's tax law will decrease consumer and business tax liabilities by about $14 billion in the current calendar year.

With this substantial change in income taxes completed, it is now appropriate to revise and adjust *excise taxes* as well. Some of the present excises are costly and inefficient to administer. Some impose onerous recordkeeping burdens on small business. Some distort consumer choices as among different kinds of goods.

Within the revenue requirements for continued progress toward a balanced budget, I believe it is vital that we correct the most pressing of these deficiencies this year. I plan to transmit to the Congress recommendations to repeal some excise taxes and reduce others. In addition to improving the tax system, the recommended changes will increase purchasing power and stimulate further growth in the economy.

These changes should become effective July 1, 1965. They will reduce tax liabilities on a full-year basis by $1.75 billion. Revenues collected by the Treasury in 1966 will be reduced by $1.5 billion.

My *other major revenue proposals* this year involve important activities financed through trust funds.

I am recommending prompt enactment of a hospital insurance program for elderly persons, who are finding hospital and medical costs far greater than their ability to pay. This program should be self-financing, with a combined employer-employee payroll contribution of 0.6 per cent on the first $5,600 of income to start in calendar year 1966.

I am also recommending an increase from $4,800 to $5,600 in the wage base on which social security taxes are paid. This would take effect on January 1, 1966, and would be coupled with a smaller increase in the payroll tax than is scheduled at that date under existing law. These changes will provide the funds for the needed increases being proposed in old-age, survivors, and disability insurance benefits.

While I am recommending reductions in certain excise taxes, I am also proposing increases in certain other excise taxes which are in the nature of *user charges*. The excise taxes for which I am recommending reduction or repeal are not associated with the provision of particular government services. However, certain existing excises on transportation are in effect a charge for the use of facilities and services provided by the government. In these cases, I am proposing changes in *user charges for transportation* so that different modes of transportation can compete on more equitable and efficient terms and users of special government services will pay a greater share of the costs.

The estimated cost of completing the Interstate Highway System — which is financed by highway user taxes — has recently been increased by $5.8 billion. To avoid serious delay in completing the system while remaining on a pay-as-you-go basis, I will include in my excise tax proposals specific recommendations for increasing certain highway user charges.

In contrast to the users of the highways, the users of the airways and inland waterways bear considerably less than the full cost of the government investments and services provided them. Accordingly, I am recommending increased or new taxes on aviation gasoline and jet fuels and a new tax on air freight for commercial aviation. Receipts from the existing two-cent tax on aviation gasoline should be kept in the general fund rather than transferred to the highway trust fund, and the five per cent ticket tax on air passengers should be made permanent. A fuel tax for inland waterway users is also being proposed.

I will continue to press for *other user charges* in government programs where benefits are provided to specific, identifiable individuals and businesses. Fairness to all taxpayers demands that those who enjoy special benefits should bear a greater share of the costs. Legislation is needed for some of the charges, such as patent and meat inspection fees. In other instances, equitable user charges will be instituted through administrative action.

I will also present recommendations to correct certain abuses in the tax-exempt privileges enjoyed by private foundations.

New Obligational Authority

This budget includes new obligational authority for 1966 of $106.4 billion in the administrative budget.

- $93.5 billion of this requires congressional action this year.
- $12.9 billion represents permanent authorizations that do not require further congressional action, mainly the appropriation for interest on the public debt.

Most of the $34.5 billion in new obligational authority recommended for 1966 for trust funds represents revenues from special taxes which are automatically appropriated.

New Obligational Authority
Fiscal years.   In billions

Description	1964 actual	1965 estimate	1966 estimate
Total authorizations requiring current action by Congress:			
Administrative budget funds	$87.9	$94.5	$93.5
Trust funds	.4	1.4	.5
Total authorizations not requiring current action by Congress:			
Administrative budget funds	13.2	12.8	12.9
Trust funds	31.2	30.3	34.0
Total new obligational authority:			
Administrative budget funds	101.1	107.3	106.4
Trust funds	31.5	31.8	34.5

The 1965 estimate in the administrative budget includes $6.0 billion of recommended supplemental authorizations. These authorizations will provide funds for several programs for which I am requesting immediate consideration and enactment — for example, housing activities and aid to Appalachia. The new obligational authority and related expenditures under these supplemental proposals are reflected fully in the estimates presented in this budget.

Reducing Government Costs

As we focus attention on improving the quality of American life, we must also see to the quality of American government.

The tasks we face are formidable. They require new dedication, new vision, and new skills. We have neither the resources nor the right to saddle our people with unproductive and inefficient government organization, services, or practices.

This must be a year of renewal — a year that will be long remembered for what we accomplish in bringing the public service to its highest state of readiness.

To realize this renewal, action will be necessary on a wide front. I pledge that this administration will strive to conduct the work of the government by the same exacting standards that would apply in the most expertly managed private business.

Government organization. We must reorganize and modernize the structure of the executive branch in order to focus responsibilities and increase efficiency. I will shortly propose certain reorganizations which will constitute the initial and most urgent steps that I deem necessary to consolidate functions and strengthen coordination of related activities.

I will ask that permanent reorganization authority be granted to the President to initiate improvements in government organization, subject to the disapproval of the Congress.

Controlling employment. In this budget, as in the budget for 1965, I have insisted upon stringent criteria to control the growth of federal civilian employment. It is important that we have enough people to carry on the government's business efficiently, but we must also see that we have no more employees than we need.

Realistic guidelines and goals have been established to aid administrators in the effective management of the government's large and diverse work force. Controls on employment have been established for each agency. To remove the guesswork from determination of employment needs, agencies are installing improved work measurement systems, and the Bureau of the Budget is providing advice and assistance in introducing measures of productivity into agency management systems. The result of such efforts has been and will continue to be a reduction in the size of the federal work force relative to the work being accomplished. The effectiveness of these controls may be seen in the fact that had federal civilian employment kept its 1955 relationship to total population, federal employees would have totaled 2,747,000 on June 30, 1964, more than 275,000 above the actual number as of that date.

Modest and highly selective increases in employment are proposed in the budget for 1966, mainly to carry out new and expanded programs recommended in this budget and to reduce excessive overtime in the Post Office Department. At the same time, we will take full advantage of every opportunity to keep the work force at minimum levels by eliminating functions, consolidating operations, closing unnecessary offices and installations, and abolishing vacancies. Total civilian employment proposed for 1966 is about 1 per cent above the totals for the current year, and I am confident that we will be able to keep actual employment somewhat below these estimates.

Management improvement and cost reduction. The past year has been a successful one from the standpoint of improved management and cost reduction. Next year will be still better.

Led by the outstanding performance of the Department of Defense, government agencies last year undertook cost reductions that saved almost $3.5 billion. These economies were not easy to come by. They have resulted from the concentrated work of government officials and employees in all agencies, large and small. They reflect a wide variety of actions ranging from the abolition of reports and other publications to the introduction of computers, the application of modern business equipment, the adoption of new purchasing methods, and decisions to close major installations.

I am counting heavily on the continuation and acceleration of cost reduction and management improvement efforts. Every dollar saved in this way can be put to better use in carrying on more urgent business. And today every dollar is important. Among other things, we must:

- Continue our war on excessive paperwork.
- Increase our capacity to find and correct management weaknesses throughout the government.
- Reexamine our career services, making certain that they are all they should be with respect to selection, training, placement-promotion, rotation, retirement, and removal.
- Seek legislation that will remove legal barriers to efficient operation.

I have instructed the Director of the Bureau of the Budget to give direction to a comprehensive, government-wide cost reduction program to be put into effect in every department and agency. In general, this program will require the head of each agency to:

- Take personal charge of cost reduction efforts.
- Set specific goals for reductions in cost.
- Reassess priorities for all programs and operations.
- Identify and remove roadblocks to economy.
- Verify reported savings.

I believe the Congress and the American people approve my goals of economy and efficiency. I believe they are as opposed to waste as I am. We can and will eliminate it.

Conclusion

Since I sent you my first budget a year ago:
- 4 million Americans have been born.
- 3.2 million young people have reached college age.
- 1.7 million new families have been formed.
- 1.3 million persons have entered the labor force.
- 1.5 million persons have reached retirement age.

Thus, our nation faces growing responsibilities. But we also possess growing resources to meet them.

One result of our expanding economy is a larger revenue potential. This means a potential for:
- Necessary increases in federal expenditures.
- Reductions in taxes.
- Reductions in the public debt.

No one of these goals is paramount at all times. Each must be balanced against the others to assure our continued progress toward a Great Society.

This progress does not rest on economic growth alone. It is aimed at improving the quality of our way of life. And it is aimed at insuring that all Americans share in this way of life.

The federal government must do its part.

This does not mean simply spending more.

It does mean spending more on some new and vital activities. But it also means cutting back or eliminating activities which are less urgent or no longer necessary.

Where there is waste, to end it; where there are needs, to meet them; where there are just hopes, to move toward their fulfillment — that is the object of the budget which I now submit to your consideration.

LYNDON B. JOHNSON

January 25, 1965

Political Implications of Budgetary

Reform ❦ Aaron Wildavsky

A large part of the literature on budgeting in the United States is concerned with reform. The goals of the proposed reforms are couched in similar language — economy, efficiency, improvement, or just better budgeting. The President, the Congress and its committees, administrative agencies, even the interested citizenry are all to gain by some change in the way the budget is formulated, presented, or evaluated. There is little or no realization among the reformers, however, that any effective change in budgetary relationships must necessarily alter the outcomes of the budgetary process. Otherwise, why bother? Far from being a neutral matter of "better budgeting," proposed reforms inevitably contain important implications for the political system, that is for the "who gets what" of governmental decisions. What are some of the major political implications of budgetary reform and where should we look to increase our knowledge about how the budget is made? We begin with the noblest vision of reform: the development of a normative theory of budgeting that would provide the basis for allocating funds among competing activities.

A Normative Theory of Budgeting?

In 1940, in what is still the best discussion of the subject, V. O. Key lamented "The Lack of a Budgetary Theory." He called for a theory which would help answer the basic question of budgeting on the expenditure side: "On what basis shall it be decided to allocate X dollars to Activity A instead of Activity B?" Although several attempts have been made to meet this challenge, not one has come close to succeeding. No progress has been made for the excellent reason that the task, as posed, is impossible to fulfill. The search for an unrealizable goal indicates serious weaknesses in prevailing conceptions of the budget.

If a normative theory of budgeting is to be more than an academic exercise, it must actually guide the making of governmental decisions. The items of expenditures which are passed by Congress, enacted into law, and spent must in large measure conform to the theory if it is to have any practical effect. This is tantamount to prescribe that virtually all the activities of government be carried on according to the theory. For whatever the government does must be paid for from public funds; it is difficult to think of any policy which can be carried out without money.

The budget is the life-blood of the government, the financial reflection of what the government does or intends to do. A theory which contains criteria for determining what ought to be in the budget is nothing less than a theory stating what the government ought to do. If we substitute the words "what the government ought to do" for the words "ought to be in the budget," it becomes clear that a normative theory of budgeting would be a comprehensive and specific political theory detailing what the government's activities ought to be at a particular time. A normative

Reprinted from the *Public Administration Review*, the journal of the American Society for Public Administration, Vol. XXI, No. 4, 1961, pp. 183–185, 187–188, 190, by permission of the publisher.

theory of budgeting, therefore, is utopian in the fullest sense of that word; its accomplishment and acceptance would mean the end of conflict over the government's role in society.

By suppressing dissent, totalitarian regimes enforce their normative theory of budgeting on others. Presumably, we reject this solution to the problem of conflict in society and insist on democratic procedures. How then arrive at a theory of budgeting which is something more than one man's preferences?

The crucial aspect of budgeting is whose preferences are to prevail in disputes about which activities are to be carried on and to what degree, in the light of limited resources. The problem is not only "how shall budgetary benefits be maximized?" as if it made no difference who received them, but also "who shall receive budgetary benefits and how much?" One may purport to solve the problem of budgeting by proposing a normative theory (or a welfare function or a hierarchy of values) which specifies a method for maximizing returns for budgetary expenditures. In the absence of ability to impose a set of preferred policies on others, however, this solution breaks down. It amounts to no more than saying that if you can persuade others to agree with you, than you will have achieved agreement. Or it begs the question of what kind of policies will be fed into the scheme by assuming that these are agreed upon. Yet we hardly need argue that a state of universal agreement has not yet arisen.

Another way of avoiding the problem of budgeting is to treat society as a single organism with a consistent set of desires and a life of its own, much as a single consumer might be assumed to have a stable demand and indifference schedule. Instead of revenue being raised and the budget being spent by and for many individuals who may have their own preferences and feelings, as is surely the case, these processes are treated, in effect, as if a single individual were the only one concerned. This approach avoids the central problems of social conflict, of somehow aggregating different preferences so that a decision may emerge. How can we compare the worth of expenditures for irrigation to certain farmers with the worth of widening a highway to motorists and the desirability of aiding old people to pay medical bills as against the degree of safety provided by an expanded defense program?

The process we have developed for dealing with interpersonal comparisons in government is not economic but political. Conflicts are resolved (under agreed upon rules) by translating different preferences through the political system into units called votes or into types of authority like a veto power. There need not be (and there is not) full agreement on goals or the preferential weights to be accorded to different goals. Congressmen directly threaten, compromise, and trade favors in regard to policies in which values are implicitly weighted, and then agree to register the results according to the rules for tallying votes.

The burden of calculation is enormously reduced for three primary reasons: first, only the small number of alternatives which are politically feasible at any one time are considered; second, these policies in a democracy typically differ only in small increments from previous policies on which there is a store of relevant information; and, third, each participant may ordinarily assume that he need consider only his preferences and those of his powerful opponents since the American political system works to assure that every significant interest has representation at some key point. Since only a relatively few interest groups contend on any given issue and no single item is considered in conjunction with all others (because budgets are made in bits and pieces), a huge and confusing array of interests are not activated all at once.

In the American context, a typical result is that bargaining takes place among many dispersed centers of influence and that favors are swapped as in the case of log-rolling public works appropriations. Since there is no one group of men who can necessarily impose their preferences upon others within the American political system, special coalitions are formed to support or oppose specific policies. Support is sought in this system of fragmented power at numerous centers of influence — Congressional committees, the Congressional leadership, the President, the Budget Bureau, interdepartmental committees, departments, bureaus, private groups, and so on. Nowhere does a single authority have power to determine what is going to be in the budget.

The Politics in Budget Reform

The seeming irrationalities of a political system which does not provide for even formal consideration of the budget as a whole (except by the President who cannot control the final result) has led to many attacks and proposals for reform. The tradition of reform in America is a noble one, not easily to be denied. But in this case it is doomed to failure because it is aimed at the wrong target. If the present budgetary process is rightly or wrongly deemed unsatisfactory, then one must alter in some respect the political system of which the budget is but an expression. It makes no sense to speak as if one could make drastic changes in budgeting without also altering the distribution of influence. But this task is inevitably so formidable (though the reformers are not directly conscious of it) that most adversaries prefer to speak of changing the budgetary process, as if by some subtle alchemy the irrefractible political element could be transformed into a more malleable substance.

The reader who objects to being taken thus far only to be told the obvious truth that the budget is inextricably linked to the political system would have a just complaint if the implications of this remark were truly recognized in the literature on budgeting. But this is not so. One implication is that by far the most significant way of influencing the budget is to introduce basic political changes (or to wait for secular changes like the growing industrialization of the South). Provide the President with more powers enabling him to control the votes of his party in Congress; enable a small group of Congressmen to command a majority of votes on all occasions so that they can push their program through. Then you will have exerted a profound influence on the content of the budget.

A second implication is that no significant change can be made in the budgetary process without affecting the political process. There would be no point in tinkering with the budgetary machinery if, at the end, the pattern of budgetary decisions was precisely the same as before. On the contrary, reform has little justification unless it results in different kinds of decisions and, when and if this has been accomplished, the play of political forces has necessarily been altered. Enabling some political forces to gain at the expense of others requires the explicit introduction and defense of value premises which are ordinarily missing from proposals for budgetary reform.

Since the budget represents conflicts over whose preferences shall prevail, the third implication is that one cannot speak of "better budgeting" without considering who benefits and who loses or demonstrating that no one loses. Just as the supposedly objective criterion of "efficiency" has been shown to have normative implications, so a "better budget" may well be a cloak for hidden policy preferences. To propose that the President be given an item veto, for example, means an attempt to increase the influence of the particular interests which gain superior access to the Chief Executive rather than, say, to the Congress. Only if one eliminates the element of conflict over expenditures, can it be assumed that a reform which enables an official to do a better job from his point of view is simply "good" without considering the policy implications for others.

. . . .

What Do We Know About Budgeting?

The overriding concern of the literature on budgeting with normative theory and reform has tended to obscure the fact that we know very little about it. Aside from the now classical articles on Congressional oversight of administration by Arthur MacMahon, an excellent study of internal budgetary procedures in the Army by Frederick C. Mosher, and an interesting case history by Kathryn S. Arnow, there is virtually nothing of substance about how or why budgetary decisions are actually made. Of course, the general literature on decision making in national government provides some valuable propositions, but it is not keyed-in to the budgetary process. Yet the opportunities for developing and testing important propositions about budgetary decisions are extraordinarily good and I would like to suggest a few of the many possible approaches here.

How do various agencies decide how much to ask for? Most agencies cannot simply ask for everything they would like to have. If they continually ask for much more than they can get, their opinions are automatically discounted and they risk a loss of confidence by the Budget Bureau and Appropriations sub-committees which damages the prospects of their highest priority items. The agencies cannot even ask for all that they are authorized to spend because their authorizations commonly run way ahead of any realistic expectation of achievement. At the same time, they do not wish to sell themselves short. The result is that the men who make this choice (an official title is no certain guide to whom they are) seek signals from the environment — supporting interests, their own personnel, current events, last year's actions, attitudes of Congressmen, and so on — to arrive at a composite estimate of "what will go." A combination of interviews, case studies, and direct observation should enable the researcher to determine what these signals are, to construct propositions accounting for the agencies budgetary position, and to generally re-create the environment out of which these choices come.

Once having decided what they would like to get, how do agencies go about trying to achieve their objectives? Today, we do not even have a preliminary list of the most common strategies used by participants in trying to influence budgetary outcomes. Again, the techniques listed above should bring the necessary data to light.

Perhaps a few examples will demonstrate the importance of understanding budgetary strategies. There are times when an agency wishes to cut its own budget because it has lost faith in a program, for internal disciplinary reasons, or because it would like to use the money elsewhere. If the agency is particularly well endowed with effective clientele groups, however, it may not only fail in this purpose but may actually see the appropriation increased as this threat mobilizes the affected interests. One budget officer informed me that he tried to convince the Budget Bureau to undertake two projects which the agency did not want but which several influential Congressmen felt strongly about. Otherwise, the official argued, the Congressmen would secure their desires by offering additional projects to their colleagues. The Budget Bureau turned him down and the result was nine unwanted projects instead of two.

The appearance of a budget may take on considerable importance, a circumstance which is often neglected by proponents of program budgeting. Suppose that an agency has strong clientele backing for individual projects. It is likely to gain by presenting them separately so that any cut may be readily identified and support easily mobilized. Lumping a large number of items together may facilitate cuts on an across-the-board basis. Items lacking support, on the other hand, may do better by being placed in large categories so that it is more difficult to single them out for deeper slashes.

We might also inquire (through questionnaires, interviews, direct observation, documentary research) about the participants' perceptions of their roles and the reciprocal expectations they have about the behavior of others. In speaking to officials concerned with budgeting I was impressed with how often the behavior they described was predicated on a belief about what others would do, how they would react in turn, how a third participant would react to this result and so on. Budgetary items are commonly adjusted on the basis of mutual expectations or on a single participant's notion of the role he is expected to play. I strongly suspect, on the basis of some interviewing, that if we studied conceptions of role prevalent on the House Appropriations Committee, their transmittal to new members and staff, and the consequent resistance of members to seeing party as relevant to choice, we would understand a great deal more about the characteristic behavior of many members as budget cutters.

My interviews suggest that the administrator's perception of Congressional knowledge and motivation helps determine the kind of relationships he seeks to establish. The administrator who feels that the members of his appropriations sub-committees are not too well informed on specifics and that they evaluate the agency's program on the basis of feedback from constituents, stresses the role of supporting interests in maintaining good relations with Congressmen. He may not feel the need to be too careful with his estimates. The administrator who believes that the Congressmen are well informed and fairly autonomous is likely to stress personal relationships and demonstrations of good work as well as clientele support. Priority in research should be given to study of these perceptions and the ways in which they determine behavior.

Another approach would be to locate and segregate classes of administrative officials who are found by observation to have or not to have the confidence of the appropriations committees and to seek to explain the differences. For if there is any one thing which participants in budgeting are likely to stress, it is the importance of maintaining relations of confidence and they are highly conscious of what this requires. Since it appears from preliminary investigation that the difference is not accounted for by the popularity of the agency or its programs, it is possible that applications of some gross psychological and skill categories would reveal interesting results.

Many participants in budgeting (in the agencies, Congress, the Budget Bureau) speak of somehow having arrived at a total figure which represents an agency's or an activity's "fair share" of the budget. The fact that a fair share concept exists may go a long way toward explaining the degree of informal coordination that exists among the participants in budgeting. Investigation of how these figures are arrived at and communicated would help us understand how notions of limits (ceilings and floors) enter into budgetary decisions. A minimum effort in this direction would require the compilation of appropriations histories of various agencies and programs rather than just individual case histories which concentrate on some specific event or moment in time. Investigation of the Tennessee Valley Authority's experience in securing electric power appropriations, over a twenty-five-year period, for example, reveals patterns and presents explanatory possibilities which would not otherwise be available.

By its very nature the budgetary process presents excellent opportunities for the use of quantitative data although these must be used with great caution and with special attention to their theoretical relevance. Richard Fenno has collected figures on thirty-seven bureaus dealing with domestic policies from 1947 to 1958 from their initial estimates to decisions by the Budget Bureau, appropriations committees in both houses, conference committees, and floor action. Using these figures he expects to go beyond the usual facile generalizations that the House cuts and the Senate raises bureau estimates, to the much more interesting question of determining the conditions under which the patterns that do exist actually obtain. Although such data do not by any means tell the whole story, they can be used to check generalizations about patterns of floor action or conference committee action which would not otherwise be possible.

.   .   .   .

The Goals of Knowledge and Reform

Concentration on developing at least the rudiments of a descriptive theory is not meant to discourage concern with normative theory and reform. On the contrary, it is worthwhile studying budgeting from both standpoints. Surely, it is not asking too much to suggest that a lot of reform be preceded by a little knowledge. The point is that until we develop more adequate descriptive theory about budgeting, until we know something about the "existential situation" in which the participants find themselves under our political system, proposals for major reform must be based on woefully inadequate understanding. A proposal which alters established relationships, which does not permit an agency to show certain programs in the most favorable light, which does not tell influential Congressmen what they want to know, which changes prevailing expectations about the behavior of key participants, or which leads to different calculations of an agency's fair share, would have many consequences no one is even able to guess at today. Of course, small, incremental changes proceeding in a pragmatic fashion of trial and error could proceed as before without benefit of theory; but this is not the kind of change with which the literature on budgeting is generally concerned.

Perhaps the "study of budgeting" is just another expression for the "study of politics"; yet one cannot study everything at once, and the vantage point offered by concentration on budgetary decisions offers a useful and much neglected perspective from which to analyze the making of policy. The opportunities for comparison are ample, the outcomes are specific and quantifiable, and a dynamic quality is assured by virtue of the comparative ease with which one can study the development of budgetary items over a period of years.

The Hoover Commission Recommendation

for a Performance Budget

The budget and appropriation process is the heart of the management and control of the executive branch.

There is a great need for reform in the method of budgeting and in the appropriation structure.

The federal budget is an inadequate document, poorly organized and improperly designed to serve its major purpose, which is to present an understandable and workable financial plan for the expenditures of the government. The document has grown larger and larger each year as the government's requirements have increased, but its general framework and method of presentation have not changed. The latest budget document, that for 1949-50, contains 1,625 closely printed pages, with about 1,500,000 words, and sums covering thousands of specific appropriations.

There is no uniformity in the schedules of appropriations. Some appropriations represent huge sums, others small amounts. Appropriations for the same service appear in many different places. Much of this results from historical accident.

The Bureau of Indian Affairs, for example, had approximately 100 appropriation titles and subtitles for the expenditure during the fiscal year 1947-48 of about $50,000,000. The largest appropriation item for this bureau amounted to more than $11,000,000, while the smallest item was $114.53.

At the other extreme, perhaps, is the Veterans' Administration, which has an appropriation item of more than a billion dollars for "salaries and expenses," a title which indicates nothing whatever of the work program of that organization.

A Performance Budget

Recommendation No. 1: *We recommend that the whole budgetary concept of the federal government should be refashioned by the adoption of a budget based upon functions, activities, and projects; this we designate as a "performance budget."*

Such an approach would focus attention upon the general character and relative importance of the work to be done, or upon the service to be rendered, rather than upon the things to be acquired, such as personal services, supplies, equipment, and so on. These latter objects are, after all, only the means to an end. The all-important thing in budgeting is the work or the service to be accomplished, and what that work or service will cost.

Under performance budgeting, attention is centered on the function or activity — on the accomplishment of the purpose — instead of on lists of employees or authorizations of purchases. In reality, this method of budgeting concentrates congressional action and executive direction on the scope and magnitude of the different federal activities. It places both accomplishment and cost in a clear light before the Congress and the public. . . .

To indicate the deficiencies of existing practices, we may cite here the National

From Commission on Organization of the Executive Branch of the Government, *Budgeting and Accounting*, (Washington D.C., Government Printing Office, 1949), pp. 7–13.

Naval Medical Center at Bethesda. This hospital now receives allotments from twelve different Navy appropriation titles such as:

Secretary's Office — Miscellaneous Expenses, Navy

Bureau of Ships — Maintenance

Bureau of Ordnance — Ordnance and Ordnance Stores

Bureau of Supplies and Accounts — Pay, Subsistence, and Transportation

Bureau of Supplies and Accounts — Maintenance

Bureau of Supplies and Accounts — Transportation of Things

Bureau of Medicine and Surgery — Medical Department, Navy

Five Other Similar Appropriation Titles

We propose, for instance, that by using performance budgeting, the costs of operating the Bethesda Center, along with those of other comparable Naval hospitals, would be shown as an identifiable program under one appropriation title for "Medical Care." ...

The idea of a performance budget is not new. It has been adopted in the modernization of budgets by some states and several municipalities.

The performance budget does not change or shift legislative responsibility; control by the Congress still lies in the power to limit expenditures by appropriations. Performance budgeting gives more comprehensive and reliable information to the President, the Congress, and the general public, and helps the individual congressman to understand what the government is doing, how much it is doing, and what the costs are. Supporting schedules can be fully provided, and in more understandable and effective form.

One of the primary purposes of the performance budget would be to improve congressional examination of budgetary requirements. Such examination should be largely on the level of accomplishment, and for this reason the Congress needs to know clearly just what the whole of the expenditures is and what the executive and administrative agencies propose to do with the money they request. In the Bethesda case mentioned above, the Congress under the new system would have presented [to it] the cost of operating the hospital in detail, so that the Congress might readily compare such cost with that of the preceding year or with the costs of other comparable hospitals.

The Bureau of Ships in the Navy Department, for example, is financed by twenty-seven appropriations, many of which, as shown in the budget, have no apparent connection with the Bureau. Efforts have been made to resolve this confusion through the working out of an adequate budget structure. The ideas thus developed have been applied in part to the new Air Force estimates as set forth in the budget in 1949-50.

In a detailed example, given at the end of this part of the report, of the effect of performance budgeting on the Forest Service, our task force points out that the real operating cost of the Forest Service for the management and protection of the national forests does not appear in full under that heading in the budget, but actually is included in several other places. The total operating cost for the national forests, as displayed by the performance budget, would be shown as about $43,000,000 instead of only $26,000,000 as indicated under the present appropriation headings in the budget.

The New Approach

Indeed, the first task of the Appropriations Committee is to review what has been accomplished and what is proposed for the future period, the latter always being examined in the light of the past experience. The approach which we propose should enable these committees more easily to decide the basic expenditure issue each year; namely, just what should be the magnitude of the many federal programs.

The performance budget would make it possible for the budget document to be submitted and acted upon in a shorter length of time. It would not delay or hamper the action of the Congress on the Budget. It would assure more complete expenditure estimates and more accurate revenue figures for the next budget period.

Executive and legislative review of functional estimates and program justifications under the performance budget should center around two basic questions:

First: What is the desirable magnitude of any major government program or function in terms of need, relation to other programs, and proportion of total governmental expenditures? This is essentially a question of public policy, and must be answered by the responsible officials of the executive branch and eventually by the Congress.

Second: How efficiently and economically can an approved government program be executed? In other words, can the same amount of work be performed satisfactorily under different arrangements or through improved procedures at less cost?

The performance budget would enable administrators to place responsibility upon subordinate officials for the clear execution of the provisions made by the Congress. It would also simplify the reporting and accounting system.

Appropriation Structure and Performance Budgeting

The present appropriation structure underlying the budget is a patchwork affair evolved over a great many years and following no rational pattern. In some areas of the budget, there are entirely too many appropriation items; in others perhaps too few. Some appropriation items are exceedingly broad in scope; others are narrow on account of excessive itemization. Appropriations for a particular function appear in different places. In spite of recent simplifications, the language of some appropriation items remains a jungle of detailed provisions. Many of these detailed prescriptions would seem to be susceptible of more or less uniform treatment in codified form.

The appropriation structure not only affects the presentation of the budget estimates, but runs to the root of management and fiscal responsibility. Departmental management is complicated and fiscal responsibility is diffused when single bureaus or functions are financed from diverse appropriations.

The appropriation structure is further complicated by several different kinds of authorizations such as annual, no-year, and permanent appropriations, reappropriations, contract authorizations, and appropriations to liquidate contract authorizations. Congress, the press, and the public are therefore often confused about the total amount of appropriations in any major appropriation bill. Certainly a comprehensive survey of existing appropriation practices looking toward simplification of appropriation structure, language, and procedure is long overdue. The revision of these practices should be made along the general lines and in accordance with the underlying purpose of the performance budget.

Recommendation No. 2: *We recommend to the Congress that a complete survey of the appropriation structure should be undertaken without delay.*

USDA's Pioneering Performance Budget

✥ RALPH S. ROBERTS

The pains of adjustment to performance budgeting experienced by most federal agencies in the past decade have not been suffered as severely by the U. S. Department of Agriculture. While the title, performance budgeting, was new to the Department, the functional concept was not. A 1907 report indicates that each bureau of the Department then had a project system developed on a functional basis which enabled the Department head "to coordinate and direct the work of the several bureaus to the greatest possible advantage." At that time the system embraced over 1,300 projects, and new ones were not added without first being brought to the attention of the Secretary.

In the early 1930's, the Department's Budget Office, with the assistance of bureau heads, developed a Uniform Project System and a budget structure that would permit presentation of the Agriculture budget on a functional basis and would relate projects more precisely to substantive programs and the appropriation structure. In simple terms, the Uniform Project System involves three basic categories:

Financial Projects — the first breakdown under an appropriation item — are the basis for financial control and fund accounting (equivalent to what has become "activities" in the President's printed budget)

Work Projects are well-defined continuing activities within the framework of the parent "financial project"

Line Projects are segments of a "work project" limited in the scope of their objectives and usually of limited duration.

This system established uniform categories and terminology throughout the Department for the structural elements of functional budgeting. It related individual projects directly to appropriations or other funds, provided for use of components of the system in program planning as well as budget preparation and review, and prescribed the form and content of formal project descriptions and reporting. By 1935 the system had developed to the point that it could be reflected in printed budget schedules and other budgetary material furnished the Bureau of the Budget and congressional committees.

The advantages of the system — conveying an understanding of financial needs in terms of work to be done and ends to be achieved — were immediately recognized. Thereafter the congressional subcommittees handling the Agriculture appropriation bill gave primary attention to this phase of the presentation; only occasionally were questions asked or attention otherwise directed to the budget schedules indicating how the money would be spent for personal services, supplies, and other aids to getting the job done.

From time to time the Department project system and its application have been reviewed to make it more useful for program management as well as budgetary administration. Throughout, the effort has been directed toward what the late William A. Jump, the Department's first budget officer, described as "a universal language for a program of work discussion so that the Congress, the Budget Bureau,

Reprinted from the *Public Administration Review*, the journal of the American Society for Public Administration, Vol. XX, No. 2, 1960, pp. 74–78, by permission of the publisher.

the Department, the bureau, and the public could all speak the same tongue." "This," said Jump, "would help remove mystery and confusion from public activity where mystery and confusion are not appropriate."

Facilitation of this universal language undoubtedly is the greatest value of performance budgeting. But from it flow other advantages and benefits.

Serves General Management Needs

Experience in the Department of Agriculture has demonstrated conclusively that functional or performance budgeting contributes to program planning and management. By breaking the total program into manageable project units, the Department has a basis for the establishment of meaningful goals related directly to the authority and purpose of each agency and for reporting work accomplishment in relation to appropriate financial and administrative plans and objectives.

Such budgeting has assisted decision-making by prescribing meaningful categories adapted to the needs of successive levels of supervision, management, and executive and legislative review. The supporting structure of the system (project categories, related organizational units, administrative and financial responsibility, and fund accounting) is rationally integrated from the broadest areas of work to the most detailed. This integration permits budgetary and management data flowing from the system to be utilized effectively in a form appropriate to the decision-making level involved. In research work, for example, the "line projects" represent the work being carried out under a research leader or supervisor and is the basis for performance reporting and direct supervisory control. Since there are over 3,000 current research line projects it is evident that line projects, while essential for supervisory and coordinating purposes within a limited area of research, are much too detailed for other management purposes and for budget decisions at higher administrative levels. Consequently, budget planning and decisions are based on "work projects," within the USDA research agency, and on "financial projects," at the Department level. The "financial projects" are justified to the Bureau of the Budget and Congress, though in certain cases groups of related "work projects" might be presented.

Across agency lines within the Department, coordinated data are available from these same sources for the development of special analyses on program subjects having interrelationships. For instance, one of the broad objectives of the Department of Agriculture can be described as "research and education." Seven of the seventeen agencies of the Department have major program responsibilities in this broad area. Each year, the budget presented to the Congress is supported by a special analysis reflecting in financial terms the total scope of the Department's research and education programs over a ten-year period.

The basic structure necessary for an effective performance budget has contributed in a very material way to general executive direction and to appropriate coordination of management responsibilities. It has provided the primary tools through which the substantive program can be planned and carried out with a common knowledge and understanding of the scope and ends to be achieved on each project. It has served as an important aid in clarifying legislative and executive intent for the project administrator or supervisor and has insured consistency of budget and management decisions at all operating levels.

Performance budgeting has forced the public administrator to look more carefully at organizational structure and to organize around rational and logical aspects of the program he is administering. This has undoubtedly contributed to more effective organization and improved management. The very process of identifying program elements and relating them simultaneously to goals, program and financial planning, and organization, tends to assure the execution of management responsibility to a degree that might not otherwise exist. The process has quickly revealed weaknesses in the interrelationships of these elements of management, particularly in a growing organization. When projects or activities are related directly to both organizational structure and financial planning, effective reorganization is facilitated — the "building blocks" can be identified quickly and re-arranged without losing identity or integrity. In 1953 when the Department of Agriculture effected a substantial reorganization, it relied heavily on its budgetary project system for information essential to putting together related activities and services.

Facilitates Decentralization of Responsibility

The increasing bigness and complexity of government today demand decentralization of management and operating authority. The existence of a budgetary process, properly developed along functional lines, creates a management framework and climate that encourages decentralization.

In the Department of Agriculture the Uniform Project System is used as the instrument for establishing the limits of discretion available to agency administrators in adjusting program operations to meet changing conditions.

Immediately after the appropriation act is passed by the Congress, each agency is required to submit a plan to the Secretary reflecting its proposed distribution of appropriated funds by financial projects (or sometimes work projects), which reflects legislative action on proposals in the President's budget. These proposals are called Project Obligation Estimates. Once these estimates are approved for the year, agencies are given the flexibility to shift up to 10 per cent of the funds available for each project without further clearance with the Secretary. The Secretary's Office must approve adjustments in excess of 10 per cent. This procedure provides assurance that agency program plans are in accord with Department policy and congressional intent while permitting considerable flexibility to enable program administrators to meet changing conditions. Agencies in the Department have established similar procedures to further decentralize program decision-making to field installations and other subordinate operating units. Since lines of administrative responsibility, performance reporting, and fund control are directly related to the same project categories used in the formulation of the budget estimates and in the Project Obligation Estimates, the system provides the means for both decentralizing decision-making and monitoring it.

Congressional Acceptance

Experience has demonstrated that this decentralization is not limited to the executive branch; it has been equally apparent in the legislative-executive relationship. The Project Obligation Estimates referred to above also serve as a key device for ensuring and facilitating the carrying out of congressional intent.

Whenever the committees on appropriations determine that program modifications should be made, they customarily so indicate in the report that accompanies the appropriation bill. The directive, for example, may be to initiate a new activity or to shift emphasis between existing projects. Related funds may or may not be added by the committees. In either event, the procedure in the Department assures that the directive is reflected in the revised program plans for the year.

Over the years, the committees on appropriations have developed a confidence that congressional intent will be faithfully carried out by the Department. They therefore do not feel the need for detailed appropriation "line-item" control. This confidence has been reflected in the consolidation and reduction in the number of appropriation items and the elimination of detailed limitations in appropriation language that frequently circumscribed desirable management flexibility. An example involved a reorganization which consolidated a number of specialized research bureaus into the Agricultural Research Service. The appropriation structure and financial project categories for research were streamlined and the budget presentation simplified. During hearings on the 1956 Budget, the House committee on appropriations explored in detail the workings of the Uniform Project System in the research area, with particular interest in the procedures for initiating, coordinating, reviewing, and terminating work at the line project level. Committee members apparently were reassured that the system was operating effectively and focused on the broader categories of work in subsequent years.

Problems and Pitfalls

While performance budgeting has its advantages and benefits, it also has its problems. Some of these are transitional and are involved only in the development of the system; others are perennial in character.

In converting to the performance concept, agencies were confronted immediately with the problem of selecting appropriate, adaptable functional categories. Ideally, these classifications — the heart of performance budgeting — should follow organizational and management lines of responsibility. Philosophers and natural scientists, however, long ago discovered that the diverse world of reality does not always lend itself to neat and discrete categories most useful for classification purposes.

In the Department of Agriculture, the ideal of uniform, logical functional patterns for budgeting, organization, and management has not been fully realized. Nor is it likely ever to be achieved completely in this or any other large agency of government. Programs such as those in Agriculture, and the varied management techniques and methods most adaptable to each, are too diverse and unlike to be forced into a strictly uniform mold. In broad outline the approach is applied uniformly. In the application of detail, however, the uniformity achieved is one of degree. In a research program, for example, the functional concept and the breakdown of the program of work into definitive manageable units can be carried out to a greater degree than in an operating program such as that of price supports in the Commodity Credit Corporation. Similarly, in some agencies it has been possible to have an exact correlation of functional projects or groups of related functional projects with organizational units. In others, because of the nature and scope of the program, functional areas more logically cross organization lines.

Performance budgeting does not solve the greatest problem in budget decision-making — the comparative evaluation of projects, functions, or activities. Unfortunately, some people think it does. Although performance budgeting aids such determinations by bringing functions or activities into sharper focus, more frequently than not the functions or activities are not comparable. Thus, management must rely on other tools and techniques to decide whether funds might result in greater public benefit if applied to one function or activity rather than another.

Ponderosity is one of the most difficult continuing problems in the management of any system of effective performance budgeting. Program administrators and operating people develop a certain amount of annoyance about the burden of maintaining the required records. Eternal vigilance is necessary to prevent the sheer weight of paper work from overshadowing the value of the system. Once the performance budget concept was adopted throughout the executive branch and formally implemented in the 1951 budget, there was a natural tendency to refine and extend the classification of budget activities wherever possible. This resulted to some extent in development of functional classifications to assemble detail beyond what budget making or efficient management demanded.

On the other hand, the system can become so skeletonized that it fails to inform adequately. It must be strictly utilitarian for operating and management purposes — it is not enough that it serves only as an aid to budget presentation.

This problem of ponderosity has been aggravated in varying degree in federal agencies by the recommendation of the second Hoover Commission in 1955 that performance budgeting be administered on an "accrued expenditure" and cost basis, a concept which has not been accepted wholly as essential in some agencies or by congressional appropriations committees.

Performance budgeting also tends to encourage overdecentralizing, over-simplifying appropriation structure, and consolidating of functional categories for purely budgetary purposes or for ease in supporting the budget with cost data. Take care also that there is not too much performance budgeting. In an attempt to make the most of the functional concept there can develop inevitably a tendency to carry the process to an extreme conclusion. Unless this tendency is curbed, an agency might over-extend itself in decentralizing program administration, simplifying appropriation structure, and consolidating functional categories for purely budgetary purposes or for building-in cost accounting support. In so doing there is a risk of obscuring important program and management considerations in the very process of attempting to bring them into sharper focus.

The federal budget now contains certain functional classifications developed by the Bureau of the Budget for special analysis. One primary classification is "Agriculture and Agriculture Resources," which is divided into five sub-functions. It is conceivable that the Department's budget presentation and appropriations could be limited to these broad categories. While such categories have some use for illustrating certain relationships, they are much too broad to reveal the significant program activities of the Department or to serve as a firm basis for budgetary decisions and management control.

A Tool — But Only a Tool

On the whole, performance budgeting, including its essential supporting structure, is proving to be a valuable tool for effective budget decision-making at all levels of large complex operations. Moreover, when properly developed and understood, it can serve important management needs beyond those related directly to the budget process. However, it is only a tool — it is not a panacea. Whether it is a manageable or unwieldy one depends largely on the skill of the tool maker. How effectively it is applied depends on the skill, imagination, energy, and strength of purpose of the user.

Performance budgeting has not and cannot of itself reduce government expenditures, as many of its advocates once believed. Nor will it provide a guarantee that government funds will be spent most wisely and effectively, as many of its supporters hope. No mere technique can ever provide such assurance. The most advanced and imaginative budgetary techniques developed or yet to be developed will prove inadequate substitutes for responsible public administration.

Program Packages and the Program Budget in the Department of Defense

❧ ROBERT J. MASSEY

For at least a half century reformers have been seeking means for optimum — or at least more "rational" — allocation of public resources among competing uses. It has been widely assumed that the goal could be achieved if budgets could be organized so that benefits were clearly related to their costs. This concept has been termed the *program budget*.

The goal of the program budget was implied in the report of the Taft Commission of 1912. The recommendation of the first Hoover Commission for "a budget based upon functions, activities, and projects" led to the implementing legislation of the Budgeting and Accounting Procedures Act of 1950. Even though significant progress has been made, the benefits achieved did not measure up to the high hopes of the budget reformers.

The Quiet Revolution

Now, innovations in defense planning-programming-budgeting are yielding the fruits of a workable program budget. The new system is known officially as *programming*, and more popularly as the *program packages*.

Many normally well-informed observers of developments in public administration were unaware that a significant development had occurred, even months after *programming* was substantially implemented. Because of the unorthodox ancestry of the *programming* innovations, theoretical discussion in professional journals, which so often precedes significant advances, was almost completely lacking. Even today, the small amount of theoretical material available is largely devoted to explanation of what has been implemented.

Programming grew from a unique union of RAND Corporation theories with Special Projects Office (Polaris) practice. The aims and philosophy of programming were set forth in *The Economics of Defense in the Nuclear Age*. This book was written by Charles J. Hitch and several of his associates from the Economics Division of RAND Corporation before Mr. Hitch became Comptroller of the Department of Defense (DOD). The administrative mechanisms — which make achievement of the goals enunciated in *Economics of Defense* possible — were developed under the direction of Hugh McCullough, Mr. Hitch's deputy for programming, after Mr. Hitch took office as DOD Comptroller. When Mr. Hitch recruited him, Hugh McCullough was top civilian official on Admiral Raborn's management team as Director of the Special Projects Office, Plans and Programs Division. The entire Fleet Ballistic Missile system effort had been called a *program package* and the subsystems *program elements* since the early days of the program.

Reprinted from the *Public Administration Review*, the journal of the American Society for Public Administration, Vol. XXIII, No. 1, 1963, pp. 30–34, by permission of the publisher.

The "Balanced" Budget

The prime aim of both the *program budget* and the *program package* is a *balanced* budget in the sense of an allocation of resources such that no improvement in total benefit could be gained by shifting resources from one program to an alternative.

Principal mechanism for allocating resources — for attempting to achieve balance — in the Department of Defense, as in most organizations, has been the budgetary process. However, the annual budget had serious limitations for the balancing task in the modern military environment, where major weapon systems have such enormous costs and long development lead-times.

The budget's orientation along functional lines — military personnel, operations and maintenance, research and development, procurement, and military construction — made it difficult to relate cost *inputs* with the military capability *outputs*.

Perhaps a more serious deficiency was the budget's short-range view. The budget for any year was largely a reflection of decisions made in previous years and, for the most part, outside its disciplining framework. If a balanced program did not result from those program decisions made outside the budgetary process, the defect could not be remedied in the process of preparing the budget for the year the major payments fell due. In its overriding emphasis on the single upcoming fiscal year, the budget process proved a poor vehicle for the all-important long-range choice of strategies and weapon systems.

Traditionally in the Defense Department, military planning and budgeting have been treated as independent activities, the first falling primarily within the province of the military side of the house; the second a concern chiefly of the comptroller. Planning was done in terms of military forces and major weapons systems projected over a period of five to ten years, while budgeting covered only the one year ahead. Military plans were prepared without systematic consideration of resource limitations and the costs of the plans generally exceeded any budgets the President was willing to request or Congress approve. Only when it came time to budget for a one fiscal year increment of the long-range programs were cost implications fully worked out.

Furthermore, the focus of balancing efforts was directed toward internal balance within each Service. Even if this goal had been achieved the military forces required to carry out major *national* military missions — which all involve *inputs* from more than one Service — would, in all probability, have remained unbalanced.

Budget Decisions Are Program Decisions

In view of these limitations of the annual budget, Mr. Hitch sought to exploit to the fullest the tools of financial management as aids for making the decisions required to develop a balanced set of programs, *but to use them outside the narrow confines of the annual budgetary process.*

The prime publicly announced goal of the *program package* approach was to "bridge the gap" between planning and programming on the one hand and financial management and budgeting on the other, "to introduce economic resource considerations into the decision-making process in a timely and meaningful manner."

Mr. Hitch has pointed out that budget decisions are inherently program decisions. Through *programming* he seeks to make the reverse also true, to have program decisions consciously made as budget decisions. Ideally a decision to embark upon a program should be a specific decision to include the funds to carry it out in the budget as submitted by the Department of Defense.

The Program Package and Program Effectiveness

One of his first steps in "bridging the gap" was to tie cost *inputs* with the *outputs* of military forces. These groupings were called *program elements*. A *program element* was defined as "an integrated activity, a combination of men, equipment and installations, whose effectiveness can be related to our national security policy objectives." Examples of such forces are B-52 squadrons, infantry battle groups, and combatant ships taken together with all the equipment, men, installations, supplies, and support required to make them effective military forces.

Costs are projected five years into the future and forces three years more. Hitch stated that, ideally, full lifetime costs of weapon systems should be projected before the decision is made to procure them for inventory. However, in view of the admittedly primitive state of the art of long-range cost projections, five years was selected as long enough to give a feel for the long-range costs implied, but not too long for them to be reasonably valid.

For effectiveness comparison — the measure of the value of forces — each *program element* must be described both in terms of its physical characteristics as well as its capabilities. This information "should be explicit and concrete, using quantitative comparisons and examples in place of generalized, qualitative evaluations."

A most important aspect of effectiveness measurement is the requirement that it be traced to *basic national security objectives*. It is not enough that a weapon system have spectacular performance, or be capable of enormous destruction. It is not even enough that it be a clearly superior replacement for a system currently in the inventory. The big tests now, for old systems as well as new ones, are: what contributions can it make to the jobs which must be done to carry out United States national security objectives? and, how does it compare, on a cost and effectiveness basis, with the available alternative ways of performing those military tasks?

Through *programming* the legitimate and worthwhile goals of *unification* can be achieved without establishing a super-bureaucracy to sap the lifeblood of the nation's defense establishment and paralyze its decision-making processes.

In order to facilitate the achievement of program balance through *rational trade-offs*, *program elements* are grouped into *packages*, or *major programs* oriented around a military mission or set of related purposes. Each package contains elements from more than one Service. The first four *program packages* are defined in terms of major military missions: Strategic Retaliatory Forces (SAC, Polaris); Continental Air and Missile Defense Forces; General Purpose Forces, the means to fight so-called "conventional war"; and Airlift and Sealift Forces. The next three major *program packages*, Reserve and Guard Forces, Research and Development, and General Support, are designed to support the first four mission-oriented packages. The General Support package is the "all other" grouping which includes items, such as the service academies, which cannot be charged meaningfully against the other *packages*. The last two packages are Civil Defense and Military Assistance.

Rational Analysis in Place of Hectic Chaos

Once a set of approved programs, fully costed and with revenue requirements within the limits of anticipated resources, have been developed, the preparation of the annual budget is a relatively orderly and painless process. "There should be no need," Mr. Hitch has said, "for a hectic and hurried *program* review crammed into a few weeks in the midst of the annual budget review." The budget making phase should consist essentially of converting a one year slice of approved long-range programs into appropriate budget format and supporting detail.

The determination of military requirements — the analysis of the military jobs to be done — and reconsideration and modification of the approved force structure, is now a year-round process. A reporting and control system has been established through which performance is measured against the approved program plans. Monthly reports relate physical and financial progress against established program milestones. In the event of variance beyond specified thresholds, the Service involved must submit a program change proposal, thus initiating new program decisions at the Secretary of Defense level.

In summary, the new procedure is designed to:

Provide for more orderly, continuous program review in contrast to the hectic program-budget review crammed into just a few weeks of the year, which had, in the words of Mr. Hitch, "been the practice in the past";
Disclose the full financial implications of program decisions;
Keep future military planning roughly in balance with probable resources and dollar availabilities — thereby minimizing the number of false starts and reducing the number of marginal and excessive support programs; and,
Promote unified, balanced *over-all* defense programs in place of *unilaterally* balanced Army, Navy and Air Force programs.

In his 1961 statement to the Jackson Subcommittee of the Senate on National Policy Machinery, Mr. Hitch put *programming* in perspective this way:

These improvements, of themselves, will not make the hard decisions easy, nor will they make simple the complex problem of formulating national defense policy. What they will do, we hope, is facilitate the rational analysis of national security problems. They will make us aware of the full cost implications of the choices we make. They will permit us, in shorter time and with greater accuracy, to cost out the various policy alternatives presented to the National Security Council for its consideration. I feel very strongly that whether one is choosing among particular items of equipment or among various policy proposals, it is extremely useful to array explicitly the alternatives and their respective costs and effectiveness. The procedures we are developing will promote this way of looking at defense problems, this way of deciding how best to defend the security of the United States.

Cracks in Program Budget Theory

Now that the *programming* system is in operation — though not yet fully perfected to the satisfaction of its architects — it may be asked why it took so long to arrive at this reasonably straightforward means of achieving the goals of the program budget. The reason most previous attempts to achieve a true program budget were not successful may be traced to some fundamental flaws in program budget theory, flaws which *programming* by-passes.

For years most critics, including the Second Hoover Commission, assumed that the program budget could become a reality only when agencies were reorganized so they could function along major-purpose lines.

It was also assumed that little significant progress toward a *program budget* could be achieved without willing congressional participation. Mosher held that "The Army, Navy, and Air Force can do little until the Budget Bureau and the appropriations committees are prepared to review budgets of the kind suggested here (program budgets)." There have been many indications that Congress was not ready to approve a true program budget, since it is not a particularly productive framework for detailed evaluation of performance.

Various critics have recognized that the program budget, while well suited for selecting programs, was inadequate for program control or performance evaluation. To meet this problem, Smithies proposed a two-budget system of the program budget for internal decision making and submission to Congress, and an "administrative budget" for program control and performance evaluation. Hitch's approach separates the budget into two elements somewhat along the lines Smithies recommended, but in the inverse order. The program budget is used for program decision making within the Department of Defense, with the annual budget submitted to Congress in the traditional format.

Great Ideas Are Simple

This separation of the decision-making budget from the budget going to Congress made it possible to place the reforms in effect without prior congressional approval. As a matter of fact, implementation was well along before Mr. Hitch or any other defense official made any formal presentation of the *programming* system to any congressional committees. The first explanation of the system to any congressional committee was made July 13, 1961 to the Subcommittee on Department of Defense Appropriations of the House Committee on Appropriations. This briefing, which unfortunately was not published, was made almost three months after the *programming* system was unveiled within the Department of Defense.

Even if Congress had given à *carte blanche* for unlimited reorganization, it is probable that the fruits sought through the program budget would still have remained out of reach. Mosher pointed out an inherent contradiction in the concept of the program budget. He said programs are not separate and discrete, but interwoven in such a way that a logical program budget for one program would preclude logical program budgets for other activities. For instance, if the Commanding General of Fort Benning had a true program budget for his activity, he would be free to effect trade-offs between troop medical facilities and any other part of his program, such as training ammunition. However, such a budget would compromise the Surgeon General's program budget.

Hugh McCullough discussed the same problem in an interview with the author. When asked if he thought the *program packages* would lead to a program budget, he replied that if by such a term was meant a budget along the lines of the *program packages* and *program elements*, the administration did not intend to seek such a change. He pointed out that some activities which are good *programs* for administration cross several *program elements*. He gave as an example a radar which might be installed on ships which were in many different elements and packages. He considered the existing budget at least as well suited for administration as a program budget along the lines of the packages and elements. Logical programs, such as the Mark 46 torpedo, are now managed as integrated programs with their costs assigned statistically to the appropriate *program elements*.

Mr. McCullough also said the administration did not intend to seek program lifetime funding, or any extension of the funding period. He pointed out that any extension of the funding period would have the disadvantage of impairing freedom to make program changes in response to changing conditions. In short, once the major program decisions were removed from the confines of the preparation of the annual budget, the traditional budget was found to be quite satisfactory for its purposes.

New Fields to Conquer

The problems which *programming* is designed to solve are not unique to defense administration. Every responsible manager must allocate limited resources among competing needs. If *programming* proves successful in its prototype tests in the Department of Defense, its spread throughout the Federal Government should follow in due course. In his testimony before the Jackson Subcommittee on "The Budget and the Policy Process," Budget Director David Bell displayed a comprehensive understanding of the *programming* innovations and said of them ". . . this is clearly the correct direction to move."

How to Improve the Financial
Management Improvement Program

✢ L. N. TEITELBAUM

The Joint Financial Management Improvement Program started about thirteen years ago as a joint effort of the Bureau of the Budget, Treasury Department, and General Accounting Office. The program has been responsible for significant developments and changes in approach to activities in federal agencies generally termed financial management.

The program emphasizes the necessity of establishing financial management systems of maximum usefulness within each agency that are appropriately responsive to executive and legislative needs. It encourages the use of modern accounting, budgeting and related reporting systems, along with the application of sound organization and internal control concepts and practices best suited to agency needs.

Since the inception of the program, there have been substantial changes and progress toward accrual accounting practices and cost-based budgeting; integration of accounting and finance functions with budgeting and reporting activities in many agencies; expanded use of automatic data processing systems; and reductions in paperwork. While there is not complete unanimity about how far some of the goals, such as accrual accounting and cost-based budgeting should be carried, there is more or less general agreement that significant improvements have been achieved by many agencies under the aegis of the program.

Accountants, auditors, and budget personnel have an important role to play in this improvement effort. Financial management functions cut across and affect all operations. Because these information-gathering and analytical functions provide data which are essential for sound decision-making, accountants, auditors and budget personnel should employ the most modern tools available to compile and analyze the information; to recommend both the best solutions to financial management problems and alternative actions available; and to participate in measures designed to reduce costs and streamline operations.

"How to Improve the Financial Management Improvement Program," by L. N. Teitelbaum, from *Federal Accountant* (March, 1962), pp. 80–90. © 1962 by the Federal Government Accountants Association. Reprinted by permission.

Financial Management — Its Objectives and Scope

A study of the statements in Bureau of the Budget Bulletin No. 57-5 and numerous pamphlets and articles leads one to the conclusion that the Joint Program goes beyond improvements in budgeting and accounting systems. The changed and expanded scope of the improvement program includes all other ". . . tools to assist in improved *planning, execution, and control of operations* and thus encourage better management in the executive branch" (emphasis supplied).

The above conclusion is also supported by secondary evidence such as the fact that the "Joint Program for the Improvement of *Financial Management* in the Federal Government" was originally called the "Joint Program for Improving Accounting in the Federal Government." The significance of the change in the scope of the program, as well as in the title, may not be fully recognized of the most important and significant business developments of our day." It is common knowledge that a number of the progressive and better known graduate schools of business and others which consider themselves innovators in the field of higher business education are concentrating their course material on the use of quantitative controls in business and are emphasizing mathematical and statistical techniques for managerial decision-making purposes.

Progressive business and professional accounting and management firms have recognized the values of these statistical and mathematical techniques and are allocating increased funds for research, development, tests and application of these methods in their operations and services. Significantly, many companies and public accounting firms have either established or are expanding their so-called "operations research" or "management service" divisions in order to meet the demand for better and more scientific management.

Need for Organized Direction

In order to promote wide and effective application of these modern scientific tools to financial management problems, strong central direction is needed. Since leadership in improving accounting and budgeting is already provided through the joint efforts of three central agencies — the Bureau of the Budget, Treasury Department and General Accounting Office — it is logical that promotion of and guidance in the use of these analytical methods be furnished by one of the three agencies, preferably the Bureau of the Budget. This agency is most directly concerned with the managerial and financial affairs of the Executive Branch of the government and should be the bellwether in this area of development.

Wherever centered, it is essential that a competent and skilled group or team be organized and properly staffed to promote and guide this effort. Experience over the past ten years has shown and understood. A brochure, The Joint Program for Improving Accounting in the Federal Government — Its Scope, Objectives, Concepts and Methods, published jointly by the Bureau of the Budget, the Treasury Department and the General Accounting Office in May, 1958, describes the scope of the program as follows:

When this program got underway, the accounting practices of the government were the first to be given attention. . . . However, it was early recognized that if full benefits were to be obtained from the accounting changes being made, the *area of improvement* effort would have to include budgeting, reporting, and *related control procedures* in relation to program planning and execution. This was one of the early significant benefits of the joint nature of the program. As a result, the program has *broadened in scope to encompass these elements of financial management.* (Emphasis supplied).

If this interpretation is correct, the time has arrived to recognize that "better management" and "improved planning, execution and control of operations" cannot be obtained solely through accounting and budgeting changes. Fortunately developments during the last ten years in the field of general business management have provided a rich source of scientific tools and analytical techniques which, if effectively applied to appropriate financial management areas in the federal government, could have a profound effect on improving management practices and results. The use of these in the solution of business management problems is spreading rapidly, particularly in private business, under such names as "operations research," "management science" and "advanced management methods." Because they involve the use of mathematical and statistical techniques, their nature tends to be obscured or misunderstood and they frighten off many of those involved in financial operations.

Nevertheless knowledgeable observers report (a) that industry, particularly big industry, is experiencing a virtual revolution in industrial management based on mathematical and statistical handling of business data, facilitated by the use of electronic computers; (b) that the growth in the use of these tools ". . . is probably the most important business development of the last decade . . ."; and (c) that ". . . today, . . . it is fair to state that its [operations research or the scientific method] use is one that the analytical approach to solving business problems is almost always a team effort. The responsibility is assigned to a group of people carefully selected as to background and experience. In the financial management area trained technicians — statisticians, mathematicians, and perhaps industrial engineers — should team up with accountants and other financially oriented personnel to stimulate and direct the agencies in the proper application of these analytical methods.

Inasmuch as the basic vehicles for effective financial management are sound accounting and budget systems, and a full understanding of their meaning and purpose is necessary, it is suggested that the leadman or manager of the group be an accountant of wide experience in government operations. It would, of course, be highly desirable if this leadman also had a knowledge of and experience with these statistical and mathematical tools as they are being utilized in business management.

A central group or team is not an unusual or revolutionary organization. As stated previously, many companies already have established comparable units. Some Federal agencies also have units of this general nature usually known as operations analysis, management analysis or management services, but there seems to be no coordinated direction of these efforts, nor is the work tied directly to the financial management program.

Such a group or team must be of proper size and composition so that it can work directly with the executive departments; advise and encourage them in setting up sound programs, including educational and training programs; assist them in *actual demonstrations* of the usefulness and effectiveness of these methods in solving a wide variety of management problems; and act as a focal point for exchange of experience and testing of results. If the experience of private industry in the past ten years is any criterion, it can be shown that the cost of staffing and operating such a unit would be offset many times by the savings and reduced costs resulting from the use of these advanced techniques. Considering the size and complexity of government operations, the potential for improvement through the use of these scientific management methods is at present almost unlimited.

Many federal accountants have been reading literature on this subject, taking courses, and participating in institutes and seminars, and thus have gained some familiarity with basic concepts and theory. The next step, however, is the difficult one: how to get started; how to define the problem; how to plan and apply the appropriate techniques to actual problems; and how to test and evaluate the results. While individuals sometimes bravely strike out for themselves, the risk is great that without competent guidance and direction the techniques may not be properly applied, or the wrong method used, and result in disappointments and failures which may do much harm.

A central unit could provide a practical program of study, training and implementation. It would increase the chances of obtaining useful results and become a valuable clearing-house for exchange of information. Such a central group would act as a guidance unit to groups and individuals within agencies and among agencies, and point out ways that these effective tools can be used in day-to-day work. This approach would appear to be superior to the alternative of setting up independent units in each agency to "go it alone," or for individuals to try to use these techniques on their own initiative and learn by trial and error.

There is considerable evidence of a real need and demand for a competent consulting service group in the federal government available to financial type personnel. Officials in many agencies and organizations seem interested in utilizing these scientific management techniques, but find it difficult to locate knowledgeable and experienced personnel within their own organizations to advise and assist them in planning and carrying through applications to their work. These agencies do not have the trained personnel, and may not have the funds to organize and staff special units for this work. Also, it would be much more efficient and less costly to have a central organization to which all the federal agencies could turn for advice, assistance, encouragement and stimulation.

It is possible that some agencies could be persuaded to set up their own units to promote and direct these developments, but it would take many years before the practice would become prevalent and it probably would be confined mainly to larger organizations. Experience indicates that unless there is strong leadership, guidance, assistance and actual demonstrations by a central organization charged with clear responsibility for such a program, the use of these techniques in financial activities will make little headway. As an observer and promoter of one such program in an agency, the author has found that without leadership and backing from top management, and an adequate staff of competent personnel, the program makes little progress.

Nature and Use of These New Techniques

What are these mathematical and statistical tools, and to what type of business problems can they be applied? There are many analytical techniques and a full description of them would require a thick volume or possibly several. Perhaps brief descriptions and examples of a few of these techniques and the types of problems to which they have been applied may suffice to give a picture of their tremendous potential and versatility.

Probability and statistical decision theory and methods are widely used in making scientific analyses which have practical application in minimizing operating costs, construction or capital outlays, or purchase costs. They are used to improve inventory control and budget management. Whenever decisions must be made with incomplete information and under conditions of uncertainty — conditions which are encountered very frequently both in business and in government — these modern scientific techniques have proved to be highly effective in solving practical problems. Statistical sampling techniques alone, which are included under this heading, are utilized extensively by business and government in quality control operations and, in recent years, in many accounting and auditing areas.

Linear programming is a systematic mathematical procedure for solving numerous business problems which are concerned with the most efficient use of men and material. A large variety of business problems which are too complex or too large to resolve by intuitive means can be solved by the computational methods of linear programming. This objective tool rules out subjective solutions and provides mathematically supported best solutions to problems of allocating limited resources (for example, scarce materials, plant capacities or labor skills) among competing or interrelated requirements. Many successful applications of mathematical programming techniques can be found in budgeting, production planning, materials handling and market research — all fields which provide excellent opportunities for using these techniques to advantage.

Correlation and regression techniques are useful in predicting future events. Correlation may be defined as the study of the extent of interrelationships between variables, that is, interrelationships between two or more events, systems or things. Regression is the further study of these interrelationships between variables for the purpose of estimating the value of one variable or predicting one event from observation of other related variables or events. This type of analysis is used, for example, to predict future manufacturing overhead rates from programmed production volume.

Waiting lines or queueing theory is another special statistical method for dealing with business problems which require balancing of services available with services required. Determining the correct capacity of services or facilities is important in minimizing costs and eliminating bottlenecks. In most instances these determinations can be made only in terms of probabilities, and therefore can be made only by statistical methods. Experience and systematic study of waiting lines have shown that intuitive decisions are often quite erroneous. Thus queueing has been used effectively to determine the minimum facilities necessary to eliminate costly waiting time or demurrage costs for: railroad cars and trucks waiting to load or unload; airplanes stacked over a field waiting to land; airplanes loaded and waiting to take off; purchased items accumulated in receiving areas for counting or quality inspection; and people waiting in cafeteria lines or at check-out counters in super-markets.

There are other effective "operations research" techniques available and in use, such as Learning Curves and Time Series Analysis. In some cases it may be appropriate to use these and other techniques in combination to obtain the best solutions to a particular problem.

Summary

The challenge facing accountants, auditors and budget personnel was clearly stated by Chairman John W. Macy of the U. S. Civil Service Commission in his keynote speech at the Tenth Annual National Symposium of the Federal Government Accountants Association:

Now we are on the threshold of a new wave of managerial advance in which we will draw heavily upon a new concept of science in management. Contributions by mathematicians, statisticians, industrial engineers, and such social scientists as psychologists and economists, are converging to provide new approaches to solving intricate management problems. . . . The ever broadening challenges of management, together with use of the new tools explored in this symposium, make it possible for accountants, budget personnel and auditors to make their full contribution to solution of the massive and myriad problems inherent in the direction of the nation's public business.

The question is whether the professional accountants in government recognize the challenge that confronts them and will grasp the opportunity to participate in the "new wave of managerial advance." If the opinion of competent observers that the new management technology is accomplishing revolutionary changes in the shape and scope of business management is accurate, it behooves the accounting profession to take immediate steps to take part in these changes. In the past, professional accountants participated substantially in financial management decision-making and problem-solving. It should be clear that unless they are prepared to use the new tools and learn the new skills, there is a danger they will lose their position in the management function.

Relationship of Budget Planning to Long-Range Planning ❖ Elmer M. Staats

As the recent report of the Subcommittee on Policy Making Machinery of the Senate Government Operations Subcommittee so aptly states: "*The task confronting us is harshly plain — to outthink, outplan, outperform, and outlast our foes.*" This report asserts that the key problem facing the President is the need for developing a forward plan of where we aim to go in the world and the road we propose to take to get there. In the view of the Subcommittee this requires mapping "a course of action which puts first things first, which separates the merely desirable, and which distinguishes between what must be done today and what can wait until tomorrow."

Many difficult questions must be answered if the objective of the report is to be realized. What trends can we foresee for our country's steady economic growth and expansion? What public and private policies will be necessary to achieve these expectations? How much of our financial and human resources should be devoted to national security? What types of weapons should be concentrated on and how fast should they be developed? What resources will be required in meeting our nation's needs for jobs, education, food, water, energy, and a high standard of living?

To obtain help in answering these questions the President seeks advice from various sources, such as the Bureau of the Budget, the Council of Economic Advisers, the National Security Council, and the Defense, State and other Departments, in addition to his own staff aides. And none of us should forget the large role that Congress plays in deciding these questions.

The challenge which confronts us is not solely in the domain of the Bureau of the Budget, nor limited to the budget process itself. Of necessity, a great deal of the

"Relationship of Budget Planning to Long-Range Planning," by Elmer M. Staats, from *Federal Accountant* (March, 1962), pp. 27–35. © 1962 by the Federal Government Accountants Association. Reprinted by permission.

responsibility in meeting the world challenge of diverse ideologies falls on the shoulders of the officials in the various federal departments and agencies. It is at the agency level that there must be fusion between the program planning and financial planning organizations; long-range planning must become a built-in habit of management if the needs of Presidential leadership are to be met. It therefore is most essential that every agency recognize and accept the fact that annual budgeting, with the primary emphasis on past events, is no longer adequate under present day conditions.

New Longer-Range Approach to Budgeting Needed

If we are to meet the problems and make the decisions I have already noted, we must come up with a more effective approach — one which looks to the future instead of to the past. We must, in other words, develop the means of relating the budgetary process more closely with long-range planning and objectives.

More particularly, it seems to those of us working in the Bureau of the Budget that we can do a better job if we have continually before us projections of programs and their likely costs, and of potential revenues under alternative assumptions about tax laws and economic conditions. We believe these projections should extend at least five years in the future. When they place primary emphasis on needed forward decisions and alternative choices to be made, they offer important assistance to the decision maker; they shift the emphasis from the record of the past to an examination of future trends and issues likely to be faced.

While these concepts are not new, we are just starting to put them to work in the government in a systematic and formal way. Maurice Stans, the Budget Director in the closing days of the Eisenhower Administration, released for the first time a government-wide official projection of the federal budget for the period 1960-1970. The expenditures were projected on three different bases — called high, medium, and low. I am sure it will be of no great surprise to learn that all three assumptions yielded federal expenditure estimates which rose steadily over this ten-year period.

The approach for this ten-year projection followed closely that of the Committee for Economic Development study of 1959 headed by Otto Eckstein of Harvard University. That study grew out of Committee interest in the subject of tax reform and was directed because of "the continued absence of any long-term budget estimates from the government." This important organization of business leaders recommended that the Congress "have before it estimates of revenues and expenditures not only in the coming year but also for four or five years ahead." It emphasized that this is "particularly important at the present time, and we strongly urge the President to make such estimates available."

This is understandable when we recognize that in less than 40 years our population will double and the economic output of our country will reach and pass the trillion dollar annual level. In the international arena, the same population trend will be at work with the added factor of the rise of nationalism coupled with the drive to close the gap between the "haves" and the "have nots."

If we are to make sensible decisions about the federal budget — expenditures and revenues alike — we must think in terms, not of annual budgets only, but of the budget outlook for a span of years. It should be clear that many decisions which we make today will affect federal expenditures and our domestic and international posture for years to come. When we start on a Polaris submarine program or adopt a commitment for the manned exploration of the moon within a decade, we are in fact committing future resources. The same applies to other programs of the federal government, for example, atomic energy, economic assistance to foreign governments, public highways, education, research, and aids to business and to agriculture.

Thus officials in the departments and agencies, as well as officials in the Executive Office of the President, are faced with various choices and alternatives. Both need *all* the information available to facilitate the difficult task of deciding the nature, scope and phasing of the various competing programs which will best serve the needs of our nation.

Budget Decisions and Long-Range Planning

The federal government has to fall in line with business, universities and other forms of enterprise in laying out forward programs and investment plans on a long-term basis. This does not mean that the forward "projections" are sacrosanct. Such projections must be flexible and subject to continuous reassessment to assure meeting changed economic, international and other conditions as they arise.

Long-range planning must become a part of the budget process, which is an integral part of the decision-making process. This marriage of "planning" and "budgeting" must begin at the "grass roots" level in the respective departments and agencies. The program people, planners and budget staff in the various federal agencies must work as a team to exercise continuing surveillance of their respective programs. The programs must be reviewed and evaluated at the departmental level in relation to the objectives of the department, not only in terms of the needs of today or next fiscal year, but also in terms of the overall departmental goals at least for several years ahead. Programs established many years ago must be re-evaluated in light of conditions of today and the years ahead. Evaluations must be made between "desirable" programs and "essential" programs. Nonessential programs must be eliminated or curtailed. New techniques and methods must be initiated to assure the maximum return for every tax dollar spent.

Not the least of the values of the forward projection process is the identification of problems needing further study and of information to be collected either by the Budget Bureau or by the interested agencies. Some of these matters relate to organization and management, others to substantive program matters. Most involve matters that could not be satisfactorily handled in the pressure period of the budget season. More than a hundred studies and projects were initiated this year in the budget preview process, such as a study of the long-term future of the Atomic Energy Commission program on civilian reactors, the possibility of obtaining more private participation in Small Business Administration loans, duplication in the field of weather research and observations, and so on.

And then there is the problem of reviewing priorities among agencies. It is natural that each agency considers its programs to be the most important. However, the individual agency is not in a position to arrive at many assessments for the government as a whole. This formidable responsibility of allocating our national resources among the various federal programs necessarily falls on the shoulders of the President.

Thus the development of national program goals and forward planning falls within the orbit of the Presidency — the one institutional organ of our government with the perspective to accept this role. The decisions and results will not always be perfect, nor will they be universally acceptable. One President's view of the responsibilities of government and the efforts of which our society is capable will differ from those of another President. External events, both domestic and international, will have an impact on the nature of our national goals and the direction of our efforts to achieve them. We must recognize that there are imperfections in the long-range planning and budgetary processes. However, decisions must be made, and we must go forward using the best tools at our disposal and making refinements as we gain more experience.

Budget Decisions and Long-Range Economic Fiscal Policy

There is a second aspect of long-range budgeting and planning in addition to the use of the budget as an instrument for coordination among different programs, namely the relationship between budgetary decisions and long-range economic fiscal policy.

With regard to the fiscal policy, the Kennedy Administration has accepted as a basis for its budget and fiscal decisions the conception that the levels of federal expenditures and receipts should be related to the state of the national economy. This conception may be described — in its simplest terms — as the philosophy of balancing the federal budget over a period of years rather than attempting to balance the budget each year regardless of prevailing economic conditions.

The application of this philosophy can be illustrated by the experience of the Eisenhower Administration during the years 1957 through 1960. Federal revenues declined, as national production and income fell. To offset the recession, it was deemed desirable to increase federal expenditures, both to relieve distress and to stimulate recovery. The effect of increased expenditures coupled with declining revenues resulted in a deficit in 1959 of $12.4 billion, the largest peacetime deficit in our history.

Based on the economic conditions of the time, it was decided that the wisest fiscal policy was not to try to balance the budget in fiscal year 1959. Such an effort would only have contributed to further depressing economic conditions throughout the country rather than stimulating recovery from the existing recession and thus would have been self-defeating. There seems to be no question that a deliberately unbalanced budget was sound fiscal policy for that year.

On the other side of the coin, federal revenues rose by $10 billion in fiscal year 1960, reflecting the economic recovery which began in 1959. This sizeable increase in revenues resulted in a balanced federal budget in fiscal year 1960, despite the large deficit of the previous year. Some economists argue that the federal budget changed too sharply from a large deficit in 1959 to a surplus in 1960, and that this abrupt shift contributed to the short and unsatisfactory recovery we had late in 1959 and in 1960. I do not intend to take sides on this argument; my purpose is to illustrate the essential philosophy of both the Eisenhower and the Kennedy administrations, which is to balance the budget, not every year, but over the years to help even out the peaks and valleys of the business cycle.

This policy is now very widely accepted. Long-range budget planning, looking ahead over a period of several years, is essential, it seems to me, if we are to apply a budget policy which calls for balancing the budget over the business cycle.

Other Factors Affecting Budget Decisions

External factors, such as the Berlin crisis, must be considered as they inevitably affect budget decisions. Defense expenditures, of necessity, depend on the strategic situation in the world which can change rapidly, as we have witnessed in recent months. Closely related are changes in defense requirements and technology. We are already building second-generation missiles before the first-generation missiles have even come off the assembly line. The missiles which we are contracting for at the present time may be relatively obsolete in two, three or four years. At that time, we may be producing something quite different at costs unknown today. Similarly, our long-range revenue and expenditure projections are heavily dependent on a variable economic condition in the future and therefore are subject to a large margin of error.

At this point you may ask whether it is worth the time and effort to go through such exercises of long-range forecasting. It seems to me that the answer is still an unequivocal "yes." It is of utmost importance that we develop, to the best of our ability, forward projections covering several years, based upon specified assumptions. It is true, of course, that such assumptions must be revised from time to time, and they may have to be in alternative forms. Forward budget figures should be considered as projections based on certain assumptions and will require revision as these assumptions change. They are neither predictions nor precise blueprints about an uncertain future.

Two-Stage Budgeting

I previously referred to the ten-year projections made under Mr. Stans' direction. I believe this was a useful exercise and should probably be repeated at certain intervals. However, due to the many uncertainties as the time interval is lengthened, ten years is probably too long a period to work with for most programs on a regular basis. For this reason, the Budget Bureau is now experimenting with five-year projections. We are trying to ascertain whether it is feasible and useful to have at all times a set of figures which carries us five years into the future. A series of alternative figures were developed on this basis and used in the decision-making process for the 1963 federal budget.

From here on, the budget will be formulated in two stages. In the first of these stages, the Bureau of the Budget will develop for the President an informed estimate of revenues and expenditures over a five-year period, not for the purpose of freezing budget totals but to illuminate for the President the major issues and program developments which will arise in that period and influence the level and trend of the budget. The Bureau will do this as a staff job for the President, with full benefit of the thinking and long-range plans of the departments and agencies, where such thinking and such plans are available.

The second stage will embrace the customary cycle under which the agencies receive planning targets and prepare their estimates for formal review and decision, leading up to the submission of the budget to Congress for enactment.

The principal changes from past practice are these:

• The planning figures given to the agency heads in the summer months will not be ceilings, but rather planning guides which may be adjusted by the agency without violating Holy Writ.

• These planning figures will emerge from a very different process than before, namely a five-year forward look.

• There will be no formal agency submissions in the spring to stake out bargaining positions in anticipation of budget ceilings, but rather there will be an identification of trends, changes, priorities and issues.

We think it is this kind of material that lends itself to thoughtful decision-making and to the evolution of understandable forward goals and choices.

Agency Understanding Required

If our efforts to broaden the outlook of the budget process to produce long-range effects are to succeed, we must all understand that a great deal is being asked of us. The budget process cannot create forward plans and goals where none exist. The budget process cannot stand in the place of the program executive, just as the Budget Director cannot stand in the place of the agency head. The budget process has developed a high degree of skill in translating requirements into costs, and in projecting those costs in a fairly sophisticated way, related to economic and other factors. But the key to the whole understanding lies in the response it evokes in the departments and agencies in the sense of creating or strengthening the environment and the machinery for looking ahead, for program planning.

The challenge, then, runs not to the Bureau of the Budget nor necessarily to the budget process itself. It runs to the agencies and to the people who work there. If departmental officers do not grasp the significance of this opportunity, if budget and fiscal people insist on taking a limited approach to financial management, if program planning and fiscal officials continue to talk in different dialects and operate from different perspectives — then we will be tragically late in organizing ourselves to recognize new problems in the world and in space, and in responding with new ideas.

On the other hand, if this summons to long-range planning and budgeting succeeds in supplying the perspective we know is necessary, if it sharpens the contrast among alternatives, if it orients our decision-making toward meeting the needs of the future, then we will know it has been worthwhile.

Not long ago the National Planning Association announced plans for a "Center For Priority Analysis" in a little booklet entitled *Unlimited Needs and Limited Resources*. This title could aptly describe the problem I have been discussing in this article. It is increasingly apparent that national decisions must be based on an evaluation of the best available projections of national needs and resources. Budgeting is but a device, both at the departmental and national level, to weigh choices and to determine priorities.

This concept makes budgeting, aided by long-range planning, a device to assist the President in forward planning and decision-making. It is a concept requiring ingenuity, teamwork and cooperation on the part of all in the federal service, to develop long-range plans and projections to the best of our ability as an integral part of the budgetary and decision-making process. If we effectively make use of it, we can then reply "yes" to Senator Jackson's Subcommittee's challenge and say that we are indeed helping our free society organize its human and material resources *"to outthink, outplan, outperform, and outlast our foes."*

7

Administrative Regulation

As government has increasingly provided services to the public, government has increasingly engaged in the regulation of the economic activities of society. Governmental agencies play a large regulatory role in such areas as transportation, public utilities, business structure and practices, banking and investment, labor relations, agriculture programs, and health and welfare. A large body of rules and regulations has grown up administered under powers delegated to various agencies. The performance of these functions calls primarily for people who are specialists in areas which grow quite complex and technical.

Much of the regulatory activity is carried on by the independent regulatory commissions. These organizations have been given a degree of independence while remaining in the executive branch of government. Thus their relationship to the President is different from that of other agencies. Their independence is protected by the Congress, but the President exercises some influence upon them through the budgetary process.

As the regulatory process has grown more complicated, the procedures of some of the agencies have become cumbersome, and their decisions are delayed for long periods of time. Others have become so engulfed in details that they have neither the energy nor the initiative for creative planning. The creation of a permanent conference of experts has been suggested as a solution to some of these problems rather than the creation of a czar to preside over the regulatory process.

Perspectives for the Study of Government Regulation ❖ EMMETTE S. REDFORD

Much of the study of regulation in the past twenty-five years has been focused on the activity of administrative agencies. Official and academic studies of this kind have been made frequently. The President's Committee on Administrative Manage-

Reprinted from *Midwest Journal of Political Science*, Vol. VI, No. 1 (February, 1962), by Emmette S. Redford by permission of the Wayne State University Press and the author. Copyright 1962 by Wayne State University Press. Pp. 1–18.

ment, the Attorney General's Committee on Administrative Procedure, task forces of the first and second Hoover Commissions, and James M. Landis, as President-elect Kennedy's agent, presented reports in 1937, 1941, 1949, 1955, and 1960, respectively. These reports have been supplemented by studies in congressional committees such as those recently under way in the Government Oversight Subcommittee of the House Committee on Interstate and Foreign Commerce and the Carroll subcommittee of the Senate Judiciary Committee. Academic interest in agency administration has been demonstrated in such studies as Herring's trail-blazing *Public Administration and the Public Interest* in 1936, Sharfman's monumental five volumes on the Interstate Commerce Commission from 1931 to 1937, Cushman's *The Independent Regulatory Commissions* in 1941, and somewhat later, Bernstein's *Regulating Business by Independent Commission* in 1955 and my *Administration of National Economic Control* in 1952. In all of these studies attention has been centered primarily on administrative operations.

In what is perhaps the most useful single reference on regulation, Merle Fainsod in 1940 concentrated attention on whether the administrative agencies could have any independent force and effect; but he recognized also other perspectives for study, namely interest pressures and institutional forces. I think it is time to consider again perspectives from which adequate understanding of the significance of government regulation can be obtained.

The perspectives need to be broader than those of agency administration alone. They should provide a view of all that happens when a decision to regulate is made: What fashioned this decision and the subsidiary decisions on scope and methods of public control? What has fashioned the subsequent lines of policy? What has been the content of policy? What techniques of regulation have been employed? Who got what out of the process? What have been the elements of determinism and what have been the possibilities of pliability by human action? The answers to such questions will not be found by analysis of agency action alone. They will be found in a varied set of factors operating from outside and from within a structure of many interacting organizations.

Perhaps the most fruitful way to study these factors is to isolate an area of service to the public and see what determines the course of action in this area. One such area of service, for example, is domestic commercial supply of air transport. This is a sufficiently distinct area of service to be viewed as a universe of social action. It does, of course, overlap with or merge into other universes of social action. Thus, it overlaps military air transport and merges into total aviation supply, domestic and international, and beyond that into total transportation supply. Yet there is a domestic commercial aviation industry and this is regulated, and these two facts create a universe of social action which can be studied as a sample of the regulatory process.

Such a universe of social action, i.e., an area of economic function under public regulation, cuts across various institutional universes such as Congress, the executive branch of the government, and the corporate system, and generates its own institutional mechanisms, such as companies, trade associations, public administrative agencies, and congressional subcommittees. In this enveloping universe, partially and vaguely independent of other economic universes, slicing across institutional forms and generating new ones, an elaborate complex of social phenomena develops. There will be responses to external stimuli, motivations crystallizing into institutional activities, and interaction among points of decision and action.

The study of the complex of phenomena in an area of economic supply under public regulation will transcend economics. It will be seen that activity within the universe will be determined quite meagerly by market forces. The study could be called political economics, indicating that the supply of the service was influenced by political forces; it could more appropriately be called political sociology, indicating that the supply of the service was encompassed in a complex of social forces and that the focus of attention was the generation and impact of political intervention. It is this latter feature which puts the subject on the agenda of political science, though it can be on the agenda also of sociology and of economics.

The basic assumption behind the current statement of perspectives for study is that understanding of the governmental aspects of regulation is possible only by analysis of the whole complex of forces in which political structures operate. Other assumptions relate to the purposes of research for understanding. It is assumed that there are three. One is scientific, i.e., to provide a basis for prediction of what will happen in this universe of social action or in other economic universes in which public regulation exists. Even though no methods of hard science — e.g., no mathematical equations or no controlled experiments — are employed, depth in perception may bring understanding of the confines of possibility and the directions of movement. Thus, anyone who analyzes the belief patterns behind the system of regulation in this country, as revealed in separate economic universes, will be able to predict certain lines of action unless or until those belief patterns are altered. To be specific, as long as the belief pattern that regulation should be fair is accompanied by the tightly-wedded belief that fairness is attainable ordinarily only by judicial processes, then the dampening hand of procedure will impair efficiency in regulation. A second purpose is utility. If an accumulation of analyses of regulation does not support unqualified determinism, this is no argument that the studies should not have been made. Against the diminished opportunity for prediction, there may be an increased opportunity for utility. Where understanding produces knowledge of limits and possibilities of change, then it serves the purpose of the policy maker. The third purpose is moral. To the extent that analysis reveals possibilities of pliability in human affairs, to this extent opportunity is provided for man to make choices in terms of his moral purposes — in terms of his concept of public interest or of other standards of public morality.

Beyond the broad and general perspectives stated above, five particular perspectives for study may be outlined. If the first three of these conform to a biological model, this is, I believe, accidental. It implies no organismic assumption and I trust no effort to twist mechanically analysis of social data into line with methods of inquiry in natural sciences. The use of two models in the discussion is itself recognition that we may draw from various analogies without yielding to any.

I

Ecology is an essential element in study of behavior in the functioning of a regulated industry. The environmental factors influencing behavior may be classified as technology, resources, general (societal) institutional organization, and belief patterns. Technology includes both the industrial arts and the managerial arts. The latter in turn include general managerial methodology and regulatory techniques. Resources include both materials and finances; involved also are special resources such, for example, as availability or limitation of air space. Institutional organization encompasses the standing arrangements through which society has ordered its affairs. Fused with these arrangements are the shared attitudes called "rules of the game" by David Truman, "systems of belief" by Clyde Kluckhohn, and "general ideological consensus" by Gabriel Almond.

Environmental factors may be almost as deterministic of regulatory activity as soil, water, and temperature are of the growth of animal or plant organisms. Consider, for example, the story Warner Mills tells of martial law in East Texas in 1931. A vast new reservoir of oil resource is discovered, above this reservoir the rights of ownership are divided among thousands of small tract holders, the legal rule of capture gives each owner a right to sink wells for capture of the oil, the shallowness of the oil resource and the developments in technology make capture possible with a small investment, new refineries crop up quickly to purchase the oil and run it to independent filling station operators, the results in six months are a decline in the price of oil from over a dollar to 10 cents a barrel and the end is not yet in sight, a major industry of a state is demoralized and the solvency of the state treasury is threatened, and the Supreme Court of the United States has said that the powers of production control are reserved to the states. Under these conditions was it not inevitable that the responsible state officials would search for ways to limit the production of oil? One may say that to determine inevitability he would have to look at the interest configuration resulting from these factors. This is true, but the fact remains that the situational factors determined what the dominant interests would be. The perspective for research must, therefore, reach to the situational factors, to the setting from which a problem arose for those having political power or influence. Technique of control also was fashioned out of the setting. The courts found that the production of oil beyond market demand called for storage in earthen tanks and that this produced overground physical waste; subsequently, the engineers discovered that unlimited flow of oil from the field resulted in decline of the water pressure which forced out the oil, and hence that limitation of production was necessary to prevent underground waste. Thus, law and engineering science came to the side of the dominant interests. The point is that it was immaterial who was governor or who sat on the regulatory commission. Environmental factors determined that proration would be the policy of Texas; all else was detail.

. . . .

Responsible decision makers know that they must assess the factors in the situation which produce a problem and determine the limits and possibilities of action. The limits are the realm of determinism; the possibilities lie in the area of pliability within which human beings may at the moment have some opportunity for manipulation. All the factors are not understood by a look only at the interests created; some lie deeper in the environment which creates and gives force to interests. The realistic student will look at all the factors which will be assessed by the decision maker and at all those factors which, whether known to the decision maker or not, will determine or confine his judgment. The response of men to environment is the first perspective of study in regulation.

II

Anatomy is a second element for study. Anatomy includes all the structural arrangements within the universe of social action. The study of the structure of a regulated sphere of economic service will aim toward discovery of the centers of decision and action, and toward determination of those which carry weight in the trend of events.

The most significant centers will ordinarily be organizational units representing social groupings. If a particular individual acquires influence it will usually be the result of his role in a strategic position as the representative of a group. Search may therefore be directed toward discovery of strategic organizational positions.

In studies of regulation it has usually been assumed that the commissions were strategic organizations worthy of study. This apparently is true, but it may also be true that the strength of their position can be exaggerated. There may at times be other organizational centers, within or outside the government, which will carry more weight in significant developments, even in government policy. Adequate understanding of government regulation can be attained only if the impact of the various organizational centers is considered.

The anatomy of a universe of social action will differ from that of an animal organism in at least two respects. The universe of social action within which the organizational centers operate is not a closed structure like an animal organism. In addition, there are no rigidly fixed positions of the organizational centers with relation to each other. Their positions are only loosely fixed and may shift with changes in the interaction of forces. They do have differentiated functions which fix to an extent positions with relation to other organizational centers; and they do contribute, through exercise of functions and through shifting lines of communication with other centers, to the activity of the universe.

By resorting to a different kind of model, we may visualize a sea of fluid substance. Its shore lines are set in the main by environmental factors, though these may be modified by action within the sea. Within this sea are whirlpools of activity. Each whirlpool with all the enveloping influences impinging upon it and effects issuing from it is a universe of social action. Within and around the whirlpool are floating, i.e., active, organisms. The floating organisms are the structural aggregations of power and influence. Each of these organisms has some effect upon the whirlpool. Some are large, continuously active, and move near the center of the whirlpool. Size, proximity, and activity are indexes of influence, though perhaps not the only indexes. Potentiality for influence on movement creates strategic position. Strategic positions are the primary centers of influence on action. Beyond the strategic positions are other positions operating more remotely, less actively, or less continuously on the whirlpool. These may be primary centers of influence on other whirlpools of activity with only a secondary influence on the whirlpool of our interest. But all the organisms are floating, sometimes remote from the whirlpool or for other reasons unable to exercise strong influence on its motion, at other times closer to the center of the whirlpool or exerting additional activity from its previous position.

Each universe of social action is affected by a multitude of floating organisms. This is merely to say that in any continuous functional area, such as supply of an economic service, there are many centers of decision and action which have influence on the course of events. If one is to study the operation of the system, he must isolate the strategic centers from which most influence may be exerted.

It has been said that the organizational centers will have differentiated functions. The centers and their functions will have been established by formal and informal allocation. By deliberate, i.e., formal action, or by the concurrence of events, i.e., informal action, the centers will have been created and will have functions, power and influence. The most familiar aspect of allocation is delegation through formal process. Congress allocates functions to a Civil Aeronautics Board and other administrative agencies, and to units within agencies — such as examiners. Within the agencies other allocations are made by internal delegation. Allocations are often the result of the formation of representative organization. Thus airlines form an Air Transport Association and pilots an Air Line Pilots Association, and these associations are allocated or assume functions. Other allocations issue from the constitutional and political system which produces such strategic centers as the presidency, the Congress and its committees, and the courts. Still other allocations result from the background of institutional habit and belief patterns. Most significant of all perhaps is the allocation of functions between the corporations supplying service and the public regulatory agencies, and this allocation will be affected as much by the background of environmental factors as by the express terms of statutory delegations.

. . . .

The internal study of the separate centers of influence will be meaningless unless related to the total complex of forces affecting the whirlpool of activity. This means, for example, that no center of influence — not even a regulatory commission — can be studied fruitfully without analysis of its position with respect to other structural centers. Regulated service is not supplied to the public under a monolithic structure. Pluralism is the central fact in the anatomy of regulation. I have suggested, for example, that if one is to understand the public control of commercial aviation he may usefully consider that the centers of influence are arranged in a parallelogram, with the influence coming from four corners, namely, community, congressional, executive, and industry aggregations.

III

The study of anatomy will unavoidably be interlaced with that of physiology. Physiology is function and process. It is activity. It is interaction among components. It is structure activated into movement.

In biological science there are many approaches to understanding of life processes in organisms, such as study of physical process, of chemical substance, and of electrical impulse. Similarly, the state of our present knowledge supplies a number of avenues to understanding of activity and movement within universes of social action.

One is study of interests, including their generation and the ensuing processes of conflict and accommodation. The term interest refers to the concern which some individual or group of individuals has with respect to what occurs. Once a technological development occurs there is a response from individuals. The development creates new visions of opportunity or of threat to existing status, and hence motivations, expectations (positive or negative), impulses to activity. These result for some individuals in definitive interests to be revealed in lines of activity. It results also in development of aggregations of interest and in crystallization of new centers of organization or use of existing centers. Thus, with the development of technology of air transport the motivations of individuals led to formation of companies and of trade associations. Almost as soon as the industry was born there were these two levels of structure. Other interests, such as that of the national community in use of the technology for national defense or of the local communities in obtaining air service, used immediately existing structure such as committees of commerce in the Congress. Ultimately, the technological developments in a setting of adequate resources generated many new interests which in turn pushed out a multitude of organizational centers. Ecology produced a new anatomy. This was accomplished by a physiological process in which interests were as vital as electrical impulses in the atom.

Each organizational entity itself becomes a center of two types of physiological process. One is internal, the other external. Roles established within the organization create cellular units within which motivations and impulses to action develop. These motivations and impulses may result from interests developed within the organization, but they may be supported by professional or other types of association with groups outside. At any rate, there will be a process of conflict and accommodation within the organization. Both the organization itself and the cells within will distribute impacts on the outside, thus contributing to the process of group conflict and accommodation in the universe of social action.

This whole process of interest generation and interest accommodation is perhaps the most important clue to understanding the process of regulation. It is, I submit, with apologies to some of my colleagues, not the only clue. Interests arise in a setting. The interests of the entrepreneurs in commercial aviation were generated by technological development, made possible by resources, and protected by the institutional habits and belief patterns of a capitalistic society. Once generated every interest is, in turn, hedged not only by other interests but by the confinements of evolved structure. There is restriction on interests as well as service to them in group aggregations formalized in organization. The impacts of environment and organization should also be studied.

. . . .

A second approach to understanding of activity is through study of communications. Communications erect a web of links between the structural units in the anatomical system — connections between the floating organisms in and around the whirlpool of activity. Where channels of communications are fixed and continuous they may be regarded as part of the anatomical system itself, but there is likely to be much fluidity in the communications network. Communications make the current of action in the whirlpool of activity dependent upon interaction among the influence centers. The complexity of the interaction system is enhanced by the fact that communication links will be established between component cells of the separate major organizational groupings. Some of these groupings are themselves highly pluralistic with limited, perhaps negligible, hierarchical control over the establishment of communication lines from cellular units to similar units in other organizations.

One effect of the communication system may be to blur the distinction between private and public action, for the resulting action may be compounded of influences from both sources. Moreover, where affinity on point of view exists, as among examiners, agency lawyers, and practitioner associations, then the communication channels may not need to be strong in order to create a consolidated effect of considerable weight.

. . . .

Yet there is another route to understanding of the physiology of regulation which may produce profound knowledge about the regulatory process. This is decision making. We have long been familiar with formal study of process flow, i.e., the procedure through which actions are taken or decisions made. More recently we have been introduced to a case approach in which attention is focused on the making of a particular decision or a series of decisions. The merit of the method is that, since it encompasses the total flow of influence, it may increase depth of perception about all the factors — whether environmental, anatomical or physiological —

which can be isolated by the researcher. The danger is that, unless skillfully used, it may not reveal typical situations and processes; and the limitation is that it may not by itself provide basis for generalization. In the design of work by the Regulatory Cases Subcommittee of the Inter-University Case Committee a great effort has been made to insure choice of cases which would illustrate typical situations, and writers of cases have been encouraged to reveal through the case presentations the extent to which patterns of activity were typical.

. . . .

IV

The fourth element for study is policy. Policy is the substance of what happens in the universe of social action, or in larger encompassing universes. It is another dimension, different from process.

The search for policy is an important part of the analysis of regulation. Policy is the meaningful result of environment, anatomy and physiology; policy is index of development; policy is determiner of the future. A policy is both stage of development and molder of activities. To find policy is merely to mark what is important, to mark the points of regularity, order and consistency in the universe of action. To find that there is a gap in policy is to find that there is no system, no rhythm, only activity, where that gap exists.

Policy may be inherent in institutional system and belief patterns and discoverable by study of these. It may be found in moments of decision or it may be discoverable out of a slide of events. It may be prospective in that it fixes a new line of development or it may be retrospective in that it crystallizes a tendency.

One feature of policy is that it tends to be decisive. There is determinism in policy. It marks what is accepted, what will be applied. When it is confirmed by consonance with other policies, by concurrence with the basic institutions and ideals of society, and by time and application it becomes part of the hardened and durable substance of social control. It is, I suggest, a more significant clue than organization to the understanding of the molding and channeling of tendency.

An important characteristic of policy development, as Lindblom has told us, is that it is incremental. Ordinarily, each policy decision is an addition to policies determined before. This is the meaning of what Simon has called the decision tree. Certain decisions build a trunk, others a major branch, and others smaller branches. If we vary the analogy, to blend with our previous model, we may say that choice and events create first the shore lines of the environmental sea in which the whirlpools occur, and then a stream out of the whirlpool, and that subsequently a tributary system develops as the stream moves onward. Lawyers would explain the phenomenon in terms of concepts and standards, then leading decisions, then refinements of these, then applications of law.

The durability and the significance of policy may be determined by its place on the decision tree, as Simon puts it, or on the shore lines, as I put it. A small change in the current from the whirlpool may cause water down the stream to shift from one tributary to a new one; but only a major revolution in technology, interests, and/or beliefs can change the shore lines of the sea or agitate the whirlpool enough to create new shore lines at the point of exit from the pool.

It follows then that the student seeking understanding must be time conscious, that is, history conscious. This history consciousness will give perspective. It will place things in order. Thus, in seeking for understanding of the universe of action represented in regulated commercial aviation the student will seek not only understanding of whirlpools of activity but shore lines on the sea and down the stream of movement issuing from the whirlpool. He may find that certain policies were fixed by the belief patterns already existing when the universe began to develop — that the main ingredients of regulatory policy are imbedded in the nation's past and fixed by the shore lines of the sea. Beyond this he may look for policy issuing from the whirlpool and follow it through the tributary system. He may find historic moments, as when policy was crystallized in the Civil Aeronautics Act of 1938; as when the Civil Aeronautics Board decided in 1941 that there were enough trunkline carriers already in existence; as when the Board decided in 1955 to expand competition among the trunklines; as when Congress determined that permanent certificates should be granted to local service airlines; as when by the concurrent activities of industry, congressional and executive centers a decision was made in the Federal Aviation Act to have a common system of air traffic control for military and civil aviation.

The aim of both analytical and historical perspectives is to fix attention on major elements and trends. Analytical perspectives which fix the strategic points in anatomy and the meaningful processes of interest accommodation, communications, and decision making may keep the student close to the center of the whirlpool of activity which he seeks to explain. Historical perspectives may lead him away from the streamlets at the end of the tributaries — back to the shore lines of institutional patterns, beliefs and basic policy, and enable him to see lines and stages of development.

V

The final element in perspectives for study is evaluation of results of activity and movement in the universe of social action. This will form the basis of another paper, but a few aspects of the perspective may be noted summarily.

The student of the universe of social action will be able on the basis of his analysis of setting, structure, and operation to define the attributes of the system he is studying. The system is one which combines in some way private and public activity in the supply of an economic service. It conforms to a general model of socio-political action which is referred to as regulated economic service and stands somewhere on a continuum, as Dahl and Lindblom have put it, between polar systems of public and private enterprise. It will exhibit certain special characteristics defined by such things as the allocation of function between public and private structures, the means by which public functions are exercised, and the interrelations among the parts of the system. Its features will be subject to specification.

The results of the system may have two types of meaning. The first is the significance of the system for the purposes it serves, and the second is its significance as a pattern for organization of other services.

There are two complementary sets of questions which are central to the inquiry on significance. The first set relates to beneficence: Is the stream of movement insofar as it is determined by public policy beneficent? Are there parts of the stream which are beneficent and others which are not? Should the system as a whole, or parts of the system, be copied, or be avoided in other areas of service? The second set of questions relates to potentials for modification: Are defects correctable? Are lessons of experience in the universe of action transferable to another universe? Are there areas of pliability and if so what are the conditions prerequisite to manipulation within such areas?

These questions may be answered in part — in large part — by reference to process. Has the process been one by which new technology could be absorbed? Has it been one by which interests could be reconciled in a way which appeared to them to be fair — in other words, has there been due process? Has the process been one which has not aroused criticism and demand for change?

The student may justifiably, however, seek for answers in substance of action as well as in process of action. Even the statement of process questions assumes substantive goals: absorption of technology, fairness, avoidance of revolutionary methods of change. In addition, specific aims of policy may be touchstones of evaluation. If "fair and reasonable" price is stated by statute to be an objective of policy, may the student not be interested in knowing whether the objective is attained? Or whether it can be attained under the system of social action which exists? If the technology of air transportation offers potential for safe, speedy, convenient, inexpensive service for most distance transportation of passengers, then the student may justifiably see if the socio-political system of supply has provided such service. He may do this, not because he assumes it is his business to determine goals, but because as a researcher he is searching for significance and believes that whatever has significance may have utility for those who have responsibility for policy.

The search for significance leads inevitably to the search for standards of judgment. The standards of judgment, relating to process and substance, will constitute some view of public benefits worthy of attainment.

VI

The perspectives of study set forth in this paper may appear to be too broad for practicable use. It need not, however, be assumed that perspectives for study should be stated in terms of what one individual can do in a brief span of time, though I must say that I have seen at least three students accomplish in dissertations a large part of what is here sketched. Moreover, studies of segments of a universe of social action will be most fruitful when pursued with comprehension of the full dimensions of meaningful inquiry. Finally, partial and reasonably accurate knowledge about big things may be more significant than complete and fully accurate knowledge about little things.

The Future of the Regulatory Agencies

❖ JAMES M. LANDIS

Some months ago I submitted to the President a report dealing with the regulatory agencies of our government. I was literally amazed at the reception that that Report got not only from the professions and the mass of our governmental personnel but also from the general public. It is of some interest to speculate on the causes for that reception.

"The Future of the Regulatory Agencies," by James M. Landis, from *Federal Accountant* (September, 1961), pp. 79–85. © 1961 by the Federal Government Accountants Association. Reprinted by permission.

One of them seems to me to be that the public began to appreciate the vast areas of authority that these agencies possessed with regard to our economic life. Even the legal profession has barely recognized this fact since the tendency of practitioners in administrative law is to center their work on few of these agencies, having only a vague knowledge of the workings and jurisdiction of the others.

A second reason seems to be public recognition of the fact that there was a tremendous amount of fragmentation of regulatory concern in areas in which some development of national policies was essential if we were to increase the pace of our national growth. The public had become conscious of the erosion that has been occurring in our railroad traffic since the end of the Korean War. Despite the significant increases in our gross national production bringing with it vastly increased demands for transportation, the total ton mileages carried by the railroads was actually declining. In the passenger field, conditions were even worse. Inter-city service and particularly commutation service was being crippled. We in New York, for example, despite rapid growth of such suburban areas as Rockland County, were substantially deprived of commutation service down the west side of the Hudson River. Nor did the development of the highway program prove a solution to the problem. Traffic congestion characterized the points of entry into our cities, parking space was at a premium, and parking rates skyrocketed. In respect to the carriage of goods, trucking concern after trucking concern went bankrupt. Despite substantial increases in air traffic, the carriers had their difficulties. One today is virtually bankrupt and others that were showing financial profits are now showing continuing and heavy financial losses. Our system of local air service is likely to require a subsidy of some $80,000,000 this coming year, and several of our unsubsidized all air cargo carriers have been forced to discontinue their activities. The simple remedial measures that have been employed of raising rates and fares — measures employed with a frequency never paralleled in our history — failed to bring any solution to this problem.

Our maritime commerce presents much the same picture More and more the carriage of goods by sea is falling into the hands of foreign flag carriers, despite our policies of subsidizing construction and operation.

In the field of communications the emergence of a host of new nations threatens the continued use of those frequencies that we have been accustomed to using, unless somehow we find new frequencies and new means of communication that hitherto have not been utilized. In television we still have to find an economic viability for the UHF band.

In energy, prices for natural gas have more than doubled. The future for hydro-electric power is not what it was in Theodore Roosevelt's day, not even what it appeared to be in the days of the initiation of TVA or the Columbia Basin Project. The development of atomic energy for peaceful purposes is, from an economic as well as, I believe, a scientific standpoint, still in its initial stage. For the next decade or two it is unlikely that we will find cause to abandon even for the large industrial consumer the use of coal, oil and natural gas. The hydrogenation of coal, namely exploding it rather than burning it so as to eliminate costs of transportation that now represent some 40 per cent of the price of the product and a process that is believed to increase significantly the energy derivable from coal, has not been developed, despite the origination of the concept some thirty years ago.

Were our traditional regulatory methods capable of surmounting these problems, my report would have been meaningless. Not only have they failed to do so but there have been serious and damaging failures in the very operation of these traditional processes. Chief among these is the matter of delay. I realize full well the necessity of accumulating the necessary facts upon which rational and sensible decisions can be made and the time necessarily spent in doing so. But decision requires two other qualities — courage and imagination. These factors seem to me to have been lacking to some degree in the administrative process during the past decade. They should be present, in my opinion, at every level of that process — the early stages of negotiation, the hearing examiner level, and the top agency level. Procedures, bureaucratic procedures, have been developed and become crystallized that may assure what might be called "safety" in decision, but these procedures place a tremendous check upon the other qualities of courage and imagination. Just as private enterprise must fall or rise upon judgments based on these qualities, government to an extent must take the same risks.

A word more about my report. Misinterpretations of my suggestions are rife. I have been reported as in favor of a Ministry or Department of Transportation. Quite the contrary is true. I have suggested that an effort be made on a purely voluntary basis to coordinate the efforts of the various agencies active in this field. The success or the failure of that effort in any particular area may show empirically the need for some statutory authority to be lodged somewhere, but the necessity for such statutory authority will not be the product of some ivory tower or egg-head thinking but a demonstration arising out of the facts of a trial and error process.

I have been reported as urging the creation of an Office of Transportation in the White House. Quite the contrary is so. I believe instead that the function of co-ordination is properly under the Constitution a function of the Executive. It is an error, in my opinion, to assign to some agency this duty of coordination. I have yet to see an Agency or a Department offer in the public interest to give up its juris-diction over any specific area on the ground that it can be done better by some other agency. Parkinson's Law militates against any such effort. On the other hand, the Office of the President, which is responsible for the faithful execution of our laws and also the formulation of over-all policies, can view the problem objectively and can best make decisions, referable to the Congress if necessary, as to how best to organize our governmental machinery to effect the desired results.

I have also been reported as suggesting or seeking to become a czar with respect to the regulatory agencies. Nothing has been further from my thoughts. Indeed, I deplored those instances where the Executive sought to inject its own opinions into the disposition of controversies before certain agencies. Adjudication simply ceases to be adjudication if it ceases to be independent. This is the basic principle that the Supreme Court of the United States has enunciated in the *Morgan* cases. And it is right. It was not only the intent of Congress in establishing these agencies that adjudication should be an independent act, but it is the dividing line between de-mocracy and dictatorship.

On the other hand, I think gains have already been made. Whether they were stimulated by my suggestions or whether they derived from previous consideration of the problems is utterly unimportant. The fact is that they have been made. The Interstate Commerce Commission, for example, has broadened extensively the power of boards of employees and hearing examiners to make final decisions subject only to discretionary review by the Commission itself, thus relieving the Commission members of time-consuming details that impinged unnecessarily upon their ability to handle really important matters. The central tragedy of life, as Ralph Waldo Emerson remarked — a remark so apt for our regulatory agencies — is that a day holds only 24 hours. The Civil Service Commission has recently acceded to a request of the Interstate Commerce Commission to upgrade its hearing examiners so that the encouragement to join that corps is substantially increased. I would add as a footnote to that observation that the policy of grading hearing examiners on the bases that the Civil Service Commission has previously operated shows in my opinion a misunderstanding of their function and the dignity that must attend their position.

The Federal Communications Commission has now determined to make some review of the practices of licensees seeking renewal of their licenses. If these licenses were originally granted to them upon their representation of their proposed program content, their ability to live up to these promises bears some relationship to their privilege to keep a frequency that others are aspiring to. This is not a suggestion of censorship but simply a determination between competing licensees as to which one should in the public interest be granted a frequency that can only be utilized by one.

The Securities and Exchange Commission announced recently that it would introduce the practice of thrusting upon individual Commissioners the responsibility of preparing individual opinions with respect to Commission decisions. This is a change in procedure that I have long advocated. The anonymity that lies behind *per curiam* decisions, written by staff members whose names are unknown, who may never have heard the arguments and who are told how to decide before they may have even read the briefs of the parties, is a definite violation of the basic principles of the *Morgan* case. Yet that practice has characterized most of our agencies for decade after decade. Moreover, the practice destroys the value of precedent upon which the predictability of administrative law depends. I know that in my tenure on the Civil Aeronautics Board I tended to have little respect for decisions whose source I could not discover other than that they were written by the staff.

But much more needs to be done. There is the problem of overlapping jurisdictions. These are called "concurrent" jurisdictions by those who seek to defend them, and these concurrent jurisdictions are said to have a certain value. They do have a value to the men operating under Parkinson's Law but they are a distinct obstacle to the trade or the persons upon whom they operate. I was somewhat shocked and surprised to read the other day a defense of the concurrent jurisdiction exercised by the Federal Trade Commission and the Food and Drug Administration over false and misleading advertising in the food, drugs and cosmetic field by Professor David Cavers, when I recall that in 1934 he spearheaded valiantly but unsuccessfully an attempt to bring the entire field within what was then the jurisdiction of the Pure Food and Drug Administration. It may be that my criticism stems from the fact that I have only grown older but not wiser.

There is the further problem of trying to develop the necessary facts in certain types of controversies by means other than the cumbersome method of examination and cross-examination of witnesses. Business judgments involving millions and millions of dollars are not arrived at in this fashion, and yet many of the decisions of our administrative agencies are in essence business judgments where facts themselves are not in dispute. It may be that the Administrative Procedure Act of 1946 forecloses other than a judicial approach to these problems. Probably the institution of trial by jury in lieu of trial by battle had similar obstacles to overcome. Probably the organized legion of professional champions opposed that innovation as much as, I presume, our organized bar would resist any departure from our traditional judicialized methods of establishing not merely facts but economic hypotheses.

Some 25 years ago accountancy could scarcely be called a profession. Since the passage of the Securities Act of 1933, it has become one. The prescription of standards by the Securities and Exchange Commission, complemented by the same move on the part of the American Institute of Accountants, buttressed by the enforcement of these standards by both the Commission and the Institute, has made of the accountants a profession comparable to that of the law. Medical experts, traffic experts, statisticians, may, perhaps, be amenable to some similar development and some similar disciplines, so as to obviate the clashes in testimony that add to records and obfuscate the true issues.

There are two further prime considerations that I believe deserve mention. The first is personnel. Without adequate personnel, whatever else we choose to do is meaningless. I have on several occasions likened the selection of personnel to man our important agencies to the selection of personnel to fill our federal judgeships. Recently I had the occasion to discuss the subject with an old friend of mine, a long time practitioner before these agencies and a former president of the American Bar Association. We agreed on the fact that as much intelligence, as much courage, had to characterize the appointment of men to our regulatory agencies as to judgeships. He then remarked that really more was needed. Judges, he said, because of our traditions are not only truly independent but are traditionally immune from political pressures and *ex parte* representations. Members of the regulatory agencies, he said, have also to have the stamina and fortitude to stand up to these pressures, whatever ethical codes will be promulgated. More imagination is also required of them because they have to guess the future as well as determine the equities of past conduct. I think both you and I can admit that that thesis has validity.

Secondly, there is the difficult but essential problem of developing national policies in fields where the development of policy has been made impossible by the fragmentation of concern over that field by the creation of regulatory agencies having only a partial and in a sense a legalized prejudiced concern with their particular jurisdictions. No one can fail to recognize the difficulties that attend an objective of this character. Apart from its intrinsic complexity, there are innumerable bureaucratic pressures, inter-agency rivalries, and competing demands on the part of vested interests. But somehow or other we must succeed. For, in my opinion, the destiny of these United States lies in that effort — the effort to shape our forms of government so that our philosophy of governmental support of individual effort, of private enterprise, can effectively promise more for the benefit, economically and spiritually, of mankind than the philosophy of those other governments who would sacrifice the many to the ambitions of the few.

A Look at the Federal Administrative
Agencies ❖ HENRY J. FRIENDLY

For the first item in a bill of particulars, let me nominate delay. I wonder whether law students still are taught, as we were, to contrast the celerity of those Mercury-like and wing-footed messengers, the administrative agencies, with the creeping and

"A Look at the Federal Administrative Agencies," by Henry J. Friendly, from *Columbia Law Review* (April, 1960), pp. 432, 434–446. Reprinted by permission of the author and publisher.

cumbersome processes of the courts. If they are, they have a rude awakening ahead, on both counts. To borrow Mr. Churchill's phrase, the regulatory agencies often tolerate delays up with which the judiciary would not put.

This is nothing new. Mr. Henderson was complaining about it in 1924. The Task Force of the Hoover Commission found in 1955 that "the delays in the final decisions of cases now pending before the Federal Communications Commission and Civil Aeronautics Board are such as to require, in the opinion of the task force, investigation by the Congress and corrective action by the agencies concerned," and that in at least five other agencies "an unreasonable amount of time apparently is consumed in certain types of proceedings." I know not what the Federal Communications Commission did in the light of this goad, but if any "corrective action" was taken by the Civil Aeronautics Board, practitioners before that body were not aware of it.

. . . .

Even as an outsider, I could venture some suggestions. One is that the agencies should take a less egalitarian notion as to proceedings before them. I would not be understood as condoning any violation of law, however petty. But since time and manpower are limited, there might be sense in the CAB's getting important rate and certificate cases decided even if a possibly unlawful but harmless interlocking directorate continues, in the FTC's making more rapid progress with its Clayton Act docket even if useless cures for baldness cause some hopes to be blighted and dollars to be wasted or some abridged or retitled paperbacks do not announce their character with the *ne plus ultra* of clarity, and in the NLRB's dealing with problems that affect large sections of labor and industry even if the employer of a dozen or so workers is not properly admonished for his refusal to bargain. Here again I think the agencies could take a leaf out of the judicial book. Heavily burdened courts do manage to expedite the cases most in need of expedition. I am thinking not merely of matters of great public importance such as the *Steelworkers* case or our Circuit's recent brushes with New York State's wiretapping and the picketing of an Arab ship, but of commercial litigation. In a recent copyright infringement suit, the total time from filing in the Southern District of New York to final decision by the Court of Appeals was less than two months.

Second, as already indicated, I think the agencies have gone overboard in their zeal for a record that will drain the last dregs from the cask — and sometimes a good many staves as well. The form of judicial procedure has created an illusion of the possibility of achieving certainty and, with this, the pursuit of every byway *au bout*. When the issue is whether John killed Mary, or even whether John promised Mary to marry, a fair degree of certainty ought usually to be attainable and no effort can be spared in the attempt to attain it. Some administrative proceedings may present issues of this sort, e.g., revocation of an airline pilot's license or certain unfair labor practice cases. But it simply is not possible for anyone to predict with complete accuracy the flow of air travel between two continents several years hence, much less how this will be divided among various airlines, or what the revenues and expenses of operating a pipeline will be. The agencies should do more to limit the time-consuming efforts of the parties and the agency staffs in obtaining the appearance of exactness when appearance is all there is.

Some attempts to compel expedition by legislative or judicial sanctions have been made or discussed. The FCC is required to expedite its business with the objective of rendering a final decision within three months from the date of filing on all original applications, renewals, and transfer cases in which it is not necessary to hold a hearing, and within six months from the final date of the hearing in all hearing cases. I leave it to practitioners before that agency to say what effect this has had. We are all familiar with time limitations on the power to suspend tariff changes by carriers and equally so with the way in which administrative agencies prolong these. I doubt the ultimatum "Let there be speed" will mean "and there was speed." I find even less promise in the suggestion of the Hoover Commission that "courts should be authorized upon proof of irreparable damage to issue mandatory injunctions to agencies to proceed to a decision upon a showing of undue delay." The time and effort required to debate whether there has been undue delay had better be used to avoid it.

The second item in my bill of particulars is the failure by administrative agencies to take hold of basic problems before these have reached a stage of crisis. Here also I think the agencies have suffered from overemphasizing a supposed likeness to the courts. Courts are not expected to initiate new measures, save perhaps as to procedure and practice; they make their contribution to law reform by deciding specific cases brought to them for adjudication, whereas other groups have the responsibility for initiating new legislative measures. Administrative agencies have the opportunity and the responsibility to make policy in advance. Public attention is now focused on the failure of the FCC and the FTC to do this in the field of television; but they are by no means alone. Surely the ICC, which had been granted broad new powers in 1920 so as to put "the railroad systems of the country more completely than ever under the fostering guardianship and control of the Commission," was not without responsibility for failing to take action that might at least have lessened the force of the wave of bankruptcies that hit the railroads in the 1930's. The thoughtful memorandum submitted to the President by Mr. Louis Hector when he resigned from the CAB lists examples from that agency. I shall cite only one. For years the Board and the Department of State have been proceeding on an *ad hoc* basis in the exchange of air rights with foreign nations. Congress, the carriers, and the executive branch have urged the need of a basic policy review. Two years ago, the State Department offered to finance a study by independent consultants. The CAB declined the offer, on the basis that it could do the job itself. The study was not even started until more than a year later — the pressure of litigated cases always wins over projects such as these — and if there has yet been any conclusion, I have not seen it. Meanwhile important decisions must be taken. I am sure that those adept in other fields could multiply examples.

A third item in the bill of particulars is the *ad hoc* character of administrative determinations and the consequent failure to let the industry and the agency staff know where they stand. Even though it be impossible to devise a precise mathematical formula, should not the Civil Aeronautics Board, after more than twenty years, have been able to announce some understandable criteria as to the amount of airline competition that it deems consistent with sound economics? The CAB's recent answer to Mr. Hector reveals that the Board now has under way "a jet study, the results of which may, among other things, have a significant relationship to policies relating to route structure, fares, and the economics of route development." This is good news, but the jets did not burst in 1960 upon a hitherto unsuspecting world, and decisions of the five preceding years, made on the basis of piston engine economics, may prove of doubtful validity in the jet age.

A subhead under this item is the practice, indulged in some agencies, of having opinions manufactured by opinion-writing sections. Mr. Landis, certainly no foe of the administrative agencies, called attention to the evils of this a score of years ago. The practice has not improved with age — indeed, it has become worse as a result of the action of certain agencies, adopted, in the case of the CAB, as a means of preventing leaks, of announcing conclusions before the opinion is written. I can not subscribe to this apparent view that the best way to stop leaks is to sink the ship. What would you think of a court that regularly said, "We have decided thus and so — our law clerks will find reasons to support this later"? Here is one instance in which the agencies, which so like to be considered as courts, would do well to emulate them.

You may have wondered why I have as yet said nothing on the currently topical subject of pressure. Of course, this is an evil and a great one. Indeed, its worst result is not even the wrong decisions that pressure sometimes produces but rather its effect in making the right type of man unwilling to accept or retain appointment to the agencies. However, we will be wise not to become hysterical. Discriminating analysis is required if, in a righteous effort to eradicate unwholesome pressure, we are not to drain off the baby with the bath water.

What are compendiously called "pressures" on administrative agencies are, in fact, of many different types. Sometimes they come from elements in the industry; sometimes from legislators, governors, mayors, or other local interests; sometimes they appear to come from the latter but are, in fact, generated by the former. Sometimes, and this is a form that needs a good deal more study, pressure comes from the agency staff — and here again this may be either spontaneous and sincere or stimulated and synthetic. I trust no one is so naive as to think the separation of staff function decreed by the Administrative Procedure Act really works. To be sure, the staff lawyer who has appeared at the hearing is not likely to stride into the office of a commissioner and tell him how to decide the case. The process is more subtle — the word is likely to pass from the lawyer to another staff member, then perhaps to another, and finally to the commissioner's assistant — and all this may, or may not, be altogether innocent. I once suggested to Professor Jaffe of the Harvard Law School that a good subject for a paper in his seminar would be "The Influence of the Car Pool on Administrative Law"; perhaps we should add the cocktail party and the Saturday night poker game.

Now let me tempt fate and say that by no means all these activities that are subsumed under the opprobrious term "pressure" are either evil or avoidable. Here again, the analogy to the courts can be pressed too far. After some doings of the last months one hesitates to utter the truism that administrators should not live in isolation from the industry — but one can remain on the side of the angels by quickly adding that nature has provided other places than yachts where isolation can be overcome. Indeed the best possible place is the commissioner's office, and with the commissioner's staff present. Of course, an airline president should not talk to a CAB member about a case pending for decision. But he definitely should keep the members abreast of his equipment plans, his visions, and his difficulties, both technological and economic, even though it is quite unrealistic to suppose that such discussions may not lead to general talk about matters that may later figure more specifically in cases that go through the hearing process. With the right kind of administrator there is no harm in this. No one would have hesitated to talk that way to Joe Eastman. No possible damage would have been done, for the Commissioner would have accepted nothing on the basis of mere statement by an interested party, but would have taken what was said as a subject for personal inquiry — and if any attempt had been made to go too far, it would have been prevented or, if not preventable, would have had an effect opposite to that desired. Neither would opposing interests have been concerned; for they would have had complete confidence that nothing in the world could affect Mr. Eastman's exercise of his powers in what the Supreme Court has called "the coldest neutrality." There is a good deal of nonsense current that an administrator cannot be truly judicial if he knows anything of a broad economic problem other than what comes from the record and briefs. No such intellectual asepsis is demanded; on matters such as these the judge is required to be neutral, not sterile, when he dons the robe.

Similarly, one neither can nor should try to outlaw all attempts by legislators or local interests to affect administrative action. A senator, a governor, or a mayor may have highly legitimate interests in a new television station, a new air service, or a new supply of natural gas. Indeed, these interests actually may be more important than those of the rival litigants. Generally, to be sure, the legislator's or executive's interest should be in the service rather than in who provides it, but even this may be an oversimplification in some cases. The agencies ought not be deprived of the information as to the nature and extent of the public need that they can get from officials thus intimately concerned, provided, of course, the concern is real. Proper zeal for fair treatment of private interests seeking a license thought to be valuable should not lead us to forget that the real issue is the public need. The problem is not whether public officials should act in such a case, but how.

The initial burden rests on the public official himself. He ought to satisfy himself that the need for which he is being asked to speak is the real need of all his constituents, and not simply the selfish desire of some. Often this will end the matter, as in the notable case, cited by Mr. Landis, in which Senator Norris of Nebraska declined to lend his name to a constituent who wished him to request "expedition" — a euphemism evidently used even in those days — on a financial matter, of no true local concern, under investigation by the SEC. If he decides on intervention, it should be done in public — best of all by appearing at the hearing and subjecting himself to cross-examination on the same basis as any other witness, and never, of course, by the secret meeting or telephone call. There must also be a willingness to accept the administrative determination without reprisal or threat of reprisal — whether in the more obvious forms of denunciations in the Congressional Record and objections to reappointment or confirmation, or by the more subtle means of a hostile attitude toward agency appropriations. I can not overstress this, particularly as it affects the most important of all problems in this area — the ability to recruit and retain able administrators. One could make a good case that the troubles of the administrative agencies began with the reprisal meted out to Commissioner Esch in 1928 for his vote in the *Lake Cargo Coal* case. You may think such self-denial to be a counsel of perfection, but it was followed by Congress from 1887 until the late twenties.

III

I shall end my bill of particulars here, and turn to the more constructive but harder subject of what we should do about it. It is easy for those experienced with the agencies to be defeatist. They have seen, all too often, symptoms of what a distinguished practitioner of our city, whose anonymity I had better preserve, has called the law of progressive deterioration of regulatory agencies. The author works this out with some elaboration. The agency begins in a crusading spirit. Able commissioners accept the challenge of public service. Excellent men join the staff, motivated by the same challenge, by the excitement of working with great chiefs, and perhaps by the more selfish but in no way unworthy desire of staking out a claim in a new field. Then the big problems are solved, and it becomes apparent the little ones will not be overcome in a hurry. At this point, according to the law, decay sets in. The initial commissioners go back to their business or to more stimulating roles in government; they are replaced by men seeking the job rather than sought by it. The able members of the staff gravitate to the industry under regulation; the less able ones are pushed to the top by seniority, and their places are taken by men who lack the maturity and zeal of their predecessors. In initially strong bodies the rate of deterioration is lineal; in weak ones it is geometrical. Ultimately the agency becomes what Toynbee would call a fossil — it really is dead but doesn't know it. So, at least, readeth the law.

I think the "law" is useful as a picture not of what always has happened or must happen — certainly the ICC resisted it for many years — but of what may happen if we do not take measures to arrest the ailment. Mr. Hector, in the provocative memorandum to the President that I have mentioned, proposed radical surgery. The agencies, he says, have been given a job for which they are not suited. He therefore proposes a division of their work into three parts: policy making, which he would transfer to the executive branch; adjudication, which he would transfer to an administrative court; and enforcement, which he would transfer to the Department of Justice. The second of these suggestions, in a more limited form, was made by the Hoover Commission five years ago.

Not only do I question the feasibility of such a separation, I think it would do positive harm. The line between policy making and adjudication is altogether too shadowy to afford a basis for separation — unless adjudication is limited to those cases, too few to be of concern, in which the only problem is whether the facts require the application of some specific rule of law. And the proposal would destroy what is one of the greatest merits of the administrative agency, its combination of legislative, executive, and judicial attributes.

Let me illustrate this from the field of railway rates. If the question is whether a shipment comes within one classification of a tariff or another, that is adjudication clearly enough, with no element of policy making. But a case concerning the fairness or the prejudicial character of rates involves elements of policy, and this even though it arises as a demand for reparations. The policy considerations inherent in such proceedings range from the trivial to the gravest, as in cases relating to the overall rate level or to differentials, or the lack of them, between different parts or between traffic that has or has not moved all the way by rail. To call such cases adjudication and place their decision in an administrative court would deprive the public of the benefits of the very expertise that is a principal *raison d'etre* of the regulatory agency. Moreover, reparations cases and cases involving future rates cannot possibly be divided — often a single case will involve both; yet the fixing of future rates is surely not a "judicial" function.

Let me take as another illustration one that Mr. Hector brings forward in support of his proposal — an airline route case. In his view, as I understand it, the determination of what new air service should be provided is a policy matter for the executive, the choice of carrier or carriers an adjudicative matter for the administrative court. In fact, in many cases the two issues intertwine. The very reason for the new service may be the ability of one airline to afford the public a new through service because of other routes that it already has. But even when separation is feasible from a formal standpoint, how can one characterize as adjudication and not policy making a decision whether the service should be operated by an existing airline or by a newly organized enterprise, or the weight to be given to better immediate service to the public as against the benefits thought to be ultimately realizable from fortifying weak carriers against the strong? To analogize decisions on such matters to the ordinary work of the courts is to let words and methods obscure substance.

The Hoover Commission cited as another example of judicial action the finding of an unfair labor practice by the NLRB. At first sight this seems a better case, since unfair labor practice proceedings often turn on who did what to whom. But here too, once we go beyond the simplest case, the line between policy and adjudication becomes blurred. Take the problem of union-operated hiring halls. After years of dealing with this on the basis of investigating whether discrimination was practiced in each case, the NLRB decided on a different tack. In the *Mountain Pacific* case, it announced that its experience had led it to conclude that any exclusive union hiring hall was discriminatory unless the hall displayed prescribed signs advising applicants of their legal rights. Certainly this is policy, and it smacks of legislation rather than adjudication. But, apart from the question of retroactivity, which led the Ninth Circuit to refuse to permit its application to the past, and without commenting on the merits of the particular ruling, is this not, as the Court of Appeals intimated, the type of thing that agencies with expert knowledge of and responsibility for a particular field ought to do? Also, even when the existence of an unfair labor practice is solely a question of fact, there is the important question of the remedy. By imposing ineffective remedies an administrative court could effectively frustrate policy, whereas by imposing penalties out of relation to the crime it might build up resentments which would lead to a demand for legislative change that a more expert administrator would have avoided.

Separation of the prosecuting function could be more easily achieved. But even this would have its problems, and the agency charged with overall responsibility should be better able to distinguish between technical violations for which censure or a small penalty would be appropriate, and deliberate and serious breaches for which the law should be enforced to the hilt.

I do not mean my attitude to Mr. Hector's affirmative proposals, as distinguished from his critical analysis, to be taken as implying a belief that by a series of lucky accidents we have achieved the finest conceivable form of organization and live in the best of all possible administrative worlds. Doubtless there are many functions now vested in regulatory agencies that could be moved to the advantage of all. The transfer of most of the CAB's functions with respect to air safety to the Federal Aviation Agency by the Federal Aviation Act of 1958 is an example. I have long wondered why the ICC, primarily an economic regulatory agency, should be burdened with the administration of the Safety Appliance Act. I gather the changes whereby administrative tasks formerly performed by the Maritime Commission have been assumed by the Maritime Administrator have been beneficial. Surely these do not exhaust the possibilities. But I would operate on an individual basis, and when this minor surgery is finished, the major problems will remain.

Neither do I find much hope in a nostrum that has been widely peddled — better hearing examiners and more respect for their determinations. No one can be against better hearing examiners, although my own experience has made me think many of the present ones are too much maligned. But the same considerations that oppose a separation of adjudication and policy show the limits on deference to decisions by hearing examiners. Here again any reform can be but modest. In those few cases in which the agency is simply applying a definite rule to the facts, the decision of the hearing examiner should be conclusive unless the commission grants review, and it should exercise great abstinence in doing that. In the cases in which fact finding and policy determination are mingled, deference should be paid to the examiner's findings on the facts; and it would be well if examiners were encouraged to devote more effort to this part of their work and were required to set out their findings in numbered form, rather than to spend time and thought, at least in the great cases, in preparing arguments and conclusions to which the commissioners surely will not and perhaps ought not give much weight. If anyone thinks this is denigrating the examiners, let him read Judge Frank's eloquent statement as to the "grave importance of fact finding" and recall Chief Justice Hughes' remark that "An unscrupulous administrator might be tempted to say 'Let me find the facts for the people of my country, and I care little who lays down the general principles.' "

Reforms such as these may help in a small way to make the job of the agency more doable. So also might a revision of the regulatory statutes wherein Congress would make some standards governing the agencies slightly more specific. Somewhat larger staffs with higher salary ceilings, and perhaps more non-seniority positions at the top, may help also, although we would do well to ponder Professor Parkinson's teachings before going too far on this road. The Interstate Commerce Commission's invitation to practitioners to study its procedures and performance is a healthy step, which other agencies might well emulate. But in the last analysis there is only one answer, albeit a trite one — get better men as members of the commissions and keep them there. Commissioner Eastman said it all in the address delivered on the twenty-fifth anniversary of his appointment to the ICC: "[G]ood men can produce better results with a poor law than poor men can produce with a good law."

There is no reason to suppose we can not get such men. Indeed, we have had them. Where would one find a brighter galaxy than the early chairmen of the SEC? How could one have secured a finer man than Paul Herzog, later Associate Dean of the Harvard School of Public Administration, to chair the NLRB? Could the CAB possibly have had members more superbly qualified than the late Edward Warner, a pioneer in both the technological and economic aspects of air transportation and later the choice of the world as President of the International Civil Air Organization, and George Baker, Professor of Transportation at the Harvard Graduate School of Business Administration. Many of us could name others. The trouble is not that we can not get some good men for the administrative agencies, but that we do not get enough and when we get them we do not hold them. The stars twinkle and then go out. As against the thirty-year average of Eastman, Aitchison, and Meyer on the ICC, and the eight and a half year average for the Commission's first fifty years, the average tenure on the CAB has been four and a half years.

This, I suggest, is the direction in which efforts must be principally directed. The bar and to some extent the public jealously watch appointments to federal judicial office. The President and his Attorney General know that a small but articulate group is ready to praise good judicial appointments and to criticize bad ones. Why do not the lawyers who practice before administrative agencies — not just those representing industry, but also those representing labor, consumers, and local interests — organize themselves to perform a similar critical function? Indeed they have a double task. Before they can be effective with the appointing power they must convince their clients that the latters' private interests will be better served by the choice of men for disinterestedness and ability rather than for a supposed predisposition, which, oft as not, is being equally cherished by the other side. Why should not the committees of the Senate that pass on the confirmation of these appointees assume a more positive role — not in pushing particular candidates, which is the executive's responsibility, but in maintaining standards, as the Judiciary Committee does with the courts, and this not so much by the traumatic course of refusing confirmations, although, of course, that prerogative is not to be relinquished, as by advance notice as to what type of men will and what will not be challenged? Beyond this Congress has another role. It must exercise its essential functions of oversight and criticism with caution and restraint. It must look at how the agency is doing its job in general, not at whether a decision has hurt some constituents of a particular legislator in a particular case. There must be no penalty on courage to offend when the public interest requires. That is what we expect and have largely obtained from the federal judiciary, and we would improve the quality, and independence of our administrators by borrowing, at least in part, one of the features that has brought it about.

I do not suggest life tenure for commissioners, but I do suggest a much longer term — say ten years, and I mean a full ten years in every case even if the new appointment comes as a result of death or resignation during a term. I know the objection to this. To paraphrase Mr. Justice Holmes, five years of a bad commissioner "are enough." But I think the prospective gains outweigh the losses. Some have suggested coupling a longer term with ineligibility for reappointment and a liberal pension. There might be merit in this, but I should like first to see whether we can not accomplish the same objective by a long term and by drawing more heavily on the great source of manpower being produced by the compulsory retirement plans of our universities, industry, labor, and government itself. These plans are constantly turning out able men who are eager for constructive activity and whose pensions make the smallness of federal salaries of little consequence. The answer sometimes given to this suggestion — that if a man is too old for his former employer, he is too old for a new one — is altogether too facile. Many plans retire executives not at all because their individual usefulness has ceased but in order to create room at the top and to avoid the need for painful choices; neither of these considerations is applicable when an outstanding and vigorous man of sixty-five is selected for government service. And no commissioner can be quite so free from fears about reappointment as the man who, because of his age, does not want it.

IV

The administrative agencies are here to stay. They are essential to the working of our private enterprise system. We can not cure their ills by major revamping of the structure — there are no panaceas in the medicine chest. We can restore their prestige and efficiency by a determined, nonpartisan effort to man them again with the sort of members who made the Interstate Commerce Commission what it was when my generation came to the bar — and to keep them that way. The job can be done, but it will not be done unless lawyers concerned with the agencies spend more time and effort on this sort of approach rather than in carping criticism and in chasing reorganizational rainbows.

The Executive and the Regulatory

Agencies ❖ ELMER M. STAATS

SENATOR [JOHN A.] CARROLL. If these agencies are independent, as I believe them to be, why do they have to clear with the Bureau of the Budget for their appropriations?

MR. [ELMER M.] STAATS. Well, of course, Mr. Chairman, the agencies, with the exception of the Federal Reserve Board, I believe historically, have come within the framework of the Budget and Accounting Act.

The agencies' appointments are made, of course, by the President, with the approval of the Congress.

So, to that extent, they are a part of the procedure of the executive branch with respect to the review of their financial and their personnel requirements, and to that extent the President has an interest and a concern with respect to the efficiency and the effectiveness of their operations.

SENATOR CARROLL. Is the budget of an independent agency — their requests for money to run their agency — entirely under the control of the President or the Bureau of the Budget?

MR. STAATS. Well, it is controlled through the operation of the Budget and Accounting Act which means, of course, it is not only subject to the review of the Bureau of the Budget and the President, but also by the Appropriations Committees of the House and Senate.

In other words, they follow the same procedures that are followed with respect to any other agency such as the Department of Agriculture or Department of the Interior.

SENATOR CARROLL. Has this continued for a long period of time?

MR. STAATS. This has been true since 1921.

SENATOR CARROLL. I see.

Then in all these independent agencies, therefore, they do have to submit their budget requests, their budget estimates, to the Bureau of the Budget?

MR. STAATS. That is correct.

SENATOR CARROLL. And receive approval?

MR. STAATS. Right.

SENATOR CARROLL. Do you know of any cases where you have — I say you, I mean the Bureau of the Budget has — denied their requests for more money, for more money for more employees?

MR. STAATS. I am quite certain, Mr. Chairman, that there have been cases, as I believe there will be this year, where we will have honest differences of opinion as to the growth of their workload in a given year which would result in some differences of view as to how many additional personnel they should be financing for that current year. . . .

The Appropriations Committees, I think, by and large, have been more conservative in their estimates on the need for personnel than we have been.

Testimony of Elmer M. Staats in U.S. Congress (Senate), Federal Administrative Procedure, *Hearings before the Subcommittee on Administrative Practice and Procedure of the Committee of the Judiciary,* 86th Cong., 2nd Sess. (1960), pp. 22, 23, 32–35, 42–46.

We have made a little analysis going back for the past six years with respect to the seven agencies that I have mentioned here, and the appropriations actions of the Congress have tended to reduce the estimates of the executive branch for these agencies.

Now, this is not true for every single year of that period, but if you take it for the full period of the six years, the net result has been a reduction by the Congress of the estimates submitted by the Bureau. . . .

I know Senator Magnuson over on the Senate side here has also been studying this problem under the leadership of General Doyle who has organized a staff directed to precisely the same kind of problem that we have been concerned with, namely, how can you provide for more expeditious and effective management of these regulatory commissions and boards?

SENATOR CARROLL. For example, I observe in your statement that you had such a survey made of the Federal Power Commission in 1953. . . .

If my memory serves me correctly, the Federal Power Commission has got a backlog of some 3,000 cases involving hundreds of millions of dollars. This is not just some small rate case, not some small airline, but this goes to the real question of what I would consider to be, not the interest of one private person in an adversary proceeding but it may be, the interest of a whole community or of a whole state.

Some of these cases have been held up for years. At one time I was present at one of these appropriations hearings urging more money for these commissions, if they need more money, need more staff to do their job.

And you say that the jurisdiction of the Bureau of the Budget is such that you can reduce or you can recommend the reduction, I assume, to the President of their budgets. He usually takes the recommendation of the Bureau of the Budget. . . .

SENATOR CARROLL. You have read some reports of men who profess knowledge in this field, and I am sure have it, who talk about abolishing regulatory agencies, the regulatory system, and putting a part of it in the executive branch, another part of it by creating administrative tribunals, courts, and the enforcement end of it going to the Department of Justice.

As I understand it, you are not getting into that field at all. What you are talking about is within the present framework?

MR. STAATS. That is correct.

SENATOR CARROLL. Do you think they can streamline procedures, preserve due process, speed up their procedures and their actions to eliminate the backlog?

MR. STAATS. That is right.

SENATOR CARROLL. Is this the basic viewpoint of the Bureau of the Budget?

MR. STAATS. That is right. We have addressed ourselves to the problems within the existing framework, and I think your statement is quite correct.

SENATOR CARROLL. Now I think we ought to say for the record the Bureau of the Budget has how many employees?

MR. STAATS. For all of our activities, including the clerical and administrative, we have about 425 employees in the Bureau of the Budget.

SENATOR CARROLL. And a part of your function is when the various budget estimates are sent to you you have groups of people or a task force or an individual who makes investigations into the requests of the various agencies?

MR. STAATS. That is correct. . . .

SENATOR CARROLL. You do that in a fashion a little bit different from the way the Congress operates, but you are checking and you are "watchdogging" to see if you cannot cut down their estimates if you can?

MR. STAATS. We give them advice, we give them help where we can, and sometimes we turn loose some of our able people to serve in these agencies.

The top administrative man in the ICC is a former employee of the Bureau. I think he has done a fine job.

We are losing one of our other able people to become the Director of Administration for the Federal Power Commission within the next couple of weeks. This is the kind of relationship that we have built up over a period of time, and we hope that our role has been one of help and advice and constructive effort rather than of a control function.

SENATOR CARROLL. Well, I feel personally that, of course, I think you are performing a very valuable service. There are some members of Congress, however, who feel that the Bureau of the Budget is taking a little bit too much power unto itself about certain budget matters, but this is understandable that there would be that feeling in certain instances.

But I want to ask you just one or two more questions about these surveys. You have had a recent survey come out on CAB, have you not?

MR. STAATS. Yes, that is correct.

SENATOR CARROLL. What did that cost?

MR. STAATS. The contract on that was $50,000 — excuse me, $53,200. . . .

SENATOR CARROLL. Is this a management group?

Now, the reason I ask these questions is because I want to be helpful to Judge Prettyman or Dean Landis or whoever handles it in the future from the executive side. . . .

Obviously, we have seen all these congressional committees year after year making reports, and sometimes I hope they have been helpful, but if we are going to attack this problem we have got to hit it head on, and we have got to spend some money in these management surveys, and it has been my information that they had such a survey in the NLRB that has been helpful. . . .

SENATOR CARROLL. Would you say of all your contracts in this last group, how much money are you spending?

MR. STAATS. On the contracts for the six agencies they amounted to $292,200. . . .

.   .   .   .

SENATOR CARROLL. I suppose if any decision were to be made by the Bureau of the Budget as to whether you would be in favor of administrative courts or the separation of these important functions this would really have to come from further study and probably from the President himself?

MR. STAATS. I believe that would be a fair statement, yes. . . .

SENATOR CARROLL. Any questions, Dean?

MR. LANDIS. I would like to ask a few of Mr. Staats.

I suppose you are aware that the basic statutory procedures, insofar as there are statutory procedures governing the disposition of the matters that flow before the administrative agencies, come from the Administrative Procedure Act of 1946.

There are in constituent statutes every now and then little items dealing with the procedure before those agencies.

But I think it is fair to say that the basic statutory requirements come from the Administrative Procedure Act of 1946.

Do I understand then that the position of the Bureau of the Budget is that that act has been harmful to the administrative agencies in their handling of the matters before them?

MR. STAATS. I think, Dean Landis, our general conclusion has been that in most instances the difficulty has come from statutes which go beyond the Administrative Procedure Act.

The case of the Federal Communications Act would be a case in point.

MR. LANDIS. Well, now, let us be specific on that. In the case of the Federal Communications Commission just what kind of statutory procedure is there which you believe to be harmful?

MR. STAATS. The Federal Communications Act of 1934, Section 409, provides that:

In any case of adjudication, as defined in the Administrative Procedure Act, which has been designated for a hearing by the Commission, no person who has participated in the presentation or preparation for presentation of such cases before an examiner or examiners or the Commission, and no member of the Office of the General Counsel, the Office of the Chief Engineer, the Office of the Chief Accountant shall, except to the extent required for the disposition of ex parte matters as authorized by law, directly or indirectly make any addition of presentation respecting such case unless upon notice and opportunity for all parties to participate.

Now this, I think, may be a somewhat extreme case, but I think the Chairman of the FCC has testified before Congress with respect to the difficulty arising from the kind of detailed procedural proscription which has been enacted here. He testified as follows, he says:

Intermeshed in all of this was the 1952 congressional act requiring complete separation of the Commission from its general counsel, its chief engineer, and all of its operating personnel, except a small review staff which was mandated never to make a recommendation on a case. Thus, shorn by statute of all staff advice, backlogged by many hundreds of competitive applications in hearings, and further prevented by law from delegating to any commissioner or panel of the commissioners its adjudicatory hearing decision work, serious inefficiency inevitably resulted.

I think this may be an extreme situation, and I would not want to say that this kind of detailed proscription holds for the others, as well.

But to try to answer your question specifically as to whether we are suggesting a specific change in the Administrative Procedure Act of 1946, I think what we are suggesting is that that needs to be looked at from the standpoint of trying to adapt the Administrative Procedure Act more specifically to the needs of individual regulatory commissions.

MR. LANDIS. That provision that you cite from the Communications Act almost finds a complete counterpart in the Administrative Procedure Act, does it not?

.   .   .   .

MR. STAATS. Yes.

MR. LANDIS. Which prohibits many situations such as the sort of contact with, say, public counsel in the CAB proceedings after the hearing is closed.

It interests me that the Bureau of the Budget takes this position because certainly the bar, as a whole, seems to be taking the other position; namely, that there should be more judicialization rather than less in the disposition of these controversies.

MR. STAATS. That is correct.

MR. LANDIS. I would like to ask you a couple of questions with regard to budget procedure.

Is it customary for the chairman of the regulatory agencies to appear before the Budget in defense of his budget?

MR. STAATS. The chairman and, in most instances, Dean Landis, either the full Commission or those designated within the Commission, do appear.

MR. LANDIS. Yes. But you do have responsible officials appearing before you?

MR. STAATS. Oh, yes; and not only is there staff work done with the staff of the commissions in advance, but then there is an informal meeting or hearing with our examiners that are assigned to work with that agency on a full-time basis.

Then, finally, as we are doing just at the present time, there is an opportunity for the chairman and the members of the Commission to appear before either the director of the Bureau or myself to talk about their needs over and above what the staff is willing to recommend. . . .

MR. LANDIS. Now, let me ask this: Let us assume that the budget for some Commission is as the commissioners have recommended, say, $5 million.

As you recommend it, which is before you, it is $4 million. Do I understand correctly that the Commission, as such, cannot, in appearing before the Appropriations Committees of the House or of the Senate tell the Senate and the House what its original suggestions were with regards to its budget?

. . . .

MR. STAATS. That is not correct. That is a misunderstanding.

There has been, I believe I am correct in saying, going right back to the 1921 enactment of the Budget and Accounting Act, the procedure and the rule of all Presidents that the agencies appearing before committees should defend the President's budget, but that they are, at the same time, completely free to respond to the committee in terms of what their original request was to the Bureau of the Budget, and this is done pretty much as a standard procedure.

MR. LANDIS. Well, frankly, my experience was always this: When the Bureau of the Budget would cut the budgets I defended, you would go around and see people on the committee, the Appropriations Committee, to ask the appropriate questions so that you would then be entitled to tell what you had really recommended to the Bureau of the Budget.

MR. STAATS. They are better trained now, Dean Landis. They do it automatically. [Laughter.]

MR. LANDIS. But I understood I could not initiate a thing of that nature myself before the House Appropriations Committee.

MR. STAATS. Well, I think almost invariably the question is asked and the statement is put in the record, and this does not concern us. But the President, I think, must have the support of the executive branch, otherwise the budget does not really mean very much.

It is his budget, and in order to have the integrity of the budget there must be support for that recommendation. I think this goes back to the whole philosophy of the Budget and Accounting Act itself, but in no sense do we feel that there should be any denial to the appropriate committees of Congress of the information as to what the agency itself in the first instance requested.

MR. LANDIS. You see, I was happy to see here that you had increased certain appropriations for some of these agencies that you mentioned here, particularly the Securities and Exchange Commission.

I suppose you are aware that for several years now the Securities and Exchange Commission has been very far behind in its work; that in financial circles where normally the 20-day waiting period was as established by statute, was effective for many years, in the last few years, due to the overworked Commission, that statutory period has, in substance, been extended to 40, 50, and even 60 days.

MR. STAATS. Sixty days is what has happened in many cases that I am aware of.

MR. LANDIS. And the chairman of the Commission has pointed out publicly over and over again that this is a matter of money and money alone, that the workload per individual has increased enormously as registrations, for example, for new issues have increased enormously, and there has been no increase in personnel. . . .

MR. STAATS (continuing). There has been each year an increase, there have been increases in the staff for the SEC.

There have been some differences in the past as to the way in which this backlog could be cleaned up, and that was the part of the background on the study which was arranged for and has now been completed on the Securities and Exchange Commission.

This is a study which has been made by the firm of Booz, Allen & Hamilton. They have made some suggestions which they feel would improve the situation procedurally, but I think, by and large, to generalize, it is their conclusion that the SEC has been performing its work very effectively, and I am sure that there will be an increase in the staff for SEC in the budget for 1962 which will be presented.

. . . .

These reports that you have with regard to these agencies, are they approved by the Bureau of the Budget? Do you say this is a final report and "We hope you will adopt these recommendations?"

MR. STAATS. Well, like any other survey by an outside organization it represents the best work that can be performed by that agency.

We believe that these are very competent and responsible organizations that have made these studies.

We do not approve the reports nor do we ask the agencies to approve the reports, but we do like to use them as a basis for sitting down together with them in examining what part of it can be accepted and what part of it cannot be accepted.

MR. LANDIS. One further question on the budgets that have been transmitted to the Congress. It was never the practice that I knew of that any member of the Budget would be there to defend it, that budget before, say, the House Committee on Appropriations. You had to defend the budget that you had not made, and sometimes it was quite embarrassing.

Now, is that still the story that the people who make the budget do not defend it?

MR. STAATS. This is true, of course, with the whole government, that the agency heads appear before the Congress in support of the budget which has been approved by the President for their submission.

Our Bureau has taken the position that at any time any committee wishes to have us before them we are perfectly prepared and willing to do so; and, in fact, in the last two years there has been a move in this direction by way of an overall presentation on the budget by the Director of the Budget and his staff before the full Appropriations Committee in the House.

. . . .

MR. LANDIS. Well, frankly it always seemed to me a little rough for me to defend a budget that I had not made, and that I was rather critical of, and to be cross-examined by the subcommittee of the House, and they are tough cross-examiners,

I assure you, and to not have the guy there who really had made the budget, and he was immune from cross-examination, it always seemed a little rough.

MR. STAATS. He is not immune. [Laughter.]

MR. LANDIS. Well, he never was there, and I do not think they asked for him. . . . it does seem to me that the Budget function is very, very closely allied to the capacity of an agency to do its work.

There have been times that I have known the Budget to have said, "Well, you can't enter this field this year; you have got to put it off until next year," or something of that nature, where the mandate of the Congress is certainly that you should be moving in that field.

MR. STAATS. I think that I would be fair to say that from our point of view the number of people here involved, assuming you can get good people and train people, is not the whole answer, and I think if we felt that this was the whole answer to the problem, well then, this could be relatively easy to deal with. . . .

The Task of an Administrative Conference

❧ ROBERT KRAMER AND ARTHUR SELWYN MILLER

In December, 1962, the Administrative Conference of the United States, convened by President Kennedy in April, 1961, wound up its work and submitted its final report. Perhaps the most important part of that report was a recommendation that a permanent conference be established as a "means by which agencies in the federal government may cooperatively, continuously, and critically examine their administrative processes and related organizational problems." Since that time a number of bills have been introduced in Congress, which, if enacted, would create such a conference. On October 30, 1963, the Senate passed one of these bills. Our purpose here is to set out in brief but comprehensive form: (1) the context in which a permanent conference, if established, would operate; (2) the conceptual requirement and the basic constitutional questions involved; and (3) the problems which should be identified and resolved within the framework of a continuing conference. The exposition will focus on the functional area within which a conference would exist; there will be no attempt to make a detailed analysis of any pending proposal. Our principal conclusion is that present proposals do not seem to be adequate to the need, because the problem is far greater than many assert.

I. The Context

Necessarily, an administrative conference will be concerned with the public administration, and thus with detailed aspects of administrative law. But it is not a narrow, circumscribed view of that body of law which should be taken. Judicial review, speaking very generally, constitutes most of what is considered by textbook authors to be "administrative law." Thus Professor Kenneth C. Davis, in his well-

"The Task of An Administrative Conference," by Robert Kramer and Arthur Selwyn Miller from *The George Washington Law Review*, (December, 1963), pp. 169–192. Reprinted by permission.

known treatise, asserts that administrative law is "the law concerning the powers and procedures of administrative agencies, including especially the law governing judicial review of administrative action." This view is accepted by most of those professors of law who offer courses in "administrative law." Moreover, emphasis is placed upon procedural and constitutional questions. Administrative *law*, accordingly, is really administrative *procedure* in the commonly accepted definition — procedure, as Professor L. L. Jaffe once put it, "lifted to the level of constitutional law." By and large, the law students of the United States concentrate upon what the Supreme Court has said about administrative procedure when they study administrative law.

Such a view of administrative law states at best a partial truth, perhaps not even a half-truth. Concentration upon judicial review of administrative procedure, most of which relates to the several so-called "independent regulatory agencies," results in a failure to scrutinize the immensely important substantive policies which are administered by the executive-administrative branch of government. There is a failure, moreover, to focus upon the procedures of agencies other than the regulatory commissions — save in small part, as an occasional case may come to the fore; e.g., the recent decisions dealing with passport issuance. Additionally, within all agencies of government the only cases deemed worthy of attention are those which in some way present a "case or controversy" within the jurisdictional meaning of federal court rules. A vast area — the great bulk — of administration thus is left unstudied in the law schools.

Congress, in enacting the Administrative Procedure Act in 1946, did not take such a narrow view of administration. Save for a few relatively minor exceptions, mainly in the area of military and foreign affairs, all federal agencies are subject — at least in theory — to the provisions of that basic statute. Speaking generally, cases which have reached the federal courts in their reviewing capacity tend to come from the so-called independent agencies, rather than the departments. Nevertheless, it seems preferable that such a constricted view of administration should not be taken by a permanent conference. The full range of administration is significant. Accordingly, the basic proposition we suggest is this: The task of an administrative conference should encompass the entire spectrum of administrative activity insofar as any segment of that activity touches and concerns individuals *qua* individuals. The further suggestion is made that an unavoidable consequence of such a mission would be that the conference would have to inquire into certain substantive matters in addition to the procedural aspects which would be its chief object of concern.

If these propositions are valid, then the work of a permanent administrative conference would differ markedly from the work and activity of the Judicial Conference, and, for that matter, of the American Law Institute's various restatement projects. The Judicial Conference is concerned mainly with rules of court and ways of improving judicial procedure. But an administrative conference would have this as only one of several matters of interest. The American Law Institute's several restatement projects may provide a somewhat closer analogy, but these often are concerned with studies of what the law is thought to be in a given subject, or with codification of the law, rather than with a basic inquiry into broad legal questions. In this connection, it is not inappropriate to recall that Justice Frankfurter in 1944 stated that "there is no such thing as a common law of judicial review in the federal courts." In sum, the task of a permanent administrative conference would be different from, and probably greater than, the assigned mission of the Judicial Conference.

Dealing with the public administration involves more than a "legal" task. It includes more than procedure alone. The lawyer's focus upon procedure and some of the details of judicial review slights much of public administration, and, in the eyes of some students of public administration, may be "an offensive combination of aridity and arrogance." If war is too important to be left to the generals, then perhaps it can be said that public administration is too important to be left to the lawyers. By that it is meant that it is improper — as giving a distorted picture — to look at and evaluate any facet of the administrative branch of government through use of purely "legal" standards. Put another way, an administrative conference should not limit its scrutiny merely to the technical side of the administrative process; of necessity, it must recognize that the technical norms of procedure, including the procedure of judicial review, have important and inescapable effects upon the substantive policies which are enunciated.

As a *public law* system, the administrative process is concerned with both the *means* by which governmental (i.e., administrative) decisions are reached and their *content*. In hoary constitutional terms, delegation of power and authority to the public administration represents a marriage of "procedural due process" and "substantive due process." The issue of that marriage has been variously described as a hybrid monster (a "headless fourth branch of government"), in anthropomorphic terms (e.g., by those who speak of "the ordeal of the administrative process"), and as inevitable and indispensable (see, e.g., the Landis Report). *Because it is a system of public law in operation, the public administration presents novel problems in American government and American constitutionalism. It is unlikely that the tools and techniques of yesteryear will be adequate to the need presented by the development of the "administrative state."*

.   .   .   .

The fundamental problems which must be dealt with in any meaningful and significant scrutiny of administration are, first, the means by which responsibility and accountability may be maintained in that system and, second, the means by which the affirmative exercise of power meets reasonably adequate levels. Put another way, the basic questions are the proper control of administrative discretion and the effective exercise of power.

The urgent tasks of government must be accomplished. While it is accurate to say that the fundamental theme of American constitutionalism is control of power — through fragmentation (as in separation of powers and federalism) and through specific limitations (the Bill of Rights) — it is manifest that the affirmative duties and obligations of government in the modern era must be met. Lord Acton's oft-quoted aphorism that "power tends to corrupt," which sums up much of historical American constitutionalism, is today but a half-truth. It overlooks the fact that power will exist and will be exercised. Even more basically, it does not come to grips with the problem of the affirmative exercise of power. This is a complex and difficult matter; the system must be such as to permit flexibility and discretion while simultaneously preserving constitutional liberties and achieving the purposes and goals of governmental endeavor. Thus, the problem is doubly difficult: how to effect both accountability and the proper exercise of power.

The task of any group devoting attention to the public administration is, by any criterion, complex and continuing. Such a group must perforce proceed with care. Its recommendations should be based upon exhaustive studies and thoroughgoing analyses of designated problem areas. Those recommendations should be "practical," in the sense that they should be couched in terms of "the possible" rather than the ideal. However, an attenuated view of "the possible" should not be taken. This point will be developed more fully below. First, it is desirable to set forth in brief form what might be called "the conceptual requirement" for such a continuing scrutiny.

II. The Conceptual Requirement

Reasonably adequate accomplishment of the task of a permanent administrative conference would seem to require a comprehensive scheme of analysis. If this is not done in some complete manner, then it would be likely that important areas relevant to the group's mission would be slighted or not even considered. Such an approach would require at least the following:

(1) That the long-range goals of the administrative process generally be identified and kept in mind throughout the inquiry;

(2) That the reasons for and purposes of administration be carefully delineated, in order to provide objectives toward which given practices might be directed;

(3) That standards be established by which given practices may be evaluated in order to determine whether the long-range objectives are being attained (in whatever degree); and

(4) That factual data be developed which would provide an empirical basis for such evaluations.

In essence, what this means is that a purely "pragmatic," *ad hoc* approach is not likely to do the necessary task in an acceptable manner. Despite its historical popularity and its current vogue within the halls of government, pragmatism is not adequate to the need of government in the age of the Positive State. Far from being a philosophy, it is an excuse for not having one. The difficulties inhering in the pragmatic approach to governmental problem-solving are deep-seated and complex.

. . . .

. . . By and large, President Kennedy's Administrative Conference was characterized by long debate over whether a given set of circumstances was in fact a problem and by a general attitude that the "facts" about the public administration were all that mattered. Such an attitude enabled the conference members to approach what often were essentially fundamental problems of administration with a series of piecemeal, empirical attacks, without being burdened with even the rudiments of a thought-out plan. Pragmatism and empiricism characterized the work of the Conference.

But that is not enough. Criteria of judgment and choice must be established, by which given decisions can be weighed and determinations made as to their desirability and feasibility. The suggestion here is that this type of approach is an inescapable requirement; it is *not* suggested that the task of developing adequate standards of evaluation would be an easy one.

. . . .

(1) A distinction should be made between the problems of governmental administration which relate to the "ordinary citizen," with his relatively small, simple claims, and those which relate to the large group, with its complex demands. In other words, the techniques and methods which might be desirable and feasible for use in connection with review of orders of the FPC or ICC or NLRB might differ

from those for use in connection with actions of, say, the Department of Health, Education and Welfare (regarding the "Social Security" legislation) or the Veterans Administration (regarding veterans' claims).

. . . .

(2) The need exists for a range of devices whereby controls may be effected upon the public administration. Judicial review, at present, is about the only existing formal technique whereby external power may be brought to bear upon the administrative decision-making process. Of course, a number of "informal" techniques also are available, such as the congressional inquiry, intervention from the executive offices of the President, the *ex parte* communication, and the like. But these are not only "informal"; some, perhaps all, of them raise serious questions of propriety. The point to be made here may be stated as follows: (a) judicial review is a system of control of administration; (b) there is a need for other formal control devices in addition to judicial review; and (c) the task of a continuing administrative conference would include inquiry into the identification and analysis of such additional control techniques.

III. Problems for a Permanent Conference

From what has been said above it follows that a continuing group would be concerned with problems falling into several categories. These are listed below.

. . . .

(1) *Problems of a conceptual nature:* An adequate appraisal of existing and desired procedures, both of judicial review and other control techniques and of affirmative governance, should be based upon a prior analysis of the basic problem. Hence a first focal point of inquiry would be such questions as the following:

a. What are the long-range goals of the administrative process?
b. What are the basic reasons for and purposes of judicial review and other similar techniques of control?
c. What are the standards by which given practices may be evaluated in terms of achievement or non-achievement of the goals and purposes of administration?
d. Should the question of external controls of administration be split so as to distinguish between administrative actions touching and concerning the private individual, with relatively simple or small claims, and those touching and concerning the large pluralistic group, with complex claims (the corporation, the labor union, etc.)?
e. If so, should different control techniques be employed in each of those situations?

. . . .

(2) *Problems of a constitutional nature:* In the final analysis, problems of judicial review — of any type of control mechanism placed upon the public administration — are constitutional in nature. While administrative law usually has been defined to encompass administrative procedure, particularly that part of that procedure which has occupied the attention of the federal courts, and an immense literature has developed concerning the myriad of details of the resulting body of law, it is

fair to say that that law is still in a fluid state. It is still in a "process of becoming," and has not yet solidified into a unified body of established principles. This is true both of the constitutional questions involved in judicial review and other control measures and of the specific doctrines which have been evolved. Postponing for a moment the specific doctrines, the constitutional questions would involve such matters as the following:

a. What are the control mechanisms presently utilized vis-à-vis the public administration?
b. What is the constitutional position of the judiciary with respect to administration?
c. What other control techniques are available?
d. What has the impact of judicial review been so far as the practices and procedures of agencies and departments are concerned? In other words, there is a need for the development of empirical studies indicating what influence, if any, judicial review has had upon the public administration.
e. Is the role of the courts essentially "negative"? Although a federal court can order the termination of a given practice of administration, is it largely impotent so far as ordering affirmative action is concerned?
f. Is there a constitutional minimum of review?
g. Can Congress prevent review in certain instances?
h. What is the constitutional position of the Chief Executive so far as the agencies are concerned?
i. What other sanctions may be developed so as to ensure the proper affirmative exercise of power?

Of basic importance here would be the development of feasible and desirable alternative methods of control of administrative decision-making. In this connection, it would be desirable to have a systematic and comprehensive inquiry made into the "ombudsman" institution now employed in certain Scandinavian nations.

(3) *Problems of an orthodox judicial review nature:*
It has been stated that "the fixing of individual rights and duties without judicial supervision of legality is not consonant with the spirit of our jurisprudence." Such an attitude perhaps reflects the distrust of administration and of governmental discretion which has characterized American legal history. Nevertheless, it seems to place too much emphasis upon the judiciary and upon what courts can do. As mentioned above, there is a need for development of other control mechanisms and other sanctions whereby the public administration can be made "accountable" and can simultaneously get its job accomplished.

What, then, are specific problems of judicial review which might be considered by a continuing conference? The following are suggested:

a. *Who* can get review? The problems of standing, of intervention, of actual or remote injury or interest.
b. *When* is review in order? The problems of timing, of exhaustion of remedies, primary jurisdiction, final orders, ripeness.
c. *How* is it effected? The avenue to follow. Venue, necessary parties, mandamus, sovereign immunity.
d. *How much* review? The scope of review. Review of administrative discretion. Questions of law and of fact. The substantial evidence rule.

e. *Where?* A court? An administrative court? Some other institution?

f. *Functional areas of review or non-review.* Are certain areas of administration free from review?

These are listed in skeletal form but it should be noted that each of the categories contains a large number of important subsidiary questions. Merely to state in detail the questions involved would take, for each of them, a paper at least as long as the present one.

.   .   .   .

IV. Format and Membership of a Conference

The manner in which the task of an administrative conference is accomplished will depend in large part upon the persons who man such an organization. This in turn depends upon the format of a conference and how it will be organized. In many respects these are questions as crucial as those which have been discussed above — whether a conference should be established and its mission — and deserve mention, even though a full exposition is beyond the scope of this paper.

Much of the controversy which has developed over a permanent conference revolves around the question of membership. There is a basic difference among those who have expressed opinions on the question. One group, consisting largely of government personnel and those sympathetic to their interests, tends to maintain the need for a conference the majority of the membership of which would come from the federal agencies. On the other hand, members of the legal profession in private practice, the spokesman for whom is the American Bar Association, perceive the need for at least equal membership to come from outside government. A third suggestion, coming mainly from academic commentators, is for membership to consist not only of lawyers, but of political scientists, economists, and similar specialists from other disciplines. This cleavage between government lawyers and private practitioners is a long-standing one, antedating even the Administrative Procedure Act of 1946.

As with the other critical questions concerning a permanent conference, the resolution of the matter of membership will turn, in the final analysis, upon the operation of the political process and probably will represent the common denominator in a compromise struck between those most affected by the work of a conference: the government official and the private practitioner of administrative law. What such a compromise will produce is difficult to forecast in detail, but it does seem likely that a conference, speaking generally, will be heavily weighted with agency personnel who will be charged with responsibility of taking part in a cooperative effort to tackle some difficult problems of administrative practice.

Whether such a compromise, if it eventuates, will be satisfactory is at best doubtful. There has been little or no evidence in the past that the agencies will police themselves in any meaningful way. A conference consisting of the very administrators whose practices are under study — and thus under criticism — hardly could be expected to develop much by way of significant results. However well intended or constructive criticism might be, the consequence probably would be a defensive attitude of self-justification. It is demanding too much of human nature to ask anyone to sit in judgment of himself, for that is what a conference, if it does anything at all, will do. (By the same token, it is far from a foregone conclusion that nongovernment members should come only from that part of the legal profession which specializes in administrative practice. The range of problems a conference should consider transcends the usual expertise of the lawyer.) Should not the public administrator, to use the old saw, be "on tap" but not "on top" of a permanent conference? He should be available to provide data and information and should have full opportunity to present his views on any question and have an influence on the final decision. It may be heretical to some, but it is indeed difficult to see why a conference is needed in the first instance, if its mission would be for administrators to point out improvements to adminstrators — who, if they were genuinely interested in improvement, should have done so on their own motion prior to outside stimulus.

. . . .

A major difficulty in matters of membership and format is that the public at large — those who are generally affected, directly or indirectly, by administrative action even though the immediate impact may be upon a private litigant — has no way to be represented. The legal profession can be expected to see to it that the interests of the profession's clients are protected as well as circumstances permit; and the governmental agencies surely will battle to influence the course of conference discussions and decisions. But although they are established to further "the public interest," it is the very practices of these agencies which are at issue — practices which have resulted from the joint efforts of government personnel and lawyers appearing before the agencies. How, then, can the unrepresented multitude — the consuming public, using "consumer" in a generic sense — make its voice heard? This is a problem larger than in the comparable situation of the Judicial Conference, although there, too, a question arises. The proliferation of administration, culminating in the rise of the "administrative state," is characterized by the fact that decisions which are made there touch and concern the American citizenry generally. Few, if any, are immune from the operations of some administrative agency. The suggestion here is that a joint agency-legal profession conference will not *ipso facto* serve to protect all of the diverse interests involved.

. . . .

A joint committee of Congress could accomplish a number of important results. In the first place, it would tend to keep membership of an administrative conference aware of congressional interest in their work. Secondly, a committee could help follow through on recommendations of a conference. There must be some established way in which conclusions reached by an administrative conference can be translated into policy and practice. Many, but not all, such conclusions would require legislation; others would be handled administratively. For both categories, some technique for following through will have to be created. It is fair to say that few recommendations of either President Eisenhower's Conference on Administrative Procedure in 1953-54 or President Kennedy's Conference in 1961-62 have been adopted; those which have tend to be minor and of little consequence. The remainder, including virtually all of those about which some controversy raged, have been cast into a limbo of unconcern and disregard. That in itself is testimony that administrators are not likely to police themselves and underscores the need for some institutional device calculated to achieve adoption of recommendations.

. . . .

VI. Conclusion

This delineation of problems for a continuing conference is not intended to be definitive. The questions set out are illustrative of the need. In sum, they transcend the "housekeeping" details of government. In many respects they involve the very fundamentals of the American constitutional order. A permanent administrative conference, if it is to accomplish the task necessary, cannot avoid tackling those fundamentals. If it does not, it likely will fall into desuetude and become a mere platform for the statement of hortatory pronouncements without real substance.

In saying this, it is emphasized that we do not advocate the creation of a "super-agency" to be superimposed upon the already cumbersome administrative machinery. But we do suggest that something more than the administrative conferences of the past is necessary and something other than what has been proposed in Congress and by the American Bar Association is in order. Why not start with the formation of a permanent joint committee of Congress, similar to the Joint Economic Committee, and build from there?

8

Administrative Responsibility

One of the central problems of modern democratic politics has become the control of bureaucratic power. Attempts to provide such control have been institutionalized by a separation of powers and a system of checks and balances. The members of a neutral independent bureaucracy might well end up being responsible to themselves alone and to their own set of values and practices.

Attempts to control bureaucratic behavior have taken many forms; executive orders, congressional investigations, exposures in the press, and the rivalry among agencies themselves. The ethical and professional standards of those in the public service will be a reflection of the ethics and professional standards of the rest of society. The question is often raised as to whether those in government should be held accountable to standards of ethics and conduct higher than those in business and other areas of society. The general answer is that such higher standards are expected in government — especially in the executive branch.

The bureaucracy in the end is supposed to function in the public interest, but this is a difficult concept to define in specific cases.

Congressional Committee Members as Independent Agency Overseers: A Case Study ❧ SEYMOUR SCHER

This paper is concerned with the behavior of members of a Congressional committee in their role as overseers of an independent regulatory commission. Congressional committees seem periodically to become aware of the presence of the regulatory agencies and after a more or less spectacular examination of one or another of them, allow them to slip back to an undisturbed and unnoticed routine. Their

"Congressional Committee Members as Independent Agency Overseers: A Case Study," by Seymour Scher, reprinted by permission of the author and the American Political Science Association from *American Political Science Review* (December, 1960), pp. 911–920.

status as "independent" agencies leaves to Congress the formal responsibility both for checking on the fulfillment of their legislative mandates and for preserving them from domination by their clientele and the President. Too little notice has been taken, however, of the nature of the control of these regulatory agencies emanating from Congress.

This study results from an examination of the House Education and Labor Committee as it reviewed the performance of the National Labor Relations Board in 1953. My sources are the public hearings of the Committee in the 83d Congress and interviews with Committee members over a two-year period thereafter. This does not purport to be a study of control of even one agency through all of the routes by which Congress can assert control. Other patterns of behavior than those identified here may appear in the review by special investigative committees or appropriations committees, for example. As with all case studies, hypotheses tested in a specific situation — one standing legislative committee dealing with one regulatory agency — are, at best, suggestive rather than conclusive. They hopefully will stimulate further testing against the experience of other committees with other agencies. And it may very well be that the experience of the NLRB constitutes a very special case, because of the highly political nature of the agency and the open hostility that divided the committee.

The NLRB has been assigned regulatory functions in an area marked by continuing struggle among the regulated parties themselves and between the regulated and the regulator. Administering the rights and prohibitions of the Wagner and Taft-Hartley Acts has kept the agency in the middle of a crossfire between unions, employers, and Congressional committees. The activity of private groups, administrative agencies, and legislative committees to influence the decisions of Congress and, in turn, among affected groups and Congress to influence agency action are familiar subjects in recent scholarly writing. What is said and done by the relevant legislative committee is, to the other major contestants in the struggle, one of the most important facets of these multipartite relations. The behavior of the members of the labor committees in reviewing NLRB action is therefore a useful focus for inquiry.

The questions dealt with here are these:

How does the Congressman use his committee position for purposes of examining the performance of the independent agencies that come within his committee's jurisdiction? Do committee members in reviewing agency activity behave differently toward independent agencies with so-called judicial functions than toward other administrative agencies? What attention do committee members pay to the norms calling for special handling for the independent agency on the part of those immediately concerned with its work: Congress, as well as the President, courts, and the agency clientele?

I. Norms and Committee Members' Behavior

Clientele and Congressional efforts to influence administrative action are at least as pronounced and aggressive when aimed at the independent regulatory agencies as they are when directed at so-called executive agencies. In spite of this a feeling seems to exist that something about the independent agency's court-like functions plus its formal location outside of the President's domain entitle it to different treatment at the hands of Congress as well as the Chief Executive. This view, while originating with the reform groups that initially pressed for regulatory legislation, has since been sustained by agency officials, the organized Bar, students of administration and, through formal expressions at least, by Congressmen. Although the characterization of these agencies as independent in any important sense has by now largely been rejected by scholarly writers, the view seems to linger that agencies like the NLRB are different and should be dealt with by their clientele, the President, and their Congressional overseers in a special, careful way.

Congress, itself, gave at least tacit support to this special status in the regulatory statutes and in the Administrative Procedure Act by making agency orders subject to limited review by the federal courts. The Congressman at the legislative stage seems willing to associate himself with a norm of conduct which he apparently rejects in his later role as agency overseer. The Congressman, frequently as lawyer participating in the regulatory legislative process, formally accepts a norm that makes regulatory agency orders reviewable by courts rather than by Congressmen. However, his conception of his role as representative reviewing agency behavior — a conception that associates him with particular group and constituent interests — involves no requirement of self-restraint on his part. Acting as overseer, the norms of the representative prevail over those of the lawyer or the administrator.

The so-called independent status of the regulatory commissions is generally assumed to apply against intervention primarily by the President in their decision-making activity. The kinds of specific restraints upon Congress which this status suggests are rarely considered. One notable instance in which a Senator did recognize the formal legalistic standard for Congressional behavior toward the regulatory agency and protested departures from this norm is found in a discussion at a 1949 committee hearing between Senator Wayne Morse and NLRB Chairman Paul Herzog:

SENATOR MORSE. My question goes to whether or not you think it is a good policy to have a quasi-judicial board brought before a congressional committee and examined in regard to the reasons that may have led the Board to render a certain decision or take a certain administrative course of action.

MR. HERZOG. I have no particular personal objection to anything of that kind. I see no reason why any congressional committee can't talk to any administrator about any problem, whether it is a joint committee, watchdog committee, or whatever it is called.

The difficulty arises when the powers of a committee are created so as to make it possible for that committee to feel that it can question the Board about a decision. Yet it seems to me that once a decision is issued it is out, and the public and the press can question us.

A very offensive thing, of course, would be for the Board to be questioned or compelled in any one direction about a case before it is decided.

SENATOR MORSE. That would be bad, too, but I certainly disagree with your conclusion if you think that questioning the Board about its decisions after they are rendered will not endanger future decisions.

MR. HERZOG. Well, I didn't say I was in favor of it, Senator. I simply said that I thought if a regular committee of Congress could do it — I suppose it has been done for years with the National Labor Relations Board — I don't think it makes much difference whether it is a joint committee, or a regular committee of the Senate or of the House.

The 1958 House Legislative Oversight Subcommittee did extend its objections to *ex parte* representations directed at the independent agencies by their regulated clientele to include similar representations originating in Congress. In the Subcommittee hearings and reports, however, significantly little attention was paid to instances of Congressional intervention in these agencies' affairs. It can reasonably be concluded that Congressmen, in spite of formal disclaimers, seek to preserve for themselves the exclusive right to intervene in regulatory agency business. Their refusal to accept in practice any restraints upon their dealings with these agencies has resulted in a standard of expected behavior which the legislators insist upon from others as a means of preserving the "independence" of the agencies but do not apply to themselves in any way other than by formal declarations.

II. The House Labor Committee and the NLRB in the 83d Congress

The House labor committee in 1953 held the NLRB to account for its conduct. This was a case of Republican-Southern Democratic control over a Truman-appointed agency, but there is no reason to believe that committee review of a quasi-judicial agency in this way was not sanctioned by most of the liberal Democratic members. Nor could it be said that, given similar circumstances, they would not have conducted the same kind of examination of the administration of a Republican-appointed agency. Even though we are concerned here with the House committee in the 83d Congress, the committee's conduct represented the continuation of practices of legislative control of the NLRB that were begun in 1938, were renewed in 1940 and 1947, and were resumed with the new Act in 1948 and 1949.

The year 1953 marked the first year of a Republican national administration since before passage of the Wagner Act, and the last year in which the administration of the Taft-Hartley Act, passed by a Republican Congress with Southern Democratic help, was in the hands of an NLRB and General Counsel appointed by a Democratic President. In the course of committee hearings on revision of the labor law the Republican leadership was joined by conservative Democrats in undertaking a review of the functioning of the agency. Yet no changes in the Taft-Hartley Act emerged from this Congress and none emerged from two subsequent Congresses, at least partly because of the composition and conduct of the labor committee in the House.

The committee's balanced representation in the 83d and 84th Congresses between liberal Democrats on the one hand and Republicans and conservative Democrats on the other created an impasse on amendments that needed the support of a committee majority. This stalemate in 1953, coupled with the lack until the following year of any Presidential proposals to consider, caused the committee to give most of its attention to the conduct of the NLRB rather than to statutory revision. The committee members, with a few exceptions, used this opportunity to engage in a thorough review of the agency's interpretations of the Act.

In the three months of hearings in 1953, the House Labor Committee heard witnesses urge a variety of proposals to cure the NLRB of an alleged lack of sympathy with the Taft-Hartley Act. These included plans for "packing" the NLRB to give the new Eisenhower Administration a chance to influence the agency's policies, abolishing the Board to allow private litigation in the federal courts, and ceding to the states the federal power to regulate labor-management relations "affecting commerce." At the close of the hearings, the committee deadlocked on a proposal to transfer NLRB judicial authority to federal district courts as a means of eliminating what was termed the "Wagner-Act influence" in the agency's application of the Act. The subsequent appointment by President Eisenhower of the General Counsel and a majority of the Board had the effect of removing much of the Republican support for the court proposal.

The committee members, regardless of party, made no allowances for the judicial character of the NLRB's work. Instead, the members who took active part used the hearings (1) to make agency officials explain and defend their conduct in particular cases that had been brought to committee members' attention by constituents and other affected parties; and (2) to afford regulated groups opportunity to "retry" before the committee cases that had been lost before the Board, or to win Congressional support in cases awaiting Board or court action.

In allowing the committee to be used for these purposes, members expressed their own and what they considered to be their constituents' feelings about the way the Act was being administered. As the representative of his district and of what he considered the important group interests principally within it, the committee member was concerned with the effect of particular agency acts on these interests. The solution that he proposed for alleged agency misconduct — "packing" the Board, increasing state jurisdiction, or adjudication in federal courts — was directed at best serving these interests.

The House labor committee hearings in 1953 were dominated by the testimony of small employers. Many of them had encountered for the first time the union organizing activities that had moved from the established bargaining relationships in large industry to the task of organizing smaller enterprises. The resistance of small employers to unionization, particularly in Southern states, brought to the NLRB the kind of highly charged "unfair practice" business it had handled fifteen years earlier in conjunction with the major organizing drives of unions into large manufacturing enterprises. The committee, through the repeated election of Congressmen from "safe" districts and the working of the seniority rule, was led by conservative Republicans and Southern Democrats. They had been opposed to the organizing activity of unions in large industry in the late 1930's; they were even more so now when it extended into small industrial areas, especially in their home districts.

During the hearings the committee chairman frequently allowed, and ranking members encouraged, the detailed recitation of facts that had been in dispute in NLRB proceedings. The committee provided disgruntled litigants with an opportunity to object to trial examiners' and Board findings and to win support from committee members for the witnesses' version of conduct that had been termed unfair labor practices by the agency.

The long line of employer witnesses who told the committee of their experiences with unions and with the NLRB found committee members aligning sharply into opposing factions to support or reject the witnesses' allegations. In weighing the merits of charges of alleged NLRB misconduct, members of both parties friendly to union interests broke with colleagues sympathetic with the interests of small employers.

On the last day of committee hearings NLRB officials were given an opportunity to rebut the testimony of former parties to Board action. Agency objections to the use of the committee for reviewing Board or trial examiners' findings became lost in a voluminous file that the agency submitted for the record. There is no indication that the committee members who most severely criticized the agency for the conduct of its personnel at various levels and for its decisions in particular cases looked closely enough at the detailed agency response (admitted to the record in large part without having been heard) to notice the agency's objections to the role that the committee had played. Agency officials protested that after three months of testimony by several dozen parties to NLRB action one day would not allow the agency to answer all the criticisms of its conduct. By requesting an opportunity to defend itself, the Board, in spite of its protests, conceded that the committee would continue to simulate the role of review court while actually behaving as participant in the struggle between unions and employers, regulatory agency and regulated clientele.

In the course of the hearings none of the committee members showed any concern that specific cases, some still awaiting Board decisions, were being reviewed before the committee. Instead, eight of the ranking members of both political parties later expressed to the writer their belief in the necessity of affording dissatisfied litigants an opportunity to be heard by the committee. One junior member with prior judicial experience did admit in an interview following the hearings that he considered this practice "probably improper" but that he did not protest it during the hearings because he "had to live with these people [the committee]."

In one case still awaiting the trial examiner's findings an employer witness prefaced an uninterrupted presentation before the committee of his experience with the Board with the statement:

It is with calculated risk that I present this testimony because the unfair labor practice charge filed by the teamsters union against our company is still undecided and the decision rests in the hands of those about whom I am about to testify.

He then proceeded to recount his version of the case, indicating what he saw as a coalition against him of field examiner, trial attorney, and trial examiner for the alleged purpose of guaranteeing a finding in support of the union's charge. His statement was accompanied by one from a small businessmen's association of which he was a member, urging Congress to relinquish to the states its regulation of labor-management relations but to include labor within the scope of Federal antitrust legislation.

The attorney for one committee member's employer constituents was accorded an opportunity, in effect, to retry a case in which the Board found unlawful interference by the employer with his employees' organizing activities. The attorney found no fault with either the regional staff's or the trial examiner's procedures. His objection was to the findings of fact by the trial examiner and the Board. In lieu of compliance with the Board's cease and desist order or of taking the Board's order to a court of appeals for review, the attorney came before the committee. There he detailed the facts in his client's case, found the trial examiner ignoring the "preponderance of evidence" in finding against the client, and urged, in place of Board application of the Act, jury trial before district courts where he expected the "results would be right more often than they would go wrong."

Committee members Barden, Landrum, Gwinn, Kearns, Bosch and Wint Smith actively helped the witness develop his case, accepted his analysis of the issues involved without having seen the transcript of the Board hearings or the trial examiner's report, and promised to call the trial examiner before the committee to defend his findings. The following colloquy, after the witness had given his version of the disputed facts, is a fair example of the members' response to appeals to them from Board findings:

WITNESS. It seems to me that the preponderance of evidence rule, if you could assume your case would be decided upon it, then you would sort of know where you are. But we thought here that the overwhelming preponderance was with our client. But it was not so decided.

CONG. SMITH. Well, is not a reasonable conclusion to draw from what the recitation is in this particular case, that this trial examiner was deeply prejudiced?

WITNESS. I personally think so; yes, sir.

CONG. SMITH. Mr. Chairman, as I said a while ago, I would like to go to the zoo sometime and look at the things out there, and I would like to have this man [the trial examiner] brought up here before this committee and I would like to look at him, and I would like to ask him some questions. It is inconceivable to me . . .

CONG. GWINN. Would you suggest that the committee subpoena this trial examiner?

CONG. KEARNS. I think it would be a good idea, Mr. Chairman.

CONG. BARDEN. Apparently the only man who can explain this [Board decision] is the man who muddled it up, so I would be in favor of his [the trial examiner] coming before the committee. That is all that I have.

CONG. SMITH. You have heard of Kangaroo Courts, have you not, Mr. Robinson? WITNESS. Yes, sir.

CONG. SMITH. If that is not a Kangaroo Court, I never heard of one.

The Board, however, resisted the request for its trial examiners to appear before the committee to explain their decisions. In this particular instance a letter to the committee from the Board's chief trial examiner summarized the agency's reaction: "Whether the trial examiner was correct in his findings of fact and his resolutions of credibility is a matter for determination by the Board and the courts on the entire record." Referring to five NLRB trial examiners whose findings had been criticized in the course of the House committee hearings, the chief examiner objected to their being asked to defend their judgments before a legislative committee. In a statement which, although included in the record, was not heard by the committee, he said:

. . . From an atmosphere highly charged with conviction on both sides, the NLRB trial examiner, a fallible human being, must attempt as objectively and expertly as possible, to resolve the differences among fallible and partisan witnesses. It is understandable, therefore, that out of the thousands of litigants who have appeared before our trial examiners in the past few years there would be a few to use the forum of this committee to express their disappointment. I am sure that the lawyer members of this committee are familiar with those litigants who, faced with an adverse decision, become overcritical of a trial judge and on appeal seek to try him instead of the merits or demerits of their cause.

While appreciative of the opportunity afforded examiners to respond, nevertheless, we are troubled by a delicate and perhaps fundamental problem. Is it proper for a trial examiner bound by the statutory scheme of agency and court review provided by the Administrative Procedure Act and the Taft-Hartley Act to file a statement with this committee explaining, and to enter into a controversy concerning, the processes of decision making, particularly where the case in question is yet open for further administrative and/or judicial action? We think not. The cases are firmly settled that it is not even the function of a court to probe the mental processes of an administrative officer.

It is respectfully suggested, therefore, that the questioned action of each of the examiners can best be evaluated in the light of the entire record of the cases mentioned, and the Board would be pleased to make such complete transcripts and the intermediate reports based thereon available to the committee for such use. . . .

The committee leadership's unwillingness to credit this agency protest was apparent later from its handling of a case that became a *cause célèbre* in the relations between the NLRB and a Congressional labor committee. A small farm implement company, the Homedale Tractor and Equipment Company of Homedale, Idaho, had been found by the Board, upholding a trial examiner's findings, to have engaged in unfair labor practices involving discriminatory discharge and unlawful interference with employees' organizing activities. Refusing to comply with the Board's order, the company's co-owner, C. W. Radcliffe, related the circumstances of the case before both the House and Senate labor committees while the Board's petition for enforcement of its order was pending in the Court of Appeals.

In contrast to the Senate labor committee which allowed Radcliffe to present a statement without comment from committee members on its merits, the House committee conducted a full-scale examination of the witness. Members expressed sympathy with his version of the case without having seen or heard any of the agency's transcripts or findings. Board officials later were called to defend their findings before the committee. The hearing given Radcliffe by the House committee resulted in a complete review and judgment on the merits of the disputed facts. Radcliffe asserted that the trial examiner's and the Board's findings of unfair practice against him were not supported by evidence and that "it is the practice of [trial] examiners deliberately discrediting all of the testimony on the part of the employer and giving full faith and credit to all of the testimony on behalf of the union".

NLRB General Counsel George Bott reminded the committee that the Homedale case was then before the court of appeals, "which is where it should be if the respondent questions conclusions of law reached so far," and that, "in the meantime, it does not appear that anything would be gained by arguing the merits of this case before this committee." The committee members nonetheless pressed Board spokesmen to defend the agency's order. Apparently unsatisfied with the reluctance of these officials to interpret for it the trial examiner's and the Board's reasoning in the case, the committee voted to send a subcommittee headed by Congressman Wint Smith to Idaho for a further investigation. Congressman Smith, as with similar complaints brought to the committee, had asked for a "full and complete investigation" by a subcommittee with power to subpoena "the National Labor Relations Board and the man [trial examiner] who wrote this opinion." The subcommittee's hearings provided Radcliffe with his third opportunity to relate before a Congressional committee his view of the facts in his dispute with the Board.

The subcommittee called the Board's trial examiner to testify but found itself confronted by an examiner armed with instructions from the Board not to "answer questions relating to the mental processes by which you resolved credibility issues or evaluated or drew inferences or reached conclusions from the evidence in your judicial capacity." In addition to these instructions to the trial examiner, Board Chairman Guy Farmer sent a letter to the subcommittee in which the issue was clearly drawn between a regulatory agency with quasi-judicial functions and a legislative committee attempting to exert control through a probing of the agency's findings in a particular case. Explaining the Board's position in restricting the testimony of its trial examiner, the letter said:

Under the scheme of review provided in the Labor-Management Relations Act of 1947, the circuit court is the sole tribunal authorized to examine into the sufficiency of the findings of the Board and the trial examiner in order to determine whether the Board's order was properly issued and is entitled to enforcement.

* * * *

Court review of the findings and conclusions of the trial examiner must be based only upon the record made in the proceeding before the Board and certified to the court. Thus, even the court may not inquire into and probe the mental processes by which the trial examiner reached his conclusions. This is so because the Administrative Procedure Act and the Labor-Management Relations Act of 1947 establish the trial examiner as a judicial officer of this agency, presumed to be of high competence and integrity and required to act with independence and impartiality. . . .

To subject such an officer to inquiry and interrogation regarding the process by which he reached his conclusions in a particular case, would seriously endanger the independence and impartiality which the law and the public interest demand for the proper discharge of his duties. . . .

Respect for the processes of the court and due regard for the public interest we are dedicated to serve therefore give us great concern lest your subcommittee have in mind an interrogation of Mr. Myers [the Board trial examiner] on the issues now before the court or on the process by which he reached his conclusions. If that is the intention of the subcommittee, the Board asks that you give serious consideration to a withdrawal of the request for Mr. Myers's appearance.

In spite of the Board's position, the subcommittee attempted to persuade the trial examiner to explain his decision in the *Homedale* case. When these efforts failed, the subcommittee gave up its special inquiry and reported to the parent committee its belief that the NLRB's refusal to allow the trial examiner to answer certain questions "constitutes an improper interference with a proper function of Congress." The subcommittee felt that "It should be made emphatically clear that no officer or employee of the National Labor Relations Board has, or should have, any right to refuse to testify before your committee on grounds such as those advanced by Chairman Farmer. . . ." It further suggested the possibility of contempt of Congress proceedings against NLRB officials.

No more was then heard from the House labor committee about the *Homedale* case. The subsequent decision of the federal Court of Appeals upholding the Board's cease and desist order and the denial of *certiorari* by the Supreme Court may have served to still any further committee action.

III. Committee Members' Views of Their Role as Agency Overseers

Committee members' willingness to have the public hearings used by regulated parties to restate their differences with the agency and to win committee support for their positions, the NLRB's resistance to committee attempts at probing the mental processes of the agency's judicial officers, and the committee's reaction to the resistance, are indications of disagreement about a proper role for a legislative committee in reviewing the conduct of an "independent" regulatory agency. The writer interviewed ten members of the House labor committee in the 83d Congress to ask them their conception of their role *vis-à-vis* the NLRB. Four were ranking Republican members; six were Democrats, two of them Southerners who generally voted with the Republicans on labor questions. The interviews were conducted in 1954 and 1955, a propitious time because of the fresh recollections of the 1953 hearings and because the top-level officialdom of the agency had by then changed significantly with appointments by a Republican administration.

Committee Democrats and Republicans alike viewed their role in reviewing NLRB activity largely in terms of how the agency treated "my people." This phrase frequently became a catch-all that identified not only constituents but the larger group commitments of the committee member as well. Thus the Southern Democrat's concern for his small employer constituents typically was compatible also with his own antagonism toward the organizing activity of unions. The Northern Democrat reacted vigorously in behalf of "his people" when his own sympathies placed him in the camp of organized labor confronting what he saw as a hostile coalition of employers and an unfriendly regulatory agency.

In cases where a committee member's own constituents were adversely affected by agency action, the member's reaction was more or less vigorous depending on the extent, if any, of his personal association with the group values of employers or unions. The member's intercession with the agency for its treatment of an employer constituent took on the character of a routine inquiry when the member's own ideological predispositions were with the rights of labor. On the other hand this same member's reaction to adverse agency treatment of a union in his district bore all the earmarks of a free-swinging, no-holds-barred encounter between committee member and offending agency. Where a member's own constituents were not affected by agency decisions brought to the committee for review, the member's response to agency conduct was governed by the extent of his identification with the values of the affected groups, labor or employer. The intensity of a committee member's reaction reached its peak, then, when the case before the committee found an injured constituent's interests coinciding with the Congressman's own group values.

For the committee member there was no abstract meaning in the term "proper" when used to describe the relationship between the independent commission and the committee. Anything was proper that served to bring the agency, in its handling of cases in the regional offices or in its own orders, into accord with the members' view of how the agency should act. One Democratic member of long tenure expressed this as follows: "When the Board [the General Counsel in charge of investigation and prosecution apparently was meant here as well as the adjudicating Board] acts friendly to labor, I have no kick coming. But when they get rough with our people, I let them know."

To the committee members the NLRB was either "with them or against them." The importance of constituents in the member's attitude was such that even where the NLRB could be shown to have "favored" labor in a series of similar cases but not in one involving an important union in his district, the agency became suspect. General tendencies in agency performance were no substitute for favorable treatment in a particular case.

Where agency officials gave evidence of having "wronged" a constituent, virtually any kind of intercession by the member or the committee was considered appropriate. One Republican member, known for his coolness toward organized labor, expressed a view accepted by Democratic members known equally for their friendliness toward unions: "We never think twice about calling the Board and asking for a little special handling of some cases; not just to speed things up but to look a little differently at the case." Paradoxically, this member saw this practice as indicative of the need to take the administration of the labor act out of the NLRB's hands and place it in the Federal courts where, he explained, "such political interference isn't possible."

Only one member I interviewed found the questioning of NLRB people on particular decisions improper, and conceived of the agency as a quasi-judicial expert body responsible for its individual decisions neither to the Executive nor to Congress. The description by nine committee members of the NLRB as a "political" agency, meaning receptive to control by the dominant party and the regulated groups, served as their public justification for whatever interference with the agency the member found necessary or useful in winning favorable treatment in cases of concern to him.

Among those interviewed, only one indicated that his understanding of how the NLRB was functioning was based on information other than what he obtained from cases brought to his attention, generally through committee hearings, by constituents or by other regulated parties. All acknowledged that they had no contacts with the agency except when they called its officials personally or in committee hearings to explain the Board's handling of specific cases. Discussion of the general direction in agency interpretation of statutory provisions was, thereby, largely lost in the questioning of agency officials on their handling of individual cases.

The members' preoccupation with the particular or the local has led several of them to propose abolition of the NLRB and its replacement by litigation in the courts. The expectation, as expressed by one Southern member, was that "our people will get a better deal in the courts." Behind this belief, for many on the committee, appeared the more fundamental feeling that the agency, regardless of the Taft-Hartley Act, had served in effect as an organizing agent for unions and had been hostile to what these members considered the dominant interests in their districts. For these committee members, two animosities were blended: one toward a Federal administrative agency acting as enforcer of ground rules in labor-employer relations, and the other toward the organizing activities of unions in their districts. As one member in a pivotal position between the committee's liberal Democrats and the Administration Republicans put it, "I want my people to accept or reject unions, not have some Board force them down their throats. I don't like any federal agency sending its people into my country to handle things that are our own business and ought to be kept that way. Unions and employers ought to fight their own battles, without bureaucrats from Washington coming in and taking sides; then, if they [unions and employers] need to, they can argue it out in court."

In contrast, three liberal Democrats on the committee who also expressed concern over the effects of NLRB actions on their areas, were nevertheless not thereby persuaded to support abolition of what they termed a pro-employer Eisenhower Board. These members were willing, instead, to depend on their own ability to keep the agency apprised of their interests until the time when a Democratic administration could again appoint a "good" Board.

Evidence in this case study supports these conclusions:

IV. Conclusions

Evidence in this study supports these conclusions:

(1) Formal norms intended to restrict the Congressman in checking the adjudicatory activity of an independent commission are not, in practice, observed by him. The committee member recognizes no limitations on his behavior by virtue of the agency's judicial functions. He may or may not see a distinction between using his committee status as a weapon against an executive bureau with largely service functions and against a quasi-judicial regulatory agency. If he recognizes the distinction in words, he acts as though none exists. Agency orders equally with agency rules are fair subjects for his attention. Whether the adjudicatory determination by the agency is in process or has been completed makes no noticeable difference to him.

(2) This behavior is in keeping with his conception of his responsibility as representative of constituent and other organized interests he shares. The attitudes and behavior of House labor committee members considered here are consistent with a theory that sees groups affected by public decisions as seeking, and public officials who share their interests as providing, alternative routes to influence these decisions.

Whether these generalizations apply to the members of other committees overseeing other independent regulatory agencies remains, of course, a subject for further investigation. All case studies have their unique characteristics. It seems reasonable to expect, nonetheless, that when agencies are assigned the job of regulating powerful organized interests, committee members with fixed attitudes toward these interests are unlikely to observe rigid rules of restraint when checking on how the agencies are doing their jobs.

Presidential Order on Federal Ethics

❖ LYNDON B. JOHNSON

By virtue of the authority vested in me by Section 301 of Title 3 of the United States Code, and as President of the United States, it is hereby ordered as follows:

Part I — Policy

Section 101. Where government is based on the consent of the governed, every citizen is entitled to have complete confidence in the integrity of his government. Each individual officer, employee, or adviser of government must help to earn and must honor that trust by his own integrity and conduct in all official actions.

Part II — Standards of Conduct

Section 201. (a) Except in accordance with regulations issued pursuant to subsection (b) of this section, no employee shall solicit or accept, directly or indirectly, any gift, gratuity, favor, entertainment, loan, or any other thing of monetary value, from any person, corporation, or group which —

(1) has, or is seeking to obtain, contractual or other business or financial relationships with his agency;

(2) conducts operations or activities which are regulated by his agency; or

(3) has interests which may be substantially affected by the performance or nonperformance of his official duty.

(b) Agency heads are authorized to issue regulations, coordinated and approved by the Civil Service Commission, implementing the provisions of subsection (a) of this section and to provide for such exceptions therein as may be necessary and appropriate in view of the nature of their agency's work and the duties and responsibilities of their employees. For example, it may be appropriate to provide exceptions (1) governing obvious family or personal relationships where the circumstances make it clear that it is those relationships rather than the business of the persons concerned which are the motivating factors — the clearest illustration being the parents, children or spouses of federal employees; (2) permitting acceptance of food and refreshments available in the ordinary course of a luncheon or dinner or other meeting or on inspection tours where an employee may properly be in attendance; or (3) permitting acceptance of loans from banks or other financial institutions on customary terms to finance proper and usual activities of employees, such as home mortgage loans. This section shall be effective upon issuance of such regulations.

Executive Order 11222, issued May 8, 1965. *Federal Register*, pp. 6469–6473.

(c) It is the intent of this section that employees avoid any action, whether or not specifically prohibited by subsection (a), which might result in, or create the appearance of —

(1) using public office for private gain;

(2) giving preferential treatment to any organization or person;

(3) impeding government efficiency or economy;

(4) losing complete independence or impartiality of action;

(5) making a government decision outside official channels; or

(6) affecting adversely the confidence of the public in the integrity of the government.

Sec. 202. An employee shall not engage in any outside employment, including teaching, lecturing, or writing, which might result in a conflict, or an apparent conflict, between the private interests of the employee and his official government duties and responsibilities, although such teaching, lecturing, and writing by employees are generally to be encouraged so long as the laws, the provisions of this order, and Civil Service Commission and agency regulations covering conflict of interest and outside employment are observed.

Sec. 203. Employees may not (a) have direct or indirect financial interests that conflict substantially, or appear to conflict substantially, with their responsibilities and duties as federal employees, or (b) engage in, directly or indirectly, financial transactions as a result of, or primarily relying upon, information obtained through their employment. Aside from these restrictions, employees are free to engage in lawful financial transactions to the same extent as private citizens. Agencies may, however, further restrict such transactions in the light of the special circumstances of their individual missions.

Sec. 204. An employee shall not use federal property of any kind for other than officially approved activities. He must protect and conserve all federal property, including equipment and supplies, entrusted or issued to him.

Sec. 205. An employee shall not directly or indirectly make use of, or permit others to make use of, for the purpose of furthering a private interest, official information not made available to the general public.

Sec. 206. An employee is expected to meet all just financial obligations, especially those — such as federal, state, or local taxes — which are imposed by law.

Part III — Standards of Ethical Conduct for Special Government Employees

Section 301. This part applies to all "special government employees" as defined in Section 202 of Title 18 of the United States Code, who are employed in the Executive Branch.

Sec. 302. A consultant, adviser or other special government employee must refrain from any use of his public office which is motivated by, or gives the appearance of being motivated by, the desire for private gain for himself or other persons, including particularly those with whom he has family, business, or financial ties.

Sec. 303. A consultant, adviser, or other special government employee shall not use any inside information obtained as a result of his government service for private personal gain, either by direct action on his part or by counsel, recommendations or suggestions to others, including particularly those with whom he has family, business, or financial ties.

Sec. 304. An adviser, consultant, or other special government employee shall not use his position in any way to coerce, or give the appearance of coercing, another person to provide any financial benefit to him or persons with whom he has family, business, or financial ties.

Sec. 305. An adviser, consultant, or other special government employee shall not receive or solicit from persons having business with his agency anything of value as a gift, gratuity, loan or favor for himself or persons with whom he has family, business, or financial ties while employed by the government or in connection with his work with the government.

Sec. 306. Each agency shall, at the time of employment of a consultant, adviser, or other special government employee require him to supply it with a statement of all other employment. The statement shall list the names of all the corporations, companies, firms, State or local governmental organizations, research organizations and educational or other institutions in which he is serving as employee, officer, member, owner, director, trustee, adviser, or consultant. In addition, it shall list such other financial information as the appointing department or agency shall decide is relevant in the light of the duties the appointee is to perform. The appointee may, but need not, be required to reveal precise amounts of investments. The statement shall be kept current throughout the period during which the employee is on the government rolls.

Part IV — Reporting of Financial Interests

Section 401. (a) Not later than ninety days after the date of this order, the head of each agency, each Presidential appointee in the Executive Office of the President who is not subordinate to the head of an agency in that Office, and each full-time member of a committee, board, or commission appointed by the President, shall submit to the Chairman of the Civil Service Commission a statement containing the following:

(1) A list of the names of all corporations, companies, firms, or other business enterprises, partnerships, nonprofit organizations, and educational or other institutions —

(A) with which he is connected as an employee, officer, owner, director, trustee, partner, adviser, or consultant; or

(B) in which he has any continuing financial interests, through a pension or retirement plan, shared income, or otherwise, as a result of any current or prior employment or business or professional association; or

(C) in which he has any financial interest through the ownership of stocks, bonds, or other securities.

(2) A list of the names of his creditors, other than those to whom he may be indebted by reason of a mortgage on property which he occupies as a personal residence or to whom he may be indebted for current and ordinary household and living expenses.

(3) A list of his interests in real property or rights in lands, other than property which he occupies as a personal residence.

(b) Each person who enters upon duty after the date of this order in an office or position as to which a statement is required by this section shall submit such statement not later than thirty days after the date of his entrance on duty.

(c) Each statement required by this section shall be kept up to date by submission of amended statements of any changes in, or additions to, the information required to be included in the original statement, on a quarterly basis.

Sec. 402. The Civil Service Commission shall prescribe regulations, not inconsistent with this part, to require the submission of statements of financial interests by such employees, subordinate to the heads of agencies, as the Commission may designate. The Commission shall prescribe the form and content of such statements and the time or times and places for such submission.

Sec. 403. (a) The interest of a spouse, minor child, or other member of his immediate household shall be considered to be an interest of a person required to submit a statement by or pursuant to this part.

(b) In the event any information required to be included in a statement required by or pursuant to this part is not known to the person required to submit such statement but is known to other persons, the person concerned shall request such other persons to submit the required information on his behalf.

(c) This part shall not be construed to require the submission of any information relating to any person's connection with, or interest in, any professional society or any charitable, religious, social, fraternal, educational, recreational, public service, civic, or political organization or any similar organization not conducted as a business enterprise and which is not engaged in the ownership or conduct of a business enterprise.

Sec. 404. The Chairman of the Civil Service Commission shall report to the President any information contained in statements required by Section 401 of this part which may indicate a conflict between the financial interests of the official concerned and the performance of his services for the government. The Commission shall report, or by regulation require reporting, to the head of the agency concerned any information contained in statements submitted pursuant to regulations issued under Section 402 of this part which may indicate a conflict between the financial interests of the officer or employee concerned and the performance of his services for the government.

Sec. 405. The statements and amended statements required by or pursuant to this part shall be held in confidence, and no information as to the contents thereof shall be disclosed except as the Chairman of the Civil Service Commission or the head of the agency concerned may determine for good cause shown.

Sec. 406. The statements and amended statements required by or pursuant to this part shall be in addition to, and not in substitution for, or in derogation of, any similar requirement imposed by law, regulation, or order. The submission of a statement or amended statements required by or pursuant to this part shall not be deemed to permit any person to participate in any matter in which his participation is prohibited by law, regulation, or order.

Part V — Delegating Authority of the President Under Sections 205 and 208 of Title 18 of the United States Code Relating to Conflicts of Interest

Section 501. As used in this part, "department" means an executive department, "agency" means an independent agency or establishment or a government corporation, and "head of an agency" means, in the case of an agency headed by more than one person, the chairman or comparable member of such agency.

Sec. 502. There is delegated, in accordance with and to the extent prescribed in Sections 503 and 504 of this part, the authority of the President under Sections 205 and 208(b) of Title 18, United States Code, to permit certain actions by an officer or employee of the government, including a special government employee, for appointment to whose position the President is responsible.

Sec. 503. Insofar as the authority of the President referred to in Section 502 extends to any appointee of the President subordinate to or subject to the chairmanship of the head of a department or agency, it is delegated to such department or agency head.

Sec. 504. Insofar as the authority of the President referred to in Section 502 extends to an appointee of the President who is within or attached to a department or agency for purposes of administration, it is delegated to the head of such department or agency.

Sec. 505. Notwithstanding any provision of the preceding sections of this part to the contrary, this part does not include a delegation of the authority of the President referred to in Section 502 insofar as it extends to:

(a) The head of any department or agency in the Executive Branch;

(b) Presidential appointees in the Executive Office of the President who are not subordinate to the head of an agency in that Office; and

(c) Presidential appointees to committees, boards, commissions, or similar groups established by the President.

Part VI — Providing for the Performance by the Civil Service Commission of Certain Authority Vested in the President by Section 1753 of the Revised Statutes

Section 601. The Civil Service Commission is designated and empowered to perform, without the approval, ratification, or other action of the President, so much of the authority vested in the President by Section 1753 of the Revised Statutes of the United States (5 U.S.C. 631) as relates to establishing regulations for the conduct of persons in the civil service.

Sec. 602. Regulations issued under the authority of Section 601 shall be consistent with the standards of ethical conduct provided elsewhere in this order.

Part VII — General Provisions

Section 701. The Civil Service Commission is authorized and directed, in addition to responsibilities assigned elsewhere in this order:

(a) To issue appropriate regulations and instructions implementing Parts II, III, and IV of this order;

(b) To review agency regulations from time to time for conformance with this order; and

(c) To recommend to the President from time to time such revisions in this order as may appear necessary to ensure the maintenance of high ethical standards within the Executive Branch.

Sec. 702. Each agency head is hereby directed to supplement the standards provided by law, by this order, and by regulations of the Civil Service Commission with regulations of special applicability to the particular functions and activities of his agency. Each agency head is also directed to assure (1) the widest possible distribution of regulations issued pursuant to this section, and (2) the availability of counseling for those employees who request advice or interpretation.

Sec. 703. The following are hereby revoked:

(a) Executive Order No. 10939 of May 5, 1961.

(b) Executive Order No. 11125 of October 29, 1963.

(c) Section 2(a) of Executive Order No. 10530 of May 10, 1954.

(d) White House memorandum of July 20, 1961, on "Standards of Conduct for Civilian Employees."

(e) The President's Memorandum of May 2, 1963, "Preventing Conflicts of Interest on the Part of Special Government Employees." The effective date of this revocation shall be the date of issuance by the Civil Service Commission of regulations under Section 701(a) of this order.

Sec. 704. All actions heretofore taken by the President or by his delegates in respect of the matters affected by this order and in force at the time of the issuance of this order, including any regulations prescribed or approved by the President or by his delegates in respect of such matters, shall, except as they may be inconsistent with the provisions of this order or terminate by operation of law, remain in effect until amended, modified, or revoked pursuant to the authority conferred by this order.

Sec. 705. As used in this order, and except as otherwise specifically provided herein, the term "agency" means any executive department, or any independent agency or any government corporation; and the term "employee" means any officer or employee of an agency.

LYNDON B. JOHNSON

THE WHITE HOUSE,
  May 8, 1965.

Conflict of Interest: A Political Scientist's View ❊ NORTON E. LONG

The author of the Tenth number of *The Federalist* regarded the conflict of interests as a necessary and inevitable incident of government. This conflict was rooted in the differing conditions of men. It might be suppressed under a tyranny but it could be at best controlled and moderated under a free government. To this one might compare the view of Washington that factions might be desirable to check a monarchy but were noxious and out of place in a republic. This federalist doctrine is not dissimilar from Rousseau's concern that the disinterested general will not be perverted by the interested and partial will of all. Despite much lip service to the views that Rousseau and Washington express, satisfactory means for rendering this operational have been hard to come by. In practice the Madisonian view that faction is not only inevitable but must be introduced into the ordinary operations of govern-

"Conflict of Interest: A Political Scientist's View," by Norton E. Long, from *Social Research* (Winter, 1964), pp. 423–434. Reprinted by permission.

ment to control its effects has tended to prevail. The representation of interests has been used to resolve the conflict of interests, and out of the proceduralized conflict of interests it has been hoped that policy bearing some resemblance to the public interest would emerge.

Perhaps the extreme form of this is evinced in the tripartism of the War Labor Board and similar labor disputes tribunals. Here a body made up of management, labor, and public representatives in equal numbers will presumably reach decisions in the public interest. This is even the case where the public member is in the minority.

The conflict of interests is acceptable. A conflict of interest is not. It is expected that interests will struggle to control the government. It is even expected that they will struggle quite selfishly. It is acceptable that they should be represented in government by officials who in their official capacity will seek with might and main to further them. What is not acceptable is that officials should further their own personal interests.

Thus the late Senator Bankhead could regard it as well nigh immoral and certainly insupportable when officials of the Bureau of Agricultural Economics pretended to some responsibility to consumers as well as farmers. Doubtless a similar view would be taken in the Departments of Commerce and Labor. There seems no sense of any opprobious conflict of interest when officials in their official capacity represent sectional or functional interests. This is true not only for legislators and members of the political executive, where it seems expected, but holds for permanent civil servants as well. Doubtless the explanation for our complacence with crass interest representation stems from the view that a conflict of interests is inevitable and that through some governmental alchemy the conflict of interests is transmuted into the public interest.

Of course it is going too far to assume that it is permissible to represent any interest other than a material personal one in government. The representation of a foreign government would generally be regarded as reprehensible. Whether this would be so in all cases and at all times is disputed. Thus it might be permissible virtually to represent Nationalist China, though it would be quite clearly inadmissible to represent Red China or the U.S.S.R. Presumably, if actions were so clear-cut as to require registration as a lobbyist, they would be incompatible with government employment, at least in the executive branch. The question of whether one were or were not a lobbyist would probably entail material gain in one way or another, so that it would resolve itself into the generally disapproved category — the impermissible representation of a personal, material interest.

While it seems clear that the representation of geographic or sectional interests and functional interests such as labor, business, agriculture and the like is permissible, at least in the appropriate departments, it is not clear that ideological interests are equally tolerated. There is an impatience with the liberal proponents of public ownership in the case of Telstar that one does not sense in the equally selfish representation of other interests. Ideological interests are less tolerantly viewed and in some cases simply outlawed. In the case of communism we have an example of what may be considered a conflict of interest in which there is little if any question of personal, material interest causing the conflict. In fact, the Attorney General's list might be considered as constituting a kind of administrative finding that membership in certain organizations was prima facie evidence of a conflict of interest. The interest or interests that a member, or in some cases even a sympathetic associate of a member, could reasonably be expected to further are deemed clearly contrary to what dominant consensus is supposed to consider the "public interest."

Much of the perplexity concerning the conflict of interest lies in the ambiguity of this concept, the public interest. Professor Glendon Schubert has devoted a perspicacious volume to the review of various attempts to give positive content to this term, and his efforts largely succeed in making the darkness more visible. Nevertheless, one may hope that the approach used by Stephen Toulmin in his *Reason in Ethics* might prove helpful. Even if we cannot discover some non-material quality that we can call the public interest, we may be able to give good reasons for saying that some course of action is in the public interest and some other is not.

People have as a rule a considerable fund of experience with at least some organizations and their management. As a result they are not without ideas as to when a member is acting in the role of member with the good of the organization in view and when he is acting as a private individual with his own ends in view. This after all is what Rousseau was talking about in distinguishing the general will and the role of the citizen from that of the individual acting in his private self-regarding capacity. We do not have too great difficulty in theory in conceiving of a general interest with which an individual's conception of his own interest may conflict. The notion of selfishness is deeply rooted in the family and develops through extension. Solidarity values in the face-to-face group of the platoon are so great that their violation entails severe sanctions. Their active operation can be the essential cement of an army.

Conflict of interest in this sense implies a violation of group norms that threatens the security and cohesion of the group. Socialization into the group does the job of acquainting the member with the norms, and informal sanctions are usually sufficient for enforcement. A pluralist society with a pluralist government, multi-representative and multi-group in character, does not necessarily provide the individual public official with a clear set of unambiguous principles to guide his action.

It is the nature of such a society with such a government to embody normative conflict in its ordinary course of operation as Madison indicated it would. The very process of representing group self interest hopefully is transmuted in the governmental context into a dialectic out of which the public interest is created and re-created. Group selfishness is a fruitful agency in the search process that a dynamic political society must constantly carry on. For the individual official, from cabinet officer to policeman on the beat, the normative conflict poses dangerous ambiguities in the standards to which he must look for guidance.

When Mr. Robert Moses snorts in righteous assurance that stealing is clearly and always wrong and that our job is to employ better men at better pay who can resist temptation, he assumes a clear and unambiguous concept of stealing which is generally shared. One could never accuse Mr. Moses of any Hamlet-like contemplation of his doubts, if indeed he has any, but one might expect a sophisticated New Yorker, dealing with finance and contractors, to be less sure of the existence of a clear and unambiguous generally accepted rule on what constitutes stealing. Chester Barnard has shown that a truly thoughtful administrator is well aware of the conflicts of principles and even codes that perplex and sometimes destroy the hapless executive who needs must mediate among them. In the recent case of Mr. George Humphrey and the M. A. Hanna Co., what from one point of view may have looked like a conflict of interest leading to improper enrichment at the expense of the government, from another looks like a crass political smear designed to offset the Estes case. Either view can be given considerable plausibility.

But even if the principle concerning stealing is less ambiguous in its application than Mr. Moses would have us believe, it is pretty fundamental to the maintenance of society. Not only is it the general consensus that it is wrong to steal from the government, but that consensus, though less unequivocally, holds that it is wrong to use official government position for self-enrichment.

Much the same position is taken with respect to appropriate behavior in nongovernmental organizations. Conflict of interest in the Chrysler Corporation has many features in common with the phenomenon in government. A main danger of conflict of interest is its *threat to disintegrate the norms* that hold the organization together. While the Kantian universalization of the maxim, me first, may fail to occur, the threat of its occurrence poses the issue of *organization survival*.

A precarious system of income tax collection dependent to a large extent on unenforced citizen compliance is menaced by the revelation of special favoritism and personal dishonesty among collectors of internal revenue. Conflict of interest at one edge shades off into corruption and theft, at the other into the representation of interests. Some of the latter are viewed as legitimate, others not. Closely allied to the representation of interests, though logically distinct, are the representation of philosophical differences or even differences as to the empirical efficacy of measures.

To the liberal advocates of public ownership of the communications satellite, turning it over to private enterprise may well seem like the endowment of selfish private interests with the fruits of public research paid for by all the taxpayers. To the opponents of public enterprise, private operation may seem not only the course dictated by a public policy of private enterprise, but the only practical means of securing efficient operation. During the war many were shocked that the same government that was demanding the risk of life for a pittance from some should be paying premium wages and profits to others in order to get equally necessary contributions to the war effort. Yet both systems of securing action could be defended as appropriate and necessary, given the values and economy of incentives of the society. Given differences of political philosophy over public and private ownership and different conceptions of what it takes to achieve the ends of policy, two groups may view the same course of action as representing either the crassest form of conflict of interest or the only sane, practical way to get things done.

Although the differences do exist and will probably continue to exist as long as we have a pluralistic society, there is no reason to abandon the attempt to implement such consensus as we have and to broaden its area. Despite all differences of philosophy and policy there is undoubtedly a broad area of agreement that stealing from the government is wrong. There is probably a substantial, if less clear-cut agreement that personal self-enrichment at the expense of the government, or by privileged relation with the government is wrong. At a further remove, but still commanding considerable support, is the view that not only should these acts be avoided, but the appearance of serious temptation to commit them should be avoided. There is considerable value in reducing where possible the moral consensus to an explicit rule that can serve as an unambiguous guide to conduct. To do so in practice involves a willingness to face up to and solve incompatible societal demands and serious cleavages that amount to a double moral standard in the government itself.

The behavior of certain petty and not so petty tyrants in Congress, of which Mr. James Reston of the *New York Times* complains, evinces not so much an assertion of principle as an assertion of special privilege. As Reston points out, the same Congressmen who are highly censorious of dubious sources of income among members of the executive are adamantly opposed to full disclosure of the sources of their own revenues. It is difficult, though by no means impossible, to justify Congressional immunity to publicity concerning Congressmen's finances. But a rule of conduct that exempts the top of the organization from its operation can scarcely commend itself for more than lip service on the part of those below. The trouble with the morals of Machiavelli's prince is that they are catching. In justice to Machiavelli, he did recommend a degree of hypocrisy on the part of his prince that we sometimes lack — a decent respect for the opinions of mankind.

Mink coats and deep freezes catch the imagination of the common man like the little lies to which Hitler said he was accustomed. Multi-million-dollar nickel smelters, depletion allowances, comber contracts, leave the common man confused and bewildered. The price of the confusion may be civic alienation and despair such as Murray Levin and George Blackwood note in Massachusetts. Concern with the conflict of interest amounts ultimately to assertion and vindication of the reality and supremacy of the public interest. This last is little more than the assertion of the reality of community and the existence of standards to measure the community's good.

One cannot, of course, deny that for some people, perhaps many, and for some interests, perhaps also for many, the larger community is unreal or commands weak or little loyalty. Resident aliens who are legal citizens and possibly even public officials are altogether possible in our kind of polity. These spiritual Goths within the gates may have no more than a mercenary loyalty, if that, to the community and its government. Geographic and functional interests may subordinate their demands to the larger community not out of any sense of duty or allegiance but from sheer necessity. Allegiance even to the rules of the game of the Hobbesian rational calculus of the value of maintaining peace and order, may achieve at most a half-hearted intellectual assent. To describe this is to describe the nascent conditions for community disintegration. When a section conceives its proper good as ultimate it becomes either a worm in the body politic or secedes, physically if it can, spiritually if it cannot.

When citizens or public officials treat their self-interest as ultimate, they too become worms in the body politic. Given the prevalence of this condition, Hobbes' figure would lead one to suppose that states, at least free ones, are doomed to a more or less worm-eaten condition. Further, one man's worm is another man's martyr. The good man in Aristotle's sense is a worm in a bad society.

These considerations aside, it seems reasonable to believe that if there is to be a larger community there must be allegiance to it. This means that however hypocritical, and they are not often entirely hypocritical, arguments made by functional and sectional groups for furthering their own interests must be made in such fashion as to claim for their particular interests some color of furthering the public interest. The necessity of carrying on the debate in these terms to a degree alters the character of the debate. Naked selfishness of course remains, but it is mitigated by the need to appeal to a standard deemed persuasive to important third parties, the relevant public. That there is no non-material quality corresponding to the public interest to which we can refer does not in practice mean that to debate whether the Humphrey transactions were or were not in the public interest is an exercise in rhetorical nonsense. We can in fact give good reasons for the positions we take. Rational men may be persuaded and convinced by them.

In politics it is through this kind of reasoned discussion that consensus is developed and enlarged. Community in a sense is constantly being created and renewed. It has to be worked at, to be repaired and strengthened. Responsible attempts to give content to the public interest are a major means of transforming lip service into conviction. The function of ethics is to alter behavior and feeling so as to harmonize the relations among peoples and groups. The clarification of principles and their application in particular cases, the consideration of the conflict of principles and the criticism of principles and codes of conduct in the light of their consequences and the existential possibilities are the continuing business of moral and political philosophy. This is no mere academic exercise but is part of the dialogue of society through which the bonds that hold a community together are strengthened or weakened. The talk, in Bentley's sense, is not meaningless, but of the essence. This is the process through which the meaning of a community is developed for its members and the norms by which it is held together are crystallized and altered.

The political community is made up of individuals, the government likewise. As Barnard points out there must be a balance of satisfactions to hold any organization together. To achieve this balance individual interests as well as organization interests must be furthered. While some conception of the public interest should be among and perhaps high among the interests of the officials that make up the government, we cannot ordinarily expect this to constitute by itself a sufficient interest continuously to motivate officials. There is then a public interest in seeing to it that the government be staffed with officials with competence and motivation adequate to the performance desired. This means that occupancy of government posts must sufficiently satisfy individual interests to attract and hold the personnel the public interest requires.

Here we run into the conflict between a private economy powered by the profit motive and a heavy emphasis on money rewards as a success symbol, and public employment where the avowal of such values is denied and their practice considered reprehensible. The government is not the only institution in our society that tries to counter the business ethos with a differing value system. While it may seek through permanent career recruitment and indoctrination to instill another code, the deep interpenetration of business and government makes this difficult. What is possible in a monastery, conceivable in a military caste, and only to a limited degree possible in a university, is well-nigh impossible where the interchange of personnel is as great as it is between government and the business world. Hopefully, the code of loyalty of the business executive to the corporate interest of his business may develop to the point where the transfer of this pattern of conduct to government office will mitigate the cleavage between the formal expectations of public office and the practice of the business world.

Government in seeking to staff itself with people of competence and ability of necessity avails itself of temporary recruits — temporary in the political executive and in the permanent bureaucracy as well. Moses' concern with better pay, prestige, career opportunity and the like are part and parcel of what any organization, civil service or otherwise, does in our culture to ensure the loyalty of its members. These measures, properly and adequately pursued — and they are not now so pursued in most governments — are and always have been promising. But our type of government is, as Weber noted, not characterized by a dominant career bureaucracy. The civilian amateur and the professional who looks forward to being a civilian characterize much of it. Government is an activity that is participated in and withdrawn from. The transitory nature of the physical identification almost characterizes the sense and state of spiritual identification.

This being the case the ethos of the civilian-business birds of passage is of major consequence for the tone of the whole enterprise. If a member of the Interstate Commerce Commission becomes general counsel and vice president of a leading railroad, only the carping will think this other than due recognition of eminent legal talent. Indeed the mutual need of government, industry and functional groups requires a mutual rivalry for and exchange of talented and prestigious personnel. The representation of interests in the government leads to the problem of the agency of the representative. Is he the interests' agent, the government's agent, or his own agent playing both ends against the middle? In the case of a race relations adviser in a federal agency, the official may be an energetic and whole-souled representative of what he considers his race's interest and possibly a coincident public interest, a direct agent of the N.A.A.C.P., a convenient Uncle Tom to handle tough personnel problems, or some combination of these roles or others. The same holds for a labor adviser or any other functional or geographic representative. The conflict but illustrates the significance of the man in the middle who may become the man on his own since he has no compelling group norm to adhere to.

The biblical injunction, lead us not into temptation, has wisdom for the construction of positions, and more than routine job analysis of the role and normative conflict that may be entailed is required. We ought not to put people in positions where the conflict of codes and the conflict of interest is greater than we can reasonably expect them to handle. Barnard may well be right when he says that on examination he found more men to have failed in high positions because of promotion beyond their capacity to handle normative conflict and conflict of loyalties, than because of any initial lack of moral fiber. We need to recognize rather more frankly than we are willing to do the brutally conflicting demands that are made of people in public service.

It may not be beyond us to translate the maxim, thou shalt not steal, into a legally definite rule in government. It will be considerably more difficult to enforce a norm that says, thou shalt not use official position to enrich thyself. Since much of interest representation is designed to enrich others, it is scarcely credible that those who are enriched should forget the one responsible for their enrichment. Whoever knows the reasons for retired military men becoming such valued business executives, or what discriminates among them?

More difficult still than enforcing the commandment, thou shalt not use official position to enrich thyself, is the maxim, no one in official position should seem to be under such temptation to misconduct that his succumbing should seem highly likely to the public or to important parts thereof. If stealing and self-enrichment strike at the bonds that hold the community together, the plausible suspicion that these are widespread is almost equally destructive. Unfortunately all too frequently the very persons whose knowledge and position make them most capable of making unique contributions to important programs of the government are most open to suspicion of interested motivation in their official conduct. Bland and bluff self-righteousness such as Mr. George Humphrey's may disconcert ill-prepared senators, but it will not dispel public suspicion that a very rich man became even richer while holding important public office. It is probably true that it is idle to expect those doing business with the government to show it any special consideration. We have no well developed norms as a community that say whether one should treat the government better or worse than any other customer. It might also be said that as a government we have precious few norms on how the government as a purchaser, or for that matter as an employer concerned with problems of loyalty, should handle its ethical obligations, if indeed we think it has any.

These are questions that cannot be solved by scientific inquiry or metaphysical speculation. Science indeed may help by showing us both what is the case and what uniformities of human behavior we may expect. Ultimately, the answers will have to be of our own creating through intense discussions among ourselves as to what the political community means to us and how best we may further its ends as we agree on them. This is the business of political and moral philosophy whose office is the constant construction and reconstruction of the spiritual habitations of men that are their moral and political communities.

The Never-Ending Search for the Public

Interest ❖ Emmette S. Redford

Pendleton Herring has said, "The *public interest* is the standard that guides the administrator in executing the law. . . . This concept," he continued, "is to the bureaucracy what the 'due process' clause is to the judiciary."

There has been no history written of the concepts "public" and "public interest" in Western political thought. Such a history would undoubtedly reveal the persistence and centrality of the concepts. Cicero defined the state as a "res publica," and the Romans had a maxim that "salus populi suprema lex esto." The distinction between things public and things private formed an important part of the early history of western constitutionalism. In forging the national state, European monarchs sought to identify their regimes with the welfare of the people. Modern political theorists, e.g., Rousseau and Hegel, placed emphasis on the public interest. In the United States the Supreme Court created a judicial doctrine of the public interest, President Cleveland proclaimed the sentiment of the nation that "public office is a public trust," and politicians and writers have habitually referred to the public interest as a standard of good government.

The vitality of the concept "public interest" has not been matched by clarity in its definition. To some it is only a myth under which policy desired by the predominant will can be rationalized as that of the general interest; to others there is reality and integrity in the concept, but it is assumed rather than defined. Some, however, have sought to entrap the elusive reality in descriptive phrase.

John Dewey looked behind the term "public interest" for the meaning of the word "public." A public was created in any case where the action or nonaction of participants led to such indirect and serious effects upon others that it was "deemed necessary to have those consequences systematically cared for." A public was created by the wave of *indirect effects*, and presumably the extent or intensity of the public interest would be determined by the extent of these effects. Paul Appleby took Dewey's concept and transferred the emphasis from effects of action of others to intrinsic need: "Expanding Dewey's dictum, then, we may say that a public comes into being in recognition of some need, for the meeting of which there seems — to those constituting the public — to be no satisfactory private means."

Dewey's hypothesis, as he called it, and Appleby's variation both recognize the existence of many publics. But Dewey was seeking an explanation of the state.

"The Never Ending Search for the Public Interest," by Emmette S. Redford, from *Ideal and Practice in Public Administration* (University of Alabama Press, 1958), pp. 107–116, 118–122, 129–137. Reprinted by permission.

And so he found that many publics became merged into one: "Those indirectly and seriously affected for good or for evil form a group distinctive enough to require recognition and a name. The name selected is The Public . . . the public is a political state." This comes about because officers are created to look after public interests; these officers, or the arrangements we call government, are means of representing the many needs or interests of a public nature. Dewey's concept of many publics merges, therefore, with the older concept of the public as a politically organized society.

Naturally, interests within this society do not differ in essence, though they may in complexity and diversity, from those in other groups. Within a family there are matters of conduct of individuals which are indifferent to other members of the family, other matters on which the members have conflicting interests which must be reconciled, still others where there is a deeply-shared interest. Thus, the detailed expenditure of an allowance for one member may be within an area of indifference, the setting of allowances a subject of compromise among the many family and individual needs, and the opportunity to increase the family income a shared interest. Within other groups also there are areas of indifference, areas of reconciliation, and areas of common or shared interest. This would be true, for example, of the group of cotton producers. There are many aspects of public policy to which they are, as a group, indifferent. Included within the area of concern to them, there are deep conflicts of interest — between types of producers and between producers in different sections of the country — over production allotments, and also a common interest in the general health of the cotton economy. Similarly, within the political group there are areas of indifference — some of which are recognized by the First Amendment, areas for the compromising technique, and areas where the balancing of interests is subordinated to a dominant shared interest.

Further illustration of some of the variations in political society may be gained by a look at three approaches to the reality of the public interest. The first is through a look at those areas where there is much concentration of special interest and often much conflict among different aggregations of concentrated interest. Examples are the agricultural interest today, the conflict between shippers and railroads in the nineteenth century, and the conflict between labor and management in the twentieth. At this level of reality, a number of variations in policy making are discernible. Quite obviously, the direct interest of dominant minority or majority groups may prevail and even become the accepted view of the public interest. Herring has said that "the concept of the public interest is given substance by its identification with the interests of certain groups," and that there must be "a working relationship between the bureaucrats and special interests" which "will enable the former to carry out the purpose of the state and the latter to realize their own ends." It is possible that this identification of the public interest with group interest, and this working relationship between bureaucrats and special interests, may be carried so far that any purposes of the larger society of men will be overlooked or overstepped, and that the idea of public interest will indeed be a myth. But usually, as Herring recognized, policy making will go beyond mere identification and involve some balancing of group interests involved. Arthur Macmahon has referred to the fact that much of our legislation shows a "balancing bias" and that administrators must carry out such legislation. The balancing may be only of interests immediately involved. For example, a set of legislative provisions regarding the allocation of cotton production quotas may resolve a sectional conflict among groups of producers with virtually no consideration of the impact of the compromise upon the economy, i.e., upon interests outside those of the cotton family. In such an event the public interest is involved only in the attainment of a workable compromise of immediate group interests. There will, usually, however, be indirect effects which create publics beyond the parties directly involved, and these publics then have interests which may struggle for recognition in the balancing process. In this event, the indirectly-created interests may be only additional interests to be compromised with primary or direct interests in the fulcrum of policy formation. These "public" interests may tip the scale as between the contending interests, or force compromise of all of these to some broader standard. In the latter case the broader standard may enable an independent public interest to become an overriding interest, at least in some degree. For example, the public interest in industrial peace in wartime led to arrangements for seizure in case of public need and subsequently the public interest in peaceful settlement was worked into a whole set of arrangements for mediation, fact finding, and temporary prevention of strikes. Beyond this, in a particular labor dispute a point may be reached where the indirectly-created public interest is vital, clear, and dominant.

A second approach to the reality of the public interest is to look for the widely and continuously shared interests which arise directly out of organic developments and shared purposes. These are interests which are so widely shared that they can be, by virtue of this fact alone, called common or public interests. Examples are the interest of people generally in education, peace, a good traffic control system, and the avoidance of boom and bust in the economy. For such cases Appleby's characterization of a public seems more adequate than Dewey's. To explain the public interest in education or a good traffic control system as indirectly-created by the action or inaction of some group or groups of persons seems less cleancut than an approach which recognizes merely that developments have occurred which create a public need. The essence of the public interest is a public need, and this need is intrinsic rather than derived. The public interest has an original, primary, and inherent quality. And it may, though confronted with or supported by claims of special interest which may obtain consideration, have a central position in policy deliberations.

There is nothing mystical about the concept of shared interests within the political society. It is no more mystical than the idea of a shared interest of family members in a larger family income, or of a shared interest of cotton producers in a healthy cotton economy. It is only broader in scope, and therefore unlikely to be shared with the same degree of universality and evenness that would exist in a compact, organic unit like the family. In practice, as a consequence, the generally-shared interest may be compromised with the interests of subgroups which do not share evenly, or perhaps at all, the prevailing common purpose. Or it may be fostered by subgroups which, in addition to sharing the common purpose, also have particular interests which will be protected or advanced by action for the common welfare.

The third approach is to look at the need for machinery for representation of interests and for weighing and deciding issues. There is a public interest in the availability of adequate organization and process, measured by the needs and ideals of society, for representing claims and resolving issues. This is to say, as Locke said, that society needs a common legislator and adjudicator, or, as we could say in more modern terms, that there is a public interest in fair and effective government, including public administration. This interest may lead to arrangements for adjudication, administration, legislation, or to supralegislative arrangements which we call constitution making. This need for public mechanism (organization and process) is the highest level of the public interest and justifies our continued concern with political "science."

The public interest, then, is diverse. It is indirectly created interests struggling with other interests; again it is intrinsic, shared interests of all or most in substantive objectives; still again it is interest in machinery for fair consideration and for resolution of intergroup and public claims. It is no myth.

The problem, however, is how the public interest in a particular situation may be discovered. Walter Lippmann, who accepts the concept of public interest as central to "The Public Philosophy," defines it in terms of a manner of approach:

Living adults share, we must believe, the same public interest. For them, however, the public interest is mixed with, and is often at odds with, their private and special interests. Put this way, I suggest that the public interest may be presumed to be what men would choose if they saw clearly, thought rationally, acted disinterestedly and benevolently.

Since disinterested and benevolent thought arises only from a feeling of kinship and a capacity for empathy among men, Lippmann has, in brief, set up rationality and fraternity as routes to the public interest.

Some of us have sought to grasp the essence of rationality in pursuit of the public interest as involved in the process of decision. One feature of the process of decision is that it goes beyond and cuts across separate interest considerations. Appleby has declared: "But usually the interests umpired are so numerous and unlike that the process is not umpiring at all. Rather it is a process of distilling out of those private interests something approximating the general interest." Macmahon also sought for the kernel of rationality in decision making. Along with other perceptive comments he says, "But the essence of the public interest is *awareness of that web* ["society's seamless"] *and the constant impulse to trace things as far as possible* before acting and as a guide to action where choices otherwise unguided must be made" (my italics). Hopefully, he adds that "it is not fantastic to state this as an ideal, for it is inclination of alert and conscientious public servants." I have likewise looked for the essence of rationality with respect to the public interest. It is based on full appraisal of situational factors, interests involved, and value assumptions, and hence the public interest "may be defined as the best response to a situation in terms of all the interests and of the concepts of value which are generally accepted in our society." This response and the "tracing of things as far as possible" — producing broad and long vision — leads quite often to a formula or approach in policy which reveals more creative imagination and origination than umpiring, and which may be quite rational in its end result even though none of the contenders show much disinterestedness.

There are deep moral connotations in the concept of the "public interest." First, the concept is a democratic one. The word "public" is an inclusive term and its inclusiveness in the practice of government has expanded with the universality and equality of citizenship. The public is not a class or a group within society; it is all. The term gets a deeper moral meaning as slavery, class distinctions, and race discriminations disappear and each man becomes a first-class member of an all-embracing public. Second, the public or general interest has a certain claim to supremacy. This does not mean that claims of equity in differential justice to men shall not be recognized. A democrat and a devotee of the public interest can agree with John of Salisbury that the "prince," that is, the government, may not "have any will of his own apart from that which the law or equity enjoins, *or* the calculation of the common interest requires." He may, however, be of the opinion that there is equity itself in the claims of the common interest and that it is frequently — even generally with appropriate compromises — the highest equity because it is equity for men generally.

Democracy and the public interest are related majestic concepts in our politics: both assume equality in citizenship, though both may combine this with recognition of differential justice. And the requisite of each is the consideration of all men's claims, or to put it differently, and returning to Lippmann's definition, a certain disinterestedness and other-regardedness arising from a spirit of fraternity for all.

.   .   .   .

II

The realization of public interests in policies of government is challenged by man's egoism and society's pluralism. Our Founding Fathers were cognizant of man's basic selfishness and designed a frame of government to check its excesses. Some of them were also conscious of the essential pluralism even of the society of that day. Madison, in addition to seeing geographical alignments of interests and the class conflict between rich and poor, saw the functional divisions within the economy: "A landed interest, a manufacturing interest, a mercantile interest, a moneyed interest, and many lesser interests. . . ."

But the Founders could not have foreseen the organization of functional interests which has developed. Each functional group which becomes self-conscious organizes. The organization is lighthouse and beacon to its members to inform and warn about government; it is shield and spear in their battle to escape injury or win victories through governments. Together the organizations provide a new system of functional representation which exists alongside the sectional representation provided through geographical electoral districts.

These organizations find multiple means of access to government. They lobby before legislatures and administrations. They obtain representation within the government by membership on advisory committees, establishment of agencies to serve their interests — called clientele agencies, location of professional and supervisory personnel in agencies, and by finding legislators who serve as their virtual agents. They support these activities by cultivation of friendships, campaign contributions, and vast publicity programs. They work at whatever center in government seems most receptive or shift from one established power center to another in the three departments of governments to find a weak point in the armor which resists them.

These associations may make our government more representative, increase the knowledge available to policy makers, and provide opportunities to the administrator to win through them acceptance for public programs. But they may also destroy the independence and the vigor of public organization.

Protection against loss of efficacy and of integrity in administration due to these activities cannot be found in administration alone. The protections must be found in society, in administration, and in the operation of the government as a whole. Two questions are presented: Can we prevent the strong special interests from twisting policy for their benefit in ways which are detrimental to the public interest? Can we get a broad and inclusive, a large rather than a narrow view of the public interest? Though no complete answers can be given to these questions, it is possible to refer to a number of factors which cumulatively may give a considerable measure of protection.

First, there are safeguards in the nature of the pluralism of our society. The pluralism creates a social check and balance system which envelops, supplements, and gives reality to that within the government.

There are a multitude of associations, varying in size and cohesiveness. It is relevant, therefore, to consider Rousseau's answer to the problem of group interest. He feared that the partial interests of groups would destroy the general will to promote the common good. He said, therefore, "that there should be no partial society within the state." This, as Madison saw, is an impossible answer for a free society. But Rousseau had another answer: "If there are partial societies, it is best to have as many as possible and to prevent them from being unequal." The "desirable object would be," as Mill stated it, "that no class, and no combination of classes likely to combine, should be able to exercise a preponderant influence in the government." Though interest organizations in this country are unequal in power and influence, though many of them have worked their way into centers of government, and though dominance of government at local, state, or national levels may appear to be threatened at times by some of them, we must place part of the hope for a public-interest oriented government on the check and countercheck of these organizations upon each other, and upon the ability of government because of their multiplicity to check their particularistic inroads upon it.

Further safeguard is found in the fact that most people do not give their complete allegiance to any single association. The officers of associations may claim that they speak for all the members, but usually this is an extreme claim and the officials of government know it. An individual may be a member of a family, a church, a party philanthropic organizations, and professional, trade, or labor groups; and even though there may be a certain similarity of point of view in most of the associations to which he belongs, he may still find there is considerable variation in the policies advanced or favored by them. His attachment to his primary economic group may be qualified by his other associations. Thus, what David Truman has called multiple or overlapping memberships contribute to the safeguards of the pluralistic society.

The safeguards of pluralism could become less effective. If power should be too greatly concentrated in a few large private organizations, or the primary economic associations of men should come to have a more inclusive call on their loyalties, or if the multiple memberships of particular persons all should tend to be class memberships, then the safeguards for the public interest in the composition of society would have diminished effectiveness. But industrialization creates numerous trades and professional specialties. It creates leisure and interests beyond the economic. Its tendency apparently is to divide and redivide and to create multiple interests. If our economy remains expansive and public policy is directed toward maintenance of a fluid society, then the protections against dominance of society by particular interests may retain their vitality.

Second, beyond the diversities of the pluralistic society are the unities which arise from the common life and the common traditions and aspirations. These unities constitute the elements of monism within society. They may be viewed in two ways — as common needs or as attitudes of mind. There are factors of common need arising from the organic developments and common aspirations of men. By way of illustration, we refer to avoidance of boom and bust, opportunity for each to employ his energies in gainful endeavor, and a measure of security for all. To an extent the administrator and the politician may appeal to these our common interests and thus moderate the demands of special groups which run counter to them. The recognition of the first named of these common interests is plain common sense; the recognition of common interests like the last two is a result of the widespread acceptance of democratic ideals. But there are other ideals of our society which may limit and circumscribe at a given moment the effect of group pressure. A few examples are the idea of fair play, the concept of reasonableness, and the idea of the rule of law. When group action and group demands seem to be excessive in terms of such ideals, the shifting middle opinion in society may rally in opposition. Even more, the statesmen in legislative, executive, and judicial posts may find opportunities to erect positive standards of future conduct which conform to these common ideals (and to common interests which they represent, though perhaps remotely) and to which groups in society must make some kind of adjustment.

. . . .

The third governmental answer is comprehensive representation. By this is meant representation of the people as a whole or, differently stated, representation of all the interests of all people through one channel. It contrasts with representation of separate groups or divisions of society, whether on the basis of class, function, or section. Sectional or geographical representation may, however, approach comprehensive representation through the single-member constituency. The Congressman representing such a constituency may find that there are many diverse interests within his district, that no one of these has a majority, that there is much overlapping of memberships and many unorganized voters. As a result he becomes a moderator among group demands and searches for answers for public problems which have a broad appeal. True, the Congressman is sometimes a virtual captive of a particular functional interest, or sometimes strongly affected by class demands, and ofttimes is representative of a sectional viewpoint. But it remains true, nevertheless, that there are many districts which are almost as pluralistic as the nation and that the single-member constituency is more favorable to search by the individual representative for the public interest than any other form of representation could be.

The chief organ of comprehensive representation is the presidency. To an extent the two-party system provides comprehensive representation, but since the national party organizations are so weak and the parties are so divided in the Congress and the nation, and the majority party is so largely under the leadership of the President, the presidency becomes the center through which the nation as a whole is represented. This function of the presidency is safeguarded to the nation through the requirement of a majority electoral vote for election of its incumbent. To win a majority the candidate must bridge the interest conflict and make his appeal on the basis of generally-shared attitudes. The function is further enforced by the high responsibility of the office. Inevitably a responsible man must try to exercise its functions for the welfare of the nation. Inevitably he will be forced to try to take a broadly-gauged view of what constitutes the general welfare. The presidency is, therefore, our most democratic and our most publicly-oriented office. And its strength and its service derive from the breadth of the constituency which it represents.

The fourth answer is creative intelligence. A careful student of American government has concluded "that the development of public policy and of the methods of its administration owed less in the long run to the processes of conflict among political parties and social or economic pressure groups than to the more objective processes of research and discussion among professional groups." This is a high claim for the influence of intelligence in government. But leaving aside issues of "more or less" among factors of influence, we can agree that the creative intelligence of professional groups and of others has been an important factor in policy forma- tion. Illustrations of the fact are numerous and should deter us from seeking an explanation of the processes of government solely on the basis of pressure politics. Look, for example, at the perfection of the framework of the Public Utility Holding Company Act, and particularly at that new kernel of policy embodied in the words "single integrated public-utility system," which came from the expert consultants serving the House Committee on Interstate Commerce. Here was imagination rising from above the mountains of data accumulated by the Federal Trade Com- mission. Or look at the magnificent development of the Truman Policy and the Marshall Plan in those critical days when communism threatened to engulf Europe — a story told in part in Joseph Jones' recently published volume on *The Fifteen Weeks.* Or look at the great imagination of those men — hardly professionals, but with first-rate educations and tremendous mental resources — who developed so quickly the techniques of allocation of scarce resources and stabilization from 1941 to 1943. Or look at the story recently told by Richard E. Neustadt of all the creative analysis that goes into the production of the President's legislative program. Or look at the achievements of traffic engineers in devising means for reconciling the public interests in facilities for through traffic and local traffic, as for example in combination of high-speed, controlled-access freeways and parallel low-speed, outside lanes. The first of these examples is from the work of Congress, the next three from the work of the national executive including its administrative branches, and the last from national-state-local planning. Yet all these and others which could be recalled give hope for a large measure of that rationality which Lippmann exalted.

The opportunities for creative intelligence arise out of the complexity of the fact situations with which policy must deal. The situational factors which must be grasped are a great "complex of technologies, institutional framework, and be- havior patterns." All of the many ingredients of social and economic fact, interests, and ideals must be assimilated and a feasible and workable solution discovered. This hypothesis is offered: that the increase in the technicality and complexity of the situational factors which must be considered in policy making increases the need for and in the long run increases the opportunity for creative intelligence to play a part in the discovery and choice of solutions.

It is a hopeful sign that governments are awakening to the need for "braineries" at all important policy determining centers. It was this awakening which led Congress to provide for staff aid for itself in the Legislative Reorganization Act of 1946 and which led those participating in discussions on the Employment Act of the same year to seek to provide an "economic brain" for the President. It is this awakening which has accounted for the recommendation of staff aid for the Presi- dent in all reorganization studies of the past twenty years, and which accounted for recommendation of aides for department heads by the task forces serving the First and Second Hoover Commissions. It was this awakening which led my own State of Texas in 1949 to create two new staff groups for the Legislature — one to study the budget and the other to make studies of problems of legislation. The motivation was in part a desire to prevent further centralization in Washington by study of problems at the state level, but the soundest reason for public "braineries" in the states is to counteract the dependence of legislatures on interest groups for informa- tion and advice.

It is a hopeful sign also that there is recognition of the need for placing intelligence centers at the top levels of government hierarchies. When these centers are located for service to chief executives and department heads and to the legislative body as a whole there can be hope that the scope of and perspective in analysis will be as inclusive as the problems and the relationships affected by them.

The final answer on the questions we have presented is broad-gauged political leadership, adverted to earlier in this discussion of protections for the public interest. There are, of course, many types of political leaders. Some, undoubtedly all to some extent, follow the political weather vanes. Others, perhaps all to an extent, are sectional or group leaders. Some are petty, narrow, prejudiced — ill-suited for pursuit of rationality or fraternity. But some have the quality of statesmanship, at least on many types of measures. This is the apex of the synthesizing expertness we discussed in an earlier chapter. It is a kind of expertness which on the one hand draws from the knowledge which experts can give on what is possible and what is best and on the other hand senses the dominant demands of the people of the nation and merges the two in a compounded wisdom which may be more profound and more beneficent than that found either in the advice of the experts or the demands of the interest groups. This is the highest form of creative intelligence. There are men in high administrative posts who possess this lofty synthesizing competence — some of them new entrants into government service, others long-time members of the upper ranks of the civil service. These are our administrative statesmen. But this competence is more likely to be found in pre-eminent degree in some of our political leaders. These then are our ultimate safeguards for rationality and fraternity.

Our political system lifts politicians to this kind of competence in various ways. Some by virtue of the part of the country they represent or the diversified nature of their constituencies acquire a kind of "border state" psychology, that is, they do not react favorably to extreme sectional, group, or class demands but intuitively sense both the full scope of the nation's pluralism and the cross-sections of unity or potential compromise among its parts. The President, more than all other of our politicians, is forced toward this kind of psychology. In addition, some men though representing areas with strong sectional allegiances acquire, by virtue of the lack of a strong opposition party or of their strong personal positions, a kind of a career position in the House or Senate. Some of them become distinguished experts in areas of legislation and also rise to positions of leadership in the houses. They may be able to exert considerable influence toward a rational public policy in some areas, even though they may remain captives of sectional or group interests on other issues. Finally, conscience, the "impulse to trace things as far as possible," and the necessity of reaching agreement with other men may lead representatives to search for the public interest.

The emphasis on the function of creative intelligence at the administrative and political levels is not, in my opinion, anti-democratic. It is assumed, of course, that there is a large measure of public consensus, above the individual wills on particular issues, in favor of a government which operates for the common good. Moreover, the administrative expert operates under political controls and hence must infuse rather than dictate intelligence. The same is true of the politicians as a group, who are subject to compulsions and restraints from the electoral process. The danger to democracy at this stage in our development lies less in independence of will than in its subservience to partial groupings. The juncture of creative intelligence and the various forms of political responsibility which exist is essential for joint satisfaction of society's yearning for responsible government and for that rationality and fraternity which underlie the public interest.

III

Four conclusions may be stated as a result of the preceding discussion.

First, we may expect to find constant group effort to bend public policy toward special interests. This leads to protection or promotion of special interests and ofttimes to the injury of other particular interests or to the neglect of general interests.

Second, as a result of the limitations on the power of groups in the structure of society and in pluralistic representation and internal checks, and of the existence of unities of interest and ideal, comprehensive jurisdiction, comprehensive representation, expert analysis, and political and administrative statesmanship, we may expect to find a considerable measure of public interest focus in major public decisions.

Third, we cannot expect a full measure of consistency in public policy. In a dynamic, free, pluralistic society the balance of forces which play upon government and which interact within it is constantly shifting. Within government, moves made contemporaneously at different points may not be synchronized — may even have conflicting effects — and moves made over a period of time may reflect great changes in purposes and effects. The processes of administrative and political decision are sensitive in too many directions for men to hope or to fear for the congruency of policies anticipated in the vision of a planned society. The realized public interest in a free society is no neat package of consistent elements.

Yet rationality and order will be achieved in area after area of public affairs. What is confusion today is reduced to order tomorrow. The tempests of conflicts in interest are supplanted or reduced by law, organization and process. Policies are defined in general and then crystallized in detail; system is elaborated; structure and procedure in smoothly-operating organizations reduce yesterday's problems to routine or simple management and fashion competence for tomorrow's solutions. Man moves on to new plateaus of confusion and problem. He may hope — and this is my final point — that much rationality and fraternity are embodied in the order and regularity already achieved, and that creative intelligence and broad sympathies working through institutional organization and process will yield a satisfactory measure of public good tomorrow.